International Law in Asia

Series Editor

Eric Yong Joong Lee, #402 Taejin Bd, YIJUN Institute of International Law, Seoul, Korea (Republic of)

This series aims to provide the latest perspectives on international law in this ever changing region of Asia. Each book of this series will address specific aspect of highly contemporary global issues such as armed conflict, maritime disputes, human rights and refugee crises, sustainable development/climate change, outer space, finance and economy, trade (WTO and FTA), investment, development, technology, intellectual property, international crime, global health, regional questions, etc.

This book series invites leading international law scholars and practitioners in Asia to contribute their expertise in interpreting a wide range of legal questions that arise in relation to the above topics through an Asian lens. This series will serve as useful guide for international lawyers, diplomats, businessmen and students to understand current and future trends of international law in Asia.

Junghwan Choi
Editor

Public Maritime Law in Asia

Springer

Editor
Junghwan Choi
Law School
Dalian Maritime University
Dalian, P.R. China

ISSN 2731-8044 ISSN 2731-8052 (electronic)
International Law in Asia
ISBN 978-981-95-7036-2 ISBN 978-981-95-7037-9 (eBook)
https://doi.org/10.1007/978-981-95-7037-9

This Springer imprint is published by the registered company Springer Nature Singapore Pte Ltd.
The registered company address is: 152 Beach Road, #21-01/04 Gateway East, Singapore 189721, Singapore

Preface

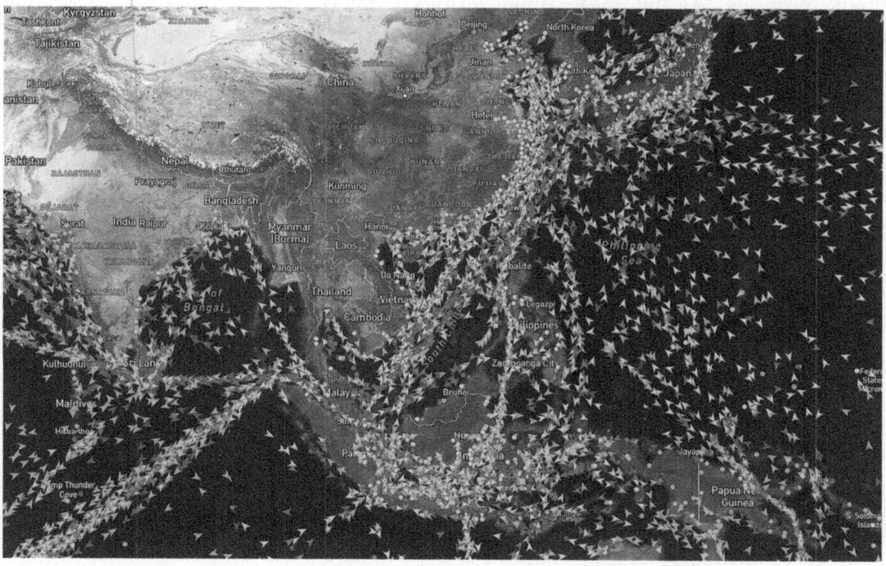

Shipping Traffic Status in Asian Shipping Routes (13 December 2025)

Asia plays a central role in the global maritime economy. According to the *UNCTAD Review of Maritime Transport 2024*, approximately 36% of the world's container cargo volume is transported through Asian ports, underscoring Asia's central position in the global maritime economy. This prominence is further reflected in fleet ownership. China, Japan, and the Republic of Korea together account for approximately 27.9% of global shipping capacity, with China alone holding about 13.3%, the largest share worldwide. Japan maintains its status as a traditional maritime power with 10.4%, while the Republic of Korea accounts for approximately 4.2%, collectively forming the core axis of the Northeast Asian maritime network.

Asia's leading position is particularly evident in port operations and shipbuilding. All of the world's top ten busiest container ports by throughput are located in

Asia, reinforcing the region's decisive role in global supply chains. Moreover, the Republic of Korea, China, and Japan collectively command approximately 95% of the global shipbuilding market, with China alone accounting for 70–74% of new shipbuilding orders in 2024. These figures clearly demonstrate Asia's overwhelming practical influence across shipping, ports, and shipbuilding. In this context, Japan, China, and the Republic of Korea, as leading maritime economies and IMO Council (Category A) members, play key roles in shaping the future of shipping, ports, shipbuilding, and maritime education and training.

Human resources remain central to the maritime industry. The global seafarer workforce serving internationally trading merchant ships is estimated at approximately 1.89 million, comprising 857,540 officers and 1,035,180 ratings. Asian seafarers account for about 44% of this total, making Asia the world's largest supplier of maritime labor. Most Asian seafarer-supplying economies are developing economies, where overseas employment in shipping plays a critical role in foreign currency earnings. At the same time, serious concerns persist regarding working conditions, onboard culture, human rights, and welfare standards. Reports by *Human Rights at Sea* reveal troubling realities, including that approximately 45% of female seafarers have experienced sexual harassment, and at least 32,000 fishermen die annually as a result of hazardous working conditions.

These vulnerabilities were significantly intensified during the COVID-19 pandemic. At its peak, over 400,000 seafarers worldwide—many of them Asian nationals—were stranded aboard ships, compelled to extend their contracts beyond the 11-month limit prescribed by the Maritime Labour Convention (MLC), 2006. An estimated 40–50% of the global seafarer workforce, predominantly from Asia, was disproportionately affected by crew change restrictions, denial of shore leave, and prolonged delays in repatriation, in some cases exceeding six months.

Against this backdrop, this volume, *Public Maritime Law in Asia*, seeks to respond to these transformations by offering Asia-centered perspectives on public maritime law. It focuses in particular on maritime safety, seafarers, marine environmental protection, and contemporary legal issues arising from structural changes in the global maritime industry.

In preparing this book, I am deeply grateful to my colleagues and to the institutional support provided by Dalian Maritime University, a leading global hub for maritime education and training and a cornerstone of China's maritime strength. The research and educational environment at this institution has contributed profoundly to my academic growth.

I also wish to highlight the important role of Korea Maritime and Ocean University within the Asian maritime industry. The collaboration between Korea Maritime and Ocean University and Dalian Maritime University will play a vital role in cultivating advanced maritime human capital capable of addressing the challenges of decarbonization and digitalization, while expanding access to high-quality maritime education for Asian seafarers, who constitute nearly half of the global maritime workforce. This academic partnership is embedded in a broader structural transformation in which the global maritime order is gradually evolving from a predominantly Eurocentric framework toward an increasingly Asia-led maritime network.

Finally, on behalf of all the authors, I extend my deepest appreciation to the Series Editor, Professor Eric Yong Joong Lee, for recognizing the significance of this volume and for his invaluable guidance and encouragement throughout the publication process.

Above all, it is my sincere hope that this book will serve as a foundation for the future development of Asia's maritime industry and for deeper regional and international cooperation.

On behalf of all authors

Dalian, P.R. China Junghwan Choi

Contents

Chapter 1
The Phenomenon of Admiralty: Its Genesis, Historical Evolution, and Usage

Proshanto K. Mukherjee

Introduction

Admiralty is unmistakably a maritime law phenomenon steeped in English legal history in juxtaposition to the Anglo-Saxon legal tradition, latterly known as the common law. It is frequently misconceived in certain quarters by individuals with a limited perception of the maritime law which is a highly specialized field. The indiscriminate and fallacious use of the appellation often inhibits its ubiquitous understanding. Unfortunately, this state of affairs prevails in jurisdictions with a narrow and distorted view of maritime law, attributable to its indigenous underdevelopment as a discipline which I have personally observed at least in one jurisdiction with which I have long been associated. In this chapter, I have ventured to clarify the misapprehensions by probing into the genesis and historical evolution of admiralty as a legal phenomenon and its usage, past and contemporary.

Following this rather brief introductory submission. I begin with a discussion of what is maritime law which is a wider macro concept within the domain of law associated with the sea stretching over millennia and then focus on admiralty as a micro phenomenon within maritime law peculiar to the law of England which has permeated historically through numerous jurisdictions embracing the common law tradition largely owing to colonialism. It is alien to the civil law system with its

Proshanto K. Mukherjee Professor of Law and Foreign Expert, Dalian Maritime University, LL.B. (Dalhousie), Ph.D. (Wales), LL.D. Juris dr. honoris causa, (Lund) Ethics Officer and Legal Adviser to the President Professor Emeritus of Maritime Law and Policy and Erstwhile Vice President (Research), World Maritime University Former Director, Postgraduate Maritime Law, Lund University Adjunct Professor of Law, Centurion University, India Chancellor, CINEC Campus Colombo.

P. K. Mukherjee (✉)
Law School, Dalian Maritime University, Dalian, P.R. China

J. Choi (ed.), *Public Maritime Law in Asia*, International Law in Asia,
https://doi.org/10.1007/978-981-95-7037-9_1

origins in Roman law except within Great Britain, which I have explained below. Given that English law is the centrepiece of the discussion, its history, at least in elementary terms, is germane to a proper appreciation and understanding of the phenomenon of admiralty. I therefore consider it incumbent on me as the (hi)story-teller to dwell briefly on the past before fast-forwarding to the present times.

As Western empires and colonialism have all but disappeared from the face of contemporary reality, it is important to note that the sovereign state of today, relevant to our central theme of discussion, is the United Kingdom of Great Britain and Northern Ireland. Essentially, Great Britain comprises Scotland, England, and Wales[1] within which Scotland is largely a civil law jurisdiction embracing the Scots Law brand of civil law, whereas England and Wales are the keepers and custodians of the common law tradition. Having said that, it is perhaps more accurate to describe Scots law as a hybrid consisting of elements of both the civil and common law.[2] It is also contextually important to note that in Scotland even though the legal system is Scots law, admiralty law and jurisdiction prevails in a manner similar to England and Wales. Another point of essential interest is that the term "common law" came into vogue only after 1066, the year which marks the landing and conquest of England by Prince William Duke of Normandy, better known as William the Conqueror, and is undoubtedly a major turning point in that country's colourful history.[3] Incidentally, Normandy was and still is a region in the northwest of France and is physically located on the French side of the English Channel.[4] Another point of interest relevant to the present discussion is that prior to the historic land mark year 1066, the legal system of England was known as "Anglo-Saxon Law" which is the term still used by many in the European civil law jurisdictions. These are historical snippets that are crucial to the understanding of admiralty law which emerged several centuries later.

The Substance and Semantics of Maritime Law

In my book *Mukherjee on Maritime Legislation*, which is the second edition of its predecessor *Maritime Legislation*, the very first chapter focuses on terminology and semantics concerning the law that governs and postulates on maritime matters across the public to private law spectrum.[5] In that chapter, I have stated that not only are there diverse views on what is maritime law, the issue appears to be semantical comprising terminological differences rather than a matter of clear and substantive

[1] https://en.wikipedia.org/wiki/United_Kingdom.

[2] https://en.wikipedia.org/wiki/Scots_law.

[3] https://en.wikipedia.org/wiki/Norman_Conquest; https://www.quora.com/How-did-common-law-develop; https://www.historic-uk.com/HistoryUK/HistoryofEngland/William-The-Conqueror/.

[4] https://en.normandie-tourisme.fr/about-normandy/some-landmarks/where-is-normandy/.

[5] Mukherjee (2021), pp. 1–5.

perception of an important phenomenon of law. I have cited an authoritative statement generated by a group of international experts in the field who have opined that "maritime law provides the legal framework for maritime transport.[6] In succinct terms, the opinion is that it is the law of maritime transportation, which in my observation is too general, decidedly narrow in scope and content and therefore inadequate. I am of the same view regarding another definition of maritime law found in a well-known text book which states that it is a "body of legal rules and concepts concerning the business of carrying goods and passengers by water."[7]

Maritime law is often highlighted as a legal discipline manifestly different from law of the sea although in literal terms, arguably, the two expressions bear the same meaning, that is, the law pertaining to matters related to the sea. This description of maritime law would arguably preclude consideration of the specific subject of law of the sea which is indubitably a branch of public international law albeit in relation to the sea, or to put it in another way, the public law pertaining to international ocean space.[8] In this characterization, the expression "law of the sea" would signify that aspect of international law which deals with the world's oceans and their multifarious uses including resources in terms of broad, fundamental principles. No doubt this would be correct in terms of usage of the expression not only in legal and academic circles but is also acceptable as such by the general public at large.

That said, there is invariably a public law and private law counterpart component to maritime law which are correlated in theory and practice. I believe this, my view, is in consonance with those of some distinguished authors, one of them being Professor F.R. Sanborn who close to a century ago in 1930, wrote:

The words "maritime law," as commonly used today, denote that part of the whole law which deals chiefly with the legal relations arising from the use of ships. But in the earlier period, of which this work treats, the law maritime had a considerably wider scope. It dealt with the primitive ancestors of some branches of our modern commercial law, dealt, too, with the germs of that public law which we today style international law.[9]

In my view, the term "maritime law" bears a broader connotation with both a national as well as an international dimension. As such, the specific term "law of the sea" is subsumed within the general notion of maritime law and its etymology which stems from the root word *mer* or *mare* in Latin meaning the sea. In Roman law, the expression is *lex maritima* as distinguished from the *lex mercatoria* which signifies the law merchant or mercantile law.

Gordon Paulsen, the author, states somewhat innocuously that the phrase "law of the sea" is different from "maritime law". The former refers to the respective rights

---

[6] *Guide-Lines for Maritime Legislation*, Third Edition, (Guidelines Vol. I); United Nations Publication, Economic and Social commission for Asia and the Pacific (ESCAP), Bangkok, Thailand, (ST/ESCAP/1076), p. 1.

[7] Schoenbaum and Yiannopoulos (1984), p. 1.

[8] Brown (1971).

[9] Sanborn (1989) Reprint, p. xvi.

of states over the world's waterways.[10] Those of a contrary view would submit that the distinction is artificial and anomalous, and in support of their proposition would point to the etymological root of the word "maritime", which derived from the Latin means "of or pertaining to the sea".[11] As noted in the text above, I subscribe to that viewpoint. Some are of the opinion that the term maritime law "… has taken on a new meaning, to refer to the entire body of laws, rules, legal concepts and processes that relate to the use of marine resources, ocean commerce, and navigation".[12] The semantic analysis so portrayed equates "maritime law" with "law of the sea" as an all-embracing term. Indeed, in *The Scotia* [13] the term "law of the sea" was used in the decision to describe what may be otherwise referred to as "maritime law" in terms of usage of terminology by most persons in the know. That said, my own observation is that in the context in which it is used in the decision, the expression "law of the sea" is seemingly simply generic and general. This is evident from the dictum of Strong J. in that case stated in the following words:

Undoubtedly, no single nation can change the law of the sea … whatever may have been its origin whether in the usages of navigation, or in the ordinances of maritime states, or in both, it has become the law of the sea only by the concurrent sanction of those nations who may be said to constitute the commercial world.[14]

In support of my personal take on the matter, I would particularly point to the phrases "usages of navigation" and "commercial world" in that dictum which lends to it a "shipping" flavour.

Another term used in this context to describe the same phenomenon is "common law of the sea". In one well-known piece of relevant literature, the author refers to "… the general maritime law; or common law of the sea and the established practices and requirements of the business".[15] The same sentiment is expressed by another noted author and in case law decisions.[16] In terms of English case law jurisprudence, a fine example is *The Tolten,* where the English Court of Appeal referred to "the general or common law of the seas".[17] There are other similar expressions in use such as "sea law" and "common or transnational law of the sea". In *MV Elisabeth* v. *Harwan Investment and Trading Pvt. Ltd.*,[18] the Supreme Court of India referred to "international common law or transnational law".[19]

Thus, it is observed that in consonance with the views of several other scholars and authors in the field, there is a public and private law dimension to maritime law

[10] See Paulsen (1983), p. 1065, where at p. 1085.

[11] Schoenbaum (1994), p. 1.

[12] *Ibid.* at p. 2.

[13] (1872), 14 Wall 170.

[14] *Ibid.* at pp. 187–188.

[15] Canfield (1922), p. 535.

[16] See for example, Mahanty (2018), pp. 2, 4.

[17] *United Africa Ltd* v. *Owners of the MV Tolten* (1946), 2 All E.R. 372 at p. 378.

[18] AIR 1990 SC 1014 at p.1036.

[19] See Mahanty, *supra*, note 16. pp. 11 and 27.

when it is viewed holistically. The public law side invariably includes law of the sea which is a branch of public international law. It also extends to regulatory maritime law largely framed through international conventions and criminal law, both of which are aspects of the penal law.[20]

A contemporary author of high academic distinction, Professor Edgar Gold, has in pointing out an anomaly, expressed a somewhat tangentially cynical viewpoint of this matter. In his observation:

> … the new law of the sea has … addressed itself to almost all areas of ocean use except the one that since before the dawn of history, has been preeminent—the use of the ocean as a means to transport people and their goods from place to place on this planet, so much more of which is water than is land. Marine transport has been discussed in an almost abstract manner, as if it did not really fit or belong within the public domain but needed to be confined to the more "private" region of international commerce, which was considered to be outside the scope of the law of the sea.[21]

A proper semantic analysis inevitably points to the inseparability of "maritime law" as an all-embracing term and "law of the sea" in the wider sense of "sea law or law pertaining to the sea". I have gleaned this particular point of view from personal communication with Professor Si Yuzhou, esteemed erstwhile President of Dalian Maritime University who subscribes to the same view. As far as the discipline of law of the sea is concerned, notably the customary international law in that field is today largely codified and entrenched in the United Nations Convention on the Law of the Sea, 1982 (UNCLOS).[22]

That said, I have expressed the view that boxing public and private maritime law into two watertight compartments is counterproductive simply because they are intimately interrelated from a practical standpoint. Thus, highlighting any superficial distinction is anomalous and inconsequential.[23] Shipping invariably involves legal transactions that concern general commercial and trade law some of which are non-maritime in scope and practical usage.[24] On the other hand, public maritime law, as I have pointed out, includes regulatory shipping law which is extensive and expansive in scope and content. It occupies a substantial place in the maritime domain and is largely established through international conventions and related instruments. This branch of public maritime law is naturally inseparable from its private law counterpart.

An interesting point expressed by Professor Gold dwells on his observation that the major maritime states found it expedient and advantageous to divide and separate maritime law into public and private counterparts to serve their national interests and policies.[25] In my own writings, I have opined that this divided approach to

---

[20] See Mukherjee (2007), pp. 463–496.

[21] Edgar Gold (1981); Introduction, at p. xix.

[22] 1833 *UNTS* 3.

[23] Proshanto K. Mukherjee, *supra*, note 5 at p. 5.

[24] *Ibid.*

[25] Edgar Gold, *supra*, note 21, at p. xix.

maritime law does not rest on objectivity but is rather a product of the perceived superiority of public power, on the one hand, and inherent biases of the commercial world, on the other.[26]

Admiralty Law and Jurisdiction

A preliminary observation is that on the private law side of maritime law, at least as far as common law jurisdictions are concerned, admiralty law and commercial maritime law undoubtedly fall within its scope in their manifold dimensions.[27] This and other observations lead our discourse into a detailed consideration of what constitutes admiralty law and admiralty jurisdiction which are interrelated phenomena within the wider scope of maritime law.

At the risk of repetition, I would venture to reiterate that "maritime law" is an all-encompassing term; by contrast, "admiralty law" is quite specific, relevant largely to common law and hybrid legal systems. The phenomenon of "admiralty" is as much a matter of jurisdiction as it is of substantive law. As such, admiralty law refers to the body of law including procedural rules developed by the English Courts of Admiralty in their exercise of jurisdiction over matters pertaining to the sea. Admiralty jurisdiction is peculiarly distinguishable from the jurisdiction exercised by typical common law courts and arguably and is the very essence of the phenomenon of admiralty. An impressive and finite description of admiralty law is that it is "a special law, a distinct entity because of its distinct origin, history, field of application and distinct courts to administer it".[28] That said, I would draw to the attention of readers the view expressed by the renowned American lawyer and author Nicholas J. Healy who has stated that "[I]n English-speaking countries, 'admiralty' is sometimes used synonymously (with maritime law) …" He then continues—"but in a strict sense the term refers to the jurisdiction and procedural law of courts whose origins may be traced to the office of Admiral." The statement is clear and instructive, and as I have alluded to above, I thoroughly agree.[29]

In terms of law, there is a substantive element to it as well as a procedural counterpart consisting of rules of the Admiralty Courts. Historically, the most distinctive characteristic of admiralty is that its origins are embedded in English history which is why it prevails overwhelmingly in common law jurisdictions. In England, the jurisdiction was distinctively different from that exercised by the common law courts, in that admiralty jurisdiction in substance and form was in some ways influenced by the European continental civil law. By virtue of this brand of jurisdiction,

---

[26] Proshanto K. Mukherjee, *supra*, note 5 at p.5.

[27] F.R. Sanborn, *supra*, note 9, p. xvi.

[28] Mahanty, *supra*, note 16 at p. 14.

[29] See *Encyclopaedia Britannica*, where Nicholas J. Healy is cited as uniting the two words in the same breath.

maritime cases were tried in the Admiralty Court, which was quite separate and different from the common law courts.[30] The jurisdiction and the law administered by the Admiralty Court with roots in England have been adopted by common law countries and territories which were former colonies of Great Britain embracing the Anglo-Saxon legal tradition.[31]

Having said that, it is of historical interest to note that whereas the predominant view postulates that admiralty, both in terms of law and jurisdiction are of English origin, the notion is also embedded in French history of the times. The superintendence of maritime affairs including protection of seafarers was entrusted to the Admirals of France. Reference is made by an eminent law historian to "a jurisdiction which ultimately assumed the name of Admiralty" further stating that it resulted from the Admiral being designated to preside over navigation and to exercise maritime power in France[32]. However, the phenomenon of admiralty was relatively short-lived in France, whereas in England it got deeply rooted especially with the prowess of England in shipping and its dominating influence as a colonial power.

It is notable that in England, the common law exerted considerable influence on the admiralty law. By contrast, in the United States much of the admiralty law retained the original flavour of the continental civil law. In the former colonial regimes of the United Kingdom in the Western world such as Canada, Australia, and New Zealand as well as in the countries of the Asian and African continents, and the many of the Caribbean Island states, the admiralty law and jurisdiction of England remain highly influential.[33] By contrast, admiralty law and jurisdiction are virtually unheard of in European continents and other countries embracing the civil law tradition because jurisdiction in that system of law, with few exceptions,[34] is inherent in the courts without heed to subject matter. The English historical background through which admiralty jurisdiction evolved is thus irrelevant.

In England, admiralty law covered those subject matters over which the admiralty court had jurisdiction. This happened historically through an evolutionary process. Aside from England, admiralty jurisdiction over substantive subject matters also evolved in the United States. In this regard, Article III of the United States Constitution provides that "judicial power shall extend . . . to all Cases of admiralty and maritime Jurisdiction". This statement of law so expressed in the supreme legislation of the land embraces both subject-matter manifested through the word "Cases", and also jurisdiction.[35] So, it can be said that in the United States, those subject matters are subject to admiralty jurisdiction which the court decides. In

[30] See https://www.fjc.gov/history/courts/jurisdiction-admiralty-and-maritime.

[31] Mukherjee, *supra*, note 5 at p. 2

[32] Reddie (1841), p. 337. See also Tetley (1989), p. 14

[33] They include *inter alia*, India, Pakistan, Bangladesh, Singapore, Malaysia, Hong Kong, Ghana, Nigeria, Tanzania, Uganda and Kenya. Also, there are many of the Caribbean states and territories such as Trinidad and Tobago, Jamaica, Grenada, The Bahamas, Cayman Islands, British Virgin Islands, Guyana in the South American mainland where admiralty law and jurisdiction prevail.

[34] In France, for example, constitutional issues are dealt with by the *Conseil d'etat.*

[35] See https://www.fjc.gov/history/courts/jurisdiction-admiralty-and-maritime.

England, by comparison, subject matters that are of a maritime character and enumerated as such by statute fall under admiralty jurisdiction. The process involves codification of the jurisprudence produced by decided cases emanating from the courts over a period of time and consolidation of the customary maritime law. Parties to a dispute cannot create admiralty jurisdiction by mutual agreement.[36] In the present scheme of things, admiralty jurisdiction over subject matters is dictated by statute.[37] All this is a part of the evolutionary process.

Admiralty law in the common law jurisdictions, as stated above, is predominantly subsumed in shipping law, which simply stated is the law relating to ships and shipping. Notably, in the latter, there are wider connotations attributable to various aspects of ships and shipping which extend to regulatory and private law within the maritime domain. This engenders probing into how shipping law interfaces with admiralty law and raises questions of terminological accuracy and clarity. The characterization of admiralty law stemming from the peculiarity of admiralty jurisdiction is an important factor in this respect. Some would distinguish admiralty law from shipping law by contending that the latter warrants a wider connotation, in that it encompasses all aspects of ships, shipping, and maritime transportation. It is both regulatory and private in scope, covering subject matters such as maritime safety and ship-source marine pollution control. It also includes commercial maritime law, maritime labour law, as well as the admiralty law as circumscribed by admiralty jurisdiction. Incidentally, and as discussed in detail below, in previous times in the United Kingdom, maritime contractual transactions concluded on land were colloquially known as “dry law” as distinguished from “wet law” signifying activities and events happening at sea such as collisions, salvage, and general average acts and sacrifices. Dry law matters fell outside the ambit of admiralty jurisdiction and were dealt with under the common law jurisdiction of the courts. That state of affairs does not prevail anymore.[38]

One distinguished author explains the contrasting notions by referring to the Indian decision *Port Maina Maritime MA* v. *Owners and Parties Interested in the Vessel M. V. Gati Majestic* as follows:

Admiralty law is that branch of law developed by the English Courts of Admiralty to exercise their jurisdiction over matters at sea, whereas shipping law encompasses aspects such as commercial maritime law, maritime safety, pollution prevention, and labour law as well as admiralty law without extending to the public international law of the sea.[39]

The explanation is indeed instructive and insightful touching on the inclusiveness of shipping law and its separation from law of the sea, a subject of public

[36] https://www.pacmar.com/story/2013/11/01/features/admiralty-jurisdiction-what-does-that-mean/191.html (per Marilyn Raia).

[37] See section 20 of the legislation presently known as the Senior Courts Act 1981.

[38] See section 20 (2)(h) of the present Senior Courts Act 1981 of the UK. With respect to the US, see for example, *Delovio* v. *Boit* (1815), 7 F. Cas. 418, 442 n.46 (C.C.D. Mass. *1815*) (No. 3,776) in which Story J. held that a marine insurance contract fell within admiralty jurisdiction.

[39] Deva Rao (2018), p. xiv.

international law. Since admiralty falls within the scope of maritime law, I have explained the nuances of that term and its all-encompassing reach together with the legal connotations. Thus, at the basic preliminary level maritime law concerns all matters maritime from a legal perspective. The private maritime law mainly concerns the commercial aspects of shipping mainly comprising carriage of goods and passengers by sea and marine insurance. Also, there is a conglomerate of uniquely maritime subject matters extending to *inter alia*, collisions, salvage, general average, ship arrest, and proprietary interests in ships such as ship ownership, mortgages, and other charges, such as maritime liens. In the common law system, these subject matters fall under the rubric of admiralty jurisdiction. Thus, in some circles within the common law system, shipping law is considered, perhaps inaccurately, synonymous with admiralty law.

The use of the colloquial terms "wet" and "dry" law as alluded to above is an interesting factor relevant to our discussion. It mainly prevails in the practice arena of the United Kingdom predominantly in the London establishment to distinguish between matters that fall under admiralty and those that do not. The distinction between wet and dry is explained by referring to subject matters that are invariably connected to happenings at sea such as collisions and salvage, which are characterized as "wet" and those that occur on shore such as conclusion of carriage of goods contracts and charterparties. In my estimation, the distinction may have some relevance to the practice and profession of the law in the field, but is not of any legal significance which is probably the reason why the jargon is absent in the maritime milieu of Canada and the United States. In those two countries, the admiralty jurisdiction encompasses both the wet and dry components, and as such, both the *lex maritima* and the *lex mercatoria* of Roman law are subsumed within the admiralty jurisdictions of those countries. Indeed, whatever might be the qualifying distinctions, they are all matters related to ships and shipping.

The Senior Courts Act 1981, which is now the statutory source of admiralty jurisdiction in the United Kingdom, also covers the "dry" subject matters except for marine insurance. In my view, given the developments in the statutory regimes in the United Kingdom as well as abroad, the "wet" and "dry" characterizations are anomalous insofar as admiralty jurisdiction is concerned.

In most instances, the expression "admiralty law" is used only in countries with an admiralty jurisdiction in their judicial systems. In other countries that are not of common law persuasion, the term "shipping law" is used interchangeably with "maritime law".

At this juncture in the discourse, it is contextually noteworthy that in China which is a country of civil law persuasion, the term "admiralty" imported from the English maritime law lexicon is used fallaciously without any clear rationale whether in terms of jurisdictional peculiarity or the substantive law. Also, it is used in conjunction with the appellation "maritime" to describe the areas of judicial responsibility of the so-called eleven maritime courts. It is also used for identifying certain maritime law subject areas in the curricula of university law schools. Unsurprisingly, it has been loosely and unwittingly mentioned that regulatory conventions of the International Maritime Organization (IMO) constitute "public admiralty law" which, in the opinion of the present author, is utterly erroneous and meaningless. It is not only a linguistic deficiency but dire lack of legal comprehension.

Historical Evolution of Admiralty

In terms of how admiralty as a phenomenon actually evolved, it is not only important to know the history but also to understand the related linguistic nuances. In English, the word "admiralty" derives from the root word "admiral"; or to be more precise, it originates in the office of the Lord High Admiral. It is said that the word comes from the Arabic through Spanish and French.[40] In my observation, it is more accurate to say that it derives from the Arabic word "Amir" which literally means, a prosperous highly placed individual of the ruling class. Although admiralty is intimately connected to ships and shipping both in substantive legal as well as jurisdictional terms, it warrants a wider connotation than what is conventionally accepted. Historically speaking, the very basis on which admiralty jurisdiction was founded in contra-distinction to the common law jurisdiction in England was the conceptually wider range of subject matters pertaining to the sea, rather than simply those related to ships and shipping, a recognizably narrower field of endeavour.[41]

One of the most prominent of the maritime codes of Europe was the *Rôles d'Oléron* or Rolls of Oléron (Rolls) considered to be among the most distinguished of the medieval maritime codes. They were highly regarded as historical and substantive legislation based on the early maritime customs and practices prevailing in the Mediterranean region. The Rolls drew from various Italian sources which were later codified. Among these was the *Consolato del Mare*.[42] One manuscript of the Rolls has been preserved to this day; it is found in a collection famously known as the Black Book of the Admiralty. This compilation is historically renowned and is the basic source of the English maritime law. Aside from incorporating the *Rôles d'Oléron*, it also drew much of its content from the Rhodian Sea Law.[43] In terms of English historical record, the *Rôles d'Oléron* were entrenched as an Ordinance and found recognition as such throughout the medieval period of European maritime history.

Historically, it was during the reign of King John in England that the *Rôles d'Oléron* acquired formal recognition through an Ordinance.[44] Thereafter, until about 1360, no court was singularly and exclusively conferred with jurisdiction over maritime causes. The common law courts and chancery courts occasionally dealt

[40] Schoenbaum and Yiannopoulos, *supra*, note 7 at p. 1, in particular, footnotes 1 and 2 at that page.

[41] *Ibid* at p. 1.

[42] *Ibid* at pp. 9–10.

[43] Gold, *supra*, note 21 at p. 39.

[44] Reddie, *supra*, note 32 at p. 418.

with maritime matters which was grossly inadequate. Aside from these tribunals, the only courts exclusively addressing maritime disputes were the courts of the seaports which operated *ad-hoc*, meaning there were sittings of these courts only as and when required. Among these, the so-called "Cinque Ports" which were ports along the English Channel became famous and prominent. There were originally only three such ports which grew to five. Eventually, there were seven such ports but then reverted back to five which is why they are known as the Cinque Ports.[45] These ports enjoyed certain benefits and privileges like tax exemption given by the monarch in return for provision of ships by the ports. The courts of the Cinque Ports enjoyed exercising jurisdiction over disputes pertaining to a wide range of maritime subject matters. Interestingly, the sittings of the seaport courts were held on the shores of the sea from tide to tide. The courts were presided over by merchants and local port officials who adopted the *Rôles d'Oléron* as the applicable laws to render justice along with local customary laws.[46]

This period in European history was occasioned by the Crusades. In England, maritime expeditions became the order of the day. In conjunction with them, shipping and commercial activities went on the rise marked by numerous ventures. Instances of piracy increased and insubordination and disorderly conduct committed by seafarers increased rapidly and became frequent bordering on rampant. As a result of these occurrences, a single judicial body was established conferred with the appropriate jurisdiction and supporting mechanisms to deal with these multifarious situations. The piracy problem became so dire that in 1337, King Edward III was forced to pay compensation to some alien merchants out of the Royal treasury, for treacherous acts committed by English buccaneers. Numerous attempts were made to control piracy which eventually culminated in the establishment of the Office of the Lord High Admiral which marked the genesis of the Court of Admiralty. Literally speaking, the term "Admiralty Court" or "Court of Admiralty" meant the Admiral's Court. As reported by James Reddie, during the reign of King Edward I, the Admiralty Court, adopted the law of the *Rôles d'Oléron* to adjudicate matters relating to private maritime law. He also reports that towards the end of King Henry III's reign, the Rolls featured as the applicable law for maritime transactions.[47]

Perhaps the most significant event concerning the phenomenon of admiralty happened in 1360 during the reign of King Edward III was when he granted a commission to John de Beauchamp as "Admiral of all the fleets of ships, south, north and west". Under this commission, the admiral was given executive powers, and most importantly, he had jurisdiction over piracy and prize cases.[48] Through another commission granted in 1386, the admiral was empowered to hear complaints "of all and

---

[45] "cinque" means five in French.

[46] Gold (1989), note 3 at pp. I-2 to I-3.

[47] See Mukherjee, *supra*, note 5 at p. 22.

[48] Prize and prize law in the maritime context referred to the substance and process involved where an enemy ship captured in a wartime situation. The capturer could claim ownership of a captured enemy ship through a judicial process known as condemnation under which the court granted legal ownership of such a ship. See Gaskell et al. (1988).

singular of such matters as belonged to the office of Admiral and to take cognizance of maritime causes and to do justice and… to do and exercise all other things which to that office appertained as of right and according to maritime laws shall have to be done".[49] Undoubtedly, these historical events indicated that admiralty as a legal phenomenon involved jurisdiction as much as substantive law which is a verity extant to this day. The jurisdiction of the Admiralty Court was eventually settled by an Ordinance of 1648 and made perpetual by several subsequent ordinances. Incidentally, it was during the reign of King Edward III in the early part of the 14th century that the *Rôles d'Oléron* received express sovereign approval as the applicable law pertaining to all disputes of a maritime nature over which the Admiralty Court exercised jurisdiction.[50] Latterly, during the reign of Kings Richard II and Henry IV, the Admiralty Court was expanded and its jurisdiction elaborated.[51]

James Reddie notes that during the reign of King Charles II, the judge of the Admiralty Court was one Sir Leoline Jenkins who was eminently qualified in the civil law and distinguished himself in maritime jurisprudence. At his instigation and under his stewardship, one Thomas Bedford translated the Black Book of the Admiralty originally written in old Norman-French into English.[52] The greatest contribution to substantive admiralty law was made by the Black Book which contained six documents or books. The first two books set out details regarding the office of the admiral and his powers. The third was a record of the 1338 inquest into the repression of crimes committed at sea. The fourth book was captioned "Laws of Oléron"; it contained thirty-five articles on private maritime law. The fifth document contained a report on the 1375 inquest made in Queensborough. It also contained eighteen articles on private maritime law which were added. They addressed matters beyond the scope of the *Rôles d'Oléron*. These were followed by sixty-three regulations dealing with inquiries into criminal and delinquent acts committed on the high seas or coasts, and also prosecutions in relation thereto.

The foregoing text shows that the wealth of admiralty jurisprudence and comprehensive legislation of the times was attributable to the establishment of the Admiralty Court and enunciation of its well-defined jurisdiction.

Statutes Pertaining to Admiralty Subject Matters and Jurisdiction

As discussed above, historically, the Admiralty Court was the court of the Lord High Admiral which was established following the problems and issues that remained unresolved by the seaport courts. Professor Wiswall reiterates that the

[49] Gold, *supra*, note 46 at p. I-3.

[50] Reddie, *supra*, note 32 at p. 418.

[51] *Ibid* at p. 420; Gold, *supra* note 21 at p. 39.

[52] Reddie, *supra*, note 32 at p. 420.

Admiralty Court belonged to the office of the Lord High Admiral who was granted the Royal Prerogative to deal with matters maritime. As such, the Admiralty Court came into existence and was empowered to adjudicate maritime disputes and deal with maritime offences which fell within the remit of the Lord High Admiral pursuant to the Royal Prerogative. Admiralty jurisdiction was thus firmly articulated.[53]

The co-existence of the seaport courts, the Admiralty Court and the Common Law Courts led to judicial rivalry and uncertainty with regard to their respective jurisdictional reaches. As a result, in 1389 and 1391, two statutes were enacted which, in essence, restrained the jurisdiction of the Admiralty Court which were limited to things "done upon the sea" which included contracts made and executed at sea.[54] Evidently, the limitations imposed by statute were not readily accepted in practice. The Admiralty Court continued to exercise jurisdiction over matters which it perceived to be maritime in character and scope. Another statute was enacted in 1400 which not only restricted in express terms the competence of the Admiralty Court to "thing(s) done upon the sea" but also provided for penalties against parties who commenced actions in the Admiralty Court which fell outside the scope of its jurisdiction.[55] This statute provided:

Whereas in the statute made at Westminster, in the 13th year of the Second King Richard, amongst other things it contained that the Admiral and their deputies shall not intermeddle from henceforth, of any thing done within the realm, but only of a thing done upon the sea, according as it hath been duly used in the time of the noble King Edward, grand-father to the said King Richard, our Lord the King, willeth and granteth that the said statute be firmly holden and kept and put in execution.[56]

Judicial rivalry between the common law courts and the Admiralty Court was quite the fabric of vibrant and interesting legal history of the times which has been excitingly recorded by legal historians. It is somewhat inconsequential as far as the present work is concerned. I would simply mention that even the subject of wreck, which is unmistakenly of maritime character, was judicially defined under the 1391 Act in *Sir Henry Constable's Case* [57] in such a way that all cases involving wrecks were removed from the admiralty jurisdiction into that of the common law. Interestingly, Professor Wiswall refers to Sir Edward Coke as the "chief antagonist of the Admiralty jurisdiction", who defined "wreck" in this case as "that cast at ebb tide upon the shelf below the flood mark". Prior to that decision, the Admiralty Court had invariably exercised jurisdiction below the high-water mark.[58]

The ordinance of 1648 c.112, decided the jurisdiction of the Admiralty court once and for all. The power of the Admiralty Court had reached its highest limit by

---

[53] Wiswall (1970), p. 4.

[54] See https://www.fjc.gov/history/courts/jurisdiction-admiralty-and-maritime.

[55] Wiswall, *supra*, note 53 *at* p. 5.

[56] 2 *Hen*. 4, c. 11.

[57] *Constable* v. *Gamble* (1601), 5 Co. Rep. 106a.

[58] Wiswall, *supra*, note 53 at p. 6. This chapter of his book contains vivid details of the feud between Admiralty and the Common Law.

that time. The jurisdiction was made perpetual by several ordinances which followed in 1651, c.3, 1654, c.21, and 1656, c.10. All the ordinances eventually expired at the Restoration of 1660. After that, the Admiralty Court's jurisdiction gradually declined and "waned into oblivion" until the 1800s.[59] During this hiatus, the Admiralty Court's jurisdiction was confined to contracts entered into and performed on the high seas, lawsuits involving seafarers' wages and torts committed on the high seas.[60]

In the early 1800s, the Admiralty Court was bi-functional. In the first instance, it fulfilled its original function as a prize court which was a wartime occupation. The other function involved the admiralty judge undertaking judicial cognizance of civil maritime causes. In performing the second function, the tribunal came to be known as the instance court. In Professor Wiswall's one of books, he notes that during that era of the most eminent Admiralty Judge, Lord Stowell, the so-called civilian function of the court was virtually dormant.[61] In his account, a detailed outline of the instance jurisdiction of the Admiralty Court is provided in the beginning of the nineteenth century.[62]. The jurisdiction covered such things as droits of admiralty.[63] It also covered civil salvage[64] and unsealed contracts entered into at sea or made abroad and recognized *prima facie* as being maritime contracts, actions for hypothecation in respect of bottomry bonds or claims for the supply of necessaries. Such actions could only be brought through actions *in rem* against the *res*. Other matters cognizable under the Court's instance jurisdiction included freight where the master had a lien against cargo for unpaid freight, seamen's unpaid wages (but not for a master) as a lien against a ship actionable *in rem,* and maritime torts such as claims in respect of collisions and personal injury.

The Admiralty Court had no jurisdiction in respect of mortgages entered into on land and at any rate did not exercise jurisdiction over mortgages made at sea. It, however, possessed power to execute judgements rendered by foreign maritime courts. With regard to charterparties, actions involving freight and general average, the Admiralty Court did not refuse to exercise jurisdiction if it so intended, and the actions could be brought *in rem* or *in personam* but *in rem* proceedings were more frequent in its exercise of the instance jurisdiction, in particular, in relation to suits

[59] See Mukherjee, *supra*, note 5 at p.38.

[60] See Gold, Admiralty Law, *supra,* note 46 at pp. I-4 to I-6.

[61] Wiswall *supra*, note 53 at p. 7.

[62] *Ibid., at* pp. 8–11.

[63] As per Professor Wiswall's account, civil droits were the Admiral's "perquisites" or proprietary rights in wrecks at sea. "Wreck" included jetsam, flotsam, lagan, derelicts and deodands. After a pirate's conviction, his goods and spoils also became droits of Admiralty. Upon payment of salvage, a droit could be claimed by its owner if it was done within a year and a day of finding. Except for deodands, the owner's sole remedy was in common law if the wreck was found ashore, but if it was retrieved from the sea and carried ashore, the remedy was in Admiralty. Unclaimed wreck was sold by Court order and the remainder of proceeds after paying out salvage accrued to the Admiralty as perquisites.

[64] Described as "endeavour so heroic that it is unrivalled in fiction"; see *The Holder Borden*, 12 Fed. Cas.331(No. 6600) (D. Mass. 1847).

involving seamen's wages, hypothecations, salvage, collisions, and droits of Admiralty. Notably, the procedural aspects in the exercise of the jurisdiction have not been altered and remain the same in the present times.

The Admiralty Jurisdiction Acts of 1389 and 1391, enacted by King Richard II, placed many restrictions on the jurisdiction of the Admiralty Court. These were removed by the first Admiralty Court Act of 1840 pursuant to a Report of the Select Parliamentary Committee in 1833. This Act expanded the jurisdiction of the Admiralty Court. However, several recommendations of the Select Committee's Report remained unimplemented by statute. For example, the Act did not restore its jurisdiction over maritime contracts, freight, and charter-parties which it previously enjoyed, but it conferred new jurisdiction relating to ship mortgages incidental to *in rem* actions, claims for provision of salvage and towage services and necessaries claims, and also for such matters as title to ships and disputes over proceeds of sales of ships.[65]

In the Admiralty Court Act of 1854, similar to the what prevailed in the common law, a penalty was introduced relating to perjury.[66] Also, one could avail of proceedings by monition as was the practice in the civil law tradition under which the Marshall could be commanded to summon the defendant personally and admonish him to appear in court and answer to the allegations. In England, monition was used by the Admiralty Court in cases involving prize and *in rem* actions for forfeiture. It operated as a court warrant in admiralty as directed by the Admiralty Marshall.[67]

The Admiralty Court Act of 1861 introduced several new procedural elements which included the court's power to issue execution writs of judgements. These were similar to the common law practice.[68] The Act also gave jurisdiction to the court over any claim for damage done by any ship. According to Professor Wiswall, this was "the most important and valuable grant" in the Act.[69] He also states that it was the illustrious Dr. Stephen Lushington who drafted most of the provisions of the 1861 Act and who took it upon himself to articulate a more expanded jurisdiction of the Admiralty Court. However, in his estimation, the Admiralty Court could not entertain claims in general average. Indeed, in observation of Professor Wiswall, the Act of 1861 Act was quite retrogressive in some respects, such as the removal of admiralty jurisdiction over cargo claims against English or Welsh shipowners. But holistically speaking, and on balance, then Admiralty Court gained more than it lost.[70]

A significant event of the times was the passing of the Judicature Acts which were enacted pursuant to the Report of a Royal Commission whose membership included Sir Robert. Three of the successive Judicature Acts rose to prominence;

---

[65] Gold, *supra,* note 21 at pp. 40–41.

[66] See *Ibid* at pp. 53 and 62–63 for further details.

[67] See *ibid.* at p. 63; see also Mukherjee, *supra,* note 5 at p.43, in particular footnote 39 at that page.

[68] Wiswall, *supra,* note 53 at p. 65.

[69] Wiswall, *ibid* at p. 59.

[70] *Ibid. at* pp. 60–61. See also p. 94.

these were the Acts of 1873, 1874, and 1875 which were intended to streamline the system. Pursuant to the 1873 Act, the central Superior Courts were consolidated into the Supreme Court of Judicature and the previous Courts of Probate, Divorce, and Matrimonial Causes and Admiralty, formed one of five Divisions.[71] In my own estimation, the subject matters of probate, divorce, and matrimonial causes being totally unrelated to admiralty, their inclusion under the same court's jurisdiction was an anomaly. But at any rate, admiralty jurisdiction became vested in a Division of the High Court of England. In 1879, the Civil Procedure Acts Repeal Act, and the 1389 Admiralty Jurisdiction Act promulgated by King Richard II were repealed, and in 1894, the Supreme Court Rules were promulgated which assigned to the Admiralty Division all of the jurisdiction conferred on the High Court of Justice of the Supreme Court, by the newly consolidated Merchant Shipping Act 1896.[72]

Attributes of Admiralty Jurisdiction and Jurisprudence

The Admiralty Court Acts over those years, as mentioned above, marked a gradual expansion of the jurisdiction of the Admiralty Court and consequently it came to be known as the High Court of Admiralty which obviously raised the judicial status of the court. The reach of admiralty jurisdiction extended to such matters as ship building, ship repairs and ship's equipment, life salvage claims and maritime liens over masters' and seamen's wages, claims relating to bills of lading and damage suffered by cargo. It is remarkable that the Admiralty Court of those times was presided over by the illustrious judges Dr. Lushington and Sir Robert Phillimore whose decisions produced the most excellent brand of maritime jurisprudence that represents the historical hallmark of English admiralty law.[73]

The Admiralty Court's location in London is also full of historical intrigue. The earliest known site of the court was Horton's Quay near London Bridge as recorded in the year 1410. Thereafter, from 1666 to 1860, it was situated in Doctors Commons, famously known as the bastion of the Admiralty practitioners and jurists.[74] It is interesting to note that the name "Doctor's Commons", which was the Admiralty counterpart to the Inns of Court out of which Barristers in the common law practised, was so named because admiralty practitioners were all qualified as Doctors of Civil Law. Academically speaking, such qualification could only be obtained from Oxford or Cambridge following some ten years of rigorous studies. Another piece of interesting information describable as a "snippet" in context is that the great icon of English literature Charles Dickens, at one time worked as a messenger at Doctor's

---

[71] *Ibid*, at pp. 100–103.

[72] *Ibid*. at pp. 138, 139.

[73] Gold, *supra*, note 46 at p. I-6.

[74] See Steel (2011), p. vii.

Commons, an experience he did not cherish. His utter dislike was reflected in one of his writings in which he wrote "let's kill the lawyers".

Dr. Lushington's retirement as admiralty judge in 1857 signified the virtual demise of the renowned Doctors' Commons which was the bastion of the admiralty practitioners and jurists, all of whom were trained in the civil law.[75] His successor, Sir Robert Phillimore was the last of the civilian judges of the Admiralty Court. One important feature of the Phillimore era was the passing of the County Courts Admiralty Jurisdiction Act in 1868. That statute conferred limited admiralty jurisdiction on the County Courts of England and Wales. It is also notable that his retirement marked the change of custodianship of the English Admiralty law from the admiralty lawyers and judges to those of common law persuasion. Appellate jurisdiction in all matters under this statute was vested in the High Court of Admiralty and under this statute, these were all cognizable by the County Courts.[76]

After several years, in 1920, the first Administration of Justice Act was enacted which conferred jurisdiction in admiralty, with some exceptions, over claims involving carriage of goods and charter-parties, and torts in connection with the carriage of cargo.[77] In 1925, the Supreme Court of Judicature (Consolidation) Act was enacted which impacted on admiralty jurisdiction as described by Professor Wiswall below:

The greatest effect of the Judicature Consolidation Act upon the Admiralty Court was jurisdictional. The inclusive grant of admiralty jurisdiction by the Judicature Acts remained the basis of jurisdiction, but additions included claims for necessaries supplied to any foreign ship *anywhere* save in her home port and questions of title arising in necessaries suits, claims for damage done *to* any ship, and claims for salvage, life salvage, and services in the nature of towage and salvage regardless of where rendered. The total admiralty jurisdiction granted was therefore all that was possessed formerly by the High Court of Justice immediately prior to the Consolidation Act, and all that unrepealed and added by the Act itself.[78]

It is notable that in this Act, the definition of "damage" included personal injury and wrongful death. Also, the definition of "ship" was expressed as "any description of vessel used in navigation not propelled by oars", a definition that remains intact to this day.[79]

The enactment of the Supreme Court of Judicature (Consolidation) Act 1928, was a landmark event. Under that Act, the Admiralty Court could entertain claims *in personam* in addition to actions *in rem*. Probably, this was instigated by the decision of the Court of Appeal in *The Sheaf Brook*[80] which held that an *in personam* claim by cargo owners against English shipowners fell outside the scope of the

---

[75] Wiswall, *supra*, note 53 at pp. 91, 96.

[76] *Ibid* at pp. 97–98.

[77] *Ibid.* at p. 138.

[78] *Ibid* at p. 141.

[79] *Ibid* at p. 143.

[80] [1926] p. 61 (C.A.).

jurisdiction conferred on the Admiralty Division by the 1925 Consolidation Act. Indeed, under this Act, the jurisdiction of the High Court could be exercised by all its constituent Divisions.[81]

At this juncture, I would venture to draw into focus the most distinctive feature of admiralty jurisdiction in contradistinction to its common law counterpart. At common law, actions can only be brought *in personam* which is similar to the civil law system. But in admiralty, actions can also be instituted *in rem* meaning actions against the *res*; in other words, the thing or object which has caused the loss, damage, or harm apart from an action *in personam* which signifies an action against a person, usually the owner of the *res*. In the maritime context, it is usually the shipowner. Both actions are available in the admiralty jurisdiction. The action *in rem* is a very useful device in the maritime context because the instrument of loss, harm, or damage is a ship which is mobile and often, the person concerned, that is, the shipowner, is unavailable or untraceable. An action *in rem* and an action *in personam* can initially proceed independently and later be joined together if and when the defendant shipowner may find it expedient and to its advantage to expose itself and defend the action *in rem* instituted against its ship.[82]

As a part of the evolutionary process relating to admiralty, the 1894 Merchant Shipping Act has stood the test of time for over a hundred years in the United Kingdom (UK). In other jurisdictions that are former British colonies, the substantive law of that legislation has been emulated or imported by reference. Relatively, recent in the United Kingdom is the Merchant Shipping Act 1995 which was enacted to replace the 1894 Act. The UK admiralty law regime is also tempered by legislation that gives effect to international conventions especially those that set out maritime law subject matters such as the Arrest Convention of 1952.[83] This convention was concluded in Brussels, the home base of the Comité Maritime International (CMI), under its auspices. The United Kingdom joined the convention shortly after it was adopted and enacted legislation to give statutory effect to it in 1956 through the Administration of Justice Act, 1956. The convention purported to create a uniform international regime for the law of ship arrest. By becoming a party to that convention and enacting the legislation to implement it, the United Kingdom was able to clarify jurisdictional issues respecting *in rem* and *in personam* actions for maritime claims for which a ship was arrestable. The 1956 Act paved the way for the recognition of new and expanded causes cognizable under admiralty jurisdiction. Following the 1952 Arrest Convention, it was able to articulate the concept of sister-ship arrest. It is notable that today there exists a more updated version of international ship arrest law in the form of the Arrest Convention of 1999. However, the United Kingdom chose not to join it.[84]

[81] Wiswall, *supra*, note 53 at p. 143.

[82] The *in- rem* action has its origins in ancient Anglo-Saxon law relating to land. See lsd.law/define/action-in-rem.

[83] International Convention for the Unification of Certain Rules of Law Relating to Arrest of Sea-Going Vessels, 1952, 439 *UNTS* 193.

[84] 2979 *UNTS* 3.

Incidentally, Article 1(1) of the 1999 Convention defines "maritime claim" by reference to a list of claims comprising some items that were conspicuously absent in the 1952 Convention. Among them are the ones mentioned in paragraphs (c) and (d) of Article 1(1). These are:

(c) salvage operations or any salvage agreement, including, if applicable, special compensation relating to salvage operations in respect of a ship which by itself or its cargo threatened damage to the environment;

(d) damage or threat of damage caused by the ship to the environment, coastline or related interests; measures taken to prevent, minimize, or remove such damage; compensation for such damage; costs of reasonable measures of reinstatement of the environment actually undertaken or to be undertaken; loss incurred or likely to be incurred by third parties in connection with such damage; and costs, or loss of a similar nature to those identified in this subparagraph (d);

The provision relating to damage to the environment noted above is conspicuously absent in the 1952 Convention and also in the Senior Courts Act 1981 implementing it. Arguably, however, "damage to the environment" can possible be accommodated within the words "any claim for damage done by a ship". All in all, it can be said that the 1999 Convention provides for more claims in respect of which a ship can be arrested than does the 1952 Convention. Similarly, it can also be said that with regard to the Senior Courts Act 1981, there are some claims which do not squarely appear in Section 20(2) of that Act.

With regard to the 1956 Act, Professor Wiswall stated in his book that "no other enactment has possessed the potential for judicial expansion of jurisdiction which is inherent in the most recent grant of jurisdiction to Admiralty, contained in Part I of the Administration of Justice Act, 1956". He commented further rather cynically that the Act made "such great restoration of jurisdiction to Admiralty that it may properly be termed 'a Coke's nightmare'."[85] In respect of the string of admiralty jurisdiction statutes enacted over the years, and the consequent entrenchment of admiralty jurisdiction, it warrants mention that in 1970, the Admiralty Court was established as a part of the Queen's Bench Division of the High Court by the Supreme Court Act, which later became the Supreme Court Act, 1981 and remained as such for more than a couple of decades. In 2009, it was renamed the Senior Courts Act, 1981 reflecting important judicial reforms which took place relatively recently.

On 1 October of that year, a landmark event took place which marked the demise of the Appellate Committee of the House of Lords, the judicial wing and institution of the Upper House of the British Parliament, which was the highest court of appeal in the British judicial system for many years. Its removal and replacement by the Supreme Court of the United Kingdom has been described as "a defining moment" in British judicial history which has had implications for the admiralty jurisdiction, among other things. It has, in essence, transformed the constitutional and legal heritage of the United Kingdom including the common law tradition itself. The Supreme Court is the highest court of the land for all civil causes within the judicial hierarchy

---

[85] Wiswall, *supra*, note 53 at pp. 149, 152.

and is also the highest court in England, Wales, and Northern Ireland for all criminal matters but not for Scotland where the High Court of Judiciary is the final court for criminal appeals. As mentioned earlier, the legal system of Scotland is Scots Law, which is largely of civil law persuasion, is best described as a hybrid legal system.

The new judicial framework, no doubt, reinforces the constitutional concept of judicial independence. In this structure, the Court of Appeal stands immediately below the Supreme Court, under which is placed the High Court within which is situated the Admiralty Court as a part of the Queen' Bench Division (now known as "King's Bench Division").

Section 20 of the Senior Courts Act currently provides the statutory foundation for admiralty jurisdiction in the United Kingdom legal system. It largely reflects the comprehensive jurisdiction which was established in the Administration of Justice Act, 1956, with some important and significant improvements added on. In Subsection 20 (1) paragraphs (c) and (d), it is provided that the admiralty jurisdiction, which the court possessed prior to its commencement, is to continue, along with any jurisdiction directed by the rules of the court to be exercised by it. The specific subject matters pertaining to the Admiralty Court's jurisdiction, are found in section 20(2). In effect, these are claims *ratione materiae*. That said, it must be noted that the jurisdiction is limited by its geographical scope of application; in other words, the *ratione loci.* It can also be restricted to certain nationalities of the litigants pointing to the application of *ratione personae* and limited to ships of certain flags.

The 1952 Convention created a uniform regime respecting claims for which ships could be arrested in state parties. It was based on the premise that arrest was only possible in cases where the claim was a maritime claim by definition in the convention. In line with the teleology of the convention, the claimant was provided with an instant security for his claim which persisted as the arrested vessel being the subject asset. In the convention, "arrest" is defined as "detention of a ship by judicial process to secure a maritime claim, but does not include the seizure of a ship in execution or satisfaction of a judgment". In terms of United Kingdom law, this meant a ship could not be rearrested for an unsatisfied judgment claim. The claimant would have to obtain an execution writ known as a writ of *fieri facias* in order to enforce the judgment.[86]

As mentioned above, the legislation giving effect to the 1952 Arrest Convention in the United Kingdom was the Administration of Justice Act, 1956 which was superseded by the Supreme Court Act, 1981, and as mentioned above, has been renamed Senior Courts Act reflecting the law reform that has subsequently taken place. The legislation in succession serves as the mechanism for the judicial founding of Admiralty jurisdiction. The 1956 Act set out certain "questions and claims" in respect of which the High Court could exercise its Admiralty jurisdiction.[87] Be

---

[86] See *The Alletta* [1974] 1 Lloyd's Rep 40 which features application of the writ of *fieri facias* and adequately explains the phenomenon.

[87] Berlingieri (2011), pp. 174–175.

that as it may, it is trite that instituting an action *in rem* is equally valid and adequate for the founding of such jurisdiction. In effect, where *in rem* proceedings have been instituted against a ship, arresting it actually provides interim relief.[88] In practical terms, however, a ship is usually arrested at the same time when a writ *in rem* is issued and served signifying the commencement of the action. As one prominent admiralty judge of recent times has stated in unequivocal terms:

The distinguishing feature of Admiralty jurisdiction, which is recognized by international convention, is that an action can be brought directly against an offending ship by arresting the ship. If the shipowner wants to contest the claim, he can do so only by submitting to the jurisdiction of the Admiralty Court which has arrested his ship.[89]

Admiralty Procedures

As mentioned above, admiralty jurisdiction comprising the substantive law exemplified by *ratione materiae* is distinctively different from the jurisdictions of courts that follow the typical common law system. It is therefore important to be cognizant of the procedural peculiarities of admiralty in the United Kingdom, where procedures for enabling efficiency and supporting functionality are promulgated as orders pursuant to the Rules of Court that are made under the Senior Courts Act, 1981 which deals with admiralty jurisdiction.[90] The rules cover several matters extending to issue and execution of warrants for ship arrests including their practical ramifications, service of writs *in rem* and *in personam* within and beyond the jurisdiction, caveats against arrests and release of ships. They also address matters pertaining to preliminary acts, security, and bail, and also the office, powers, and duties of the Admiralty Marshall who is the most important officer of the court. The procedures also cover such matters as procedures for interveners, orders for appraisement and sale of a ship and determination of priorities, orders for sales of other maritime property, and forfeiture proceedings in relation to ships. Actions pertaining to limitation of liability are also covered by the rules.[91]

These procedural matters identified above are, needless to say, also relevant to countries where the civil law system prevails but not pursuant to anything that falls under the rubric of "admiralty" jurisdiction but rather under the inherent jurisdiction of the courts which is a typical characteristic of that legal system. As such, jurisdictionally speaking, inclusive of the substantive as well as the procedural elements, they can be said to fall under the appellation "maritime".

[88] Berlingieri *ibid.*; see also Jackson (2005), p. 99.

[89] Sheen (2011), p. xv.

[90] See Order 75 of the Supreme Court Rules.

[91] See Mukherjee (2016), pp. 42–43.

Conclusion

In this chapter, I have described admiralty as a phenomenon because it is wider in scope than simply a brand of law in the maritime field. Indeed, it is the jurisdictional aspect which is equally important as the law generated by it. Arguably, it is the jurisdiction that defines its character. I have pointedly stated that the phenomenon of admiralty is only present in the common law system stemming from its origins in England steeped in English maritime history. However, it was present in France even earlier but was short-lived. Over several centuries, it has been propagated worldwide through the British colonial regimes and is vibrantly present to this day.

There is a serious semantic aspect to the term "Admiralty" which I have highlighted. The fact that historically it was established by ordinance and royal prerogative, empowering the Lord High Admiral with unrestricted jurisdiction over piracy and prize cases made it the Admiral's Court and gave it the distinctive caption "Admiralty". I have drawn to the attention of the readership the anomalous use of that term in certain quarters by those who are ill-informed regarding the law as well as the distinctive jurisdiction it engenders. I have attempted to present an adequate historical backdrop focusing on the salient features which are distinguishable from the substantive common law and draws on European continental legal practices associated with the civil law of Roman law heritage. Even so, it is doubtlessly embedded and entrenched in the common law system in view of its historical evolution and chronological development. Insofar as the jurisdictional dimension of admiralty is concerned, a distinctive feature is the availability of the action *in rem* which is virtually unheard of in the civil law system which only accommodates the action *in personam*. The phenomenon of admiralty is absent in the civil law system mainly because there is no historical foundation for it in any of the countries that follow that legal tradition.

The chapter provides a revisit to the phenomenon of admiralty residing within the wider domain of maritime law which is steeped in antiquity and rich tradition. I have attempted to trace the historical roots of admiralty law and jurisdiction and its evolutionary background refined over several centuries. In that process, I have attempted to clarify certain misunderstandings even among those who are in the field professionally and in academia. It is hoped and anticipated that this elementary effort will inspire and instigate those interested in this highly specialized field of endeavour and provide the impetus for further study and enquiry by practitioners and scholars alike into a rare area of legal persuasion. In my experience, even though admiralty is old law, it is still unfamiliar ground for many who need to be in the know.

While maritime law is unquestionably a dynamic field and is organic in terms of growth and comprehensibility, it is fertile ground for research and rethinking, especially by the younger genre of enthusiasts who are future law and policy makers. Hopefully, this chapter will contribute to a better appreciation and understanding of the varied nuances and peculiarities of the phenomenon of admiralty in the spheres of both law and jurisdiction within the wider sphere of maritime law and practice.

References

Berlingieri F (2011) *Berlingieri on arrest of ships*, 5th edn. Informa, London

Brown ED (1971) *The legal regime of hydrospace*. Stevens & Sons, London

Canfield GL (1922) Note. *Mich Law Rev* 20:535

Constable v Gamble (1601) 5 Co Rep 106a

Delovio v Boit (1815) 7 F Cas 418 (CCD Mass) (No 3776)

Deva Rao S (2018) Introduction. In: Mahanty S (ed) Maritime jurisdiction and admiralty law in India, 2nd edn. Universal Law Publishing LexisNexis, Gurgaon, p xiv

Gaskell NJJ, Debattista C, Swatton RJ (1988) *Chorley and Giles' shipping law*, 8th edn. Pitman Publishing, London

Gold E (1981) *Maritime transport: the evolution of international marine policy and shipping law*. Lexington Books, Toronto

Gold E (1989) *Canadian admiralty law, introductory materials*, 7th edn. Yvon Blais Inc, Montreal

Insurance Co v Dunham (1872) 14 Wall 170

Jackson DC (2005) *Enforcement of maritime claims*, 4th edn. LLP, London

Mahanty S (2018) *Maritime jurisdiction and admiralty law in India*, 2nd edn. Universal Law Publishing LexisNexis, Gurgaon

Mukherjee PK (2007) The penal law of ship-source marine pollution: selected issues in perspective. In: Malick Ndiaye T, Wolfrum R (eds) Liber Amicorum Judge Thomas A. Mensah: law of the sea, environmental law and settlement of disputes. Martinus Nijhoff, Leiden/Boston, pp 463–496

Mukherjee PK (2016) An introduction to maritime law and admiralty jurisdiction. In: *Admiral: a compendium*. Ghana Shippers' Authority, Accra, pp 42–43

Mukherjee PK (2021) Mukherjee on maritime legislation, 2nd edn. WMU Publications, Malmö

Paulsen GW (1983) A historical overview of the development of uniformity in international maritime law. Tulane Law Rev 57(5):1065

Reddie J (1841) An historical view of the law maritime commerce. William Blackwood & Sons, Edinburgh/London

Sanborn FR (1989) Origins of the Early English Maritime and commercial law. Professional Books Ltd, Abingdon, 1989 reprint).

Schoenbaum TJ (1994) Admiralty and maritime law, vol 1, 2nd edn. West Publishing Co, St Paul, Minn

Schoenbaum TJ, Yiannopoulos AN (1984) Admiralty and maritime law: cases and materials, Charlottesville

Sheen B (2011) *Foreword* to the First Edition of Nigel Meeson and John A. Kimbell, *Admiralty Jurisdiction and Practice*. Informa, London, p xv

Steel D (2011) Foreword to the Fourth Edition of Nigel Meeson and John A. Kimbell, Admiralty Jurisdiction and Practice. Informa, London, p vii

Tetley W (1989) Maritime liens and claims. Yvon Blais Inc, Montreal

The Alletta [1974] 1 Lloyd's Rep 40

The Holder Borden (1847) 12 F Cas 331 (No 6600) (D Mass)

United Africa Ltd v Owners of the MV Tolten [1946] 2 All ER 372

United Nations (2003) Guide-lines for maritime legislation, 3rd ed. (ESCAP, Bangkok, ST/ESCAP/1076)

Wiswall FL (1970) The development of admiralty jurisdiction and practice since 1800. Cambridge University Press, Cambridge

Chapter 2
Public Maritime Legislations in South Korea

Junghwan Choi

Introduction

A significant portion of global trade volume is transported by sea, and maritime transport continues to play a central role in world trade in 2025. This indicates that maritime transport is not merely a means of conveyance but a critical component of the global economy, serving as an essential lifeline that affects international supply chains and energy security. Such strategic importance of the oceans further underscores the necessity of laws and regulatory frameworks capable of effectively and systematically governing maritime activities.

Maritime law is a comprehensive legal system that coordinates and regulates the diverse interests and activities occurring across the vast maritime domain. It can be divided into private maritime law, which addresses civil rights and obligations concerning ships and cargo, and public maritime law, which encompasses state and international regulations aimed at protecting public interests and societal values, such as ship safety, marine environmental protection, seafarer welfare, and maritime security. This study focuses primarily on public maritime law. Public maritime law is a domain where national sovereignty intersects with international public interest, encompassing a wide range of regulations including ship construction and equipment standards, collision prevention, marine pollution control, seafarer training and labour conditions, and the state mechanisms established for their enforcement.

Junghwan Choi Xinghai Associate Professor at The School of Law of Dalian Maritime University, China. LL.M. in Maritime Law (Korea Maritime & Ocean Uni.), LL.M. in International Maritime Law with Merit (Swansea Uni., UK), Ph.D. in Maritime Law (Exeter Uni., UK).

J. Choi (✉)
Law School, Dalian Maritime University, Dalian, P.R. China
e-mail: junghwanchoi@dlmu.edu.cn

J. Choi (ed.), *Public Maritime Law in Asia*, International Law in Asia,
https://doi.org/10.1007/978-981-95-7037-9_2

By its nature, public maritime law requires international cooperation for its formation and development. Given that individual vessels navigate multiple national waters and international seas, effective regulation cannot rely solely on unilateral national measures. Major international norms are therefore designed under the auspices of international organizations, such as the International Maritime Organization (IMO). Member-states subsequently adopt and implement these norms within their domestic legal frameworks, creating a regulatory system applicable worldwide, which represents an essential model of international cooperation for the effective management of the "common oceans."

South Korea, as a major shipping power ranking among the top five in global fleet capacity and possessing a world-class shipbuilding industry, plays a leading role in the global maritime order beyond mere participation.[1] It is essential for the South Korean shipping and shipbuilding industries to proactively adopt internationally recognized standards and regulations and implement them in ways suited to domestic industrial realities in order to maintain competitiveness in global markets and achieve sustainable growth. This goes beyond mere compliance with international legal obligations; it constitutes a foundational effort to build national competitiveness.

This study aims to comprehensively examine the legislative framework of public maritime legislations in South Korea. It illuminates the institutional foundations of South Korean public maritime law, provides an overview of the current status and structure of the South Korean shipping industry, analyses South Korea's role and position within the IMO, and examines the principles and legislative processes through which various IMO international conventions are implemented in domestic law.

Institutional Framework for Maritime Legislations in Korea

Overview of Shipping Industry

Shipping industry comprises three essential components: capital, vessels, and seafarers, among which seafarers represent a critical human resource rather than merely labour. South Korea, as a peninsular nation surrounded by the sea on three sides, has developed its shipping industry into a fundamental national infrastructure sector. Maritime transport accounts for approximately 99.7 per cent of all import and export cargo and 100 per cent of essential raw materials, including crude oil, coal, and iron ore, thereby forming a vital pillar of the national economy.[2] The industry also serves as a significant foreign exchange-earning sector, contributing to the

[1] Choi et al. (2024), p. 8512.

[2] Korea Shipowners' Association, 'Korean Shipping Industry', available at https://oneksa.kr/about/shipping_industry.php (accessed 21 September 2025).

improvement of the balance of payments. In 2021, the revenue of South Korean global shipping companies reached approximately USD 35.7 billion.[3] The shipping sector's role is to create substantial employment, encompassing seafarers, cargo handling, port construction, pilotage and towage services, shipbuilding and ship equipment, and financial services, thereby demonstrating broad socio-economic contributions. South Korea possesses integrated maritime competitiveness as a seafarer country, the ship owner country, and shipbuilding country. As a seafarer nation, approximately 1,723 South Korean seafarers were employed overseas as of 2023, earning roughly USD 7.4 billion in foreign exchange from 2010 to 2019.[4] As a ship owner country, South Korea operated 1688 vessels in 2024, totalling approximately 97, 020 thousand DWT, representing about 4.2 per cent of the global fleet.[5] Key domestic shipping companies, including HMM, Pan Ocean, Hyundai Glovis, and H-Line Shipping, maintain competitive positions in the international market across multiple vessel types, such as ultra-large container ships, bulk carriers, and car carriers.[6]

According to the Review of Maritime Transport 2024 by UNCTAD, South Korea ranks as the sixth-largest ship-owning country globally, holding 4.2 per cent of the total world tonnage. The domestic fleet comprises 1688 vessels, of which 826 are nationally registered (19,896,324 DWT), while 852 are foreign-flagged vessels (77,045,438 DWT), resulting in a foreign-flagged proportion of 79.4 per cent.[7]

From a strategic perspective, the shipping industry also fulfils a national security role, transporting strategic materials and military supplies, and functioning as a 'fourth branch of the armed forces' alongside the army, navy, and air force during emergencies. South Korea's ocean-going fleet operates across the world's five oceans and six continents, serving not only as a commercial transport network but also as a maritime diplomatic envoy that enhances the nation's international standing. Since 2001, South Korea has consistently held Category A Council membership in the IMO for twelve consecutive terms (spanning over 22 years) and produced Kitack Lim as Secretary-General of the IMO (2016–2023), demonstrating its proactive role in shaping global maritime policy.[8]

South Korea has established itself as a comprehensive maritime power through the integration of seafarers (human resources), vessels (assets), and shipbuilding (industrial capacity). Nevertheless, challenges remain, including the decline in nationally registered seafarers and issues related to irregular employment, underscoring the importance of long-term workforce development and continued policy support to sustain maritime competitiveness.

---

[3] The Korea Herald, 'S. Korea's shipping industry expected to enjoy strong sales in 2021', available at https://www.koreaherald.com/article/2548088 (accessed 21 September 2025).

[4] Choi et al. (2025), p. 135.

[5] UNCTAD, *Review of Maritime Transport 2024* (2024), available at https://unctad.org/publication/review-maritime-transport-2024 (accessed 21 September 2025).

[6] Korea Shipowners' Association (n 2).

[7] UNCTAD (2024).

[8] IMO Korea, available at https://www.imokorea.org/ (accessed 21 September 2025).

Involvement in the IMO

South Korea has played a continuous and strategic role in shaping international maritime policies and regulatory frameworks through its active participation in IMO. South Korean engagement with the IMO began with the adoption of the IMCO Convention in 1948 and the establishment of the Maritime Affairs Bureau in 1955, the country's first governmental organization dedicated to maritime affairs.[9] This engagement was further institutionalized with the enactment of the Seafarers Act and South Korea's accession to IMCO in 1962, which laid the foundation for linking international maritime regimes with domestic legal frameworks.[10] During the 1960s and 1970s, South Korea adopted and acceded to key international conventions, including the International Convention for the Safety of Life at Sea (SOLAS), the Convention on Facilitation of International Maritime Traffic (FAL), the International Convention on Tonnage Measurement of Ships (TONNAGE), the International Convention for the Prevention of Pollution from Ships (MARPOL), and the International Convention on Standards of Training, Certification, and Watchkeeping for Seafarers (STCW). South Korea established a system to harmonize international norms on maritime safety, marine environmental protection, and seafarer training and certification with domestic legislation. Notably, the adoption of the STCW Convention in 1978 and the MARPOL 73/78 Protocol marked a significant milestone in strengthening South Korea's commitment to compliance with international maritime standards and environmental protection, while providing a strategic platform to enhance competitiveness in shipping, shipbuilding, and seafarer development.

In the 1980s and 1990s, South Korea pursued compliance with international norms and professional capacity building, exemplified by the establishment of the Korea Maritime Training Institute (currently the Korea Maritime and Fisheries Training Institute), the opening of the Korean Register's London office, the first implementation of Port State Control (PSC), adoption of the International Safety Management (ISM) Code, and accession to STCW-F.[11] The election of South Korea as the first C-Group Council member of the IMO in 1991, and subsequent election as an A-Group member after 2001, provided a critical opportunity to secure a voice in international maritime policy-making and regulatory formulation. These achievements allowed South Korea to project its comprehensive maritime capabilities as a seafarer nation, ship-owning nation, and shipbuilding nation on the international stage.

Since the 2000s, South Korea has taken a leading role in the adoption and domestic implementation of international regulations related to environmental protection, security, and safety, including the Anti-Fouling Systems (AFS) Convention, the International Ship and Port Facility Security (ISPS) Code, the Ballast Water

---

[9] Ibid.

[10] Ibid.

[11] Ibid.

Management (BWM) Convention, the Suppression of Unlawful Acts (SUA) Protocol, and the Hong Kong Ship Recycling Convention. In the 2010s, South Korea contributed to international standard-setting in areas such as seafarer management, environmentally friendly operations, and energy efficiency through participation in the 1995 Manila amendments to the STCW Convention, the establishment of World Seafarers' Day, the introduction of the Energy Efficiency Design Index (EEDI) for ships, and the election of Kitack Lim as the 9th Secretary-General of the IMO.[12]

In the 2020s, South Korea has further strengthened its international leadership by implementing IMO sulphur oxide regulations, commercializing e-navigation, establishing the IMO Gender Equality Award, electing the 10th Secretary-General, and adopting IMO greenhouse gas reduction strategies.[13] These efforts have positioned South Korea as a comprehensive maritime power that leads international standards in climate change mitigation, maritime safety, and environmental protection. Beyond mere international participation, these activities leverage South Korea's integrated maritime capabilities, encompassing seafarers, vessels, and shipbuilding, to influence international norms and policymaking processes. In doing so, South Korea enhances its global leadership in maritime safety, protection of the marine environment, maritime security, seafarer training and certification, and greenhouse gas reduction.

To sum up, South Korea's engagement with the IMO demonstrates a historical trajectory in which the nation has simultaneously advanced domestic maritime policy and international regulatory development, strengthened the global competitiveness of its shipping, shipbuilding, and seafarer sectors, ensured compliance with international environmental standards, secured maritime safety and security, and addressed climate change. This record exemplifies South Korea's evolution from a mere seafarer-supplying country to a comprehensive maritime nation, while providing a critical foundation for strategic influence in international maritime governance.

General Principle of Implementation of IMO Conventions in Domestic Law

According to Article 60 of the Constitution of South Korea, the National Assembly holds the authority to consent to the conclusion and ratification of treaties or legislative matters that impose significant financial burdens on the state or its citizens. Therefore, the conclusion of major international treaties requires the consent of the National Assembly. Here, the term 'legislative matters' refers to issues concerning

[12] MOF, available at https://www.mofa.go.kr/www/brd/m_4080/view.do?seq=371918&page=397&pitem=10 (accessed 21 September 2025).

[13] IMO, 'IMO gender equality award 2024', available at https://www.imo.org/en/mediacentre/pressbriefings/pages/2024-gender-equality-award.aspx (accessed 21 September 2025).

the rights and obligations of citizens. Since most treaties related to IMO Conventions affect the rights and obligations of citizens, parliamentary approval is necessary.[14]

Regarding the domestic legal effect of international norms, Article 6, Paragraph 1 of the Constitution stipulates those treaties concluded and promulgated, as well as generally recognized rules of international law, possess the same effect as domestic law.[15] Treaties are inherently self-executing and generally do not require the enactment of specific domestic legislation. However, the direct applicability of a treaty within domestic law is limited to self-executing treaties. Most international maritime treaties are self-executing, yet some require explicit or implicit domestic measures for implementation. Furthermore, even within a single treaty, it is necessary to distinguish between provisions that are directly applicable or have direct effect and those that do not. Some scholars argue that monism (adoption theory) is appropriate for self-executing treaties, whereas dualism (transformation theory) should be applied to non-self-executing treaties.[16]

Although international law and domestic law have the same formal effect, in the event of a conflict, the principles of *lex posterior* (new law prevails) and *lex specialis* (special law prevails) apply. Thus, while the domestic legal effect of international law is recognized under the Constitution, it is reasonable to consider it subordinate to the Constitution.[17] However, even though international law generally governs relations between states, provisions in treaties that require domestic legislation or the application of domestic law (e.g., UNCLOS, 1982a) may establish the precedence of the treaty (e.g., Article 4 of the Act on the Security of Internationally Navigating Ships and Port Facilities). Therefore, it is inappropriate to assert a universal hierarchy of either international law over domestic law or vice versa without considering the nature of the treaty.

Most international maritime conventions have been developed and implemented over long-standing governmental practice and are incorporated into domestic law according to each country's legal procedures. The legislative process generally seeks to harmonize international and domestic law, so the potential for actual conflict is limited. In the event of a conflict, the two norms should be interpreted in a manner that reconciles them, ensuring that neither provision is infringed, with the text interpreted in accordance with its ordinary meaning and legislative intent.

The domestic effect of international conventions can theoretically be classified under monism or dualism. In practice, South Korea generally adopts the monist approach (adoption theory), similar to the United States and Japan. However, major domestic statutes related to vessel safety and marine environmental protection, such as the Ship Safety Act and the Marine Environment Management Act, adopt a dualist approach (transformation theory) or dual legislative system, as the provisions of

[14] Korea Legislation Research Institute, 'Status of the Republic of Korea', available at https://elaw.klri.re.kr/kor_serviice/main.do (accessed 21 September 2025).

[15] MOFA, *Treaty Making by the ROK*, available at https://www.mofa.go.kr/eng/wpge/m_5439/contents.do (accessed 21 September 2025).

[16] Mendez (2013).

[17] MOFA (n 15).

international conventions are translated and incorporated into South Korean law through statutes, ordinances, regulations, and administrative guidelines.

Furthermore, when an international convention establishes standards stricter than domestic law, the Ship Safety Act (Article 5) and the Marine Environment Management Act (Article 4) provide that the convention shall take precedence. This ensures respect for the authority of international treaties while avoiding conflicts with domestic law. For this reason, South Korea's maritime legislation contains extensive subordinate regulations (e.g., ordinances), and domestic laws are enacted even for self-executing conventions to adapt them to national circumstances and to supplement measures necessary for the protection and safety of the domestic maritime industry.

Given the rapid development and frequent amendments of international maritime safety conventions, it may be difficult to obtain National Assembly approval in a timely manner. In such cases, the Ship Safety Act and the Marine Environment Management Act explicitly provide for the precedence of international conventions, thereby preventing conflicts with domestic law and ensuring uninterrupted international navigation.

IMO conventions address technical and specialized matters and are frequently revised to respond to industry requirements and international standards. As a party to these IMO conventions, South Korea has enacted and implemented domestic laws corresponding to the SOLAS Convention on maritime safety and the MARPOL Convention on marine environmental protection, which are systematically managed as shown in Table 2.1.

Role of Maritime Administrations

South Korea's maritime administrative framework is centered on the Ministry of Oceans and Fisheries (MOF) and encompasses a variety of specialized agencies and enforcement mechanisms. Each institution performs specific functions related to

Table 2.1 IMO Conventions and South Korean Domestic Legislations

Municipal Law	IMO Conventions
Maritime Safety Act, Ship Safety Act	SOLAS, 1966 LL,1972 CSC
Ship's Act	1969 Tonnage
Ship Personnel Act and Seafarers' Act	2010 STCW
Maritime Safety Act	1972 COLREG
Marine Environment Management Act	MARPOL 73/78, OPRC 1990, OPRC/HNS 2000
Ballast Water Management Act	BWM 2004
Compensation for Oil Pollution Damage Guarantee Act	1992 CLC, 1992 FUND and Protocol 2003, Bunker Convention

maritime safety, environmental protection, vessel management, and maritime accident response.[18]

As the principal administrative body responsible for maritime policy, the MOF implements policies on marine environmental protection, pollution prevention, vessel safety, and maritime disaster response under the authority of legislation such as the Marine Environment Management Act, Ship Safety Act, Marine Environment Conservation Act, Ballast Water Management Act, and Oil Pollution Compensation Act. Subordinate specialized agencies and cooperating organizations execute operational tasks in accordance with the powers and procedures defined under each law.

Maritime administrative functions originated in 1948 with the Shipping Bureau of the Ministry of Transportation and the Fisheries Bureau of the Ministry of Commerce and Industry. Subsequently, maritime affairs were managed separately under fisheries and shipping divisions, and later integrated under the MOF or shared with relevant ministries following governmental reorganization. The MOF's policy domains are extensive, covering maritime and fisheries policy, fishing village development, distribution of seafood, shipping and ports, marine environment, oceanographic surveys, marine resource development, marine science and technology R&D, and maritime safety adjudication. Regional responsibilities are delegated to local maritime and fisheries offices, while the Marine Safety Tribunal (MST) oversees adjudication related to maritime accidents.[19]

Port State Control (PSC) is conducted under Chapter 9 of the Ship Safety Act and the Guidelines for Port and Flag State Control. MOF-appointed PSC officers (Port State Control Officers, PSCOs) board foreign vessels to inspect whether ship structure, equipment, cargo transport, and seafarer competence comply with international conventions such as MARPOL 73/78 and SOLAS. Violations may result in detention or corrective orders, and objections can be submitted to the minister within 90 days. Special inspections may be conducted, and navigational suspension or corrective measures may be imposed if necessary.[20]

The Korea Coast Guard (KCG) is responsible for maritime accident prevention, law enforcement, and disaster response, executing vessel safety inspections, accident investigations, marine pollution response, emergency rescue, and lifesaving operations based on the Marine Environment Management Act, Ship Safety Act, Marine Pollution Prevention Act, and Ballast Water Management Act. In emergencies, the KCG exercises on-site command authority to minimize damage and ensure rapid response.[21]

MST, a specialized adjudicatory body under the MOF, reviews and adjudicates the appropriateness of administrative measures related to vessel and maritime accidents. Based on accident investigations, the MST performs administrative review,

[18] Ibid.

[19] Korea Maritime Safety Tribunal, available at https://www.kmst.go.kr/eng/ (accessed 21 September 2025).

[20] Lee and Kim (2024), p. 2339362.

[21] Korea Coast Guard, available at https://www.kcg.go.kr/english/main.do (accessed 21 September 2025).

dispute mediation, issuance of recommendations, and proposals for recurrence prevention measures. It handles appeals against administrative sanctions or corrective orders, assesses accident liability, and recommends improvements for vessel operation safety. Its legal basis includes regulations on the establishment and operation of the MST, the Ship Safety Act, and the Maritime Accident Investigation Act. Through integration of administrative review and judicial measures, the MST plays a central role in resolving administrative and legal disputes related to maritime accidents.[22]

In addition, the Korea Ports Authority and regional maritime and fisheries offices under MOF are responsible for the safety and environmental management of maritime facilities and ports, as well as vessel inspection and safety management.[23] Their authority derives from the Ship Safety Act, Marine Environment Management Act, and Ballast Water Management Act, enforcing safety and environmental protection in ports and coastal waters.

The division of responsibilities among these institutions and the structured enforcement of relevant laws enhance the professionalism, efficiency, and fairness of South Korea's maritime administration. This framework serves as a critical foundation for preventing maritime accidents, preserving the marine environment, and maintaining consistency in maritime safety policies.

Key Public Maritime Legislations

Maritime Safety and Security

The legal framework governing maritime safety and security in South Korea is designed to encompass both maritime safety and maritime security, regulating a broad spectrum of areas including vessel navigation safety, seafarer protection, maritime accident response, marine pollution prevention, and the security of international navigation and port facilities. Maritime safety traditionally encompasses ship design, seafarer training, passenger and cargo management, navigational safety, aids to navigation, and responses to marine pollution incidents, forming an integral component of accident prevention and disaster management systems. This conception of maritime safety is closely aligned with the standards and regulatory frameworks of IMO and is codified domestically through statutes such as Framework Act on Maritime Safety, Ship Safety Act, Seafarers Act, Water Leisure Safety Act, Ports Act, Aids to Navigation Act and which collectively establish a systematic approach to managing operational risks associated with vessels.

Maritime security is conceptualized as a broader legal regime aimed at preventing deliberate threats, including piracy, terrorism, and armed robbery, while safeguarding national sovereignty, maritime resources, freedom of navigation, and

[22] Korea Maritime Safety Tribunal (n 19).

[23] Song and Lee (2017), p. 27.

international trade. Domestically, the Act on the Prevention of Piracy Against Ships Engaged in International Navigation and the Act on the Security of Internationally Navigating Ships and Port Facilities provide the primary statutory foundation for maritime security, authorizing risk area designation, deployment of maritime security personnel, regulation of weapons use, and coordination with national security agencies to ensure operational effectiveness.

The Ship Safety Act constitutes the principal legislative instrument for regulating maritime safety.[24] It imposes obligations on shipowners, seafarers, and other stakeholders to maintain vessel seaworthiness and protect human life and property, encompassing the act itself, associated enforcement decrees, subordinate regulations, and administrative guidelines. The act prescribes comprehensive standards for maintaining vessel seaworthiness and safe navigation, including mandatory inspections and periodic evaluations to ensure compliance with minimum safety requirements.[25] Seaworthiness assessments incorporate vessel structure, equipment, crew and cargo management, and operational capabilities, with inspectors applying professional expertise to ensure sufficient safety margins.[26] Furthermore, the act integrates international law standards into domestic legislation, ensuring harmonization with global norms.

The Act on The Investigation of and Inquiry into Maritime Accidents governs incidents occurring in both maritime and inland waters, classifying accidents according to vessel or facility damage, human casualties, vessel loss, grounding, capsizing, sinking, and marine pollution.[27] Situations that may pose threats to vessels, lives, or the marine environment if unremedied are defined as "quasi-maritime accidents," with specific criteria established through Ministry of Oceans and Fisheries regulations. Empirical analysis of domestic maritime accidents indicates increasing human casualties resulting from vessel collisions, machinery failures, and structural deficiencies, underscoring the need for structural improvements in maritime safety management systems.

The Framework Act on Maritime Safety contributes to the prevention of marine accidents and the facilitation of traffic and to the protection of the lives, bodies, and property of citizens, by prescribing fundamental matters regarding maritime safety policies and systems.[28] The Act applies to South Korean-flagged and government-owned vessels, while fishing vessels are subject to the Fisheries Vessel Act. Recreational vessels are regulated under the Water Leisure Safety Act, while port-related legislation (Ports Act) and navigation-related legislation (Aids to Navigation

[24] Ship Safety Act, available at https://elaw.klri.re.kr/kor_service/lawView.do?hseq=61839&lang=KOR (accessed 21 September 2025).

[25] Ibid.

[26] Ibid.

[27] Act on the Investigation of and Inquiry into Maritime Accidents, available at https://elaw.klri.re.kr/kor_service/lawView.do?hseq=55795&lang=KOR (accessed 21 September 2025).

[28] Framework Act on Maritime Safety, available at https://elaw.klri.re.kr/eng_mobile/viewer.do?hseq=64550&key=42&type=part (accessed 21 September 2025).

Act and Hydrographic Survey Act) collectively ensure navigational safety, maritime traffic order, and environmental protection.

The Act on the Prevention of Damage to Ships on International Voyages from Piracy prescribes matters necessary to safeguard, and prevent damage to, ships on international voyages and the seafarers onboard, and offshore structures from any piracy, etc. prohibited by the United Nations Convention on the Law of the Sea, occurring on the sea outside the territorial waters of the Republic of Korea, thereby contributing to protecting the lives and property of the people and to maintaining order in international voyages[29] The Act on the Security of Internationally Navigating Ships and Port Facilities establishes preventive measures against security threats to international vessels and port facilities, including damage to vessels or facilities, smuggling or concealment of explosives or weapons, and coordination with national security agencies.

South Korea's maritime safety and security legislation can be categorized into the domains of maritime traffic, seafarers, vessels, maritime accidents, navigation, ports and shipping, fisheries, and ancillary areas. Laws directly related to accident prevention and safety are primarily concentrated in vessel and maritime accident regulation. Key statutes include the Maritime Safety Act and Open Port Regulation Act for maritime traffic, the Seafarers Act and Ship Personnel Act for seafarers, the Ship Safety Act, Fisheries Vessel Act, Fishing Charter Vessel Act, Passenger and Pilot Services Act, and Water Leisure Safety Act for vessels, the Act on the Investigation and Adjudication of Maritime Accidents and Marine Rescue Act for maritime accidents, the Aids to Navigation Act and Hydrographic Survey Act for navigation, the Ports Act, Fishing Port Act, and Shipping Act for ports and shipping, and the Fisheries Act, Meteorological Services Act, and Radio Waves Act for fisheries and ancillary matters. Human-factor-related incidents are governed by seafarer-specific statutes. Additionally, regulations concerning foreign fishing in the Exclusive Economic Zone, piracy prevention, and international ship and port security legislation supplement domestic maritime safety and security governance.

This legal framework enables integrated management of maritime safety and security, ensuring vessel operation safety, protection of human life, maritime accident prevention, and secure international navigation. These statutes guarantee the professionalism, coherence, and effectiveness of South Korea's maritime legal system, positioning the country as a robust and comprehensive maritime power.

[29] Act on the Prevention of Damage to Ships on International Voyages from Piracy, available at https://elaw.klri.re.kr/kor_service/lawView.do?hseq=59615&lang=KOR (accessed 21 September 2025).

Protection of the Marine Environment from Shipping Activities

South Korea has established a comprehensive legal framework to protect the marine environment from various pollution sources, primarily through the Marine Environment Management Act (MEM Act), which integrates technical annexes of the International Convention for the Prevention of Pollution from Ships (MARPOL 73/78).[30] Initially enacted in 1977 as the Marine Pollution Prevention Act, the legislation was fully revised on 29 January 2007, and its most recent amendment was promulgated on 31 October 2017. This analysis focuses on the regulation of marine pollution originating from ships. Article 35 of the Constitution of the Republic of Korea imposes a duty on all citizens to preserve the environment, thereby providing a constitutional basis for governmental efforts in marine environmental protection, the formulation of related legislation and policies, and the imposition of sanctions for violations.[31]

South Korea first enacted the Marine Pollution Prevention Act in 1977 in accordance with internationally established standards for marine environment management, conservation, and utilization. However, this act primarily targeted pollution from land-based sources affecting coastal areas, and thus presented limitations as a comprehensive legal instrument for the broader marine environment. To address these gaps, the MEM Act was enacted on 18 November 2007, establishing the legal foundation for the designation of sensitive marine areas and for the integrated regulation of marine pollution originating from both marine and land-based sources. The MEM Act was designed as a domestic implementation tool for international conventions, including MARPOL 73/78, the 1972 London Convention on the Prevention of Marine Pollution by Dumping of Wastes and Other Matter, its 1996 Protocol, and the Stockholm Convention on Persistent Organic Pollutants. Nevertheless, the act faced limitations in comprehensively regulating the overall marine environment, including nearshore areas. To address these shortcomings, the Marine Environment Conservation Act was promulgated and implemented in 2017, with associated enforcement decrees revised and legislative notices published.

The MEM Act provides legal mechanisms for the management of pollution sources, including ships, marine facilities, and marine areas, as well as the regulation of discharges of oil and harmful liquid substances, facilitating prevention, mitigation, response, and restoration of marine pollution.[32] The initial enactment contained extensive provisions that combined general principles with enforcement regulations, resulting in a lack of systematic organization. This issue was addressed through the 2017 amendment, whereby the Marine Environment Conservation Act governs general principles and the MEM Act governs enforcement regulations. Key principles introduced include the precautionary principle, allowing preventive

[30] Choi (2021), p. 219.

[31] Ibid.

[32] Marine Environment Management Act, available at https://elaw.klri.re.kr/kor_service/lawView.do?hseq=64109&lang=KOR (accessed 21 September 2025).

restrictions in the absence of conclusive evidence where significant pollution risks exist, the marine health and environmental quality assessment system, marine spatial management and planning, climate change adaptation measures, and the promotion of marine environmental education.

The MEM Act applies to the territorial sea, exclusive economic zone (EEZ), and submarine mineral development zones of the Republic of Korea, as well as to South Korean-flagged vessels and foreign vessels navigating or anchoring in domestic waters. Where discrepancies exist between international conventions and domestic law, the MEM Act prioritizes international standards; however, if domestic regulations impose stricter requirements, the domestic standards prevail. Measures to strengthen marine pollution prevention and response include designation of environmentally protected and special management areas, appointment of ship pollution prevention managers, technical requirement standards, and development of emergency response plans, with corresponding criminal and administrative sanctions for violations.

The technical standards and administrative provisions governing ship-related pollution prevention are articulated in the Regulations on the Prevention of Marine Pollution from Ships, promulgated pursuant to the authority of the MEM Act.[33] Technical requirements encompass vessel equipment, structural standards, inspections, documentation, certification, reception facilities, and air pollution prevention, all in accordance with MARPOL 73/78 standards. Violations may result in criminal penalties of up to five years of imprisonment or fines not exceeding KRW 50 million under Articles 126–129 of the MEM Act. In terms of ship-generated pollution, the Ministry of Oceans and Fisheries may impose an Environmental Improvement Charge on vessels discharging more than 1,000 litters of oil (Article 19). In principle, discharge of pollutants from vessels is prohibited unless specified standards are met. Article 32 mandates shipowners to appoint a Marine Pollution Prevention Manager, with additional managers designated for the transport of hazardous liquid substances. Managers are responsible for monitoring pollutant discharge, maintaining facilities, conducting training, and managing emergency response, thereby enhancing the effectiveness of the MEM Act.

The Ballast Water Management Act (BWM Act), enacted on 21 March 2017, applies to the same jurisdictional scope as the MEM Act. Certain vessels, including those not carrying ballast water, military or police vessels, and small vessels, may be exempted or subject to reduced requirements.[34] The BWM Act regulates ballast water discharge standards, technical requirements, inspections, certification, and documentation, while providing the legal basis for prohibiting discharges within domestic waters and designating special management areas. In regions requiring international agreement, such as overlapping EEZs in the Yellow Sea, unilateral designation may be limited. Violations are subject to up to one year of

[33] Ibid.

[34] Ballast Water Management Act, available at https://elaw.klri.re.kr/kor_service/lawView.do?hseq=64098&lang=KOR (accessed 21 September 2025).

imprisonment or fines not exceeding KRW 10 million, in addition to administrative penalties.

The Oil Pollution Damage Compensation Act (OPD Act), enacted in 1992, implements the International Convention on Civil Liability for Oil Pollution Damage (CLC) and the International Oil Pollution Compensation Fund Convention (Fund Convention) into domestic law. This act governs liability and compensation for oil pollution damage caused by vessels, imposing obligations on shipowners and insurers while granting national and local authorities' powers for emergency response and restoration.[35] Through this framework, rapid compensation and remediation are possible in the event of marine accidents, and, together with the MEM Act and BWM Act, the OPD Act strengthens the legal basis for prevention and response to marine pollution.

Regulations on Seafarers

The Seafarers Act of South Korea defines a seafarer as 'a person employed to provide labour on board a vessel for remuneration', emphasizing the provision of labour within the specific spatial context of a ship.[36] Accordingly, individuals providing labour for remuneration outside the ship are not recognized as seafarers under this definition. The term 'remuneration' encompasses all forms of monetary compensation provided by the shipowner in return for labour, and the seafarer is presumed to engage in specific duties or shipboard tasks, including navigation watch, radio communication, engine operation, meteorological observation, marine exploration, or passenger services. Compared to the broader definition under the International Labour Organization (ILO) Maritime Labour Convention (MLC), the domestic definition in the Seafarers Act is relatively narrow. While the MLC classifies all persons employed or engaged in any capacity on a vessel to which the convention applies as seafarers, the South Korean law imposes the stricter requirement that the labour be performed aboard the ship. Consequently, passengers, trainees, or casual visitors are excluded from the seafarer category, even if they perform activities on board.

Since its enactment in 1962, the Seafarers Act has functioned as a special law designed to address the unique nature of maritime labour, distinct from the Labor Standards Act, which governs land-based employment. While the Labor Standards Act serves as a general law regulating universal labour conditions across industries, the Seafarers Act addresses specific issues arising from the maritime work environment, including safety, service obligations, shipboard duties, crew capacity, onboard order, occupational injury compensation, and training. Therefore, in principle, the

[35] Park (2021), p. 81.

[36] Seafarer's Act, available at https://elaw.klri.re.kr/eng_service/lawView.do?hseq=53374&lang=ENG (accessed 21 September 2025).

Seafarers Act takes precedence in regulating seafarers' employment relations, while the Labor Standards Act applies supplementarily only in areas not explicitly covered by the Seafarers Act. For instance, provisions related to wages, paid leave, and injury compensation are primarily governed by the Seafarers Act, whereas issues such as termination of employment contracts or internal work rules may invoke the Labor Standards Act as a supplementary reference. In this respect, the Seafarers Act functions as a special law relative to the Labor Standards Act.

The distinctiveness of the South Korean Seafarers Act can be summarized as follows. It explicitly regulates the duties and service obligations of seafarers, taking into account the hazards and isolation inherent in maritime labour. Unlike land-based workers, seafarers live and work for extended periods in isolated sea environments, necessitating strict governance of onboard order, safety, hygiene, and operational protocols. The act embodies a dual character encompassing both labour protection and maritime safety. Ensuring the rights and working conditions of seafarers is directly linked to vessel safety and the prevention of maritime accidents; thus, the Seafarers Act simultaneously functions as labour legislation and maritime safety regulation, extending beyond mere labour conditions to encompass welfare, training, crew management, and onboard safety management. The act also aligns with international standards. South Korea has incorporated international maritime labour conventions, including the MLC, into domestic law, and recent amendments address protections for trainee seafarers, prevention of onboard harassment, and enhanced medical obligations in conformity with international norms.

The rights guaranteed to seafarers under the Seafarers Act include the right to fair working conditions, entitling seafarers to receive appropriate wages according to their employment contracts, including compensation for overtime and night work, as well as paid leave and rest periods. They are also entitled to occupational injury compensation and social security, providing protection for seafarers and their dependents in cases of injuries, illnesses, or fatalities occurring during maritime service, with safeguards exceeding those available to land-based workers. Seafarers have the right to work in a safe environment, requiring shipowners to establish safety management systems and provide necessary equipment and facilities. Additionally, they are entitled to medical care and welfare, including appropriate treatment for illness or injury, onboard medical facilities, emergency care, and coordination with shore-based medical institutions during extended voyages. The act also guarantees human rights protection, extending safeguards against harassment and violence to trainee seafarers and reinforcing procedures for remedying discrimination or human rights violations.

South Korean Seafarers Act establishes an independent regulatory framework within the special law–general law relationship with the Labor Standards Act, reflecting the unique characteristics of maritime labour while simultaneously safeguarding seafarers' rights and ensuring maritime safety. This demonstrates that the Seafarers Act is more than a maritime version of labour law; it is a specialized statute with a dual character, addressing both the inherent risks of the shipping work environment and the need for compliance with international maritime standards.

Enforcement Regime: Port State Control

The Port State Control (PSC) system refers to a regulatory framework under which port authorities inspect foreign vessels voluntarily entering their ports to ensure compliance with safety standards established by international conventions, with the overarching objective of protecting lives, property, and the marine environment within their jurisdiction. Under the PSC system, a Port State Control Officer (PSCO) boards vessels directly to conduct safety inspections. If violations of IMO conventions or deficiencies are detected, the officer may take necessary measures, including detention orders or corrective action instructions. Through this mechanism, the port state evaluates whether foreign vessels calling at its ports comply with international and domestic safety and environmental standards. Depending on the severity of identified deficiencies, corrective measures are imposed to prevent maritime accidents and to safeguard life, property, and the marine environment.

In South Korea, the legal basis for the PSC system is established under the Ship Safety Act, Maritime Safety Act, Marine Environment Management Act, Seafarers Act, Ship Crew Act, Ballast Water Management Act, Act on the Security of Internationally Navigating Ships and Port Facilities, and the Regulations on Port State Control and Flag State Control. Notably, Chapter 9 of the Ship Safety Act empowers the Minister of Oceans and Fisheries to verify the structure, equipment, cargo transport methods, and seafarers' operational knowledge of foreign vessels in accordance with international convention standards, and to take necessary enforcement actions.[37] According to this chapter, the minister may authorize subordinate officials to board and inspect foreign vessels. If a vessel fails to meet international convention standards, the minister may issue corrective actions or detain the vessel, and vessel owners may file an appeal within 90 days. The minister is required to report investigation results within 60 days (extendable by 30 days if necessary). In special cases, vessels previously detained at foreign ports are subject to special inspections upon entry into South Korean ports. Additionally, specific vessels, such as bulk carriers or hazardous cargo ships exceeding 15 years of age, may be subject to navigation suspensions or additional corrective orders.

The PSC system functions as a critical legal mechanism to ensure that port states supervise compliance of foreign vessels with safety and environmental standards, thereby strengthening maritime safety and marine environmental protection through the harmonization of international conventions and domestic law. Furthermore, as a member of the Tokyo Memorandum of Understanding (Tokyo MOU), South Korea actively participates in international cooperation to enhance maritime safety and environmental protection in the Asia-Pacific region.[38] As of 2024, Tokyo MOU member states conducted a total of 32,054 vessel inspections, identified deficiencies in 19,967 inspections, imposed detention measures on 1,189 vessels for serious

[37] Ship Safety Act, available at https://elaw.klri.re.kr/kor_service/lawView.do?hseq=61839&lang=KOR (accessed 21 September 2025).

[38] Bang and Jang (2012), p. 170.

deficiencies, and recorded a total of 77,526 deficiencies. South Korea contributes to the prevention of maritime accidents and the protection of the marine environment at the international level through these PSC activities.[39]

Emerging Challenges in Public Maritime Law

Decarbonization and Digitalization

South Korea's decarbonization strategy for the shipping sector sets proactive and ambitious targets that exceed the regulatory levels of the IMO, with the core objective of achieving net-zero greenhouse gas (GHG) emissions from shipping by 2050. In 2023, MOF announced the 'International Shipping Decarbonization Promotion Strategy', which outlines plans to reduce emissions by 60 per cent relative to 2008 levels by 2030, 80 per cent by 2040, and 100 per cent by 2050.[40] These reduction targets surpass IMO's medium-term regulatory goals, demonstrating South Korea's commitment to more stringent emission reductions than international mandates.

To achieve these objectives, the government is implementing a multifaceted fleet transition policy. This policy includes the adoption of environmentally friendly and zero-carbon fuels such as methanol, ammonia, and hydrogen, retrofits of existing vessels, construction of new eco-friendly ships, installation of green maritime equipment, and measures to enhance fuel efficiency. Furthermore, the government, in cooperation with financial institutions, is providing cost support and policy incentives to shipping companies. It is also actively promoting the development of biofuel and zero-carbon fuel production technologies, as well as the establishment of supply infrastructure. International collaborative projects are also being actively pursued, such as South Korea–U.S. cooperation on zero-carbon shipping routes.

From a regulatory perspective, South Korea has implemented the 'Standards and Methods for Ship Energy Efficiency Inspection' notice in 2023, incorporating the IMO's Energy Efficiency Existing Ship Index (EEXI) and Carbon Intensity Indicator (CII) into domestic inspection and evaluation systems. This allows for the systematic monitoring of shipowners' and operators' compliance with Ship Energy Efficiency Management Plans (SEEMP). The system also integrates the Marine Environment Management Act and the Ship Safety Act, thereby establishing a framework that simultaneously ensures marine environmental protection and ship safety.

In the field of autonomous shipping, which is recognized as a core component of digital transformation, the 'Act on the Development and Commercialization of

---

[39] Tokyo MoU, available at https://www.tokyo-mou.org/inspections-detentions/psc-database/ (accessed 21 September 2025).

[40] MOF, available at https://www.mof.go.kr/doc/ko/selectDoc.do?docSeq=49155&=&menuSeq=971&bbsSeq=10 (accessed 21 September 2025).

Autonomous Ships' was enacted in 2023 and came into effect on 4 April 2024. Article 1 of the Act explicitly states its purpose: to promote the development and commercialization of autonomous ships and related technologies, enhance maritime safety and environmental protection, strengthen the competitiveness of the shipping industry, and contribute to the national economy.[41] The act provides a comprehensive framework for the entire lifecycle of autonomous ships to achieve this purpose. It covers the establishment of a national policy committee, designation of pilot operation zones, safety assessment and certification of autonomous ships and related systems, standards for the establishment and operation of remote-control centres, protection and utilization of operational data, and liability and insurance systems. The associated enforcement decree and rules specify obligations for safety measures, accident reporting procedures, and emergency response systems.

Protecting of Seafarer's Human Rights

Internationally, the protection of seafarers' human rights has been progressively reinforced through the regulatory frameworks of the IMO and the ILO, and South Korea has incorporated these standards into its domestic legal framework. The 2024 amendments adopted at the 108th session of the IMO Maritime Safety Committee (MSC 108) revised the STCW Convention and Code to include prevention and response training for sexual assault and sexual harassment (SASH) in basic training modules, effective January 1, 2026.[42] In response, South Korea is restructuring the Seafarers Act and associated training regulations to ensure that all maritime officers complete mandatory training in gender equality and human rights. Similarly, the 2022 amendments to the ILO MLC 2006 reinforced seafarers' rights to welfare, access to medical services, and secure reporting mechanisms, which South Korea has incorporated through domestic legislative adjustments.

The most recent amendments to the Seafarers Act (Act No. 20127, promulgated January 23, 2024) focus on strengthening protections for trainee and female seafarers. These include restrictions on survivor compensation under certain conditions, enhanced medical obligations for shipowners, explicit preventive measures against onboard harassment, independent protective regulations for trainee seafarers, and mechanisms for shared supervisory and protective responsibilities among shipping companies, maritime training institutions, and MOF. The reforms recognize trainees as workers entitled to regulated working hours, rest, safety protections, and wage guarantees. They also address high-profile incidents involving human rights violations and fatalities and institutionalize protections for female seafarers by

[41] Korea Law Information Center, available at https://www.law.go.kr/LSW/lsInfoP.do?lsiSeq=257803&viewCls=lsRvsDocInfoR (accessed 21 September 2025).

[42] MOF (n 40).

prohibiting sexual harassment and assault, mandating victim protection, preventing retaliation, and requiring shipowners to implement measures against recurrence.

Overall, the recent legal developments in South Korea's Seafarers Act reflect four core pillars: trainee protection, female seafarer rights, prevention of onboard harassment and violence, and enhanced access to medical and welfare services. These reforms demonstrate the country's proactive incorporation of international maritime labour standards while addressing domestic challenges. They function as a dual-purpose legal instrument that simultaneously safeguards seafarers' labour rights and promotes maritime safety in alignment with global regulatory trends.

Conclusion

South Korea's public maritime law is structured upon the strategic significance of the shipping industry to the national economy and international trade, establishing an institutional framework to ensure maritime safety and protect the marine environment. In particular, by faithfully incorporating and implementing key international maritime conventions adopted by the IMO into domestic legislation, South Korea achieves both compliance with international norms and coherence within its domestic legal system. The foundation of South Korea's maritime legal framework comprises the Maritime Safety Act, the Ship Safety Act, and the Marine Environment Management Act, which collectively provide an integrated regulatory system for safe vessel operation, accident prevention, pollution control, and environmental preservation. Furthermore, in response to the IMO's decarbonization regulations, South Korea has legislatively supported its maritime decarbonization strategy through the enactment and implementation of the Notice on the Standards and Methods for Ship Energy Efficiency Inspection, while the 2023 enactment of the Act on the Development and Commercialization of Autonomous Ships establishes a pioneering legal foundation suited to the era of digital transformation.

As both a flag state and a seafarer nation, South Korea places significant emphasis on legislation for seafarer training and rights protection. The Seafarers Act governs seafarers' working conditions, welfare, safety, and human rights, with recent amendments addressing the protection of trainees, prevention of discrimination against female seafarers, prohibition of onboard harassment, and strengthened medical obligations. The Ship Officers Act regulates the qualifications, licensing, and training of ship officers to ensure safe vessel operations and maintain international recognition of seafarer credentials in alignment with the STCW Convention. Additionally, the Strategic Fleet system secures a national fleet of a specified scale to guarantee the country's maritime transport capacity, and the Tonnage Tax System reduces tax burdens for shipping companies, enhancing international competitiveness.

South Korea's maritime law, therefore, extends beyond traditional frameworks focused on maritime safety and environmental protection to pursue a multifaceted set of objectives: faithful domestic implementation of international conventions, safeguarding seafarers' rights and welfare, innovating legislation to accommodate decarbonization and digital transformation, and strengthening national economic contribution through fleet maintenance and enhanced shipping industry competitiveness. These legal features enable South Korea to function not merely as a compliant actor within the international maritime order but as a proactive leader, simultaneously supporting the sustainability of the shipping sector and the stable growth of the national economy.

References

Act on the Investigation of and Inquiry into Maritime Accidents, available at https://elaw.klri.re.kr/kor_service/lawView.do?hseq=55795&lang=KOR (Accessed 21 September 2025)

Act on the Prevention of Damage to Ships on International Voyages from Piracy, Available at https://elaw.klri.re.kr/kor_service/lawView.do?hseq=59615&lang=KOR (Accessed 21 September 2025)

Ballast Water Management Act, Available at https://elaw.klri.re.kr/kor_service/lawView.do?hseq=64098&lang=KOR (accessed 21 September 2025)

Bang H-S, Jang D-J (2012) Recent developments in regional memorandums of understanding on port state control. Ocean Dev Int Law 43:170

Choi J (2021) Domestic legal system of the yellow sea states for the prevention of vessel-source pollution under the UNCLOS: a comparative legal study. J East Asia Int Law 14:219

Choi J, Lim S, Lee C (2024) Comparative analysis of sustainable seafarers' employment and welfare systems in South Korea and China: contemporary issues and improvements. Sustainability 16:8512

Choi J et al (2025) The importance of career development programs for Korean seafarers: case studies from key shipping countries. Int J Contents 21:135

Framework Act on Maritime Safety, Available at https://elaw.klri.re.kr/eng_mobile/viewer.do?hseq=64550&key=42&type=part (Accessed 21 September 2025)

IMO, 'IMO gender equality award 2024', Available at https://www.imo.org/en/mediacentre/pressbriefings/pages/2024-gender-equality-award.aspx (Accessed 21 September 2025)

IMO Korea, Available at https://www.imokorea.org/ (accessed 21 September 2025).

Korea Coast Guard, Available at https://www.kcg.go.kr/english/main.do (Accessed 21 September 2025)

Korea Law Information Center, Available at https://www.law.go.kr/LSW/lsInfoP.do?lsiSeq=257803&viewCls=lsRvsDocInfoR (Accessed 21 September 2025).

Korea Legislation Research Institute, 'Status of the Republic of Korea', available at https://elaw.klri.re.kr/kor_serviice/main.do (Accessed 21 September 2025).

Korea Maritime Safety Tribunal, Available at https://www.kmst.go.kr/eng/ (Accessed 21 September 2025).

Korea Shipowners' Association, 'Korean Shipping Industry', available at https://oneksa.kr/about/shipping_industry.php (Accessed 21 September 2025)

Lee S-I, Kim I (2024) Measures to improve ship inspection system in Korea by amending administrative crime provisions of the Ship Safety Act. J Int Marit Saf Environ Aff Ship 8:2339362

Marine Environment Management Act, Available at https://elaw.klri.re.kr/kor_service/lawView.do?hseq=64109&lang=KOR (Accessed 21 September 2025)

Mendez M (2013) The legal effects of treaties in domestic legal orders and the role of domestic courts. The Legal Effects of EU Agreements

MOF, Available at https://www.mof.go.kr/doc/ko/selectDoc.do?docSeq=49155&=&menuSeq=971&bbsSeq=10 (Accessed 21 September 2025)

MOF, Available at https://www.mofa.go.kr/www/brd/m_4080/view.do?seq=371918&page=397&pitem=10 (Accessed 21 September 2025)
MOFA, *Treaty Making by the ROK*, available at https://www.mofa.go.kr/eng/wpge/m_5439/contents.do (Accessed 21 September 2025).
Park Y-S (2021) Korea oil pollution damage compensation scheme and major oil spill case review – focusing on Hebei Spirit Incident and Wuyisan Incident. Asian Bus Law 28:81
Seafarer'sAct,Availableathttps://elaw.klri.re.kr/eng_service/lawView.do?hseq=53374&lang=ENG (Accessed 21 September 2025).
Ship Safety Act, Available at https://elaw.klri.re.kr/kor_service/lawView.do?hseq=61839&lang=KOR (Accessed 21 September 2025)
Song D-W, Lee S-W (2017) Port governance in Korea: revisited. Res Transp Bus Manage 22:27
The Korea Herald, 'S. Korea's shipping industry expected to enjoy strong sales in 2021', available at https://www.koreaherald.com/article/2548088 (Accessed 21 September 2025)
Tokyo MoU, Available at https://www.tokyo-mou.org/inspections-detentions/psc-database/ (Accessed 21 September 2025)
UNCTAD (2024) Review of Maritime Transport 2024. Available at https://unctad.org/publication/review-maritime-transport-2024 (Accessed 21 September 2025)

Chapter 3
Public Maritime Legislations in China

Junghwan Choi and Xingguo Cao

Introduction

In the 21st-century global shipping industry, China has emerged as a major country of strategic importance to international maritime networks, global trade, and national economic development, fulfilling a triple role as a shipbuilding country, the ship owner country, and a seafarer country.[1] As a shipbuilding country, China has consistently ranked first worldwide in key indicators such as shipbuilding output, new orders, and order backlog, thereby consolidating its position as the global hub of ship supply. China is recognized as the world's largest ship-owning nation, operating an extensive national fleet comprised of both state-owned and private shipping companies, while utilizing its major ports to develop international shipping routes and enhance maritime transport capabilities.[2] In addition, China cultivates a substantial workforce of seafarers through education, certification, and welfare systems that conform to international standards, thereby serving as a key provider of skilled seafarers to the global shipping industry.

Junghwan Choi Xinghai Associate Professor at The School of Law of Dalian Maritime University, China. LL.M. in Maritime Law (Korea Maritime & Ocean Uni.), LL.M. in International Maritime Law with Merit (Swansea Uni., UK), Ph.D. in Maritime Law (Exeter Uni., UK).
Xingguo Cao Professor at the School of Law of DMU, China. Ph.D. in Maritime Law (DMU, China), Postdoctoral Research (CUPL), Visiting Scholar (Center for Maritime Law Studies, Tulane University, USA).

[1] Wang et al. (2025), p. 107746.

[2] Shuo Ma (2020); Cebr (2025).

J. Choi · X. Cao (✉)
Law School, Dalian Maritime University, Dalian, P.R. China
e-mail: junghwanchoi@dlmu.edu.cn; caoxingguo@dlmu.edu.cn

J. Choi (ed.), *Public Maritime Law in Asia*, International Law in Asia,
https://doi.org/10.1007/978-981-95-7037-9_3

As a member of the International Maritime Organization (IMO), China actively participates in the development of conventions and norms, incorporating major international instruments such as International Convention for the Prevention of Pollution from Ships (MARPOL), International Convention for the Safety of Life at Sea (SOLAS), and International Convention on Standards of Training, Certification and Watchkeeping for Seafarers (STCW) into its domestic legal framework to enhance ship safety, protect the marine environment, and safeguard seafarers' rights. At the same time, China maintains compliance with international standards while strengthening its maritime sovereignty and industrial strategy through key national legislation, including the Maritime Traffic Safety Law, the Marine Environmental Protection Law, and the Regulations on the Prevention and Control of Marine Pollution from Ships.[3] More recently, China has pursued policy and institutional innovations to address emerging challenges such as environmental sustainability, digitalization, and the protection of seafarers' rights, reflecting the strategic evolution of its shipping industry and maritime legal system.

Institutional Framework for Maritime Legislations in China

Overview of Shipping Industry

China occupies a strategic position in the global maritime industry by simultaneously serving as a shipbuilding nation, a ship-owning nation, and a seafarer-supplying nation, thereby reinforcing its influence over international maritime networks, global trade, and national economic development.

China has consolidated its global dominance by securing, as of 2024, a market share of 55.7% in shipbuilding output (48.18 million DWT), 74.1% in new orders (113.05 million DWT), and 63.1% in order backlog (208.72 million DWT), reflecting year-on-year increases of 13.8%, 58.8%, and 49.7%, respectively.[4] Since 2023, China has maintained a majority share exceeding 50% across all three indicators, with production concentrated in containerships, oil tankers, LNG carriers, and large bulk carriers, alongside a growing proportion of eco-friendly and high-efficiency vessels. Ship exports reached USD 31.87 billion in 2023, representing 87.4% of total output, further substantiating China's role as the principal global supplier of

---

[3] Ibid.

[4] iMarine News, "China's shipbuilding statistics for 2024 released" 21 January 2025, available at https://www.imarinenews.com/18918.html (accessed 1 September 2025); Brookes Bell, "74% of All New Shipbuilding Orders Booked by Chinese Yards in 2024" 6 February 2025, available at https://www.brookesbell.com/news-and-knowledge/article/74-of-all-new-shipbuilding-orders-booked-by-chinese-yards-in-2024-159301/ (accessed 1 September 2025); Global Times, "China leads three shipbuilding indicators for 15th year" 16 January 2025, available at https://www.globaltimes.cn/page/202501/1327019.shtml (accessed 1 September 2025).

ships.[5] China maintains one of the world's largest fleets, accounting for 309.9 million DWT in 2024, operated primarily through state-owned and private carriers. International shipping routes are anchored in major ports such as Shanghai, Ningbo-Zhoushan, and Tianjin, while governmental initiatives have strengthened strategic fleet management to sustain maritime transport capacity and facilitate trade flows.[6] From the perspective of a seafarer-supplying nation, China places a strong emphasis on the education and training of seafarers, managing over 130 maritime education and training institutions that cultivate the largest seafarer workforce in the world. According to the 2020 China Seafarers Development Report (published in June 2021), the total number of registered seafarers in China at the end of 2020 was 1,716,866, reflecting a 3.5% increase compared to the previous year. Of these, 258,896 were women, and 592,998 were engaged in international voyages, representing a 3.0% growth over the same period.[7] These seafarers serve in both domestic and international fleets and are supported by education, certification, and welfare systems aligned with global conventions such as the MLC 2006 and STCW, thereby making a substantial contribution to the international maritime labour force.

China's fleet composition highlights its structural duality: while it ranks second globally with 309.9 million GT across 9418 vessels (13.3% of global tonnage), foreign-flagged ships constitute 57.6% of its tonnage (178.3 million GT), exceeding the share of domestically flagged ships (130.7 million GT).[8] This distribution reflects the prevalence of foreign registration for large vessels owned by Chinese companies. In this context, China not only sustains sufficient carrying capacity to support its position as the world's leading trading nation but also consolidates its status as a global maritime power.

Involvement in the IMO

China acceded to IMO in 1973, at which time the People's Republic of China restored its legitimate seat in place of the Republic of Chin, acquiring the authority to participate in the formulation of international maritime norms. At the ninth IMO Assembly in 1975, China was elected for the first time as a Category B Council member, and since the sixteenth Assembly in 1989 it has continuously served as a Category A Council member, holding this status for seventeen consecutive terms.

---

[5] Ibid.

[6] Lloyd's List, "One Hundred Container Ports 2024", available at https://www.lloydslist.com/one-hundred-container-ports-2024 (accessed 21 September 2025).

[7] Ministry of Transport of China, *China Seafarer Development Report 2020* [in Chinese].

[8] UNCTAD, *Review of Maritime Transport* 2024 (2024), available at https://unctad.org/publication/review-maritime-transport-2024 (accessed 21 September 2025).

Category A, composed of ten principal maritime nations, in effect performs the function of permanent membership within the IMO Council.[9]

China's institutional engagement within the IMO is primarily exercised through the Council and the core committees, notably the Marine Environment Protection Committee (MEPC), the Maritime Safety Committee (MSC), and the Legal Committee (LEG), where China occupies a strategically significant position. In July 2025, China announced the establishment of a permanent mission to the IMO headquarters in London, with the stated aim of enhancing institutional cooperation, strengthening compliance with international maritime instruments, and expanding participation in global regulatory deliberations.[10]

The Chinese government has consistently characterized the IMO as a central UN specialized agency in the fields of maritime safety, security, and environmental protection and has declared its policy commitment to 'strengthening genuine multilateralism and promoting safe and efficient shipping in clean oceans'. China has also pursued cooperative initiatives in maritime capacity building. It has dispatched personnel for advanced training at the World Maritime University (WMU) and, in 1984, established a WMU branch campus in Dalian Maritime University (DMU) to cultivate professional expertise in international maritime affairs.

At the domestic level, China has actively incorporated IMO conventions into its legislative framework. Typical examples include the *Regulations on the Safe Management of Ships*, the *Maritime Traffic Safety Law*, and the *Marine Environment Protection Law of the People's Republic of China*. The 2021 revision of the *Maritime Traffic Safety Law* expanded its scope to encompass all waters under Chinese jurisdiction.[11] The *Marine Environment Protection Law* regulates marine pollution from ships, hazardous discharges, environmental monitoring, and emergency response, thus reinforcing the normative linkage between international environmental standards and national legislation.

Furthermore, China has articulated an active position on global governance issues such as climate change, greenhouse gas mitigation, and marine environmental protection, emphasizing the principle of 'Common but Differentiated Responsibilities'. In this regard, China's status as a Category A Council member of the IMO enables it to participate proactively in the development of international regimes on maritime safety and environmental protection, while concurrently advancing the strategic interests of its shipping industry and safeguarding its maritime rights.

[9] Embassy of the People's Republic of China in the United Kingdom of Great Britain and Northern Ireland, available at http://gb.china-embassy.gov.cn/eng/zywl/2011/201112/t20111201_3386668.htm (accessed 21 September 2025).

[10] Xinhua, "International Maritime Organization looks forward to China's continued support: secretary-general" 22 July 2025, available at https://english.news.cn/20250722/09e302b7fa854462a06993a4cd3b3899/c.html (accessed 21 September 2025).

[11] Zhang et al. (2022), p. 346.

General Principle of implementation of IMO Conventions in Domestic Law

China generally adopts international treaties and conventions into domestic law through the doctrines of incorporation or transformation. Concerning the legal basis for concluding treaties or agreements with other states or international organizations, the Constitution of China grants the State Council the authority to negotiate and conclude treaties or agreements with foreign states.[12] The right to decide on ratification and abrogation of treaties and important agreements concluded with other states is vested in the Standing Committee of the National People's Congress.[13] This procedure is expressly governed by the Law of the People's Republic of China on the Procedure of the Conclusion of Treaties. Although the Constitution does not explicitly provide that international treaties or conventions adopted by the State Council take precedence over national laws, such priority may be inferred from the provisions of specific laws. Article 5, paragraph 2 of the Constitution and Article 78 of the Law on Legislation stipulate that the Constitution has the highest legal authority, and no national law, administrative regulation, or local rule may contravene it, indicating that the Constitution prevails over all other national laws, treaties, and conventions.[14] Decisions of the Standing Committee regarding treaties or agreements with foreign states have the same force as national laws, while international treaties concluded in the name of China require examination and approval by the State Council, bearing validity and effect equivalent to administrative regulations.[15]

Following China's ratification of MARPOL 73/78 and all its technical annexes, the government enacted the Marine Environmental Protection Law in 1982, later amended in 1999. In accordance with administrative regulations, the State Council promulgated the 1983 Regulation on the Prevention and Control of Marine Pollution from Vessels. In addition, to implement the SOLAS Convention domestically and strengthen the legal framework for maritime safety, China enacted the Maritime Traffic Safety Law, which regulates vessel navigation, safety management, and accident prevention within Chinese jurisdictional waters.[16] This law sets operational standards for ships, establishes responsibilities for shipping companies and port authorities, and enforces inspections to prevent marine accidents and pollution incidents, complementing the Marine Environmental Protection Law.

Moreover, Article 26, paragraph 1 of the Constitution requires the state to protect and improve the living and ecological environment and to prevent and remedy pollution and other public hazards. This constitutional mandate underpins the enactment and continuous amendment of environmental and maritime safety legislation,

---

[12] Hanqin and Qian (2009), p. 299, 301

[13] Zou (2009), p. 935.

[14] Hanqin and Qian (2009).

[15] Ibid.

[16] Tian et al. (2023), p. 105570.

including the Marine Environmental Protection Law, the 1983 Regulation, and the Maritime Traffic Safety Law, thereby providing a comprehensive legal framework for controlling vessel-source pollution and ensuring safe navigation within China's jurisdiction.

Role of Maritime Administrations

China's maritime governance is structured through a multi-layered institutional framework, with the Ministry of Transport of the People's Republic of China (MOT), Maritime Safety Administration of the People's Republic of China (MSA), China Classification Society (CCS), the China Coast Guard (CCG), under the People's Armed Police Force of the People's Republic of China, plays a central role in regulatory, technical, and enforcement capacities.[17] MOT functions as the principal policy-making authority, responsible for formulating national maritime strategies, coordinating the development of the shipping industry, and ensuring the domestic implementation of international conventions. MOT oversees the management of ports, shipping operations, and maritime transport infrastructure, thereby aligning national maritime policies with strategic economic and trade objectives.

China MSA serves as the principal supervisory and operational agency for maritime safety, navigation management, and accident prevention. MSA conducts vessel inspections, certifies seafarers, and enforces compliance with international conventions, including SOLAS and MARPOL, as well as relevant domestic legislation. It also manages port state control activities, search and rescue operations, and emergency response measures, positioning the agency as the frontline institution for maritime safety governance within Chinese jurisdiction.

CCS, as a technically specialized organization recognized by the Chinese government, provides classification and certification services to ensure that vessels meet both national and international technical standards in construction, equipment, and safety management. CCS contributes to the domestic implementation of international regulations while supporting China's shipbuilding and shipping sectors through technical expertise and standardization.[18]

CCG complements these functions by enforcing maritime law, conducting patrols and surveillance within China's territorial waters and exclusive economic zones, and ensuring maritime security, environmental protection, and the suppression of illegal activities at sea. CCG safeguards China's maritime sovereignty and economic interests while contributing to the broader enforcement of national and international maritime regulations.

---

[17] Haoran Cui (2024), p. 6.

[18] China Classification Society, About CCS, , https://www.ccs.org.cn/ccswzen/about?columnid=201912240228526379, (accessed 1 October 2025).

These institutions constitute an integrated maritime administrative system that combines policy leadership, operational supervision, technical certification, and law enforcement. The coordinated interaction among MOT, MSA, CCS, and CCG provides a comprehensive governance framework that ensures maritime safety, environmental protection, and compliance with international standards, thereby supporting China's strategic position as a major shipping nation and its active role in global maritime governance.

Key Public Maritime Legislations

China's maritime legal framework has focused on the domestic implementation of IMO conventions, while establishing an independent legal basis to strengthen its maritime sovereignty and protect the marine environment. In particular, the Maritime Traffic Safety Law, the Marine Environment Protection Law, and the Regulations on the Prevention and Control of Marine Pollution from Ships constitute the twin pillars of China's maritime legislation, exemplifying the reconciliation of international obligations with national interests.[19]

Maritime Safety and Security

The Maritime Traffic Safety Law of the People's Republic of China was originally enacted in 1984, with the objective of incorporating SOLAS into domestic law, and was comprehensively revised in 2021. China initiated a full-scale amendment in 2017, reflecting both the evolving conditions of maritime traffic and its efforts to strengthen maritime sovereignty.[20] After nearly four years of legislative deliberation, the Standing Committee of the National People's Congress of the People's Republic of China adopted the amendment on 29 April 2021, and it entered into force on 1 September of the same year. The revised law expanded significantly from 12 chapters and 53 articles to 10 chapters and 122 articles, thereby covering the full spectrum of maritime traffic, including ships, offshore installations, and seafarers; traffic conditions and navigational safety; navigation, anchorage, and maritime operations; cargo and passenger transport; search and rescue; accident investigation and handling; as well as supervision, enforcement, and legal liability.[21]

Chapter I (General Provisions) defines the objectives of the law as strengthening maritime traffic management, maintaining order, safeguarding life and property, and protecting national interests. It specifies the law's application to waters under

[19] Li and Ingram (2013).

[20] Tian et al. (2023).

[21] Ibid.

Chinese jurisdiction and designates China MSA under MOT as the national authority responsible for maritime traffic safety. Chapter II (Ships, Offshore Installations, and Seafarers) provides for the establishment of ship inspection agencies, registration and deregistration of vessels, pollution-prevention management systems, issuance of Safety Management Certificates and Ship Security Plans, as well as the training, certification, and medical fitness of seafarers. It further codifies compliance with the Maritime Labour Convention (MLC), mandating that shipowners, operators, and managers ensure proper working conditions, occupational health, safety, and hours of work and rest. Chapter III (Traffic Conditions and Navigational Safety) regulates the establishment and adjustment of maritime functional zones, management of navigational aids, installation and operation of radio stations, dissemination of safety information, designation of pilotage districts, compulsory pilotage for specific vessels, and the setting of ship and port security levels, while affirming the continuing command responsibility of the shipmaster during pilotage. Chapters IV and V (Navigation, Anchorage, Operations, and Maritime Transport) stipulate the carriage of statutory certificates, pre-departure inspections, prohibition of coerced service, maintenance of Automatic Identification Systems (AIS) and voyage data recorders, shipmasters' authority, quarantine and reporting obligations during epidemics, adherence to watchkeeping standards, port state control, permits for calling at non-designated ports, restrictions on innocent passage of foreign vessels, and the adoption of special precautionary measures. The law explicitly codifies emergency responsibilities, such as requiring the master to take immediate measures during an epidemic, isolating infected persons, and ensuring that in cases of distress, passengers and crew are evacuated first, with the master disembarking last (Articles 40 and 74). Chapters VI and VII (Search and Rescue and Accident Investigation) establish a national maritime rescue coordination system, mandate centralized coordination of major rescue operations, require reporting of accidents to maritime authorities, and impose an obligation to submit investigation reports within ninety days. Chapters VIII to X (Supervision, Enforcement, and Legal Liability) prescribe port state and coastal state control measures, including boarding, certificate inspection, on-site examination, electronic monitoring, and questioning of relevant parties. They further authorize prohibitions on entry, expulsion, and the exercise of hot pursuit, while specifying fines and other penalties for violations by shipowners and masters. The law also contains provisions regulating the activities of foreign public vessels and warships within Chinese territorial waters and affirms the primacy of international treaties, thereby reinforcing the dual functions of safeguarding national rights and maintaining maritime order.

The 2021 revision introduced significant new mechanisms, including enhanced requirements for safety management and pollution prevention by shipping companies, ship security measures, seafarer occupational health and safety protections, overseas emergency alert and response systems, management and utilization of maritime traffic resources, mandatory reporting obligations for foreign vessels, and strengthened pilotage safety.

Protection of the Marine Environment from Shipping Activities

China's *Marine Environment Protection Law* (MEPL, enacted in 1982 and amended in 1999, 2016, revised 2023) serves as a comprehensive basic law on marine environmental protection, providing the legal foundation for the prevention of marine pollution and the conservation of marine resources, including the regulation of vessel-sourced pollution.[22]

The 2023 revision of the MEPL represents a substantial enhancement of the legal framework governing marine environmental protection. The MEPL 2023 is designed to strengthen ecological security, safeguard public health, and uphold national maritime rights, while simultaneously promoting the construction of an ecological civilization and advancing sustainable development. This revised legislation consolidates and optimizes institutional arrangements for marine environmental governance by explicitly delineating responsibilities among relevant government agencies, including ecological and environmental authorities, natural resources, maritime transport, fisheries, and the coast guard.[23] A particularly noteworthy feature of MEPL 2023 is the incorporation of the Land–Sea Coordination (LSC) principle, which integrates terrestrial and marine environmental management into a unified system, thereby reflecting China's commitment to comprehensive and systematic environmental governance.[24] Specifically, Chapter VII of MEPL 2023, titled 'Prevention and Control of Pollution from Ships and Related Activities,' mandates that all ships within Chinese jurisdictional waters are prohibited from illegally discharging ship-generated garbage, sewage, oily water, toxic or harmful substances, exhaust gases, ballast water, and sediments. Ships must be equipped with appropriate pollution prevention equipment and possess valid certificates and documentation demonstrating compliance with national pollution control regulations.

Complementing the MEPL, the *Regulations on the Prevention and Control of Marine Pollution from Ships* (enacted in 1983 and revised in 2010) functions as China's direct domestic implementation instrument for MARPOL 73/78. Article 16 requires all vessels to maintain oil and garbage record books and to be equipped with pollution-prevention facilities, thereby institutionalizing the technical requirements of MARPOL Annexes I and V. Article 37 establishes mandatory accident-reporting obligations, emphasizing a domestic reporting regime more immediate than that required by IMO conventions.

---

22 Zhu et al. (2013), pp. 73, 77.

23 Liu (2024), p. 1409772.

24 Shi and Zhuang (2024), p. 128.

Regulations on Seafarers

Since the launch of the reform and opening-up policy in 1978, China introduced elements of a market economy and achieved rapid economic growth during the 1980s and 1990s, with the shipping industry serving as a key driver. In parallel, the government actively promoted the policy of seafarer deployment abroad as a means of earning foreign currency, thereby establishing seafaring as one of the most favoured professions in China. To support this development, the Chinese government established maritime education and training institutions, including maritime universities, with a view to cultivating highly skilled seafarers (ship's officers), while also adopting legislation and social security measures tailored to the distinctive nature of seafaring labour.

Unlike many other countries, however, China has not enacted a standalone *Seafarers' Act*. Instead, seafarer-related matters are regulated within selected provisions of the *Maritime law* (enacted in 1992 and effective as of 1 July 1993). Chapter 3 of the law, entitled 'Seafarers,' contains a total of ten provisions, the majority of which concern the authority and duties of the master.[25] In addition, the *Regulations on the Administration of Seafarers*, promulgated in 2007 and amended five times up to March 2019, governs such matters as seafarer registration and qualification requirements, positions and job security, training and manning agencies, as well as supervisory and administrative mechanisms.

MOT, as the competent authority for maritime and inland waterway transport, has issued a detailed regulatory framework covering qualification, licensing, and registration requirements for both seagoing and inland waterway seafarers. These include the *Examination and Certification Rules for Seagoing Seafarers*, the *Examination and Certification Rules for Inland Waterway Seafarers*, the *Seafarer Registration Administrative Measures*, the *Pilot Registration and Qualification Requirements*, the *Seafarer's Book Administrative Measures*, and the *Minimum Safe Manning Requirements for Vessels*. To regulate seafarer welfare and working conditions, the government also adopted the *Administrative Measures on Seafarers' Onboard Working and Living Conditions*. Since 2016, the China Seafarers' Construction Workers' Union and the China Shipowners' Association have annually concluded collective agreements between seafarers and shipowners, which serve as model contracts, thereby institutionalizing both legal and social frameworks of seafarer management.[26]

Seafarers enjoy the same legal protections as shore-based workers, and shipowners are obligated to comply with the relevant laws. Recognizing the specific characteristics of seafaring, Chinese law grants certain preferential provisions and entitlements. For instance, seafarers' wages are accorded maritime lien status, enabling claims against vessels in the event of non-payment, and they are guaranteed a minimum of 2.5 days of paid leave for each month of service at sea.

[25] Zhang (2016).

[26] Jin and Choi (2020), p. 189.

Furthermore, under the preferential income tax policy for ocean-going seafarers announced on 20 November 2019, seafarers with more than 183 days of annual sea service between 1 January 2019, and the end of 2023 are entitled to a 50% reduction in taxable income.[27] While significant, this measure remains relatively limited compared to advanced maritime nations such as the United Kingdom, Norway, India, and the Philippines.

In this respect, although China has developed a legal and welfare framework to protect and support seafarers, the overall scope of such measures remains comparatively limited when evaluated against international standards.

Enforcement Regime: Port State Control

China enforces PSC regime to monitor the compliance of foreign vessels entering its jurisdictional ports with standards of safety, security, and marine environmental protection, thereby ensuring the domestic implementation of international conventions. China MSA under MOT exercises PSC authority, inspecting foreign vessels for compliance with major IMO conventions, including SOLAS, MARPOL, and MLC. According to Article 88(2) the Maritime Traffic Safety Law of China, China MSA may exercise port state control.

Furthermore, both the Regulations on the Prevention and Control of Marine Pollution from Ships and the MEPL incorporate discharges standards and pollution prevention equipment into PSC inspections. These inspections include checks on pollution prevention equipment and logbooks, thereby reinforcing the obligations set forth in MARPOL Annexes from I to V at the domestic level.

PSC in China functions not only as a mechanism for ensuring compliance with international norms but also as an enforcement instrument that concurrently strengthens national maritime sovereignty and safety management. Namely, the evolution of China's PSC system demonstrates an approach that accommodates IMO standards while accentuating domestic legal enforcement and the protection of national maritime interests.

Conclusion

China's maritime industry and maritime legal system are structured to simultaneously pursue compliance with international conventions and the advancement of national strategic interests. China strengthens vessel safety, marine environmental protection, and seafarers' rights by enhancing global competitiveness in shipbuilding, ship ownership, and seafarer supply, and by integrating IMO conventions with

[27] Ibid.

domestic legislation. In particular, as an IMO A-Group Council Member, China actively participates in the formulation of international maritime norms concerning maritime safety, environmental protection, seafarer education, and labour conditions. Through the World Maritime University and domestic maritime training institutions, China systematically cultivates professional maritime personnel and seafarers. These efforts provide a dual foundation for engagement in international maritime governance and the enhancement of domestic shipping industry competitiveness.

In addition, China has developed and refined maritime dispute resolution mechanisms through maritime courts and arbitration. Beginning with the establishment of the Beijing Maritime Court in 2018, specialized maritime courts have been set up in major port cities such as Shanghai, Guangdong, and Tianjin, facilitating the swift and professional adjudication of complex maritime disputes involving shipping, shipbuilding, insurance, and logistics. The China Maritime Arbitration Commission (CMAC) administers both English and Chinese arbitration rules and actively participates in the global maritime arbitration market through international cooperation.

Chinese public maritime legislations serve as the legal foundation for this systematic development, exerting significant influence over public functions such as maritime traffic safety, marine environmental protection, port and route management, and the safeguarding of national maritime interests. Chinese public maritime legislations extend beyond the regulation of private shipping, playing a decisive role in overall maritime governance by integrating state sovereignty, compliance with international norms, comprehensive maritime safety management, and the establishment of responsibilities for vessels and seafarers. This legal and institutional framework underpins China's global maritime strategy.

References

Brookes Bell (2025) 74% of All New Shipbuilding Orders Booked by Chinese Yards in 2024. 6 February 2025, Available at https://www.brookesbell.com/news-and-knowledge/article/74-of-all-new-shipbuilding-orders-booked-by-chinese-yards-in-2024-159301/. Accessed 1 September 2025

Cebr (2025) The Competitiveness of the UK Shipping Industry. Available at https://www.ukchamberofshipping.com/people-planet-prosperity/prosperity/the-competitiveness-the-uk-shipping-industry. Accessed 21 September 2025

Cui H (2024) A study on the interpretation and application of the 'International Concern Provisions' of Chinese Coast Guard Law. Mar Dev 2(1):6

Embassy of the People's Republic of China in the United Kingdom of Great Britain and Northern Ireland. Available at http://gb.china-embassy.gov.cn/eng/zywl/2011/201112/t20111201_3386668.htm. Accessed 21 September 2025

Global Times (2025) China leads three shipbuilding indicators for 15th year. 16 January 2025. Available at https://www.globaltimes.cn/page/202501/1327019.shtml. Accessed 1 September 2025

Hanqin X, Qian J (2009) International treaties in the Chinese domestic legal system. Chinese J Int Law 8(2):299

iMarine News, "China's shipbuilding statistics for 2024 released" 21 January 2025., Available at https://www.imarinenews.com/18918.html. Accessed 1 September 2025
Jin W, Choi J-Y (2020) A study on the problems and improvement discussion of the seafarers' act system and marine officer training in China. Cult Inter Stud Sea Port Cities (CISSPC) 22:189
Li S, Ingram C (2013) Maritime law and policy in China. Routledge-Cavendish
Liu R (2024) Revision of China's marine environmental protection law: history, background and improvement. Front Mar Sci 11:1409772
Lloyd's List, One Hundred Container Ports 2024. Available at https://www.lloydslist.com/one-hundred-container-ports-2024. Accessed 21 September 2025
Ma S (2020) Economics of maritime business. Routledge
Ministry of Transport of China, China Seafarer Development Report 2020 [in Chinese]
Shi Y, Zhuang Y (2024) China: 2023 revision to China's marine environment protection law: interpretations and implications. Asia-Pac J Ocean Law Policy 9(1):128
Tian H, Khan MI, Chang Y-C (2023) Maritime traffic law of the People's Republic of China and its implications in international law. Marine Policy 151:105570
UNCTAD, Review of Maritime Transport 2024 (2024), Available at https://unctad.org/publication/review-maritime-transport-2024. Accessed 21 September 2025
Wang Y, Mi JJ, Chen C, Ge J, Chen Y (2025) Evolution of China's shipping policies and attention: evidence from LDA analysis. Ocean Coast Manage 267:107746
Xinhua (2025) International Maritime Organization looks forward to China's continued support: secretary-general. 22 July 2025, Available at https://english.news.cn/20250722/09e302b7fa854462a06993a4cd3b3899/c.html. Accessed 21 September 2025
Zhang H, Hu H, Wang Q (2022) New developments in China's maritime traffic safety legislation: theoretical background, institutional changes, and potential implications. Ocean Dev Int Law 53(4):346
Zhang P (2016) Seafarers' Rights in China. Springer
Zhu L, Dong B, Li KX (2013) Compensation for oil pollution damage from ships in China: a way toward international standards. Ocean Dev Int Law 44(1):73
Zou K (2009) International law in the Chinese domestic context. Valparaiso Univ Law Rev 44:935

Chapter 4
Public Maritime Legislations in Japan

Unho Lee

Introduction

Japan's status as a maritime nation is both profound and indisputable. An island country with extensive coastlines and a heavy reliance on seaborne trade, Japan has developed one of the world's largest shipping industries. The vitality of its ports and the scale of its merchant fleet underscore the economic and strategic significance of maritime activities to Japan's national interests. In this context, public maritime law—the body of statutes and regulations governing maritime safety, security, environmental protection, and the welfare of seafarers—plays a pivotal role. It provides the legal architecture that ensures ships are safely constructed and operated, marine pollution is prevented or controlled, and those who work at sea are protected. Beyond domestic importance, Japan's commitment to robust maritime public law also aligns with international standards, reflecting its active participation in global maritime governance through instruments such as the International Maritime Organization (IMO) conventions and related frameworks. This thematic focus on Japan's public maritime legislation is therefore significant not only for safeguarding Japan's own maritime domain but also for its contribution to the rule of law at sea regionally and worldwide.

The chapter is structured into three main sections. Section 1 outlines the institutional framework of Japan's maritime legislation, including an overview of its

---

Unho Lee is a lecturer at the Faculty of Law of Kyushu University, Japan. He obtained LL.M. and LL.D. in the field of international maritime law (Kyushu University, Japan), with the completion of a professional research program in maritime commercial law (Korea University, South Korea).

U. Lee (✉)
Faculty of Law, Kyushu University, Fukuoka, Japan
e-mail: peter@law.kyushu-u.ac.jp

J. Choi (ed.), *Public Maritime Law in Asia*, International Law in Asia,
https://doi.org/10.1007/978-981-95-7037-9_4

shipping industry, Japan's involvement in the IMO, the principles guiding implementation of IMO conventions in domestic law, and the roles of maritime administrations such as Ministry of Land, Infrastructure, Transport, and Tourism (MLIT) and the Japan Coast Guard (JCG). Section 2 surveys Japan's key public maritime laws in four domains: (a) safety and security, including vessel and port regulations; (b) marine environmental protection, notably through the 1970 Marine Pollution Prevention Act and MARPOL implementation; (c) seafarers' rights and standards, covering qualifications, working conditions, and labour protections; and (d) enforcement and Port State Control, focusing on inspections and sanctions against substandard ships. Section 3 turns to emerging challenges in public maritime law, examining Japan's legal responses to decarbonization and digitalization—from zero-emission shipping goals to autonomous vessels and e-navigation—and to the protection of seafarers' human rights, especially highlighted during the COVID-19 crew-change crisis. The conclusion synthesizes these findings, outlines future directions for reform, and considers Japan's influence on regional maritime governance in Asia.

Institutional Framework for Maritime Legislations in Japan

Overview of Shipping Industry

Japan is one of the world's leading maritime nations, with a vast shipping industry that is integral to its trade-dependent economy. As an island country with limited natural resources, Japan relies heavily on maritime transport for both imports and exports, with 99.6% of trade by volume carried by sea.[1] Japanese shipowners collectively control roughly 12% of the world's deadweight tonnage, making Japan the third-largest ship-owning country globally.[2] The nation's extensive merchant fleet is complemented by high-volume port operations and coastal shipping networks. Japanese ports are major hubs in international trade, handling roughly 21.5 million TEUs of containers in 2023,[3] with Tokyo, Yokohama, and Kobe among the notable gateways. At the domestic level, Japan's archipelagic geography has fostered a robust internal maritime network: coastal shipping accounts for nearly 40% of all domestic freight transport in ton-kilometers (and around 80% of key industrial commodities like steel, cement, and petroleum) far outpacing rail and rivaling trucking in moving goods between country's numerous islands and coastal cities.[4] Given this

[1] Japan Maritime Public Relations Center (2024), p. 26.

[2] BIMCO, "*Japan Is World's Third Largest Shipping Nation as Owners Control 12% of the Fleet*", Shipping Number of the Week (24 April 2025), available at: https://www.bimco.org/news-insights/market-analysis/shipping-number-of-the-week/2025/0424-snow (accessed 30 June 2025).

[3] UNCTAD, "Statistical Profile: Japan (2023)", available at: https://unctadstat.unctad.org/CountryProfile/GeneralProfile/en-GB/392/index.html (accessed 28 July 2025)

[4] Japan Federation of Coastal Shipping Associations, "Coastal Shipping of Japan 2025", pp. 5–6 (2025).

economic significance, the shipping industry plays a vital role in Japan's economy, demanding a robust regulatory framework to ensure safe and efficient operations.

To support and regulate this extensive maritime activity, Japan has developed a sophisticated legal and institutional framework. Its maritime governance is characterized by strong administrative coordination, active participation in international rule-making, and comprehensive implementation of global standards. As a long-standing member of the IMO and a regular IMO Council member, Japan has helped shape many key conventions while aligning its domestic laws closely with them. The responsibilities of policy development, safety oversight, environmental protection, and enforcement are shared among specialized agencies, most notably the MLIT and the JCG. The close relationship between Japan's shipping interests and its maritime institutions ensures that the country remains deeply engaged in the evolution of international maritime law—a theme that will be explored further in the sections that follow.

Involvement in the IMO

Japan has been deeply involved in the IMO since its inception. The IMO came into being in 1958, and Japan joined as a member-state at that foundation, quickly becoming an influential participant.[5] In fact, Japan has continuously served on the IMO Council since 1958, often as a top-tier (Category A) member representing the states most vital to international shipping.[6] This long-standing council membership reflects Japan's status as a leading maritime nation, maintaining one of the top ten largest contributors to the IMO.[7] The prominence as a flag State, port State, and shipbuilder underpins Japan's strong voice in IMO deliberations and its commitment to global maritime governance.[8]

Japan has leveraged its maritime expertise to shape many of the IMO's cornerstone conventions and standards. It was one of the earliest parties to key IMO

[5] Ministry of Foreign Affairs of Japan, "Maritime Safety, Maritime Pollution Prevention and Japan's Contribution", Available at https://www.mofa.go.jp/policy/maritime/safety/pollution.html (accessed 28 June 2025).

[6] Embassy of Japan in the UK, *"Japan elected to the IMO Council Category "A" as member with the highest number of votes"* (Press Release, 1 Dec 2023).

[7] IMO, "IMO Financial Statements 2024", p. 69 (2024).

[8] Japan has ratified or acceded to most of the key IMO conventions, including but not limited to: SOLAS, MARPOL (and its Annexes), STCW (with successive amendments), FAL, COLREG, Load Lines, CSC, SAR, SUA, various pollution-control instruments (such as OPRC, AFS, Ballast Water Management, and the Hong Kong Ship Recycling Convention), as well as liability and compensation regimes (CLC/FUND, Bunker Oil Convention, Nairobi Wrecks, Athens, and the LLMC Protocol 1996), together with the Cape Town Agreement, which is not yet in force as of September 2025. For details, *see* International Maritime Organization, "Status of IMO Treaties" (Status of Conventions and Amendments), available at https://www.imo.org/en/About/Conventions/Pages/StatusOfConventions.aspx (accessed 29 June 2025).

treaties such as the SOLAS Convention on Safety of Life at Sea (1974) and the MARPOL Convention for prevention of pollution from ships (1973/78), and it implements the STCW Convention on seafarer training and watchkeeping, among others.[9] Japanese officials and experts actively participate in IMO committees to develop and refine these international rules. Notably, Japan's delegation has at times spearheaded important regulatory advances—for instance, after the 1997 Nakhodka oil spill off the coast of western Japan, Japan proposed amendments to strengthen MARPOL's pollution controls, which were subsequently adopted by IMO member states.[10] Through such contributions, Japan has consistently promoted higher safety and environmental standards. Its maritime administration also diligently incorporates IMO rules into domestic law, ensuring that global norms (from ship construction requirements to crew training standards) are upheld in Japanese waters and by Japanese-flagged vessels. This active engagement in rule-making and implementation illustrates Japan's role as both a contributor to, and a model enforcer of, IMO conventions.

More recently, Japan has been a vocal proponent of efforts to decarbonize international shipping, aligning with IMO's greenhouse gas reduction strategy and investing in cleaner vessel technologies and alternative fuels.[11] At the same time, Japan is helping drive the IMO's agenda on digitalization and automation, such as developing regulations for Maritime Autonomous Surface Ships (MASS) and promoting e-navigation systems.[12]

---

[9] Ministry of Foreign Affairs of Japan, "Maritime Safety, Maritime Pollution Prevention and Japan's Contribution", available at https://www.mofa.go.jp/policy/maritime/safety/pollution.html (accessed 29 June 2025).

[10] *Id.*

[11] This commitment has been institutionalized through Japan's "Shipping Zero Emission Project", launched in 2018 under the leadership of MLIT and JSTRA with support from the Nippon Foundation, which has carried out research on zero-emission fuels, vessel technologies, and regulatory measures necessary to achieve net zero GHG emissions in international shipping by 2050. *See* MLIT Maritime Bureau & JSTRA (Japan Ship Technology Research Association), "Toward Achieving Net Zero GHG Emissions from International Shipping by 2050", Shipping Zero Emission Project (March 2022).

[12] For example, Japan actively contributed to the IMO's Regulatory Scoping Exercise (RSE) for MASS by submitting proposals, participating in intersessional working groups, and chairing the MSC-LEG-FAL Joint Working Group on MASS to guide cross-committee coordination and the development of a goal-based regulatory framework. *See* IMO, "Development of a Goal-Based Instrument For MASS", MSC 107/5/1 (May 2, 2023).

General Principle of Implementation of IMO Conventions in Domestic Law

Japan's approach to incorporating IMO conventions is grounded in its legal framework and constitutional provisions. Formally, Japan follows an 'incorporation system'—once the Diet approves a treaty, it is considered part of domestic law by virtue of Article 98(2) of the Constitution, which stipulates that treaties 'shall be faithfully observed'. In practice, however, Japan does not rely on treaty text alone; it takes a dualist-like approach of passing detailed domestic legislation to implement the convention's requirements. This ensures that international maritime standards are given full effect in Japan's legal order and provide clear rules for enforcement by national authorities.[13]

A central principle in Japan's implementation of IMO conventions is legal harmonization: domestic laws are systematically aligned with international obligations. Japan usually enacts any necessary laws or amendments before or by the time it formally ratifies an IMO convention, so that domestic regulations take effect the moment the treaty obligations become binding.[14] For example, Japan's amendments of the Order for Enforcing the Marine Pollution Prevention Act took effect on the same dates, precisely matching the dates Annex VI of MARPOL entered into force, which synchronized domestic implementation and treaty's entry into force.[15] Similarly, Japan timed legal amendments related to the Bunker Oil Pollution Convention and the Wreck Removal Convention to coincide with their ratification dates, ensuring immediate legal applicability.[16] This proactive timing reflects a policy of no gaps in compliance, minimizing transitional uncertainty and facilitating compliance for industry and enforcement bodies alike.

Although Japanese doctrine recognizes the possibility of self-executing treaties, governmental practice generally requires the enactment of implementing legislation prior to ratification, as the mere conclusion of a treaty does not itself confer

[13] Tomoaki Shiota (2024).

[14] Jun Tsuruta (2009), p. 386.

[15] MLIT, "Regarding the Cabinet Order Partially Amending the Enforcement Order of the Act on Prevention of Marine Pollution and Maritime Disasters" [in Japanese] (Sept. 22, 2024), *available at* https://www.mlit.go.jp/kisha/kisha04/01/010922_2_.html (accessed 4 July 2025).

[16] Japan has traditionally protected victims by requiring certain ships to maintain compulsory insurance covering bunker oil pollution damage and wreck removal costs. However, cases arose in which insurance proceeds were not paid despite the existence of such contracts. To strengthen victim protection, Japan enacted the Act Partially Amending the Act on Liability for Oil Pollution Damage and Compensation for Damage Caused by Ship Oil Pollution (Act No. 18 of 2019), promulgated on 31 May 2019, to implement the Bunker Convention and the Nairobi Wreck Removal Convention. After completing the necessary subordinate legislation, Japan acceded to both Conventions. Japan P&I Club, "Ratification of the Bunker Convention and Wreck Removal Convention, and Amendment of the Oil Pollution Act in Japan" (July 3, 2020), *available at* https://www.piclub.or.jp/en/news/31553 (accessed 4 July 2025).

regulatory authority and enforcement powers upon administrative agencies.[17] Accordingly, Japan has adopted detailed implementing provisions—covering issues from discharge limits to crew standards[18]—before any administrative or penal measures are carried out. While this approach imposes burdens on legislative coordination, it ensures that IMO commitments are fully integrated into Japan's legal system. The result is a structured, timely, and legally robust implementation process that reflects both Japan's commitment to international maritime law and its domestic legal principles.

Role of Maritime Administrations

The MLIT serves as Japan's central maritime authority through its Maritime Bureau. This bureau is responsible for a broad spectrum of regulatory and administrative functions: it formulates shipping policy, licenses domestic shipping services, oversees vessel registration and inspection, and develops technical standards to ensure ships' safety and environmental compliance.[19] It also administers seafarer affairs—from training and certification of officers to labour conditions and accident compensation—thereby safeguarding the welfare and competence of crew serving on Japanese ships. In essence, the Maritime Bureau translates international maritime conventions into national regulations and coordinates their enforcement across Japan's commercial fleet and ports. To carry out these mandates, MLIT works closely with specialized agencies and recognized organizations (like the classification society ClassNK) to survey vessels and uphold standards, while engaging with international bodies to keep Japan's regulations aligned with global norms.

Equally important are the ancillary agencies. The JCG is an external organ of MLIT, institutionally situated within the ministry but operationally responsible for maritime law enforcement: it conducts patrols, ship inspections, search-and-rescue operations, while also handling hydrographic surveying and traffic management,[20] providing a constant presence to ensure vessels adhere to safety and pollution regulations. Meanwhile, the Japan Transport Safety Board (JTSB) plays a complementary investigative role. Established in 2008 to replace the Marine Accident Inquiry Agency, it conducts objective, fact-based investigations and issues safety recommendations to MLIT, thereby supporting regulatory adjustments or stronger

---

[17] Makoto Matsuda (2011), p. 318.

[18] For example, Japan amended its Seafarers Act Enforcement Regulation on 1 January 2012 and the Ships' Officers Regulation on 1 April 2014, to align domestic training and certification standards with international requirements under 2010 Manila Amendments.

[19] MLIT Maritime Bureau, "Organization and Functions of Maritime Bureau" (May 1, 2014), *available at* https://www.mlit.go.jp/common/001040099.pdf (accessed 5 July 2025).

[20] Japan Coast Guard, *"Mission"*, MLIT, *available at* https://www.kaiho.mlit.go.jp/mission/ (accessed 7 July 2025).

enforcement measures.[21] JTSB's recommendations often catalyse downstream policy responses or operational enhancements in vessel traffic regulations, crew training, or emergency procedures.

These institutions ensure Japan's maritime governance is both comprehensive and proactive. In events such as oil spills or major casualties, JCG leads emergency response and containment, while local port authorities and industry stakeholders operate within a unified response framework. Joint government–industry oil-spill committees established in major ports nationwide and the Maritime Disaster Prevention Center support rapid coordination.[22] In major incidents, the MLIT, often in coordination with the Cabinet Office, mobilizes cross-administration resources to mount an effective response. Regional Transport Bureaus deploy inspectors to conduct regular and intermediate inspections,[23] which contribute to the prevention of accidents. This integrated approach underpins Japan's consistently high performance as a flag state—rated 'all-green' in the ICS Flag State Performance Table—reflecting strong compliance with international standards.[24]

Key Public Maritime Legislations

Maritime Safety and Security

Maritime safety in Japan is grounded in domestic laws that implement IMO conventions like SOLAS 1974. A centerpiece is the Ship Safety Act (Law No. 11 of 1933, as amended) which ensures the seaworthiness of vessels and the protection of life at sea. This law prescribes technical standards for ship construction, equipment (e.g., life-saving and fire-fighting appliances), and inspection requirements in alignment with international safety conventions. Navigation safety is further reinforced by the Act on Preventing Collision at Sea (Law No. 62 of 1977, as amended), which incorporates the COLREGs 1972 rules into Japanese law. In especially congested waterways such as Tokyo Bay, the Act on Maritime Traffic Safety (Law No. 115 of 1972, as amended) provides additional traffic regulations to prevent marine accidents, and the Port Regulations Act (Law No. 174 of 1948, as amended) governs safe navigation with orderly control and administration within designated ports. Together, these laws create a comprehensive regime for vessel safety standards and operational safety in Japanese waters.

[21] Japan Transport Safety Board, "*Mission*", MLIT, *available at* https://jtsb.mlit.go.jp/mission.html (accessed 7 July 2025).

[22] International Tanker Owners Pollution Federation Limited (2018), pp. 1–2.

[23] Article 5 of the Ship Safety Act; and Articles 18 and 24 of the Regulations for Enforcement of the Ship Safety Act (Ministry of Transport Ordinance No. 41 of 1963).

[24] International Chamber of Shipping (ICS), "Shipping Industry Flag State Performance Table 2024/2025", *available at* https://www.ics-shipping.org/wp-content/uploads/2025/02/Shipping-Industry-Flag-State-Performance-Table-2024-2025-.pdf (accessed 8 July 2025).

Maritime security has likewise been strengthened through specific legislation. In the aftermath of new IMO security requirements, Japan enacted the Act on Ensuring the Security of International Voyage Ships and International Port Facilities (Act No. 31 of 2004) in 2004 to implement the ISPS Code and SOLAS Chapter XI-2 measures. This law mandates the preparation and approval of ship and port facility security plans (Article 11), requires ships entering Japanese ports from abroad to report security information to authorities in advance (Article 44), and empowers the JCG to deny port entry to vessels that pose security threats (Article 45). More broadly, the Japan Coast Guard Act establishes the JCG's authority to ensure maritime safety and public order at sea (e.g., Article 2), including powers to stop, board, and inspect vessels and to take necessary measures in situations involving danger or crimes (e.g., Articles 17–18). Through these instruments, Japan's legal framework addresses both the safety of navigation and the security of maritime transport, in line with international standards and national security concerns.

Protection of the Marine Environment from Shipping Activities

Japan has established a comprehensive legal framework to protect the marine environment from ship-sourced pollution. The cornerstone is the Act on the Prevention of Marine Pollution and Maritime Disaster (Act No. 136 of 1970), which was enacted to implement international conventions and prevent pollution from ships. In effect, it serves as the primary domestic instrument implementing MARPOL 73/78—the comprehensive global treaty regulating oil, chemical, sewage, garbage, and air pollution from vessels. The Act applies to vessels in Japan's internal waters and territorial sea,[25] as well as to Japanese-flagged ships worldwide. Over the years, Japan has updated this legislation in step with international standards. Notably, a 1983 amendment enabled Japan's ratification of MARPOL and its technical Annexes I–V. Another major revision in 2004 introduced stricter controls on ship emissions (e.g., sulfur in fuel and engine NOx limits) to implement MARPOL Annex VI on air pollution, taking effect in 2005 alongside the global entry into force of that Annex.[26] These measures collectively ensure that operational discharges of oil and other harmful substances, as well as air emissions from ships, are tightly regulated in comformity with global norms.

In addition to preventive regulations, Japan has joined international liability and response frameworks addressing marine pollution incidents. It is party to the key oil

[25] This is subject to exemptions under Article 9 (3) that explicitly exempts foreign vessels from Articles 6 and 7 (i.e. appointing oil pollution prevention manager; and establishing oil pollution prevention regulations), which is understood as reflecting a balance between Japan's environmental protection goals and its obligations under international law (especially UNCLOS and relevant IMO/MARPOL conventions). Also, Article 19 (3)–(15) and (25)–(31) may not be applicable under the special rules of Article 19(16) and (32).

[26] Tsuruta (2009), p. 386.

pollution compensation treaties—including the 1992 Civil Liability Convention (CLC), the 1992 Fund Convention and its Protocol of 2003, and the 2001 Bunker Oil Pollution Convention—which have been incorporated into domestic law via the Act on Liability for Oil Pollution Damage (Act No. 95 of 1975).[27] This ensures that shipowners are financially liable for oil spills and that adequate compensation is available to victims, with supplemental funding through the International Oil Pollution Compensation (IOPC) Fund scheme. Japan has also ratified the International Convention on Oil Pollution Preparedness, Response, and Co-operation (OPRC 1990) to bolster its national and regional readiness for marine pollution emergencies. Enforcement of these environmental protections is chiefly entrusted to the JCG. Under the Japan Coast Guard Act, one of its missions is explicitly the 'prevention of marine pollution' (Article 2). The JCG, in conjunction with other national laws (such as the Marine Pollution Prevention Act), is empowered to inspect vessels, verify compliance with anti-pollution standards, and take corrective measures or initiate investigations of suspected violations,[28] subject to jurisdictional limits.[29] Combined with domestic pollution control rules, liability/compensation regimes, and Japan's treaty obligations, this legal and institutional framework provides for significant protection of the marine environment from shipping-related harms.

Regulations on Seafarers

Japan has developed a robust legal regime for seafarers that aligns with international standards, such as the International Convention on Standards of Training, Certification and Watchkeeping for Seafarers (STCW, 1978, as amended, including the 2010 Manila Amendments) and the Maritime Labor Convention of 2006 (MLC, 2006). These global conventions set baseline requirements on seafarers' professional qualifications, training, and watchkeeping (under the STCW), as well as minimum standards for labour conditions—including employment terms, hours of work and rest, accommodation, health protection, and welfare (under the MLC). Reflecting the distinctive nature of seafaring work, Japan maintains a specialized maritime labour law regime separate from general employment law.[30] Key statutes in this regime include the Seafarers Act (Law No. 100 of 1947) and the Act on Ships' Officers and Boats' Operators (Law No. 149 of 1951), which together form

---

[27] Takahashi Hongo & Ryo Munakata, "Shipping Laws and Regulations Japan 2025", *International Comparative Legal Guides*, available at https://iclg.com/practice-areas/shipping-laws-and-regulations/japan (accessed 15 July 2025).

[28] For example, *see* Article 17 of the Japan Coast Guard Act; and Article 48(10) of the Act on the Prevention of Marine Pollution and Maritime Disaster.

[29] *See supra* note 25.

[30] MLIT Maritime Bureau, "Seafarers' Labor Handbook" [in Japanese], p. 2 (September, 2022), *available at* https://www.mlit.go.jp/maritime/content/001513926.pdf (accessed 18 July 2025).

the backbone of Japanese seafarer legislation. These laws implement the above international standards in domestic law—the former focusing on seafarers' labour rights and shipboard working conditions, and the latter on seafarer training and certification in line with STCW requirements.

Certification and Training Under the Act on Ships' Officers and Boats' Operators, Japan prescribes strict qualification and licensing requirements for shipmasters, officers, engineers, and other crew, in accordance with the STCW Convention's competency standards (e.g., Articles 4–16). This statute (and its associated regulations) governs maritime education curricula, examinations, and the issuance of certificates to ensure that all seafarers on Japanese-flagged vessels meet internationally mandated levels of proficiency. Oversight is carried out by the MLIT through its Maritime Bureau, which administers seafarer certification and training institutions. The Seafarers Act complements these provisions by incorporating safe manning rules (e.g., Article 70), watchkeeping duties (e.g., Article 117-2), and mandatory rest hours for crews (e.g., Articles 61–65)—measures that reinforce maritime safety in line with STCW and related IMO standards. Through this dual system of dedicated statutes, Japan ensures that its seafarers are competently trained and certificated in conformity with global standards before serving at sea.

Labor Rights, Welfare, and Enforcement The working conditions and welfare of seafarers in Japan are primarily governed by the Seafarers Act, a comprehensive statute that codifies seafarers' employment contracts, wages, hours of work and rest, leave, onboard living conditions, health and safety measures, and other labor rights. This law was enacted in the post-war era (building on earlier maritime laws from 1899 to 1937) to ensure that seafarers receive protections comparable to those of land-based workers, adapted to the maritime context.[31] It includes specific chapters addressing issues such as crew accommodations and provisions, medical care (Chap. 8), discipline (Chap. 3), accident compensation (Chap. 10), and special protections for young and female mariners (Chap. 9 and 9-2). Over time, Japan has augmented this framework with additional legislation—for example, a Seafarers' Insurance Act (Law No. 73 of 1939, as amended) and dedicated occupational safety regulations—thereby establishing an extensive safety-net for seafarers' welfare and social security. Following the ratification of the MLC, Japan reviewed and adjusted its laws to meet the Convention's requirements on matters like minimum age, seafarers' employment agreements, hours of rest, and onboard welfare facilities.[32] In practice, all Japanese-flag ships on international voyages (over 500 gross tonnage) must now carry a Maritime Labor Certificate and a Declaration of Maritime Labor Compliance, attesting that their crew's working and living conditions comply with

---

[31] Kengo Minami (2025), p. 16.

[32] Regarding the amendment details, *see* MLIT Maritime Bureau, "Revision of the Seafarers Act following the ratification of the Maritime Labor Convention" [Japanese] (March 2013), *available at* https://www.mlit.go.jp/common/001012029.pdf (accessed 24 July 2025).

MLC standards.[33] MLIT's Maritime Bureau serves as the chief enforcement authority, overseeing flag-State implementation and delegating inspection duties to Recognized Organizations (such as Nippon Kaiji Kyokai/ClassNK and other classification societies) for shipboard labor inspections. At the same time, Japan participates in port State control under the Tokyo MOU framework to enforce these standards on foreign ships calling at its ports—port State inspectors are empowered to verify MLC compliance and detain vessels that violate seafarers' rights.[34] Through this integrated system of stringent national laws and active enforcement, Japan upholds international norms on seafarers' certification, working conditions, and welfare, thereby safeguarding the rights and well-being of its seafaring workforce.

Enforcement Regime: Port State Control

Port State Control (PSC) serves as a critical enforcement mechanism in Japan's maritime regulatory regime, allowing Japanese authorities to inspect foreign ships in Japanese ports for compliance with international safety, environmental, and crewing standards. Although primary responsibility for a ship's compliance rests with its flag State, port State oversight acts as a vital safety net to catch substandard vessels, complementing flag State enforcement. Japan has played a significant role in regional PSC cooperation, becoming a founding member of the Memorandum of Understanding on Port State Control in the Asia-Pacific Region (Tokyo MOU) concluded in 1993. Under the Tokyo MOU framework, Japan works alongside other Asia-Pacific maritime authorities to harmonize inspection procedures, share information, and conduct periodic Concentrated Inspection Campaigns targeting specific risk areas.[35] The Tokyo MOU's New Inspection Regime adopted risk-based targeting, classifying vessels as high, standard, or low risk according to factors like ship age, flag performance, and past deficiencies.[36] This approach enables Japanese inspectors to prioritize high-risk ships for more frequent and rigorous inspections, thereby enhancing the effectiveness of preventive enforcement.

---

[33] Maritime Labor Convention 2006, Regulation 5.1.3 (1).

[34] Tokyo MOU provides that the Port State inspectors have authority to inspect for MLC compliance and detain non-compliant vessels. (*See* Tokyo MOU, "Memorandum of Understanding on Port State Control in the Asia-Pacific Region", Sections 3.1 and 3.7 of the 23rd amendment with the effect on 1 July 2025) The Tokyo MOU also participates in Concentrated Inspection Campaigns on crew wages and seafarers' employment agreements, under which inspections are conducted and non-compliances can lead to detention. (*See* Paris MOU, "Joint Concentrated Inspection Campaign on Crew Wages and Seafarer Employment Agreements (MLC, 2006)", Press Release (1 August 2024), available at https://parismou.org/2024/08/joint-concentrated-inspection-campaign-crew--wages-and-seafarer-employment-agreements-mlc (accessed 25 July 2025).

[35] For Tokyo MOU, *see* https://www.tokyo-mou.org/; for CICs, *see* https://www.tokyo-mou.org/cic-results/.

[36] https://www.tokyo-mou.org/inspections-detentions/nir/.

On the domestic front, PSC in Japan is conducted by MLIT through its Regional Transport Bureaus under the supervision of the Maritime Bureau. PSC officers stationed at the nation's major ports are authorized under Japanese law to enforce the standards of major international conventions—such as SOLAS, MARPOL, Load Line, STCW, and MLC—which have been incorporated into national legislation. PSC inspections are carried out in accordance with IMO and Tokyo MOU guidelines, beginning with checks of certificates and vessel conditions and expanding into detailed examinations where 'clear grounds' of non-compliance are found.[37] Where deficiencies pose a serious threat to safety, crew welfare, or the marine environment, the ship may be detained[38] until the deficiencies are rectified or satisfactory corrective measures are in place.[39] To promote transparency and compliance, MLIT publicly reports vessels detained in Japanese ports on its website, creating an additional deterrent against substandard shipping.[40] In this manner, Japan's PSC regime operates as an essential complement to flag state oversight, leveraging both international cooperation and domestic legal authority to ensure that foreign ships calling at Japanese ports meet applicable international standards before they sail onward.

Emerging Challenges in Public Maritime Law

The maritime sector is facing unprecedented shifts driven by global climate imperatives and rapid technological innovation. Japan's public maritime law agenda has accordingly expanded beyond traditional concerns to address new challenges such as the decarbonization of shipping and the digitalization of maritime operations. Curbing greenhouse gas emissions from ships has become urgent, given that shipping contributes roughly 3% of global CO_2 emissions.[41] At the same time, emerging technologies like autonomous vessels and AI-assisted navigation promise greater efficiency but pose complex legal and regulatory hurdles. These developments are pushing Japan to update its domestic legal framework and to play an active role in shaping international maritime rules to meet evolving environmental and technological standards.

---

[37] Tokyo MOU, "Memorandum of Understanding on Port State Control in the Asia-Pacific Region", Sections 3.1 and 3.2 of the 23rd amendment with the effect on 1 July 2025.

[38] *Id.*, at Section 3.7.

[39] *Id.*

[40] MLIT Maritime Bureau makes public the list of ships detained in Japan every month. For example, see the latest information updated in August 2025, which is available at https://www.mlit.go.jp/maritime/content/001909542.pdf (accessed 16 September 2025).

[41] UNCTAD, "2024 Review of Maritime Transport: Navigating Maritime Chokepoints", UNCTAD/RMT/2024 and Corr.1, p. xiv (2024).

Decarbonization and Digitalization

Decarbonizaing Shipping In response to the climate crisis, maritime regulators worldwide (led by the IMO) have been tightening emissions standards for ships. In 2018, the IMO adopted an initial strategy targeting a 50% reduction in shipping GHG emissions by 2050, and in 2023 it reinforced this with a new goal of reaching net-zero emissions around 2050.[42] Japan has positioned itself as a key proponent of these stronger climate commitments. Notably, in late 2021, MLIT joined forces with other states to push the IMO to adopt a 2050 net-zero target.[43] MLIT has even advocated for market-based measures like carbon pricing to ensure these goals are met.[44] This stance aligns with Japan's own pledge to achieve carbon neutrality by 2050 and adds momentum to global regulatory efforts.

On the home front, Japan is embedding international decarbonization targets into broader domestic law and policy frameworks. In 2023, the government enacted the Act on the Promotion of Smooth Transition to a Decarbonized, Growth-Oriented Economic Structure ('GX Promotion Act', Act No. 32 of 2023) to drive economy-wide green transformation, providing a legal basis for maritime emissions reduction initiatives. Under this framework, MLIT—in partnership with industry and academia—has promoted zero-emission ship concepts and undertaken R&D projects (such as the MOL 'Wind Hunter Project') and policy roadmaps, exploring hydrogen, ammonia, wind propulsion, battery/electric systems and related technologies for future deployment.[45] Japan's roadmap envisages introduction of its inaugural zero-emission ship by 2028 as a milestone toward 2050 goals.[46] At the same time, Japan's major shipping companies (including NYK, MOL and K Line) have voluntarily announced their own 2050 net-zero pledges, investing in LNG dual-fuel, ammonia-fuelled, and hydrogen-fuelled ships to complement government policy. By combining regulatory measures with industry collaboration, Japan is striving to decarbonize its maritime sector while maintaining its competitiveness as a leading shipping and shipbuilding nation.

Digitalization and Autonomous Shipping Alongside decarbonization, Japan is tackling the rise of digitalization in shipping, especially the advent of Maritime Autonomous Surface Ships (MASS). The Japanese government and private sector have launched ambitious trials of autonomous vessel technology—most promi-

[42] IMO, "2023 IMO Strategy on Reduction of GHG Emissions from Ships", Resolution MEPC.377(80) (MEPC 80/17/Add.1 Annex 15), p. 6 (2023).

[43] MLIT, "Japan sets a target for global shipping of achieving net-zero GHG emissions by 2050" (October 26, 2021), *available at* https://www.mlit.go.jp/en/report/press/kaiji07_hh_000001.html (accessed 29 July 2025).

[44] MLIT Maritime Bureau & JSTRA, "Toward Achieving Net Zero GHG Emissions from International Shipping by 2050", Shipping Zero Emission Project, p.3 and pp.47–49 (March 2022).

[45] In general, *see* JSTRA, Nippon Foundation, and MLIT, "Roadmap to Zero Emission from International Shipping", Shipping Zero Emission Project (March 2020).

[46] *Id.*, at p. 34.

nently, the Nippon Foundation's MEGURI2040 program, which serves as a roadmap for the implementation of advanced autonomous navigation on coastal routes.[47] The goal is to begin introducing fully autonomous commercial ships by 2025, aiming for as much as 50 per cent of domestic coastal vessels to operate autonomously by 2040.[48] However, Japan's existing maritime laws have yet to catch up with these technological strides. Current regulations still effectively require a human master or crew on board, meaning fully unmanned ships cannot legally set sail under present law. Legal scholars note that several core statutes—such as the Seafarers Act, the Ship Officers and Small Vessel Pilots Act, and the Ship Safety Act—would need to be amended to recognize remote operators or AI systems in lieu of onboard crew. Questions of liability in the event of collisions and the certification of autonomous navigation systems also remain unresolved under today's legal framework.

To address regulatory gaps, Japanese authorities are reviewing existing maritime laws and developing interim safety frameworks in parallel with large-scale demonstration projects for autonomous shipping. Notably, Japan has progressively developed a domestic safety framework for MASS. MLIT first issued a Safety Design Guideline for Autonomous Ships in 2020, followed by a more comprehensive "Guideline on the Safety of Autonomous Ships" in 2022, addressing design, system integration, and operational safety, including remote control and autonomous navigation. In 2025, building on the work of an expert working group established in 2024, MLIT published Safety Standards and Inspection Protocols for autonomous vessels, marking a substantive step toward formalizing concrete safety standards and inspection methodologies for commercial deployment. Internationally, Japan plays an active role in shaping emerging standards for MASS, contributing to the IMO's development of a unified MASS Code and engaging in technical cooperation with other maritime nations. For example, in 2024 Japan and the United Kingdom held joint workshops to develop an assurance framework for safe autonomous shipping, as part of aligning standards and best practices.[49, 50] By investing in both technology and rule-making, Japan seeks to ensure that the digital transformation of

[47] The Nippon Foundation, "MEGURI2040 Fully Autonomous Ship Program: Aiming to Implement Fully Autonomous Navigation", The Nippon Foundation (Tokyo, 2020), *available at* https://en.nippon-foundation.or.jp/what/projects/ocean/meguri2040 (accessed 12 August 2025).

[48] Back to Blue (Economist Impact & Nippon Foundation), "The Future of the Japanese Maritime Industry Lies in Commercialising Fully Autonomous Ships" (March 2022), available at https://backtoblueinitiative.com/the-future-of-the-japanese-maritime-industry-lies-in-commercialising-fully-autonomous-ships/ (accessed 12 August 2025).

[49] Lloyd's Register, "UK and Japan Align Efforts to Accelerate Maritime Autonomy", Press Release (8 April 2024), *available at* https://www.lr.org/en/knowledge/press-room/press-listing/press-release/2024/uk-and-japan-align-efforts-to-accelerate-maritime-autonomy/ (accessed 13 August 2025).

[50] *Id. See also*, Megumi Shiokari, "Japanese MASS R&D Projects and Approaches for Ensuring Safety", in cooperation with MLIT, The Nippon Foundation MEGURI2040, JSTRA, and NMRI (31 August 2022), *available at* https://wwwcdn.imo.org/localresources/en/OurWork/Safety/PublishingImages/Pages/MASS/10_Megumi%20Shiokari_Japanese%20MASS%20R&D%20Projects%20and%20Approaches%20for%20ensuring%20safety.pdf (accessed 15 August 2025).

shipping—from autonomous vessels to AI-enhanced port logistics—unfolds in a safe, secure, and legally sound manner. This dual focus on decarbonization and digitalization underscores the dynamic evolution of Japan's public maritime law in the face of 21st-century challenges.

Protecting of Seafarer's Human Rights

Japan is regarded as maintaining a comparatively advanced regulatory framework in the region. As discussed above, the working conditions and welfare of seafarers in Japan are principally regulated by the Seafarers Act, supplemented by the Seafarers' Insurance Act and related maritime safety provisions. Following Japan's ratification of the MLC in 2013, the domestic framework was amended to ensure compliance with international standards on employment conditions, rest hours, onboard welfare, and so on.[51]

Institutional responsibility is shared among several authorities. The MLIT oversees enforcement of labour standards and seafarers' certification, while, in cooperation with its regional offices and JCG, conducting port state control inspections under the Tokyo MOU to check compliance on foreign vessels. The Immigration Control and Refugee Recognition Act (Cabinet Order No. 319 of 1951) provides foreign crew members with short-term landing permits—up to 15 days—for crew changes or medical attention (Article 16), while the Quarantine Act (Act No. 201 of 1951) empowers health authorities to impose screenings and isolation when needed (Articles 13–15), especially in times of health emergencies. These mechanisms demonstrate how Japan integrates international obligations into domestic administration.

Despite this solid foundation, recent developments have tested the regime's resilience. Crew abandonment remains a concern: Although amendments to the MLC in 2014 required shipowners to maintain financial security for repatriation and wages,[52] abandonment cases surged globally during the pandemic,[53] and Japan was not exempt. The COVID-19 crisis also created severe repatriation barriers. While Japan initially introduced strict border controls, denying entry to many foreign nationals, it recognized seafarers as essential personnel for the purpose of controlled entry exemptions, recognizing the critical role of seafarers.[54] Nevertheless, quarantine rules and local restrictions often required ships to remain at sea for 14 days or to

---

[51] Choi et al. (2024), p. 8512.

[52] Maritime Labor Convention, Standard A2.5.2.

[53] Richard Meade, "Crew Abandonment Cases Increase 138% During Pandemic," *Lloyd's List* (14 February 2022), *available at* https://www.lloydslist.com/LL1139848/Crew-abandonment-cases-increase-138-during-pandemic (accessed 2 August 2025).

[54] IMO, "More States join IMO call to designate seafarers as key workers" (15 December 2020), *available at* https://www.imo.org/en/mediacentre/pages/whatsnew-1573.aspx (accessed 8 August 2025).

undergo onboard isolation before disembarkation, delaying crew rotations and restricting shore leave.

These restrictions had profound consequences for seafarers' mental health. Already vulnerable to stress, isolation, and fatigue, many endured prolonged contracts and uncertainty about repatriation. Reports of rising anxiety, depression, and even suicides illustrated the human costs of pandemic-era restrictions. Japan acknowledged severe crew-change disruptions during the COVID-19 pandemic and took steps (such as travel exemptions and certificate extensions) to address what many international bodies described as a humanitarian crisis.[55]

Japan's institutional response combined pragmatism with ad hoc flexibility. MLIT extended the validity of seafarer certificates that could not be renewed during travel restrictions and issued guidance allowing temporary extensions of employment contracts with compensatory leave deferred until later.[56] At the same time, the JCG maintained an intensive programme of port state control, carrying out 2958 inspections in 2022 that included checks on crew welfare under the MLC.[57] Local port authorities and welfare groups also contributed by organizing vaccination drives, delivering supplies to ships, and establishing safe transit corridors for crews. These measures helped avert a collapse of operations, but their reliance on administrative directives rather than statutory authority created risks of uneven application. The experience suggests that Japan's strong maritime labour framework should be reinforced by codified crisis protocols to ensure that fundamental seafarers' rights—particularly repatriation, shore leave, and health protection—are secured even under extraordinary circumstances.

Conclusion

Japan's public maritime law reflects a mature and comprehensive framework that underpins maritime safety, environmental protection, and labour standards. Domestically, it incorporates key international conventions such as SOLAS, MARPOL, and MLC, while tailoring them to local conditions. Laws on ship safety, marine pollution, seafarers' rights, and enforcement through port state control together provide a well-institutionalized regime. Japan's active role in the Tokyo MOU has further strengthened its enforcement record, improving compliance across the Asia-Pacific and positioning Japan as a regional leader in eliminating substandard shipping.

[55] IMO, "A humanitarian crisis at sea: all United Nations Member States must resolve the crew change crisis", *available at* https://www.imo.org/en/mediacentre/pressbriefings/pages/27-crew-change-joint-statement.aspx (accessed 5 August 2025).

[56] MLIT Maritime Bureau, "On the Handling of Matters Related to the Seafarers Act in Connection with COVID-19" [in Japanese], Administrative Notice (Issued 31 March 2020).

[57] ABS, "ABS Port State Control Annual Report" (2022), p. 18.

In this regard, Japan has been both a rule-taker, faithfully incorporating IMO conventions such as MARPOL and SOLAS into its domestic legal framework, and a rule-shaper, actively proposing amendments and contributing expertise and resources at the IMO to influence the development of international maritime regulations.

At the same time, emerging challenges test the adaptability of this framework. Decarbonization demands that Japan align domestic law with global net-zero targets, incentivize alternative fuels, and regulate low-emission technologies. Digitalization, particularly autonomous vessels and smart ports, exposes gaps in statutes that still assume human crews, raising issues of certification, liability, and cybersecurity. Meanwhile, the COVID-19 crew-change crisis highlighted vulnerabilities in protecting seafarers' rights, from repatriation and shore leave to mental health. These developments underscore that while Japan's legal regime is strong, proactive innovation is needed to address climate, technological, and human rights pressures.

Japan faces three central tasks: legal reform to integrate autonomous vessels, stronger labour safeguards for seafarers, and continuous alignment with international decarbonization standards. In pursuing these, Japan is also well placed to shape regional maritime law. Through initiatives such as the Tokyo MOU, green shipping corridors, and cooperative dialogues, Japan can share best practices and set benchmarks for neighbouring states. Ultimately, Japan's case illustrates how a forward-looking maritime legal system can ensure safety, sustainability, and dignity at sea—while contributing to a more harmonized and progressive maritime order in the Asia-Pacific region.

References

ABS (2022) ABS Port State Control Annual Report

Back to Blue (Economist Impact & Nippon Foundation), "The Future of the Japanese Maritime Industry Lies in Commercialising Fully Autonomous Ships" (March 2022), Available at https://backtoblueinitiative.com/the-future-of-the-japanese-maritime-industry-lies-in-commercialising-fully-autonomous-ships/. Accessed 12 August 2025

BIMCO, "Japan Is World's Third Largest Shipping Nation as Owners Control 12% of the Fleet" Shipping Number of the Week (24 April 2025), Available at https://www.bimco.org/news-insights/market-analysis/shipping-number-of-the-week/2025/0424-snow. Accessed 30 June 2025

Choi J, Lim S, Lee C (2024) Comparative analysis of sustainable seafarers' employment and welfare systems in South Korea and China: contemporary issues and improvements. Sustainability 16(19):8512

Embassy of Japan in the UK, "Japan Elected to the IMO Council Category 'A' as Member with the Highest Number of Votes" (Press Release, 1 December 2023)

Hongo T, Munakata R, "Shipping Laws and Regulations Japan 2025" International Comparative Legal Guides, Available at https://iclg.com/practice-areas/shipping-laws-and-regulations/japan. Accessed 15 July 2025

International Chamber of Shipping (ICS), Shipping Industry Flag State Performance Table 2024/2025. Available at https://www.ics-shipping.org/wp-content/uploads/2025/02/Shipping-Industry-Flag-State-Performance-Table-2024-2025-.pdf. Accessed 8 July 2025

International Maritime Organization (IMO). More States Join IMO Call to Designate Seafarers as Key Workers (15 December 2020), Available at https://www.imo.org/en/mediacentre/pages/whatsnew-1573.aspx. Accessed 8 August 2025

International Maritime Organization (IMO) (2023a) 2023 IMO Strategy on Reduction of GHG Emissions from Ships. Resolution MEPC.377(80), MEPC 80/17/Add.1 Annex 15

International Maritime Organization (IMO) (2023b) Development of a Goal-Based Instrument for MASS. MSC 107/5/1 (2 May 2023)

International Maritime Organization (IMO) (2024) IMO Financial Statements 2024

International Maritime Organization (IMO). A Humanitarian Crisis at Sea: All United Nations Member States Must Resolve the Crew Change Crisis. Available at https://www.imo.org/en/mediacentre/pressbriefings/pages/27-crew-change-joint-statement.aspx. Accessed 5 August 2025

International Maritime Organization (IMO). "Status of IMO Treaties," Status of Conventions and Amendments. Available at https://www.imo.org/en/About/Conventions/Pages/StatusOfConventions.aspx. Accessed 29 June 2025

International Tanker Owners Pollution Federation Limited (2018) Country & Territory Profiles: A Summary of Oil Spill Response Arrangements & Resources Worldwide (Japan)

Japan Coast Guard, "Mission," MLIT, Available at https://www.kaiho.mlit.go.jp/mission/. Accessed 7 July 2025

Japan Federation of Coastal Shipping Associations, Coastal Shipping of Japan 2025

Japan Maritime Public Relations Center (2024) Japan's Shipping: Shipping Now 2024–2025 (Data Section). Japan Maritime Center

Japan P&I Club, "Ratification of the Bunker Convention and Wreck Removal Convention, and Amendment of the Oil Pollution Act in Japan" (3 July 2020), Available at https://www.piclub.or.jp/en/news/31553. Accessed 4 July 2025

Japan Transport Safety Board, "Mission," MLIT, Available at https://jtsb.mlit.go.jp/mission.html. Accessed 7 July 2025

Lloyd's Register, "UK and Japan Align Efforts to Accelerate Maritime Autonomy" (Press Release, 8 April 2024), Available at https://www.lr.org/en/knowledge/press-room/press-listing/press-release/2024/uk-and-japan-align-efforts-to-accelerate-maritime-autonomy/. Accessed 13 August 2025

Matsuda M (2011) A practical guide to conclusion of treaties [in Japanese]. Hokkaido J New Glob Law Policy 10:318

Meade R (2022) Crew Abandonment Cases Increase 138% During Pandemic. Lloyd's List (14 February 2022). Available at https://www.lloydslist.com/LL1139848/Crew-abandonment-cases-increase-138-during-pandemic. Accessed 2 August 2025

Minami K (2025) The legal systems for the prevention of seafarer accidents in Japan. J Work Health Saf Regul 4(1):16

Ministry of Foreign Affairs of Japan. Maritime Safety, Maritime Pollution Prevention and Japan's Contribution. Available at https://www.mofa.go.jp/policy/maritime/safety/pollution.html. Accessed 28–29 June 2025

MLIT (2021) Japan Sets a Target for Global Shipping of Achieving Net-Zero GHG Emissions by 2050 (26 October 2021). Available at https://www.mlit.go.jp/en/report/press/kaiji07_hh_000001.html. Accessed 29 July 2025

MLIT (2024) Regarding the Cabinet Order Partially Amending the Enforcement Order of the Act on Prevention of Marine Pollution and Maritime Disasters. [in Japanese] (22 September 2024), Available at https://www.mlit.go.jp/kisha/kisha04/01/010922_2_.html. Accessed 4 July 2025

MLIT Maritime Bureau (2013) Revision of the Seafarers Act Following the Ratification of the Maritime Labour Convention. [in Japanese] (March 2013), Available at https://www.mlit.go.jp/common/001012029.pdf. Accessed 24 July 2025

MLIT Maritime Bureau (2014) Organization and Functions of Maritime Bureau (1 May 2014). Available at https://www.mlit.go.jp/common/001040099.pdf. Accessed 5 July 2025
MLIT Maritime Bureau (2020) On the Handling of Matters Related to the Seafarers Act in Connection with COVID-19. [in Japanese] (Administrative Notice, 31 March 2020)
MLIT Maritime Bureau (2022) Seafarers' Labor Handbook [in Japanese] (September 2022), Available at https://www.mlit.go.jp/maritime/content/001513926.pdf. Accessed 18 July 2025
MLIT Maritime Bureau & JSTRA (Japan Ship Technology Research Association), Toward Achieving Net Zero GHG Emissions from International Shipping by 2050: Shipping Zero Emission Project (March 2022)
MLIT Maritime Bureau, JSTRA and Nippon Foundation, Roadmap to Zero Emission from International Shipping (March 2020)
Nippon Foundation, MEGURI2040 Fully Autonomous Ship Program: Aiming to Implement Fully Autonomous Navigation (Tokyo, 2020). Available at https://en.nippon-foundation.or.jp/what/projects/ocean/meguri2040. Accessed 12 August 2025
Paris MOU (2006) Joint Concentrated Inspection Campaign on Crew Wages and Seafarer Employment Agreements (MLC). (Press Release, 1 August 2024), available at https://parismou.org/2024/08/joint-concentrated-inspection-campaign-crew-wages-and-seafarer-employment-agreements-mlc. Accessed 25 July 2025
Shiokari M, "Japanese MASS R&D Projects and Approaches for Ensuring Safety" (31 August 2022), in cooperation with MLIT, The Nippon Foundation MEGURI2040, JSTRA and NMRI, Available at https://wwwcdn.imo.org/localresources/en/OurWork/Safety/PublishingImages/Pages/MASS/10_Megumi%20Shiokari_Japanese%20MASS%20R&D%20Projects%20and%20Approaches%20for%20ensuring%20safety.pdf. Accessed 15 August 2025
Shiota T (2024) Implementation of Multilateral Treaties by Adopting Domestic Law: Some Japanese Cases (Research Materials 2024e-2). Research and Legislative Reference Bureau, National Diet Library, Tokyo
Tokyo MOU, Memorandum of Understanding on Port State Control in the Asia-Pacific Region, 23rd amendment, effective 1 July 2025.
Tsuruta J (2009) Japanese measures against marine pollution under UNCLOS and the IMO treaties. J East Asia Int Law 2(2):386
UNCTAD (2023) Statistical Profile: Japan (2023). Available at https://unctadstat.unctad.org/CountryProfile/GeneralProfile/en-GB/392/index.html. Accessed 28 July 2025
UNCTAD (2024) 2024 Review of Maritime Transport: Navigating Maritime Chokepoints, UNCTAD/RMT/2024 and Corr.1

Chapter 5
A Legal Analysis of the Reporting Duty for Defects in Seaworthiness Under the Ship Safety Act

You-Rak Jang

Introduction

In March 2017, the *Stellar Daisy*, a very large ore carrier (VLOC) registered under the Marshall Islands and operated by a South Korean shipping company, tragically sank in the South Atlantic Ocean near Uruguay while transporting approximately 260,000 tons of iron ore from Brazil to China. Investigations suggested that structural failure—such as deformation of transverse bulkheads or cracks in the upper deck—may have led to the vessel's rapid sinking. Of the 24 crew members, only two were rescued, and 22 including eight South Koreans, were declared missing and presumed dead.

In the aftermath, South Korean prosecutors indicted the company's CEO, head of the maritime division, and fleet superintendent for failing to report the ship's structural defects as a failure of seaworthiness under Article 74 of the Ship Safety Act.[1] In the first trial, the CEO received a suspended prison sentence; however, the

You-Rak Jang is Lecturer at Korea Maritime and Ocean University, a former Chief Officer at Haeyoung Shipping Co., Ltd., and holds a B.Sc. in Maritime Transportation Science, an LL.M. in Maritime Law, and a Ph.D. in Maritime Law from Korea Maritime and Ocean University (KMOU).

[1] Busan District Court of Korea (2020). In the first-instance ruling, the court found both the head of the maritime division and the inspection superintendent guilty of breach of trust under Article 357(1) of the Korean Criminal Act, for allowing the vessel to operate without adequate stability. However, in the appellate decision, only the head of the maritime division was held criminally liable for the offense.

Y.-R. Jang (✉)
Korea Maritime and Ocean University, Busan, Republic of Korea
e-mail: jangyourak@kmou.ac.kr

J. Choi (ed.), *Public Maritime Law in Asia*, International Law in Asia,
https://doi.org/10.1007/978-981-95-7037-9_5

appellate court overturned the decision and imposed an actual six-month prison term, citing the CEO's final responsibility for ensuring defect reports were submitted. Both the head of the maritime division and the fleet superintendent were also convicted. This case marked the first time a custodial sentence was imposed under the revised Ship Safety Act, which was significantly strengthened following the *Sewol ferry* disaster. As the ruling confirmed that failure to report vessel defects could lead to imprisonment, it garnered widespread attention from stakeholders across the maritime industry. Subsequently, the defense counsel submitted a constitutional challenge on March 24, 2020, questioning the validity of Article 74(1) and Article 84(1)(11) of the Ship Safety Act.[2]

The *Stellar Daisy* incident raised a range of critical questions, such as whether known structural issues had been reported in a timely manner and whether existing legal and regulatory frameworks were adequate to prevent such maritime disasters. This article conducts a legal-historical analysis of Article 74 of the Ship Safety Act, focusing on its evolution in defining and enforcing defect reporting obligations. It further evaluates the judicial interpretations applied in relevant case law and scrutinizes whether the law has been interpreted in a manner that supports its intended safety objectives. Moreover, the study compares maritime defect reporting framework with those of the Railway Safety Act and the Aviation Safety Act in Korea. By identifying legal inconsistencies and enforcement challenges, this paper proposes specific reforms to enhance the clarity, accountability, and effectiveness of defect in seaworthiness reporting in practice.

Evolution and Judicial Application of Article 74

Overview of Legislation of Article 74

Enacted in 1961 Under Act No. 919

The Republic of Korea enacted the Ship Safety Act on December 30, 1961 under Act No. 919, based on Japan's Ship Safety Act, in order to establish requirements for maintaining the seaworthiness of ships and ensuring the safety of life and property at sea by preventing maritime hazards. Article 13 of the Act and Articles 161 to 164 of Chapter 15 of the Enforcement Decree of the Ship Safety Act (Presidential Decree No. 651), promulgated on April 10, 1962, stipulate detailed provisions regarding defect reporting by ship crew members. Article 161 of the Enforcement Decree establishes a unique legal framework that allows crew members to report significant equipment defects directly. This system is notably absent in major maritime jurisdictions such as the United Kingdom, the United States, France, and Germany, and remains unique to Japan and Republic of Korea. Interestingly, Japan

---

[2] Constitutional Court of Korea (2024a).

continues to implement the defect reporting provisions—originally referenced during Korea's 1971 legislative revision—without substantial amendments.[3]

Under Korean law, the reporting entity is defined according to the number of crew members: for ships with fewer than 20 crew members, at least half must agree to the report; for other vessels, the minimum threshold is 10 crew members. Reports are limited to serious defects affecting seaworthiness or facilities essential for crew accommodation, hygiene, or general human safety. The reporting procedure involves the drafting of a written report by the concerned crew members, detailing the suspected defect, observed symptoms, and the background leading up to the report. This is submitted to the ship's master, who is required to attach a statement of opinion along with the ship's inspection logbook before submitting it to the relevant maritime authority.[4]

Upon receiving a defect report, the maritime authority is obligated to conduct an investigation and, if necessary, may dispatch officials to inspect the vessel. Depending on the severity of the defect, the authority is empowered to suspend the ship's navigation or impose other regulatory measures. If the report is filed immediately before the ship's departure, the law allows the master to submit the report via postal or other appropriate means after departure—except in cases where the defect (e.g., cargo overloading or improper stowage) is difficult to verify. Failure to forward the report to the authorities, despite the crew's submission to the master, constitutes a legal violation. In such cases, the shipowner or master may be subject to a fine of up to 100,000 Hwan[5] under Article 20 of the Ship Safety Act (Act No. 919).

Complete Amendment in 2007 Under Act No. 8221

In 2007, Korea fully revised the Ship Safety Act to prevent maritime accidents caused by ship defects and substandard vessels. As part of this revision, the law was amended to allow "any person" to report defects in a vessel's seaworthiness or safety equipment upon discovery. However, the law also stipulates that anyone who falsely reports a ship defect or fails to comply with a sailing suspension order issued by the Minister of Oceans and Fisheries may be subject to a fine of up to five million KRW. In addition, Article 95 of the Enforcement Rules of the Ship Safety Act stipulates the method of reporting ship defects, protection of the reporter's personal

[3] Relevant provisions include Article 13 and Article 23 of Japan's Ship Safety Act, and Article 50 of the Japanese Ship Safety Act Enforcement Regulations.

[4] Enforcement Decree of the Ship Safety Act (1962), Presidential Decree No. 651, Article 161(Report by Crew Members Regarding Equipment Defects), and Article 162 (Captain's Procedures upon Receiving the Report).

[5] Based on the 1962 currency reform in the Republic of Korea, 100,000 Hwan (the former currency unit) was converted to 10,000 Korean Won. Adjusting for an average annual inflation rate of approximately 7.3% from 1961 to 2025, this amount is equivalent to approximately 908,620 KRW in 2025. Using an estimated 2025 exchange rate of 1 USD ≈ 1300 KRW, this corresponds to approximately 699 USD.

information, and the procedure for issuing a sailing suspension order to the shipowner if the defect is confirmed after the report is received.

A comparison between the original Ship Safety Act and the fully revised 2007 version of the defect reporting provisions reveals the following key features. First, previously reporting was limited to a quorum of crew members (e.g., half of the crew on small vessels or 10 or more crew members on larger ones). The 2007 revision expanded the range of potential reporters, easing procedural thresholds and facilitating broader participation in defect reporting for maritime safety.

Second, the scope of defects subject to reporting was also expanded. The original provision limited reports to **"serious defects"** related to seaworthiness, habitability, hygiene, and other safety equipment. In contrast, the revised law permits reports for **any defects** related to seaworthiness or safety equipment, removing the "serious" threshold. Notably, Article 2 of the Ship Safety Act defines **seaworthiness** as a vessel's ability to safely navigate under certain weather and sea conditions while maintaining structural stability. However, this raises practical concerns: individuals without sufficient maritime expertise may find it difficult to accurately assess the seaworthiness of a vessel, potentially leading to **excessive or unfounded reports.**[6] However, the Act provides that a person who files a false report regarding vessel defects, or fails to comply with a departure suspension order issued by the Minister of Oceans and Fisheries, may be subject to a fine of up to five million Korean Won(KRW).[7]

Partial Amendment in 2015 Under Act No. 12999

In response to the 2014 *Sewol Ferry* disaster, the Ship Safety Act was amended to strengthen the regulatory framework ensuring vessel safety. One of the most significant changes was the transition of the defect reporting system from a permissive (voluntary) regime to a mandatory duty. As revised, the law imposes criminal liability on anyone such as shipowners, masters, and crew members who fail to report known defects related to seaworthiness or safety equipment. Under the amended Article 85, such failure is punishable by imprisonment of up to 1 year or a fine of up to ten million Korean Won (KRW). This legislative shift marks a fundamental change in the treatment of non-reporting violations, reclassifying the act from an administrative offense (administrative order violation) to a criminal offense, thereby elevating its seriousness within the legal framework.

[6] Ofurumazi et al. (2024), pp. 75–77.

[7] Ship Safety Act (2007), Act No. 919, Article 20 (Penalty Provisions).

Judicial Interpretations and Applications of Article 74

Judicial Interpretation of "Defects Affecting Seaworthiness" Under Article 74 of the Ship Safety Act[8]

Evidence indicates that the defendants were clearly aware of structural defects in the vessel, particularly the deformation of the transverse bulkhead located between Ballast Tanks No.3 and No.4. This awareness was established through a series of internal inspections, external expert evaluations, and formal approvals that took place between May and July 2016. While docked in Lumut, Malaysia, the fleet superintendent directly observed the deformation during an on-site inspection. He subsequently submitted a formal report recommending a professional safety inspection and early drydocking. The report was approved by the head of the Maritime division and reviewed by the CEO. Concurrently, an external inspection in Singapore revealed severe corrosion and weakening of the bulkhead, concluding that immediate reinforcement and hull thickness measurements were necessary. These findings were formally recorded in the company's risk management documentation and reviewed by the executive safety committee. Subsequently, on July 5, 2016, the fleet superintendent submitted an emergency repair request explicitly warning that continued navigation would pose significant safety risks. This request was approved the same day by both the head of maritime division and the CEO. This sequence of events confirms the defendants' actual knowledge of the vessel's compromised seaworthiness and the urgent need for corrective action.

The court of first instance provided an important interpretation of Article 74(1) of the Ship Safety Act, which imposes a legal obligation to report defects affecting a vessel's seaworthiness. The court held that a "defect in seaworthiness" should be interpreted as any deficiency that impairs the vessel's ability to safely navigate and, if unaddressed, poses a material risk of maritime accident or hazard. Importantly, this concept is not limited to situations of total unseaworthiness and is not negated simply because the master subjectively believed the vessel to be fit for voyage. Applying this legal standard, the court determined that the deformation of the bulkhead on the *Stellar Daisy* constituted a reportable "defect in seaworthiness" under Article 74(1). The failure to report this defect to the Minister of Oceans and Fisheries within a reasonable time frame, measured against societal expectations, constituted a violation of the statutory reporting obligation.

Based on this reasoning, the court found the CEO of Shipping company, the Head of the maritime division, and the fleet superintendent guilty of failing to comply with the reporting requirement under Article 74(1). The sentences were as follows: the CEO received a six-month prison term, suspended for 1 year; the Head of the maritime division was given a 1-year prison sentence, suspended for 2 years; and the fleet superintendent was fined KRW three million. This ruling reinforces the broad construction of "defect in seaworthiness" under Ship Safety Act. It also

[8] Busan District Court of Korea (2020).

affirms the personal criminal liability of corporate decision-makers who fail to act on known deficiencies affecting vessel safety, regardless of the ship's location or voyage stage.

Appellate Clarification on the Interpretation of "Defect in Seaworthiness[9]

In the appellate proceedings, the defendants challenged the legal interpretation of the term "defect in seaworthiness" as provided under Article 74(1) of the Ship Safety Act. They contended that the term should be narrowly construed to mean a total absence of seaworthiness—namely, a condition in which the vessel is entirely unfit for navigation—rather than a partial or remedial deficiency that may still allow for continued operation. On this basis, they requested the appellate court to revisit the trial court's ruling, arguing that the lower court had impermissibly expanded the scope of reportable defects beyond the intended statutory limits. Additionally, the defendants argued that the duty to report a defect in seaworthiness arises only when such a defect is recognized **prior to departure**. In their view, because they became aware of the alleged structural issues only **after** the vessel had departed port, the statutory reporting obligation did not apply. They further claimed that the reporting requirement under Article 74(1) should not extend to vessels engaged exclusively in international voyages between foreign ports. Since such vessels do not call at Korean ports and the Minister of Oceans and Fisheries is effectively unable to exercise jurisdiction to issue a sailing suspension order, they asserted that the legal framework could not impose a meaningful or enforceable duty to report.

The appellate court rejected this argument. It held that, according to the text and legislative purpose of the statute, a "defect in seaworthiness" refers to a **condition where the vessel's hull, engine, equipment, documentation, or crew composition lacks sufficient capacity to ensure safe navigation for a given voyage, and which—if left unaddressed—could result in maritime accidents or hazards.** Thus, the term encompasses **partial deficiencies**, not just total failures. The court emphasized that **transverse bulkheads in cargo holds and ballast tanks,** as well as the **main deck and internal partitions**, are critical structural components. Their **deformation, cracking, or perforation** can compromise longitudinal strength and lead to water ingress, posing serious threats to navigation safety. Given these risks, the court found that the observed structural damage—such as **deformed transverse bulkheads and cracked deck structures**—constituted a "defect in seaworthiness" within the meaning of Article 74(1). Accordingly, the appellate court upheld the lower court's finding of guilt for all defendants based on their failure to report these structural defects within a reasonable period.

---

[9] Busan High Court of Korea (2021).

Legal Interpretation of "Defect in Seaworthiness" Under Korean Maritime Law: Supreme Court's Clarification[10]

In their appeal to the Supreme Court, the defendants argued that the lower court had erred in interpreting Article 74(1) of the Ship Safety Act by broadly construing the term "defect in seaworthiness" to include minor or partial deficiencies, rather than limiting it to total unseaworthiness. They claimed this interpretation violated the principle of legal certainty. Additionally, they asserted that the reporting duty arises only if the defect is recognized prior to departure, which the lower court failed to properly examine. They also alleged that the appellate court's evidentiary assessment lacked rational justification, thereby breaching procedural fairness. Based on these grounds, the defendants sought reversal or retrial.

The Supreme Court of Korea reaffirmed its established precedent that there is no absolute or fixed standard for determining seaworthiness; rather, it must be assessed relative to the specific voyage and operational conditions.[11] In addition, the Court provided a significant legal interpretation of the term "defect in seaworthiness" as stipulated in Article 74(1) of the Ship Safety Act, in the context of a case involving the failure to report structural defects on a merchant vessel engaged in international trade. Article 74(1) of the Ship Safety Act imposes a statutory duty to report any "defect in seaworthiness" or defect in safety equipment to the Minister of Oceans and Fisheries. The Court held that the term defect should be understood in its ordinary linguistic meaning—i.e., any flaw, deficiency, or incompleteness—and thus covers both significant and minor shortcomings in a vessel's navigational capability. Under the statute, the duty to report extends beyond catastrophic structural failures to include any deficiency that, if unaddressed, could compromise a vessel's ability to safely withstand expected maritime conditions. Even non-extreme deficiencies fall within the scope of reportable 'defects in seaworthiness' if they pose a potential risk to maritime safety during a specific voyage. Also, The Supreme Court upheld the appellate court's factual findings and legal interpretations were within the bounds of judicial discretion and did not violate the rules of logic or experience. Though some expressions in the appellate judgment were suboptimal, the ultimate legal conclusions were found to be sound. Arguments newly raised at the Supreme Court stage—such as claims regarding the temporal scope of recognition, alleged exemption due to repair efforts, or misinterpretation of Article 326(4) of the Criminal Procedure Act—were dismissed as inadmissible since they were not previously raised on appeal. Finally, the Court noted that complaints about the severity of the sentence (including fines and suspended prison terms) did not meet the statutory threshold for appellate review under Article 383(4) of the Criminal Procedure Act, as none of the sentences imposed exceeded 10 years of imprisonment.

This ruling underscores a broad and functional interpretation of "defect in seaworthiness" under Korean law. It affirms that the legal duty to report encompasses

[10] Supreme Court of Korea (2024).

[11] Supreme Court of Korea (1996a).

any meaningful deficiency that may compromise the safe navigation of a vessel. The decision further illustrates the Korean judiciary's emphasis on preventive safety measures within the framework of maritime regulatory compliance, even when jurisdictional challenges exist.

Constitutional Review of the Legal Clarity of "Defect in Seaworthiness" Under the Ship Safety Act[12]

The petitioners challenged the constitutionality of Article 74(1) and Article 84(1)(11) of the Ship Safety Act, focusing particularly on the phrases referring to "defect in seaworthiness." Their argument centered on two major constitutional principles: the principle of legal clarity under the rule of law (*nullum crimen sine lege certa*) and the principle of proportionality between criminal responsibility and punishment.

Under the Korean Constitution, criminal punishment must be proportionate to the offender's culpability. Even where the purpose of punishment is legitimate, a sanction that exceeds what is appropriate to the offender's conduct may violate the constitutional principle of proportionality. In this context, the Constitutional Court of Korea reviewed whether Article 74(1) of the former Ship Safety Act—which imposes a duty to report "defects in seaworthiness"—and the associated penalty provision violate this principle.

First, the Court held that the term "defect in seaworthiness" refers to deficiencies that materially impair the minimum performance required for a vessel to ensure safe navigation. This interpretation is grounded in the technical inspection standards set forth in the Ship Safety Act.[13] The Court concluded that the term can be construed with sufficient clarity to exclude trivial or minor deficiencies that do not directly affect navigational safety.[14] Therefore, concerns about over-penalization due to vague statutory language were deemed unfounded.

Second, the petitioners argued that extending criminal liability to agents, employees, and other personnel associated with the shipowner was excessive. The Court disagreed, emphasizing that the legislative intent behind the provision was to deter a persistent and dangerous industry practice in which structural defects were deliberately concealed for economic gain, resulting in catastrophic maritime accidents. Given this legislative objective, extending the reporting obligation to affiliated personnel was considered proportionate and justified.

Third, pursuant to Article 14 of the Korean Criminal Act, negligence-based offenses are punishable only where explicitly provided by law. The Court found no

[12] Constitutional Court of Korea (2024a).

[13] International Maritime Organization (2023), emphasizing PSC inspections checking ship condition and equipment compliance, including identification of deficiencies; Shen et al. (2020), pp. 1120–1121.

[14] Constitutional Court of Korea (2024b).

textual or structural basis to interpret Article 74(1) as imposing liability for negligent omissions. As such, the reporting obligation is limited to intentional (*dolus*) violations, and any prosecution must demonstrate that the accused had actual knowledge of the defect in seaworthiness. This element of intent further mitigates concerns about disproportionate punishment.

Fourth, the Court reaffirmed that legislative bodies enjoy broad discretion in defining crimes and penalties, particularly in areas that involve complex policy judgments. As previously held by the Court, the setting of legal sanctions must consider various factors, including the nature and gravity of the offense, prevailing social norms, public sentiment, and broader criminal policy objectives.[15] Given the heightened risk and irreversible damage associated with maritime accidents, the Court concluded that criminal sanctions for failing to report defect in seaworthiness constitutionally justifiable.

Fifth, the penalty clause under Article 84(1) of the Act prescribes a choice between imprisonment of up to 1 year or a fine not exceeding ten million Korean won. The absence of a mandatory minimum sentence allows judges to tailor penalties based on factors such as the severity of the defect, the defendant's role, and the potential or actual harm caused. Moreover, the availability of suspended sentences or judicial leniency ensures that the punishment remains proportionate to the offender's culpability.

Lastly, while the petitioners cited the Aviation Safety Act—which imposes only administrative fines for similar reporting omissions—as a comparator, the Court rejected this analogy. It emphasized that aircraft and ships differ fundamentally in structure, operation, regulatory environment, and the nature of associated risks. Therefore, equal treatment under the law cannot be presumed solely on the basis that both are modes of transportation.

In conclusion, the Constitutional Court held that the duty to report defects in seaworthiness under the Ship Safety Act, and the associated criminal penalties, do not violate the principle of proportionality. The provisions reflect a legitimate legislative aim of maritime safety and offer a balanced mechanism for deterring deliberate omissions without imposing unjust or excessive punishment.

Critical Evaluation of the Constitutional Court's Reasoning

Ambiguity in the Definition of "Defect in Seaworthiness" and the Principle of Legal Clarity

The Constitutional Court of Korea held that the term "defect in seaworthiness" is a generally accepted legal concept, encompassing any deficiency in a ship's structure, equipment, documentation, or crew that materially affects its ability to ensure safe navigation. However, However, when assessed against the constitutional principle

[15] Constitutional Court of Korea (2010, 2023).

of legal clarity (*nullum crimen sine lege certa*), this interpretation becomes problematic.[16]

First, the statute lacks a clearly defined scope. It fails to specify the precise moment when the duty to report arises, and it does not establish objective criteria to distinguish between reportable and non-reportable defects. Neither the primary legislation nor subordinate regulations provide a concrete framework to guide interpretation or enforcement.[17] Second, the provision permits excessive administrative discretion. The open-ended and broadly formulated language allows for highly variable interpretations by the Ministry of Oceans and Fisheries and law enforcement authorities, increasing the risk of arbitrary or inconsistent application of criminal sanctions.[18] Third, the foreseeability of the law is undermined, especially for non-expert actors. Although the statute potentially subjects agents, employees, and general staff members of shipowners to criminal liability, it implicitly assumes that such individuals possess the technical knowledge and legal capacity to determine whether a specific condition qualifies as a "defect in seaworthiness." This presumption places a disproportionate and unfeasible obligation on non-experts without adequate technical qualifications.[19]

In summary, the Court's reliance on the presumed expertise and awareness of regulated parties to justify the flexible and contextual interpretation of the statute effectively dilutes the constitutional requirement of legal foreseeability. Legal clarity requires that criminal provisions be clearly defined so individuals can foresee the consequences of their conduct.[20] The Court's reasoning, however, deviates from this standard by legitimizing an overly indeterminate statutory formulation.

Disproportionality Between Criminal Liability and Culpability

The Constitutional Court also ruled that the challenged provision does not violate the constitutional principle of proportionality, as it applies only to intentional violations and allows for flexible sentencing. Nevertheless, this conclusion warrants further scrutiny.[21]

First, the statute risks expanding liability without ensuring substantive effectiveness. In situations involving agents or employees of a shipowner—or ships operating exclusively on foreign routes—reporting a defect may be practically meaningless, as the Ministry may not have the legal authority to enforce corrective measures such as detention. Holding such individuals criminally liable in these contexts creates a

[16] Hornopparat (2017), pp. 51–56.

[17] Ibid, p.51 l; Lee (2025a), pp. 14–17.

[18] Lee (2016), pp. 8–10; FAO (2003), pp. 3–7; Soyer (2014), pp. 112–129; Hornopparat (2017), op cit pp. 55–57.

[19] Kassem (2006), pp. 14–15, 22; Daniels (2012), pp. 14–18.

[20] Re (2019), pp. 1509–1516.

[21] Daniels (2022), pp. 83-85; 93–96.

disconnect between responsibility and regulatory effectiveness.[22] Second, the unequal treatment between ships and aircraft raises concerns of legislative consistency and fairness. Under the Aviation Safety Act, the failure to report technical defects is subject only to administrative fines. By contrast, the Ship Safety Act imposes criminal penalties for comparable conduct without providing a compelling justification for this disparity. The principle of equality before the law suggests that materially similar conduct should attract equivalent legal consequences unless objective differences warrant distinction.[23]

In light of these issues, the criminal penalty imposed for violations of the reporting duty—though pursuing a legitimate public interest in maritime safety—does not fully satisfy the requirements of appropriateness and minimal intrusion under the proportionality principle. The legislature should consider adopting a more calibrated approach that differentiates sanctions based on the severity and context of the violation.[24]

Comparative Analysis of Defect Reporting Obligations Under the Aviation and Railway Safety Laws

The Aviation Safety Act

The Republic of Korea initially enacted the Aviation Act in 1961 to establish a legal framework for ensuring the safety of aircraft and regulating air transport operations. However, due to the Act's complexity and its limited adaptability to rapidly changing international standards, the government promulgated a separate statute, the Aviation Safety Act, in 2016, focusing exclusively on aircraft safety.[25] The Aviation Safety Act imposes a legal obligation to report any failures, defects, or functional impairments (hereinafter referred to as "reportable aviation safety hazards") affecting aircraft or related components. It also provides the legal basis for administrative sanctions in cases of noncompliance.

---

[22] Maria (2012); Khan et al. (2020), pp. 378–379; Busan High Court of Korea (2021). The court held that when a report of a defect in seaworthiness is submitted, the Minister of Oceans and Fisheries has the authority to impose corrective measures—including voyage suspension, reporting or document submission orders, and repair or remedial actions. Accordingly, the court ruled that the Ship Safety Act is applicable even to vessels located in foreign ports.

[23] Jang (2022), pp. 98–102.

[24] Lee et al. (2019), pp. 99–100.

[25] Ministry of Government Legislation, purpose of enactment of No.14116.

Reporting Obligations and Responsible Parties

The Act classifies the responsible parties based on the cause or context of the defect: First, in cases of design or manufacturing defects, the obligation to report lies with certified manufacturers. Entities holding certificates such as Type Certificates, Supplemental Type Certificates, Production Certificates, or Technical Standard Part Approvals must report any reportable aviation safety hazard caused by their certified aircraft, equipment, or parts.[26] Second, if a defect occurs during operation or maintenance, the duty to report falls on the aircraft owner or operator, or on certified maintenance organizations.[27] This includes commercial air transport operators, aircraft users, or individuals or organizations with legal rights to use large aircraft or helicopters.[28] Third, when an accident or safety hazard occurs—or when an aviation personnel becomes aware of such an event—it is their duty to report it.[29] This reporting obligation applies to aviation personnel[30] who either caused or became aware of an aircraft accident, serious incident, or any other reportable safety hazard under the Aviation Safety Act. However, individuals who fall under Article 33 of the Act are excluded from this obligation.

Scope of Reportable Events

The Act classifies reportable aviation safety hazards into seven categories, encompassing a total of 36 detailed scenarios.[31] These categories include: In-flight incidents, Takeoff and landing events, Ground operation failures, Pre-flight preparation hazards, Aircraft fire or damage, Airport and navigational service disruptions, Other safety threats.

[26] Article 33(1) of the Aviation Safety Act.

[27] According to Article 8 of the Enforcement Decree of the Aviation Safety Act of Korea, the term includes: domestic air transport operators, international air transport operators, small-scale air transport operators, aircraft utilization business operators, persons who own or lease and are entitled to use an aircraft with a maximum take-off weight exceeding 5700 kg, and persons who own or lease and are entitled to use a helicopter with a maximum take-off weight exceeding 3175 kg.

[28] Article 8 of Enforcement Decree of the Aviation Safety Act.

[29] Article 33(2) of the Aviation Safety Act.

[30] Pursuant to Article 134(3) of the Enforcement Rule of the Aviation Safety Act of Korea, the term "relevant aviation personnel" includes: (1) aircraft captains, (2) aircraft maintenance technicians, (3) air traffic controllers, (4) persons responsible for managing and maintaining airport facilities under the Airport Facilities Act, (5) persons responsible for the installation and management of navigation safety facilities under the Airport Facilities Act, (6) dangerous goods handlers, (7) aircraft handling personnel engaged in loading management for aircraft weight and balance under the Aviation Business Act, and (8) ground support personnel providing power to aircraft or guiding aircraft for safe movement on the ground.

[31] Article 74(1) of the Enforcement Rule of the Aviation Act and listed in Annex Table 20–2.

Reporting Deadlines

The reporting deadlines are defined based on the nature and timing of the incident: Immediate reporting is required for certain severe cases involving fire, airport facility failure, or navigational disruptions.[32] Within 72 h: This applies to most operational defects, including in-flight, takeoff/landing, ground operation, and miscellaneous hazards.[33] Within 96 h: Specifically applies to incidents involving aircraft fire or mechanical failure.[34] Weekends and public holidays are excluded from the time calculation, and in cases of injury, communication failure, or other unavoidable circumstances, the deadline is extended to 72 h from the moment the impediment is resolved.[35]

Sanctions for Noncompliance

Under Article 166(4) of the Aviation Safety Act, failure to report or false reporting of an aviation safety hazard, as stipulated in Articles 33 and 59, is subject to an administrative fine of up to KRW one million.

The Railway Safety Act

The Republic of Korea initially enacted the Railway Act in 1962 to promote efficient railway operations and the welfare of the public. However, due to increasing structural complexity and evolving technical and social safety risks, the government restructured the legal framework by enacting the Railway Safety Act in 2004. The purpose of this legislative reform was to more effectively prevent railway accidents and respond promptly when safety threats arise.[36] Under the Railway Safety Act, individuals and entities are obligated to report railway accidents, equipment defects,

---

[32] Pursuant to Article 74(1) and Annex Table 20–2, item 6 of the Enforcement Rule of the Aviation Safety Act, immediate reporting is required in the following cases: (a) when airport navigation facilities fall below the required operational standards or cease to operate; (b) when a runway, taxiway, or apron suffers significant damage or catches fire; (e) when radio communication facilities prescribed under the Airport Facilities Act experience operational failure or interruption.

[33] In accordance with Article 74(1) and Annex Table 20–2 of the Enforcement Rule of the Aviation Safety Act of Korea, reporting is required in the following categories of occurrences:(1) incidents occurring during flight; (2) incidents occurring during take-off or landing; (3) incidents occurring during ground operations; (4) incidents during pre-flight preparations; (6) failures related to airport and air navigation services;(7) other hazardous occurrences not specified in the above categories.

[34] Pursuant to Article 74(1) and Annex Table 20–2, item 5 of the Enforcement Rule of the Aviation Safety Act of Korea, reporting is required in cases involving aircraft fire or mechanical failure.

[35] Article 134(4) of the Enforcement Rule of the Aviation Act.

[36] Ministry of Government Legislation, purpose of enactment of No.7245.

and emerging safety hazards, with clearly defined legal responsibilities and penalties for noncompliance.

Reporting Obligations and Responsible Parties

The Act classifies the responsible parties based on the cause or context of the defect. First, in cases of design or manufacturing defects, the obligation to report lies with certified manufacturers. Entities holding certificates such as Type Certificates, Supplemental Type Certificates, Production Certificates, or Technical Standard Part Approvals must report any reportable aviation safety hazard caused by their certified aircraft, equipment, or parts.[37] Second, in the event of a railway accident,[38] the railway operator and related parties are required to report the incident. If a railway accident prescribed by Presidential Decree occurs—such as an accident involving death, injury, or damage to property in connection with railway operation or railway facility management—the railway operator and the railway facility manager must report the occurrence.[39] Third, In cases where a railway safety hazard arises, any individual who becomes aware of the hazard or reasonably anticipates its occurrence may voluntarily report the matter. Specifically, if a person has caused, observed, or foresees an event, situation, or condition that poses a threat or potential threat to railway safety, that individual may voluntarily report such information to the Minister of Land, Infrastructure and Transport.[40]

Scope of Reportable Events

Under the Railway Safety Act, the obligation to report varies depending on the type of occurrence, such as mechanical failures, accidents, or the emergence of safety hazards. First, manufacturers or entities that have obtained type approval or manufacturer approval for railway vehicles or railway products are required to report certain types of failures. Specifically, a report must be made when a defect, failure, or functional impairment of a railway vehicle or component arises due to: (i) a design or manufacturing deviation from the approved specifications, or (ii) the need for defect correction or compensation for damages.[41] In addition, certified railway

---

[37] Article 33(1) of the Railway Safety Act.

[38] According to Article 1–2 of the Enforcement Rule of the Railway Safety Act, railway accidents are classified into two categories: railway traffic accidents and railway safety accidents. Railway traffic accidents refer to incidents related to train operations, including collisions, derailments, train fires, and other railway traffic incidents. Railway safety accidents involve accidents related to railway facility management, including railway facility fires, damage to railway infrastructure, and other railway safety incidents.

[39] Article 33(2) of the Railway Safety Act.

[40] Article 61–2(2) of the Railway Safety Act.

[41] Article 87(1) of the Enforcement Rule of the Railway Safety Act.

vehicle maintenance organizations are subject to mandatory reporting obligations under the following circumstances: (i) when structural damage to a railway vehicle necessitating heavy maintenance occurs; (ii) when a critical component failure arises that has a significant impact on operational safety; and (iii) when cracks, permanent deformation, or corrosion in the structure of the railway vehicle exceed the maximum allowable limits prescribed by technical standards.[42] Railway operators and related entities are required to report certain types of serious incidents. These include (i) train collisions or derailments; (ii) fires occurring on railway vehicles or trains that result in service interruption; and (iii) incidents related to the operation of railway vehicles or trains that cause either three or more casualties (deaths or injuries) or property damage exceeding 50 million KRW. In such cases, the railway operator must promptly report the occurrence to the relevant authorities, in accordance with the statutory reporting obligations.[43] Lastly, the risk factors subject to voluntary reporting are categorized into the following areas: safety management, railway operations, railway vehicles, roadbed, track, and structures, as well as electric power for railways, signaling, and communications.[44]

Reporting Deadlines

Under the Railway Safety Act, when a mechanical failure or defect occurs, the responsible party is required to report the issue within seven days from the time the defect is recognized.[45] In contrast, in the event of an accident or similar incident, immediate reporting is mandated within 30 minutes of the occurrence.[46] On the other hand, safety hazards may be reported voluntarily, and such reports should be made in accordance with the relevant guidelines, following the prescribed procedures and methods.

Sanctions for Noncompliance

Article 82 of the Railway Safety Act stipulates that any person who fails to report or makes a false report in violation of Article 61(1) or Article 61–2 shall be subject to an administrative fine of up to ten million Korean won.

---

[42] Article 87(2) of the Enforcement Rule of the Railway Safety Act.

[43] Article 57 of the Enforcement Decree of the Railway Safety Act.

[44] Article 88(1) Annex Table 45–19 of the Enforcement Rule of the Railway Safety Act.

[45] Article 11 of the Guidelines on Mandatory Reporting of Railway Accidents, Failures, and Vehicle Defects, and Voluntary Reporting of Railway Safety Hazards.

[46] Article 4 of the Guidelines on Mandatory Reporting of Railway Accidents, Failures, and Vehicle Defects, and Voluntary Reporting of Railway Safety Hazards.

Cross-Sectoral Review of Safety Legislation: Ship, Aviation, and Railway Defect Reporting

The Republic of Korea has enacted and enforced the Ship Safety Act, Aviation Safety Act, and Railway Safety Act with the aim of preventing safety accidents involving major public transportation modes such as ships, aircraft, and railways. To achieve this objective, each statute imposes various legal duties on those responsible for maintaining and managing transportation safety. Notably, each law mandates the obligation to report malfunctions, defects, functional failures, or accidents to the relevant authorities. However, important distinctions arise in how each statute defines the reporting responsibility.

Reporting Obligations and Responsible Parties

The Ship Safety Act stipulates that any person who discovers a defect in a vessel's seaworthiness or safety equipment may report it to the Minister of Oceans and Fisheries. Accordingly, the reporting obligation appears to extend to all stakeholders who are reasonably capable of identifying such defects—such as the shipowner, company personnel, ship inspectors, the captain, or crew members. However, in the absence of clear criteria for determining whether a defect in seaworthiness or safety equipment exists, these stakeholders may face legal uncertainty and pressure stemming from the fear of being punished for failing to report. This legal ambiguity creates a burden and difficulty in fulfilling the duty to report. Moreover, if there is a disconnect between those who are actually responsible for reporting and those subject to punishment, it could foster mistrust among stakeholders.

In contrast, the Aviation Safety Act and the Railway Safety Act clearly designate the responsible party for reporting based on the cause or circumstances of the safety hazard, malfunction, or accident. Accordingly, the Ship Safety Act is considered problematic in that the scope of reporting subjects is overly broad. This broad designation makes it difficult for individuals to recognize that they themselves bear the duty to report, and to faithfully fulfill that duty with due diligence.

Reporting Obligations and Responsible Parties

While the Ship Safety Act imposes a duty to report vessel defects, it fails to clearly specify the key subject of such reporting—namely, what exactly constitutes a reportable defect. The concept of "seaworthiness" is inherently broad, and the Supreme Court of Korea has held that there is no definitive or absolute standard for determining whether a vessel is seaworthy.[47] Instead, such determination must be

[47] Supreme Court of Korea (1996a), addressed the issue of seaworthiness. Similarly, Busan High Court (2021), held that a defect in seaworthiness constitutes a lack of seaworthiness, and if left unaddressed, may pose a risk of maritime accidents or hazards. The court determined that such circumstances require appropriate repairs or corrective measures.

made on a relative basis, depending on the specific and individual circumstances of each voyage. Accordingly, determining whether a vessel possesses seaworthiness is inherently uncertain and presents practical difficulties. Furthermore, the Ship Safety Act does not provide a definition of "safety equipment," and the term is mentioned only in Article 74. Despite the fact that failure to report defects in seaworthiness is treated as an administrative crime under the Act, the lack of clear standards for assessing the seaworthiness of a vessel and the condition of its safety equipment raises serious concerns under the principle of *nullum crimen sine lege* (no crime without law).[48]

In contrast, Article 74(1) and Annex Table 20–2 of the Enforcement Rule of the Aviation Safety Act explicitly categorize mandatory reportable aviation safety occurrences into seven distinct areas, providing detailed classifications. Similarly, the Railway Safety Act clearly defines the types of mechanical failures, accidents, and safety hazards subject to mandatory or voluntary reporting through its Enforcement Decree, Enforcement Rule, and relevant guidelines.

Reporting Deadlines

The Ship Safety Act, the Aviation Safety Act, and the Railway Safety Act each impose reporting obligations, and failure to comply with these obligations—or submitting false reports—may result in administrative penalties or sanctions. Specifically, the Aviation Safety Act and the Railway Safety Act stipulate precise reporting deadlines based on the type of occurrence, such as immediate reporting, within 72 h, or within 96 h, in order to ensure prompt response and action. The Railway Safety Act also clearly sets out reporting timeframes depending on the nature of the incident, such as accidents, operational failures, or vehicle malfunctions.

In contrast, the Ship Safety Act imposes a duty to report defects in seaworthiness or safety equipment but does not specify a concrete timeframe for such reporting. As a result, it is generally viewed as less effective than the Aviation Safety Act or the Railway Safety Act in ensuring timely notification.

Sanctions for Noncompliance

While the Aviation Safety Act and the Railway Safety Act impose administrative fines (as administrative order sanctions) for violations of reporting obligations, the Ship Safety Act treats the failure to fulfill the reporting duty more severely,

[48] The principle of clarity, which derives from the broader principle of ***nullum crimen sine lege*** (the principle of legality), requires that the elements of a criminal offense and the degree of punishment be defined with sufficient clarity and precision. This ensures that individuals can foresee the legal consequences of their actions and make informed decisions about their conduct. This principle was affirmed by the Supreme Court of Korea (2014) (Case No. 2013Do12939)

imposing administrative criminal penalties.[49] The Ship Safety Act provides for the reporting of vessel defects. In this context, "reporting" refers to notifying the administrative authority of the existence or non-existence of a specific fact or legal relationship. Such reporting is self-executing and does not require a separate approval, permission, or authorization process—it simply involves informing the relevant administrative office of the matter. However, under the current legal framework, some reports—such as those requiring corrective measures—are also used as a basis for administrative authorities to take necessary actions upon recognizing the reported facts.[50]

The Aviation Safety Act and the Railway Safety Act both establish reporting obligations. In this context, a reporting obligation refers either to: (i) the duty of a subordinate administrative body to report certain matters to a higher administrative authority, or (ii) the requirement imposed on individuals, corporations, or organizations entrusted or delegated by an administrative authority to report specific matters or submit data as part of general supervisory functions. Accordingly, under the Aviation Safety Act, if the Minister of Land, Infrastructure and Transport receives a mandatory safety report or otherwise becomes aware of a relevant aviation safety issue, the Minister may conduct an investigation to verify the facts and determine whether there has been a violation of the Act.[51] Under the Railway Safety Act, upon receiving an accident report, the Minister of Land, Infrastructure and Transport may, if deemed necessary, issue instructions to the railway operator or other relevant parties regarding accident response and recovery measures.

Under the Ship Safety Act, any person who discovers a defect in a vessel's seaworthiness or safety equipment is required to report it to the Minister of Oceans and Fisheries. In response, the Ministry may require the submission of reports or materials, issue voyage suspension orders, or take measures related to repair reports. In this respect, the reporting obligation under the Ship Safety Act is not fundamentally different in nature from the reporting obligations under the Aviation Safety Act and the Railway Safety Act. Nevertheless, the legal framework distinguishes between these obligations by labeling them as "reporting" in the Aviation and Railway Acts and as "notification" in the Ship Safety Act. This distinction results in unequal treatment, as violations of the reporting obligation are subject to administrative fines,

---

[49] Acts that directly infringe upon administrative objectives or the public interest are treated more severely and are subject to administrative criminal penalties. However, in cases where the violation merely poses a risk of disrupting administrative order, and the misconduct is based on an objective breach of order rather than subjective elements such as intent or negligence, the act is sanctioned through administrative fines as a form of administrative order penalty. Korea Institute of Criminal Justice Policy (2009), pp. 3–4.

[50] Under the current legal system, more than 1300 types of reporting systems are in operation. These can be categorized into: self-executing reports, reports requiring acceptance or review (i.e., approval-type reports), and information-providing reports, as well as reports pertaining to violations of statutory obligations. Legislation Research Center (2020) Guidelines for Legislative Drafting and Review, p. 87.

[51] Article 60 of the Aviation Safety Act; Guidelines for Fact-Finding Investigations in Air Traffic Services (Directive No. 320).

whereas violations of the notification obligation are subject to administrative criminal penalties. This discrepancy raises concerns regarding fairness and consistency.[52]

Conclusion

The Ship Safety Act in Korea was established based on Japan's Ship Safety Act, and the ship defect reporting system was also directly inherited and stipulated from the Japanese model. Over time, as society has evolved, the Ship Safety Act has undergone numerous amendments. Accordingly, the ship defect reporting system has also experienced significant revisions in terms of the reporting entities, subjects, deadlines, and associated penalties. However, various issues have been identified in the understanding and implementation of these mandatory reporting regulations.

In particular, the 2005 full revision of the Ship Safety Act (Act No. 82221) aimed to enable effective fact-checking and corrective measures regarding defects in seaworthiness and safety equipment of ships. As part of this revision, the law was amended to allow any person to report ship defects. However Seaworthiness is inherently a relative concept, assessed in the context of each voyage's specific operational and environmental conditions,[53] Judging defects in a vessel's seaworthiness should be no different. Nevertheless, the current provision requires that anyone who discovers a defect in a vessel's seaworthiness or safety equipment must report. This poses institutional risks, as individuals without maritime expertise may make inaccurate assessments. As a result, public officials in the Ministry of Oceans and Fisheries are obligated to promptly verify each report, which could lead to unnecessary administrative burdens and potentially disrupt the smooth operation of vessels.

To mitigate such risks while preserving the current reporting framework, it is essential to address the underlying legal ambiguities and structural issues embedded in the system. Specifically, the issues identified above—regarding the reporting entity, subject, deadline, and penalties—should be resolved through targeted legislative and regulatory amendments. First, it is necessary to establish a clear definition of the reporting entity. The Constitution and the Criminal Act of Korea proclaim the principle of the rule of law and adopt the principle of *nullum crimen, nulla poena sine lege* (no crime or punishment without law). Accordingly, individuals must be able to understand which actions are prohibited and what sanctions may follow such

[52] In general, violations of reporting obligations are subject to administrative fines. However, when the reporting requirement carries significant policy importance, failure to comply may be punishable by administrative criminal penalties. For example, Article 45 of the Livestock Products Sanitary Control Act stipulates that a person who has obtained a business license must report any suspension, resumption, or closure of business, or any minor changes to licensed matters. Failure to comply with this reporting requirement is punishable by imprisonment of up to one year or a fine of up to ten million Korean won.

[53] Supreme Court of Korea (1996b) and Busan High Court of Korea (2021).

actions through the interpretation of the law itself, enabling them to make autonomous decisions regarding their conduct. However, the current Ship Safety Act lacks clarity regarding the scope of "any one," who are both the obligated reporters and subjects to punishment. While the rationale for broadening the subject of ship defect reporting to "any person" and the potential public interest benefits of such a change cannot be overlooked, it is nonetheless necessary—following the examples of the Aviation Safety Act and the Railway Safety Act—to clearly specify the obligated parties. In particular, those who bear direct responsibility for ship safety, such as ship personnel and inspectors, should be explicitly designated as responsible reporting entities.

Second, it is necessary to enumerate and clearly define the subjects of mandatory reporting. The Constitutional Court of Korea has held that, while it is impossible for all laws to specify every element in complete detail, legal provisions do not violate the principle of clarity if an average person with sound common sense and a reasonable legal conscience can sufficiently understand to whom the law applies and what specific conduct is prohibited.[54] However, "Article 74 of the Ship Safety Act imposes a reporting duty based on subjective judgments regarding broadly defined defects in seaworthiness and safety equipment. Due to the relative and ambiguous nature of these concepts, the scope of reportable conditions becomes overly broad, raising constitutional concerns regarding the principle of legal clarity (*nullum crimen sine lege*).[55] In determining the scope of reportable ship defects, the Minister of Oceans and Fisheries, upon receiving a report, may issue a sailing suspension order if the defect is deemed serious enough to pose a risk to the vessel or its crew should the vessel continue its voyage. Therefore, the primary causes of such sailing suspensions should serve as important criteria in this assessment. In addition, it is necessary to analyze both international conventions—such as the International Convention for the Safety of Life at Sea (SOLAS)—and relevant domestic legislation pertaining to seaworthiness and safety equipment, in order to classify defects and apply risk assessment[56] and time management concepts.[57] Based on this, the scope of defects in seaworthiness and safety equipment should be categorized into the following types: (i) structural defects of the hull, (ii) equipment-related defects of the hull, (iii) machinery and electrical system defects, and (iv) human (crew-related) errors. These categories and their specific details should be clearly stipulated in Article 95 of the Enforcement Rule of the Ship Safety Act.

---

[54] Constitutional Court of Korea (1996).

[55] From the perspective that it violates the principle of legal clarity, Park (2024). From the perspective that it does not violate the principle of legal clarity, Lee (2025b).

[56] Risk assessment means categorizing identified hazards by combining the frequency (probability of occurrence) of an accident and the intensity (severity) of its impact on the organization, thereby determining the type and level of risk involved. Mousavi et al. (2017), pp. 1377–1378.

[57] Time management refers to the deliberate allocation and distribution of time: redistributing available time according to the priority, objectives, and activities associated with identified risk factors to maximize efficiency. Typically, this approach employs the Eisenhower Matrix Callula (2024), p. 154.

Third, the reporting deadline must be clearly stipulated. The ship defect reporting system is designed to ensure vessel safety under the Ship Safety Act and other related laws. It aims to address cases where defects in a vessel's seaworthiness or safety equipment are not properly recognized or remedied. In such cases, the Ministry of Oceans and Fisheries may issue a detention order based on the judgment of an authorized official, thereby preventing maritime accidents and safeguarding vessel operations. Therefore, in order to operate the defect reporting system effectively and achieve its intended purpose, it is necessary to mandate prompt reporting upon discovery of defects in seaworthiness or safety equipment. To this end, Article 95 of the Enforcement Rule of the Ship Safety Act should clearly specify the reporting timeline as follows: (i) If a defect in seaworthiness or safety equipment is identified and cannot be immediately rectified onboard, the defect must be reported within 72 h of its discovery (excluding any hours that fall on Saturdays or official public holidays). (ii) If the person who becomes aware of the defect is unable to report it within the deadline due to injury, communication failure, or other unavoidable circumstances, the report must be submitted within 72 h from the moment such impediment is resolved.

Lastly, it is necessary to ease the punitive provisions. The reason for including penal provisions in administrative statutes stems from the notion that criminal penalties serve as one of the primary means to ensure the effectiveness of such regulations. Unlike punishments for natural crimes, administrative offenses are generally established as a means to secure compliance with obligations designed to achieve the intended purposes of the law. As such, they function as sanctions for noncompliance and are typically based on broad legislative discretion.[58] The Constitutional Court of Korea also regards matters related to administrative penal provisions as falling within the scope of legislative discretion, to be determined comprehensively by the legislature in consideration of the nation's history and culture, the prevailing social conditions at the time of legislation, public values and legal sentiment, the nature and circumstances of crimes, the legal interests to be protected, and the anticipated effect on crime prevention.[59] As a result, growing awareness of safety issues—particularly following the *Sewol* Ferry disaster—has led to a legislative trend of strengthening mandatory obligations and punitive provisions related to ship safety under the Ship Safety Act. However, the expansion of criminal liability and the imposition of harsher penalties often reflect a reliance on symbolic criminal law, based on the questionable belief that increasing statutory punishments alone can resolve systemic problems.[60] Many scholars have raised concerns about the actual effectiveness of such legislative measures.[61]

---

[58] Choi (2015), pp. 30–31.

[59] Constitutional Court of Korea (1995).

[60] Hassemer and Yoon (2008), p. 224.

[61] Choi (2003), pp. 158–160.

There has been ongoing criticism that administrative criminal penalties under maritime laws, including the Ship Safety Act, are excessively severe.[62] More specifically, the Ship Safety Act, Aviation Safety Act, and Railway Safety Act all impose obligations to report or notify authorities of defects in their respective transport systems. Despite the similar legislative purposes and protected legal interests among these statutes, the legal consequences differ: under the Ship Safety Act, failure to report defects in seaworthiness is treated as an administrative crime (punishable by criminal penalties), whereas under the Aviation Safety Act and the Railway Safety Act, similar failures are classified as administrative violations (subject to administrative fines).

Although it might be argued that the legislative approach under the Ship Safety Act was influenced by the severity of the *Sewol* Ferry disaster, the legal comparison reveals an inconsistency. For example, the offense of failing to report a defect in seaworthiness under the Ship Safety Act is punished on par with serious violations such as operating a vessel in violation of the terms or capacity stated in its inspection certificate, operating a vessel without a valid inspection certificate, or falsifying or tampering with draft markings. While the duty to report defects in seaworthiness is intended as a supplementary mechanism to prevent maritime accidents, compliance with inspection certificates and safe vessel operation is a fundamental requirement for ensuring maritime safety. Therefore, treating the failure to report defects in seaworthiness as legally equivalent to these core violations is not a reasonable approach. The excessive reliance on the deterrent effect of criminal punishment, coupled with administrative convenience, has led to over-criminalization. This trend imposes a heavy burden on criminal justice institutions and contributes to the unnecessary criminalization of ordinary citizens. Therefore, for minor violations such as the failure to fulfill a simple reporting obligation—where the infringement on administrative objectives is minimal—it would be more appropriate to impose an administrative fine rather than criminal penalties.[63]

The current structure of the ship defect reporting system under the Ship Safety Act in Korea reveals several critical shortcomings in terms of legal clarity, fairness in enforcement, and proportionality of punishment. Ambiguous definitions of reporting entities, overly broad categories of reportable defects, and harsh punitive measures—especially when compared to parallel systems in the aviation and railway sectors—undermine the legitimacy and effectiveness of the system. Without clear legal boundaries and a balanced application of administrative responsibility, there is a risk of over-criminalization and diminished public trust in maritime safety governance.

To enhance the practicality and legal soundness of the ship defect reporting system, it is essential to refine the scope of reporting obligations, introduce specific risk-based classifications of defects, and revise the reporting deadline provisions.

[62] See: Choi and Lim (2019); Choi et al. (2021); The Cargo Times (2020), http://www.cargotimes.net/news/articleView.html?idxno=63063.

[63] Korea Institute of Criminology and Justice (2009), p. 118; National Assembly Legislative Research Office (2011), pp. 502–503.

Moreover, the punitive regime should be realigned to reflect the administrative nature of reporting duties, limiting criminal sanctions to severe violations and adopting administrative fines for minor infractions. This approach would uphold the rule of law, promote efficient maritime safety management, and strike a more reasonable balance between legal enforcement and operational reality.

References

Busan District Court of Korea (2020) Decision of Feb 18, Case No. 2019GoHap50

Busan High Court of Korea (2021) Decision of May 26, Case No. 2020No151

Choi SY (2003) A critical review of symbolic criminal law. Comp Criminal Law Rev 5(2):158–160

Choi HY (2015) A Study on the Improvement of Administrative Penal Provisions, Korea Legislation Research Institute, Research Report No.2015–09, pp. 30–31

Choi SY, Lim CH (2019) Problems and improvement measures of punitive provisions under maritime law. Maritime Law Rev 31(3)

Choi SY et al (2021) Study on the propriety of punitive statutory penalties. Korea Maritime Officer Association

Constitutional Court of Korea (1995) Decision of Nov 13, Case No. 94Hun Ga3

Constitutional Court of Korea (1996) Decision of Dec 20, Case No. 93Hun-Ba65

Constitutional Court of Korea (2010) Decision of July 29, Case No. 2009Hun-Ba53

Constitutional Court of Korea (2023) Decision of June 29, Case No. 2020Hun-Ba489

Constitutional Court of Korea (2024a) Decision of May 30, Case No. 2020Hun-Ba234

Constitutional Court of Korea (2024b) Decision of Oct 26, Case No. 2024Hun-Ga1

Daniels S (2012) The criminalisation of the ship's master. PhD thesis, Solent University, pp. 14–18

Daniels S (2022) Responsibility and accountability in maritime law: criminalisation of the ship's master, 1st edn. Informa Law from Routledge, pp 83–85. https://doi.org/10.4324/9781003266839. 93–96

Eisenhower Matrix Callula B (2024) A structural framework for effective time management in dynamic work environments. APTISI Transactions on Management:154

FAO (2003) Administrative sanctions in fisheries law, FAO Legislative Study No. 8, pp. 3–7

Hassemer W, Yoon YC (2008) The symbolism in symbolic criminal law, trans. by Yoon, Y. C., Yongsan Law Review, 5, 2, p. 224

Hornopparat NN (2017) The relevancy of seaworthiness and its deviation in the 21st century. Int J Crime Law Soc Issues 4(2):51–56

International Maritime Organization (2023) Port State Control: Procedures, A.1185(33)

Jang YR (2022) A study on the Improvem_ent of defect reporting under article 74 of the ship safety act. J Maritime Law Rev 44(2) Korean Maritime Law Association:98–102

Kassem AH (2006) The legal aspects of seaworthiness: current law and development. Doctoral thesis, Swansea University, pp. 14–15, 22

Khan A, Usman M, Amjad S (2020) Jurisdictional challenges in prosecuting maritime crimes: a comparative analysis. Int Rev Soc Sci 8(11):378–379

Korea Institute of Criminal Justice Policy (2009) Study on the Standardization of Statutory Penalties in Administrative Criminal Provisions I, pp 3–4

Korea Institute of Criminology and Justice (2009) Improvement measures for statutory penalties in administrative criminal provisions I. Korea Institute of Criminology and Justice, Seoul, p 118

Lee J (2016) A study on the formation of the theory of discretionary acts in German administrative law, Doctoral thesis, Seoul National University, pp. 8–10

Lee J (2025a) A study on the reporting obligation and legal liability of Shipowners regarding defects in seaworthiness. Ministry of Government Legislation, pp 14–17

Lee JW (2025b) A study on the duty of reporting defects of seaworthiness of vessels and legal responsibilities of Shipowners, legal review no.708. Ministry of Government Legislation
Lee S, Kim J, Yoo J (2019) An exploratory study on the justification of penal legislation for ship inspectors. J Ocean Policy Res 34(2):99–100
Legislation Research Center (2020) Guidelines for Legislative Drafting and Review, p. 87
Maria PH (2012) Investigation crime at sea-whoes jurisdiction?, Standard-club, chrome-extension://efaidnbmnnnibpcajpcglclefindmkaj/https://www.standardclub.com/fileadmin/uploads/standardclub/Documents/Import/publications/bulletins/split-articles/2012/1557758-investigating-crime-at-sea-whose-jurisdiction.pdf?utm_source=chatgpt.com
Mousavi M, Ghazi I, Omaraee B (2017) Risk assessment in the maritime industry. Eng Technol Appl Sci Res 7(1):1377–1378
National Assembly Legislative Research Office (2011) Legislative theory and legislative practice. National Assembly Secretariat, Seoul, pp 502–503
Ofurumazi RP, Ifiokonko et al (2024) An analysis of the impact of condition surveys in determining the seaworthiness of vessel before purchase. Global J Manag Bus Stud 12(1):75–77
Park YS (2024) A critical review on ship's seaworthiness reporting system. J Korea Maritime Law Assoc 46:No.3
Re RM (2019) Clarity doctrines. UC Law Rev 86:1509–1516
Shen JH, Liu CP et al (2020) Ship deficiency data of port state control to identify hidden risk of target ship. JMSE 9(10):1120–1121
Soyer B (2014) Maritime liabilities in a global context. Informa Law, London, pp 112–129
Supreme Court of Korea (1996a) Decision of Oct 11, Case No. 94Da60332
Supreme Court of Korea (1996b) Decision of Oct 11, Case No. 94Da60332.
Supreme Court of Korea (2014) Decision of January 29, Case No. 2013Do12939
Supreme Court of Korea (2024) Decision of Jul 11, Case No. 2021Do7251
The Cargo Times (2020) Seafarers Forced to Leave Their Livelihoods Due to Harsh Sanctions, last accessed 5 Aug 2022

Chapter 6
Current Safety Issues of Car Ferries in South Korea and Northeast China and Their Improvements

Junghwan Choi and SangSeop Lim

Introduction

In 1993, South Korea and China signed the Agreement on Maritime Transport, aiming to bolster marine transportation efficiency between the two nations.[1] Through Annual South Korea-China Maritime Transportation Meetings, they have exchanged information on establishing and operating container and ferry routes. This collaboration has led to significant achievements in the Korea-China routes, including market stability, equitable opportunities for national shipping firms, and improved shipping services. Notably, the Korea-China ferry market has become the world's largest, mostly in the Yellow Sea region, owing to well-managed marine routes,

Junghwan Choi Xinghai Associate Professor at The School of Law of Dalian Maritime University, China. LL.M. in Maritime Law (Korea Maritime & Ocean Uni.), LL.M. in International Maritime Law with Merit (Swansea Uni., UK), Ph.D. in Maritime Law (Exeter Uni., UK).
SangSeop Lim Professor at the Division of Navigation Convergence Studies, Korea Maritime and Ocean University, Busan, Korea. B.Eng. in Navigation Science (KMOU); M.Sc. and Ph.D. in Shipping Management (KMOU).
This is an updated and revised version of the author's article "Life cycle assessment for environment-friendly ferry service: A case study between South Korea and China "published at Regional Studies in Marine Science (Vol. 89, 2025) under the official permission of Publication company and Co-Autor.

[1] Database of Japanese Politics and International Relations (1993).

J. Choi
Law School, Dalian Maritime University, Dalian, P.R. China
e-mail: junghwanchoi@dlmu.edu.cn

S. Lim (✉)
Division of Navigation Convergence Studies, Korea Maritime & Ocean University, Busan, Republic of Korea
e-mail: limsangseop@kmou.ac.kr

J. Choi (ed.), *Public Maritime Law in Asia*, International Law in Asia,
https://doi.org/10.1007/978-981-95-7037-9_6

proximity-driven demand, and efficient transportation methods.[2] Since 2013, ten ferry routes have connected Incheon Port with various Chinese ports, including Weihai, Tianjin, Qingdao, Dalian, Dandong, Yantai, Shidao, Yingkou, Qinhuangdao, and Lianyungang. Three of these ports/routes (Yingkou, Dalian, and Dandong) are situated in the Northeast three provinces of China, acting as crucial nodes in the Maritime Silk Roads and logistic hubs for inland cargo from Northeast China and the Far East.[3] Given the strategic importance of Northeast China, South Korea has acknowledged the region's significance.[4] However, with most South Korea-China car ferries exceeding 20 years in age, safety management for aging vessels has become a growing concern.[5] Additionally, current policies in South Korea and China impose age limits on passenger ships, prohibiting ferries over 30 years old from operating. Considering that vessels on routes in Dalian, Yingkou, and Dandong are over 25 years old, special attention to safety management and discussions on alternative vessel construction are necessary.[6]

Moreover, the International Maritime Organization (IMO) adopted a net-zero emissions strategy by 2050 at the IMO MEPC 80th meeting. Thus, transitioning to eco-friendly vessels and fuels should comply with international decarbonization mandates.[7] Shipping is responsible for approximately 3% of global greenhouse gas emissions, with a 20% increase over the past decade.[8] Given the global move toward decarbonization, China and South Korea may need to introduce alternative-fueled ferries for operations in the Yellow Sea.

Against this backdrop, this study aims to examine the current safety issues of car ferries operating between South Korea and China and to analyze the regulatory and legal frameworks governing them. In particular, it identifies limitations in the safety management of aging vessels, evaluates the adequacy of existing regulations, and explores possible improvements. Furthermore, it seeks to propose policy and legal measures to enhance maritime safety, such as strengthening bilateral cooperation, establishing a joint safety management framework, and encouraging the construction of new eco-friendly ferries for Korea-China routes.

The subsequent sections of this paper will be organized as follows: Section One will review the existing literature on ferry operations and maritime safety, highlighting the regulatory and legal gaps this study aims to address. Section Two will outline the research methodology and analytical framework employed. Section Three will present the findings of the safety issue analysis, followed by a discussion in

[2] Jung et al. (2014), p. 81.

[3] Fan et al. (2024), p. 1.

[4] Choi and Lim (2023), p. 121; Incheon Port Authority, available at http://www.icferry.or.kr/eng/intrl/nvg/realtimelist.do?menuKey=560 (accessed 13 February 2024).

[5] Jeon et al. (2017), p. 145.

[6] Incheon Port Authority (2023).

[7] IMO, "IMO Strategy on Reduction of GHG Emissions from Ships. Resolution MEPC.377(80), adopted on 7 July 2023", available at https://wwwcdn.imo.org/localresources/en/MediaCentre/PressBriefings/Documents/Resolution%20MEPC.377(80).pdf (accessed 21 September 2025).

[8] UNCTAD (2024).

Section Four that interprets the results in the context of regulatory implications and recommendations for policy and legal reforms.

Literature Review

Geographic, Socio-Economic, and Cultural Significance of Three Chinese Northeast Provinces from the South Korean Perspective

China is South Korea's largest trading partner, with the Korean economy heavily dependent on imports of raw materials and intermediate goods from China. They also pointed out that Northeast China serves as a transport hub connecting Russia, Mongolia, and the Korean Peninsula, facilitating trade in multiple directions.[9] The region's geopolitical importance for South Korea is further emphasized by the implementation of South Korea's New Northern Policy and China's Belt and Road Initiative. According to KITA statistics (2021), South Korea's foreign trade dependency reached 69.6%, with intermediate goods accounting for 66.5% of exports and 47.1% of imports globally. This high trade volume underscores the logistical significance of the region, particularly in the context of maritime transport.[10]

Northeast China is geographically bordered by North Korea, Russia, and Mongolia, establishing close ties with other Northeast Asian countries such as South Korea and Japan through marine transportation.[11] In addition, the Northeast three provinces of China—Liaoning, Jilin, and Heilongjiang—serve as vital connectors between the Korean Peninsula and the Eurasian continent. The interests of numerous Northeast Asian countries converge in these areas, making them a primary focus for the diplomatic efforts of previous South Korean governments, particularly in the context of inter-Korean relations with China. These provinces have developed South Korea-China relations over the past three decades, leveraging their significant Korean Chinese population.[12]

The close ties with Northeast China are rooted in its pivotal role in mitigating tensions and conflicts among Northeast Asian countries.[13] Geographically bordered by Russia and North Korea, cooperation with this region is indispensable for bilateral and multilateral cooperation efforts involving North and South Korea, China, and Russia.[14] The region's proximity to Russia and North Korea enhances its role as a nexus for trilateral and multilateral cooperation in Northeast Asia. Economically,

[9] Choi and Lim (2023).

[10] Korea International Trade Association (KITA) (2021).

[11] Zhang and Qin (2022), p. 311.

[12] Lee (2019), p. 1.

[13] Armstrong (1990), p. 35.

[14] Lee (2019).

the region's ports, such as Dalian and Yingkou, serve as major nodes for multimodal logistics, handling approximately 28% of Sino-Korean seaborne trade.[15]

The Northeast region boasts superior access to Mongolia, Russia, and northeastern Japan compared with other Chinese regions, enabling it to leverage logistical advantages in trade with its Northeast Asian neighbors.[16] Lee and Park (2018) implied that culturally, Northeast China exhibits high linguistic and cultural homogeneity, preserving traces of the ancient Korean peninsula's tangible and intangible cultural heritage, as well as the modern anti-Japanese independence movement. Northeast China has played a pivotal role in diplomatic and cultural exchanges. Thus, it is a strategic region necessitating cultural exchange and cooperation, capitalizing on its cultural homogeneity.

Current Status of Ferry Operation

South Korea and China forged the Agreement on Maritime Transport between the Government of the Republic of Korea and the Government of the People's Republic of China in May 1993, following the establishment of diplomatic relations in August 1992. This agreement bolstered friendly relations and enhanced cooperation in marine transport, emphasizing reciprocity and equality to improve efficiency in the shipping industry between the two nations. The primary agendas of the South Korea-China Maritime Transportation Meeting include sharing the maritime transportation policy direction, establishing and operating container and ferry routes, and addressing mutual concerns.[17]

According to Incheon Port Authority statistics (2023), there are ten ferry routes connecting Incheon Port and China, established through the South Korea-China Maritime Transportation meeting in 2013: Weihai, Tianjin, Qingdao, Dalian, Dandong, Yantai, Shidao, Yingkou, Qinhuangdao, and Lianyungang.[18] In 2022, Qingdao, Shidao, Yantai, and Weihai ports in Shandong province recorded the highest trade volumes, followed by Lianyungang in Jiangsu province. Notably, three of these ports—Yingkou, Dalian, and Dandong—serve as pivotal nodes in the Maritime Silk Routes and logistic hubs for inland cargo from Northeast China and the Far East.[19]

Incheon Port, a major player in South Korea's maritime trade landscape, handled 61,633 tons of seaborne trade in 2022 (Table 6.1), constituting approximately 13% of the nation's total cargo volumes.[20] Alongside Pyeongtaek·Dangjin Port, Incheon

---

[15] Incheon Port Authority (2023).

[16] Wang (2013), p. 137.

[17] Incheon Port Authority (2023).

[18] Ibid.

[19] Ibid.

[20] Ibid.

Table 6.1 Container Freight volume transported by South Korea- China Ferries (unit: TEU)

	2018	2019	2020	2021	2022
Total	431,676	406,431	416,767	494,666	463,649
Dalian	20,800	20,011	19,638	19,796	24,687
Dandong	23,294	24,649	20,262	21,942	5482
Lianyungang	51,549	44,893	54,797	67,199	58,517
Qingdao	62,398	59,807	66,577	77,606	80,508
Qinhuangdao	38,999	20,851	33,749	45,090	37,728
Shidao	90,438	65,745	75,261	92,699	83,519
Tianjin	32,385	36,401	3700		
Weihai	66,496	66,188	70,919	74,531	69,354
Yantai	38,517	39,595	43,801	60,796	72,391
Yingkou	26,800	28,291	28,334	35,009	31,464

Source: Incheon Port Authority (2023)

Port contributes to around 20% of South Korea's overall cargo volume. Established in 2015, Incheon Port boasts modern infrastructure, including berth facilities tailored for the largest container ships and automated unloading equipment. Additionally, it features an international passenger terminal and cruise terminal, designed to position the port as a global marine tourism hub. In 2022, the port handled a total container cargo volume of 3,193,000 tons, with approximately 60% of this volume originating from trade with China, amounting to 1,945,000 tons, which is attributed to the port's advantageous geographical location (Fig. 6.1).[21]

However, the expansion of ferry operations has been accompanied by increasing environmental concerns. Existing literature has primarily focused on the economic benefits and logistical efficiency of these routes, while largely neglecting the environmental impacts, such as greenhouse gas emissions, marine pollution, and ecological disturbances.[22] For instance, the Incheon-Qingdao ferry route alone is estimated to emit over 12,000 tons of CO_2 annually, with the majority of vessels operating on diesel fuel and lacking advanced emissions control systems.[23] Moreover, 78% of ferries in operation exceed 15 years of service, further exacerbating their environmental footprint.[24]

Although recent technological advancements-such as the introduction of electric and low-carbon ferries in pilot projects-demonstrate the feasibility of sustainable alternatives, there remains a lack of comprehensive studies applying these solutions to Sino-Korean ferry routes. Furthermore, policy frameworks such as IMO 2050 decarbonization targets and Korea's Green New Deal highlight the urgency of

[21] Ibid.

[22] Kim et al. (2018), p. 1.

[23] Lee et al. (2021), p. 5568777.

[24] Korea Pro (2024).

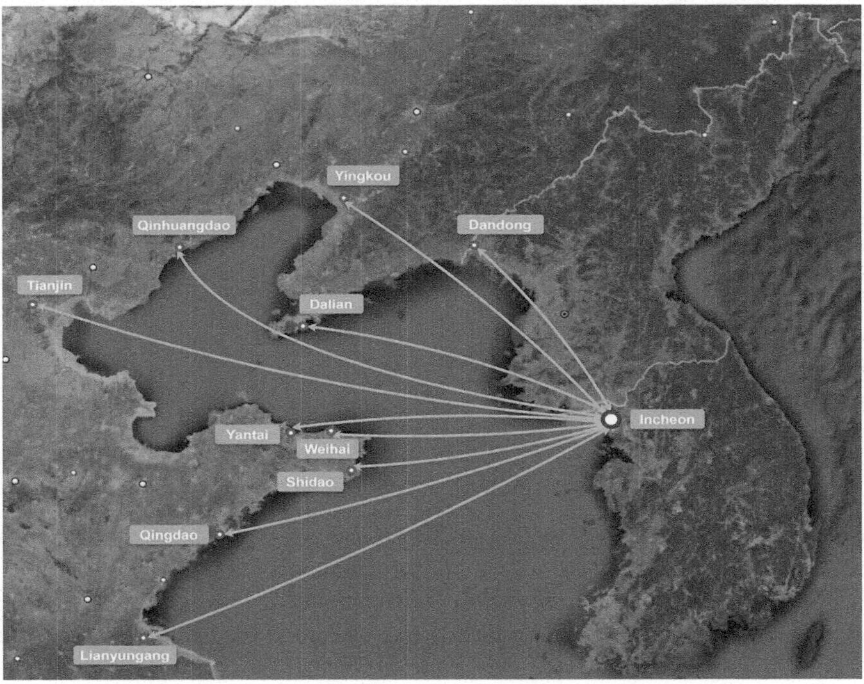

Fig. 6.1 Ferries Routes between South Korea and China (created by Authors)

transitioning to eco-friendly maritime transport, yet practical implementation and empirical assessment are limited.

Contemporary Issues

Decarbonization in International Shipping and Its Implications for the China–South Korea Ferry Route

The IMO made a significant stride towards environmental sustainability by declaring the 2050 Net Zero in International Shipping through the adoption of the 2023 IMO Strategy on Reduction of GHG Emissions from Ships at the 80th Maritime Environment Protection Committee (MEPC 80th) on July 7.[25] This declaration prompted a comprehensive revision of the 2018 Strategy, which aimed to slash GHG emissions by 50% by 2050 compared to the 2008 baseline. Additionally, the revised strategy outlined indicative checkpoints for GHG reduction, targeting

[25] IMO (n 7).

20–30% reduction by 2030 and 70–80% reduction by 2040. Currently, carbon emissions from the marine transportation sector contribute to 3% of global carbon emissions,[26] with most of the world's cargo-carrying fleet consisting of over 100,000 freight vessels powered by diesel engines, posing a significant pollution risk.[27] In response, the IMO extended its GHG emission regulations, previously applicable to newly constructed vessels, to include ships currently in operation from January 1, 2024.[28]

Alternative fuel and renewable energy usage are considered as practical countermeasures to combat carbon emissions in the shipping industry, encompassing various technologies, including transitioning from the current HFO to alternative fuels such as LNG, methanol, bio-oil, hydrogen, and ammonia, as well as utilizing electricity (batteries) and wind power.[29] Notably, large global shipping companies are increasingly inclined to replace their old vessels with alternative-fueled ships, with LNG-fueled ships comprising a significant portion of new orders.[30] LNG has relatively low fuel costs, given the existing production and supply infrastructure.[31] Consequently, shipping companies are actively replacing outdated vessels with alternative-fueled counterparts to comply with stricter environmental regulations imposed by the IMO. Methanol-fueled ships have also gained prominence, partially influenced by Elon Musk's initiatives. According to Clarksons Research, a UK-based provider of maritime market data and intelligence, global shipbuilders have secured orders for a total of 539 alternative-fueled vessels since 2023, with 125 vessels designated for methanol fuel.[32] The International Transport Forum (ITF) emphasizes that these alternative fuel and clean energy-based vessels will contribute significantly to achieving GHG reduction targets in the shipping sector by 2035. Particularly noteworthy is the ITF's suggestion for vessels and shipping based on ammonia/hydrogen to comprise 80% of the entire marine transport sector by 2035.[33]

This global trend exerts significant external pressure on the China–South Korea ferry route, which, as a component of international shipping, is directly subject to evolving environmental regulations. While alternative fuel technologies like LNG, methanol, and ammonia have been introduced, their adoption on the China–South Korea route is still non-existent.

The decarbonization imperative is closely associated with global regulatory trends and highlights the urgent need to transition to eco-friendly ferries on the China–South Korea route. This transition is critical for compliance with

[26] Su et al. (2024), p. 1.

[27] Jacoby (2022).

[28] IMO (2018).

[29] EMSA (2024).

[30] Safety4Sea (2023).

[31] Lee et al. (2020), p. 102220.

[32] Clarkson (2024).

[33] ITF (2018).

international standards, reduction of environmental impacts, and long-term sustainability of maritime transport in the region.

Safety Issues Related to Age Limits for Car Ferries

South Korea's policy concerning the age limit of passenger ships is grounded in the Marine Transportation Act, with further specifications provided by the Enforcement Regulation of the Marine Transportation Act. According to these regulations, passenger vessels are restricted to 20 years of age or less.[34] However, vessel operations exceeding this age limit may be extended in one-year increments for up to five years, provided they undergo inspections in compliance with the Ship Inspection Standards and are deemed fit for safe operation. For vessels over 25 years old, extensions are subject to evaluation based on both Ship Inspection Standards and Ship Management Assessment Standards.

China's regulations on the age limit of passenger ships are outlined in the Provisions on Old and Worn-out Transportation Vessels of The People's Republic of China. These regulations enhance the management of aging transport vessels, optimize water transportation infrastructure, elevate vessel technology, ensure water transportation safety, and foster water transportation sector development. The Provisions classify old vessels into five categories based on ship age and type, establishing criteria for vessel age within these categories (Article 4). South Korea--China car ferries fall under Category 2, covering various maritime transport vessels, including container and passenger ships, cargo and passenger ships, passenger ferries, sightseeing ships, and those aged over 10 years. Specific age limits apply to vessel purchase or lease, special periodic surveys, and mandatory decommissioning, with vessels over 24 years old subject to special periodic surveys and potentially extending operational life up to 30 years under China's age limit policy (Table 6.2). International Council on Clean Transportation (ICCT) indicated that vessels older than 20 years consume 15–20% more fuel compared to newer models, which directly leads to higher emissions and reduced operational efficiency.[35]

One pressing safety concern for South Korea-China ferries is the age of vessels, with many exceeding 20 years. This aging fleet poses ongoing safety risks. Phased replacement of these aging vessels, guided by policies restricting vessel age, is a viable strategy to enhance safety management. On June 2024, six out of the ten South Korea-China ferries, operating primarily from Incheon Port, were over 20 years old. Notably, the Jinchon Ferry, servicing the Incheon-Tianjin route, surpassed 30 years of age and has remained suspended since January 2020 due to a management dispute among shareholders. Additionally, three ferry routes in the

[34] Enforcement Rule of Marine Transportation Act of Republic of Korea, available at https://elaw.klri.re.kr/kor_service/lawView.do?hseq=56966&lang=ENG (accessed 8 March 2024).

[35] ICCT (2013).

Table 6.2 South Korea-China Ferries Details

Name	Company	Line	G/T	Speed	Capacity	Age	Active/ Inactive
ARAFURA LILY	Yingkou Ferry	Yingkou	12,304	17	394	**27**	
XIN YU JIN XIANG	Quinin Ferry	Qinhuangdao	12,304	20	376	28	
BIRYONG	Dain Ferry	Dalian	14,614	20	510	**27**	
XIN XIANG XUE LAN	Hanjoong Ferry	Yantai	32,729	21	700	4	
HUADONG PEARL VIII	Huadong Ferry	Shidao	35,092	22	1500	7	
NEW GOLDEN BRIDGE VII	Weidong Ferry	Weihai	30,322	23.5	724	5	
NEW GOLDEN BRIDGE V	Weidong Ferry	Qingdao	29,554	23	660	26	
MV. TIAN REN	Jinchon Ferry	Tianjin	26,463	23	800	33	Inactive
HARMONY YUN GANG	Lyg Ferry	Lianyungang	35,187	18.5	1080	5	
ZI YU LAN	Lyg Ferry	Lianyungang	16,071	18.5	392	28	
ORIENTAL PEARL VI)	Dandong Ferry	Dandong	16,537	25.5	800	**28**	

Source: Incheon Port Authority (2023)

Northeast three provinces rely on vessels over 25 years old, necessitating the replacement of these aging ships. The aging fleet's impact on safety and service quality is a significant challenge for the South Korea-China ferry routes.

Operational Profitability Concerns

The profitability of China–South Korea ferry operations has come under increasing pressure due to a combination of external economic factors and internal operational challenges. The aftermath of the COVID-19 pandemic has seen a 30% year-on-year decline in cargo volumes and a slow recovery in passenger numbers, with average boarding rates remaining at only 20% of pre-pandemic levels.[36]

Container transport volume on the 15 ferry routes between South Korea and China decreased to 524,800 TEU, marking a 16% decline from 622,800 TEU in 2022, and recording the lowest volume performance since 2017.[37] South

[36] Maritime Press (2023).

[37] *Shipper's Journal* (n.d.).

Table 6.3 Number of maritime passengers carried by Soth Korea- China Ferries (Unit: Person)

	2015	2016	2017	2018	2019
Total	816,409	920,391	600,365	809,056	1,027,019
Dandong	147,473	154,185	89,517	104,062	119,617
Dalian	53,406	91,077	40,750	38,034	75,665
Yingkou	52,932	50,221	13,496	9332	47,883
Qinhuangdao	45,421	51,379	16,459	25,101	11,907
Tianjin	66,314	72,447	26,576	74,204	101,953
Yantai	75,837	87,494	48,550	70,053	85,851
Weihai	131,530	198,467	136,605	126,127	140,089
Shidao	122,113	150,261	143,747	172,123	200,728
Qingdao	70,075	75,416	41,197	76,251	94,855
Lianyungang	48,308	49,444	43,468	113,769	148,471

Source: Incheon Port Authority (2023)

Korea-China maritime passenger tourism experienced a significant increase in the number of maritime passengers in Dalian, Dandong, and Yingkou before the onset of COVID-19. Notably, among the ten routes between China and South Korea, the Northeast region (comprising Dalian, Dandong, and Yingkou) exhibited a dominant presence in terms of maritime passengers (Table 6.3).

Aging vessels further compound these challenges by incurring higher maintenance costs-estimated to be 40% greater than those of newer ships-and by failing to meet increasingly stringent environmental regulations, which may result in substantial financial penalties for non-compliance.[38] The adoption of eco-friendly ferries presents a strategic opportunity to enhance profitability. Newer vessels, particularly those utilizing renewable energy, offer significant reductions in fuel costs (up to 35%) and are likely to attract environmentally conscious customers, thereby improving service quality and market competitiveness.[39]

Recommendations for Sustainable Environment-Friendly Car Ferries

The Need for Public Policy for South Korea-China Maritime Transportation Cooperation

Given the financial constraints and operational challenges faced by Korean and Chinese ferry companies, the construction of eco-friendly vessels, particularly those using LNG and methanol, ammonia, or hydrogen-powered vessels and comes with a high cost, is anticipated to be challenging. Based on the decarbonization trend in

[38] Alandia (2022).

[39] Moon et al. (2025), p. 41.

the shipping industry, South Korea and China have implemented domestic policies to address this issue. However, as neighboring countries sharing sea areas, they need to establish a comprehensive and cooperative policy framework to facilitate the introduction of net zero emission car ferries.

In January 2019, South Korea enforced the Act on Promotion of Development and Distribution of Environmentally Friendly Ships of the Republic of Korea, enacted in December 2018. Under this Act, the government mandates the establishment of the "Basic Plan for Environmentally Friendly Ships" every 5 years. On December 23, 2020, the Ministry of Oceans and Fisheries and the Ministry of Trade, Industry and Energy formulated the First Basic Plan for Development and Distribution of Environmentally Friendly Ships, covering the period 2021–2030.[40] This plan outlines measures to promote the distribution of environmentally friendly ships, with the government providing financial suppor t(Baek et al. 2022). In the public sector, 388 vessels will be converted to environmentally friendly ships, including replacing and constructing 199 old vessels and renovating 189 vessels less than 10 years old.[41] Additionally, in the private sector, the proportion of environmentally friendly vessels among newly constructed ships, approximately 164 per year, will increase by up to 20%, with a total of 140 vessels expected to become environmentally friendly by 2030. Regarding LNG, plans include securing the foundation for private investment by diversifying means of supply through bunkering vessels and onshore terminals, expanding supply capacity, and LNG-fueled ships.

At the 75th Session of The United Nations General Assembly, China committed to peak carbon dioxide emissions before 2030 and achieve carbon neutrality before 2060.[42] The document "Responding to Climate Change: China's Policies and Actions," released by the State Council Information Office of the People's Republic of China on October 27, 2021, outlined policy measures to achieve carbon neutrality in coastal shipping. China aims to strengthen support for green finance by introducing policies supporting climate investment and financing, developing a standard system for climate investment and financing, actively promoting green credit, and bolstering support for green bonds. Additionally, China seeks to secure low-carbon transportation modes, support research and development initiatives, reduce taxes on clean-fuel ships, and phase out old ships.[43]

South Korea and China are facing limitations in technical capabilities and policy support to achieve carbon neutrality, particularly in their coastal vessel operations. To address this challenge, cooperation between the two nations is crucial. Initiatives such as declaring green shipping corridors for the South Korea-China ferry routes through the South Korea-China Maritime Transportation Meeting are essential. A green shipping corridor involves implementing diverse environmentally friendly

[40] Ministry of Oceans and Fisheries (MOF) (2023).

[41] Ibid.

[42] UN News (2021).

[43] State Council Information Office of the People's Republic of China (2021).

technologies, such as fuel facilities for eco-friendly ships and port electrification, to reduce GHG emissions across maritime transport.

Financial Assistance

Financial assistance is crucial alongside policy support for the construction of eco-friendly ships. The Ministry of Oceans and Fisheries provides subsidies of approximately 10% of the new ship price to business operators who dismantle or sell old ships and replace them with eco-friendly vessels through the Korea Ocean Business Corporation (KOBC n.d.). Moreover, South Korea plans to expand government subsidies and establish a public fund of up to KRW 4.5 trillion to support subordinated loans.[44] To further stimulate private investment in vessels, the country intends to offer benefits such as reduced financing interest rates through green finance, issuance of green bonds, and the introduction of security tokens.[45]

Considering the nature of South Korea-China ferry companies, which include small and medium-sized shipping firms and Korean-Chinese joint ventures, tailored financial support plans are essential. Special guarantees via public funds and the leasing of environmentally-friendly vessels built by public ship owners should be explored. Additionally, a green financial support system between South Korea and China to initially aid in the construction of eco-friendly car ferries sailing between the two countries should be established. The South Korea-China car ferries operating in the Northeast three provinces of China are managed by joint ventures between the two nations. Given that all these vessels are over 25 years old, urgent action is required to build replacements. A successful decarbonization strategy in international shipping hinges on the construction of environmentally friendly vessels and close cooperation between the private sector and government in providing financial support.

Conclusion

This study explores the current safety and regulatory issues concerning South Korea-China car ferries, particularly those operating between Incheon Port and ports in China's Northeast three provinces. It makes a meaningful contribution to the field by addressing a critical research gap: the lack of legal and policy-focused studies examining the safety management of aging international ferry routes in this strategically important Northeast Asian corridor. While previous research has largely centered on European ferry systems or domestic Korean shipping, this study

---

[44] Yum (2022).

[45] KDI (2024).

is among the first to systematically evaluate the regulatory frameworks and safety challenges of international ferry operations between South Korea and Northeast China.

This study is summarized as follows. First, South Korea and China signed the Agreement on Maritime Transport in 1993 to enhance marine transportation efficiency between the two countries. Since 2013, ten ferry routes have been established through the South Korea-China Maritime Transportation Meeting, connecting Incheon Port to destinations such as Weihai, Tianjin, Qingdao, Dalian, Dandong, Yantai, Shidao, Yingkou, Qinhuangdao, and Lianyungang. Among these routes, three (Yingkou, Dalian, and Dandong) are situated in China's Northeast three provinces, serving as key logistics hubs for inland cargo from Northeast China and the Far East. However, the operation of vessels over 25 years old on these ferry routes raises concerns about compliance with international safety standards and national regulations, both of which impose age limits that prohibit the operation of passenger ships over 30 years old. This situation emphasizes the urgent necessity of vessel replacement and improved safety management.

The key findings of this study indicate that aging vessels on South Korea-China ferry routes require enhanced safety oversight and timely replacement to prevent maritime accidents and ensure passenger protection. In particular, bilateral cooperation between South Korea and China is essential to strengthen regulatory enforcement, establish joint safety management systems, and promote the construction of new vessels. Furthermore, given the global move toward decarbonization and the IMO 2050 net-zero strategy, any replacement vessels should also align with international environmental and safety standards.

Given the pivotal role that South Korea-China ferries play in diplomatic relations, cultural exchange, and economic development, policy support and cooperation between the two countries are essential for facilitating the replacement and construction of environmentally friendly vessels in alignment with international decarbonization goals. Advancing and disseminating green ship technologies-such as hydrogen fuel cell propulsion and ammonia fuel propulsion systems-will be crucial for leading the adoption of eco-friendly solutions in the shipping and shipbuilding industries of both nations.

References

Alandia (2022) Evolving Ship Design & Maintenance https://alandia.com/article/evolving-ship-design-maintenance/. Accessed 21 Sept 2025

Armstrong C (1990) South Korea's "Northern Policy". Pac Rev 3(1):35

Choi J, Lim S (2023) Analysis for Circumstance of Maritime Transport in the Chinese Northeastern Three Provinces Towards Sustainable New Northern Policy. J Korea Soc Comp Information 28(4):121; Incheon Port Authority http://www.icferry.or.kr/eng/intrl/nvg/realtimelist.do?menuKey=560 accessed 13 Feb 2024

Clarkson (2024) Green Technology & Alternative Fuel Uptake. https://www.clarksons.com/home/news-and-insights/2024/green-technology-alternative-fuel-uptake/, Accessed 21 Sept 2025

Database of Japanese Politics and International Relations (1993) The Agreement on Maritime Transport between Government of the Republic of Korea and Government of the People's Republic of China. Ministry of Foreign Affairs of ROK. https://worldjpn.net/documents/texts/CHKR/19930527.T1E.html. Accessed 21 Sept 2025

EMSA (2024) 'Alternative Sources of Power'. https://emsa.europa.eu/sustainable-shipping/alternative-fuels.html. Accessed 2 Feb 2024

Enforcement Rule of Marine Transportation Act of Republic of Korea. https://elaw.klri.re.kr/kor_service/lawView.do?hseq=56966&lang=ENG. accessed 8 March 2024

Fan H, Lyu J, Wang S, Gong X (2024) Leverage Rule-Based Bayesian Network on Assessing Straits/Canals Resilience Performance on a Risk Coupling Analysis Perspective. Marit Policy Manag:1

ICCT (2013) Long-term potential for increased shipping efficiency through the adoption of industry-leading practices International Council on Clean Transportation White Paper https://theicct.org/wp-content/uploads/2021/06/ICCT_ShipEfficiency_20130723.pdf. Accessed 21 Sept 2025

IMO (2018) Initial IMO Strategy on Reduction of GHG Emissions from Ships

IMO, 'IMO Strategy on Reduction of GHG Emissions from Ships. Resolution MEPC.377(80), adopted on 7 July 2023' https://wwwcdn.imo.org/localresources/en/MediaCentre/PressBriefings/Documents/Resolution%20MEPC.377(80).pdf. accessed 21 Sept 2025

Incheon Port Authority (2023) 2023 Incheon Port Major Statistics https://www.icpa.or.kr/article/list.do?menuKey=3864&boardKey=224. Accessed 21 Sept 2025

ITF (2018) Decarbonising Maritime Transport: Pathways to Zero-Carbon Shipping by 2035. https://www.itf-oecd.org/sites/default/files/docs/decarbonising-maritime-transport-2035.pdf. accessed 21 Sept 2025

Jacoby M (2022) The Shipping Industry Looks for Green Fuels. Chemical and Engineering News https://cen.acs.org/environment/greenhouse-gases/shipping-industry-looks-green-fuels/100/i8. accessed 21 Sept 2025

Jeon H-D, Park Y-S, Oh Y-S (2017) A Study on the Improvements of the Safety Management of Korea-China Car Ferries through a Review of Age of Ships. Maritime Law Rev 29(2):145

Jung H-J, Jo G-S, Yeo G-T (2014) An Analysis on Efficiency of Car-Ferry Shipping Companies in Korea-China routes. J Shipping Logistics 301:81

KDI (2024) Korea Unveils Roadmap for Net Zero in Shipping by 2050. https://www.argusmedia.com/en/news-and-insights/latest-market-news/2422258-korea-unveils-roadmap-for-net-zero--in-shipping-by-2050. accessed 21 Sept 2025

Kim Y-S, Hong J-P, Shimo H-W et al (2018) Study on a Fully Electrified Car Ferry Design Powered by Removable Battery Systems. J Ocean Eng Technol 35(1):1

KOBC (Korea Ocean Business Corporation). n.d. "Environment-Friendly Ship Support Program." https://www.kobc.or.kr/ebz/eng/contents.do?mId=0301020000

Korea International Trade Association (KITA) (2021) South Korea's Export Sector Signals Caution with Its Heavy Reliance on China, Prompting an Urgent Need to Fortify Supply Chain. https://www.kita.net/board/totalTradeNews/totalTradeNewsDetail.do?no=72941&siteId=1. Accessed 21 Sept 2025

Korea Pro (2024) South Korea and China extend ferry lifespan to 15 years to stabilize routes. https://koreapro.org/2024/09/south-korea-and-china-extend-ferry-lifespan-to-15-years-to-stabilize-routes/. accessed 21 Sept 2025

Lee, M-g, Park E-H (2018) Seoul's City Diplomacy towards the Three Northeastern Provinces of China: Strategies and Policies (The Seoul Institute, 2018). available at https://www.si.re.kr/bbs/view.do?key=2024100039&pstSn=1904290006 (accessed 8 March 2024)

Lee J (2019) Korea's New Southern Policy: Motivations of "Peace Cooperation" and Implications for the Korean Peninsula. The Asian Institute for Policy Studies Issue Brief:1

Lee H-J, Yoo S-H, Huh S-Y (2020) Economic Benefits of Introducing LNG-Fuelled Ships for Imported Flour in South Korea. Transp Res Part D: Transp Environ 78:102220

Lee H, Pham H-T, Chen M, Choo S (2021) Bottom-Up Approach Ship Emission Inventory in Port of Incheon Based on VTS Data. J Adv Transp:5568777
Maritime Press (July 2023) Interview—Park Jun-young, Chairman of the Korea-China Carry Association. https://www.haesainfo.com/news/articleView.html?idxno=38619. accessed 21 Sept 2025
Ministry of Oceans and Fisheries (MOF) (2023) Eco-Friendly Ship Policies. https://www.mof.go.kr/doc/ko/selectDoc.do?docSeq=48839&menuSeq=971&bbsSeq=10. accessed 21 Sept 2025
Moon H, Park W, Hendrickson T et al (2025) Exploring the cost and emissions impacts, feasibility and scalability of battery electric shipping. Nat Energy 10:41
Safety4Sea (2023) Clarksons Research: 2023 Saw 539 New-Build Orders for Alternative Fuelled Vessels. https://safety4sea.com/clarksons-research-2023-saw-539-newbuild-orders-for-alternative-fuelled-vessels/. accessed 21 Sept 2025
Shipper's Journal (n.d.) Container Shipping Volume between South Korea and China Has Reached Its Lowest Point in Six Years. http://www.shippersjournal.com/news/article.html?no=28435. accessed 21 Sept 2025
State Council Information Office of the People's Republic of China (October 2021) Responding to Climate Change: China's Policies and Actions. http://www.ncsc.org.cn/yjcg/cbw/202111/P020211117406748792288.pdf. accessed 21 Sept 2025
Su M, Lee H, Wang X, Bae S-H (2024) Fuel consumption cost prediction model for ro-ro carriers: a machine learning-based application. Marit Policy Manag:1
UN News (2021) China headed towards carbon neutrality by 2060; President Xi Jinping vows to halt new coal plants abroad. https://news.un.org/en/story/2021/09/1100642. accessed 21 Sept 2025
UNCTAD (2024) Review of Maritime Transport 2024: Towards a Green and Just Transition https://unctad.org/publication/review-maritime-transport-2024. Accessed 21 Sept 2025
Wang B (2013) Logistics development at Dalian port to revitalize Northeast China. Ritsumeikan J Asia Pacific Stud 32:137
Yum J (2022) Korea's Green Shipping Pathways: The Korean Shipping Landscape and Policy Recommendations for Ocean-Climate Leadership in Shipping. Pacific Environment https://www.pacificenvironment.org/wp-content/uploads/2022/12/sfoceng-PE-shipping-report_1208%EC%B5%9C%EC%A2%85.pdf. accessed 21 Sept 2025
Zhang Y, Qin J (2022) Development of Transportation Logistics under the Belt and Road Initiative with Northeast China as an Example. In: The Belt and Road: Industrial and Spatial Coordinated Development. Springer Nature, p 311

Chapter 7
Ship Collision Under Chinese Maritime Law: Legislation and Judicial Precedents

Jiancuo Qi

Introduction

In April 2025, the Maritime Safety Administration of the Ministry of Transport issued the *Marine Safety Bulletin*,[1] which shows the collision accident has in trend to increase. Records from the Shanghai Maritime Court's handling of ship collision cases[2] over the past four years reveal that the annual number of ships entering and leaving the Shanghai Port is more than 1.5 million. During this period, the court has dealt with 203 cases involving various types of ship collision disputes. Navigation has been inherently risky since antiquity, as the unique conditions at sea—coupled with natural disasters and accidents—have led to damage to ships, cargo, and passengers. These incidents often give rise to maritime disputes concerning the allocation of liability. Such maritime events can significantly impact national interests, especially when international parties are involved, influencing both foreign-related maritime legislation and the promotion of shipping business.

Ship collisions can result in massive damage, personal injuries, and environmental pollution. Furthermore, wrecked ships that have sunk, whether due to collision or intentional disposal, pose continued threats to navigation safety and the marine environment.[3]The principles governing ship collisions have evolved from ancient

Jiancuo Qi. B.A. (Dalian Maritime Univ.), LL.M. (Swansea U.), Ph.D(Korea Univ.).

[1] Marine Safety Bulletin by the Maritime Safety Administration of the Ministry of Transport on Recent Collisions Between Commercial and Fishing Vessels. Available at: https://news.sol.com.cn/html/2025-04-28/A37FCE04B4F9463D9.shtml.

[2] Minghua (2019), p. 3.

[3] James (2013), p. 9.

J. Qi (✉)
COSCO (H.K) Shipping Co, Ltd., Hongkong, P.R. China

J. Choi (ed.), *Public Maritime Law in Asia*, International Law in Asia,
https://doi.org/10.1007/978-981-95-7037-9_7

maritime practices and customs, eventually becoming codified in modern maritime law.[4] A key milestone occurred in 1840[5] when Trinity House formalized existing maritime customs in regulatory form. Later, the 1846 Steam Navigation Act (SNA) incorporated these regulations, giving them statutory force and imposing penalties on shipmasters who violated them.[6] With the advancement of technology and shipping practices, the International Regulations for Preventing Collisions at Sea (COLREG),[7] first adopted in 1972 under the auspices of the IMO, replaced the earlier 1960 Collision Regulations. Since 1980, these regulations have been incorporated into Chinese law.

To regulate ship collisions and the damages resulting from such accidents, the Chinese government has enacted various statutes, including the Maritime Code of the People's Republic of China (1992),[8] and has ratified key international conventions such as the 1910 Collision Convention[9] and the 1972 COLREG. Chapter VIII of the 1992 Maritime Code governs ship collisions and applies to all vessels[10] navigating the sea and adjacent navigable waters,[11] except for military and government vessels.[12] Additionally, the Supreme People's Court of China has issued several judicial interpretations that clarify the application of relevant laws. This paper provides an in-depth analysis of China's legislative and judicial framework concerning ship collisions, focusing on applicable domestic laws, the allocation of collision liability, and compensation for damages.

Applicable Laws on Ship Collisions in China

China's maritime legal framework is comprehensive, encompassing international conventions, domestic maritime legislation, basic civil laws, administrative regulations, and judicial interpretations issued by the Supreme People's Court.

The 1992 Maritime Code stipulates that international treaties acceded to by the People's Republic of China shall prevail over domestic laws in cases of conflict. Specifically, Article 142 of the Application of Law in Civil Relations with Foreigners asserts that international treaties will take precedence unless China has made a

---

[4] Nicholas J. Healy, "Maritime Law," *Encyclopædia Britannica*. Available at: https://www.britannica.com/topic/maritime-law.

[5] Aleka (2013), p. 388.

[6] Ibid.

[7] *Convention on the International Regulations for Preventing Collisions at Sea*, 1972 (COLREGs).

[8] *The Maritime Code of the People's Republic of China*, adopted November 7, 1992, entered into force July 1, 1993.

[9] *Convention for the Unification of Certain Rules with Respect to Collision between Vessels*, Brussels, September 23, 1910 (adopted by China in 1994).

[10] Yuzhuo (2015), p. 637.

[11] China Maritime Code (1992) [CMC 199], Chap. VIII [Collision of Ships].

[12] Ibid.

reservation[13]on the provisions in question. This approach is consistent across various domains of Chinese law, such as the 1982 Trademark Law and the 1984 Patent Law, which adopt provisions from international conventions.[14]

As a result, international treaties that China has ratified have direct domestic legal effect.[15] If discrepancies arise between international treaties and domestic laws, the provisions of the relevant international treaty will apply.[16] However, despite the clear tendency toward prioritizing international conventions, China's legal system has not yet fully integrated these treaties into the broader domestic legislative framework, and there remain areas in which the rules on ship collisions require further development.

When it comes to the 1910 Collision Convention, Chinese law stipulates that its provisions shall apply if they differ from domestic law. However, Chapter VIII of the 1992 Maritime Code serves as a special law governing ship collision disputes and takes precedence over the 1910 Collision Convention. Thus, in cases of ship collision disputes, Chinese courts primarily apply the 1992 Maritime Code, with international conventions acting in a supplementary capacity where the Code lacks specific provisions.

In addition to the 1992 Maritime Code and the 1910 Collision Convention, general tort law is also applicable to ship collision disputes in China, particularly when determining liability. China's adoption of the 1972 COLREG further regulates vessel maneuvering and the assessment of liability in ship collision cases.[17]The COLREG serves as the global standard for maritime conduct, with some variations allowed by local regulations. Ships navigating through different jurisdictions must adhere not only to the COLREG but also to any specific local navigational rules.

Furthermore, all ships, as defined by the 1992 Maritime Code, must comply with the provisions of the COLREG, with failure to do so constituting prima facie evidence of negligence. Although the COLREG does not directly create civil liability, it plays a critical role in determining fault and liability in ship collision cases. The Application of Law in Civil Relations Concerning Foreign Affairs[18] and Chapter XIV of the 1992 Maritime Code guide Chinese courts in determining the applicable law in international ship collision disputes. When determining the law governing a ship collision case, courts consider the law of the location where the incident occurred, while cases involving collisions on the high seas fall under the jurisdiction of the court hearing the case.[19] Additionally, the Regulations for Preventing

---

[13] CMC 1992, art. 268(1).

[14] Civil Law of the People's Republic of China, art. 142.

[15] The Trademark law of People Republic of China, 1982, revised in 1993, 2001, 2013, 2019.

[16] The Patent Law of People Republic of China 1984, revised in 1992, 2000, 2008.

[17] *The Esso Brussels* (1972) (Q.B.).; it was held that the Colregs and unwritten rules of good seamanship were only applicable insofar as the law of the place of the collision made them so.

[18] Both two laws regulate the application of law in relation to foreign related matters.

[19] 1992 CMC, art 273.

Collisions on Inland Waters (1991) apply to incidents occurring in inland waters,[20] providing a framework for liability distribution in such cases. Lastly, the China Maritime Traffic Safety Law[21] offers specific guidelines for navigating safety, investigation, and legal liability related to maritime incidents.

Ship Collisions in the 1992 CMC

Articles 1 and 13 of the 1910 Collision Convention establish the scope of ship collisions and related damages, yet they do not explicitly define the term "ship collision."[22] Article 165 of the 1992 CMC, however, offers a more precise definition, stating that a "collision of ships" refers to an incident arising from the physical contact between ships at sea or in other navigable waters adjacent thereto.[23] Furthermore, Article 170 stipulates that the provisions of this chapter apply not only to the ships involved but also to other ships, persons, and goods on board that have suffered property losses due to improper operations or non-compliance with navigational regulations, even if no actual collision occurs between vessels.[24]

The definition of "ship" in the 1992 CMC specifically excludes military and public service vessels, as well as small vessels of less than 20 tons gross tonnage,[25] thereby excluding collisions between military or official vessels from the scope of the 1992 CMC.[26] In contrast, the 1972 COLREG (Convention on the International Regulations for Preventing Collisions at Sea) applies to all vessels navigating the high seas or waters connected to the high seas that are navigable by seagoing vessels.

While the 1992 CMC mandates physical contact for a collision to occur, it is important to note that it also addresses situations where no direct physical contact occurs between ships. According to Article 170, it is not necessary for a direct collision to take place for the affected party to claim damages. The law allows for claims based on improper maneuvers or non-compliance with navigation rules by another vessel, even if no collision actually occurred.[27] In the case of MV Jia Yang 6,[28] the Wuhan Maritime Court ruled that although no direct collision took place between MV Jia Yang 6 and MV Shunjiang 2827, the avoidance maneuvers taken by the vessels led to subsequent damages and collisions with other vessels. As a

[20] Order No. 30 of the Ministry of Communications of the People's Republic of China (1991).

[21] Maritime Traffic Safety Law of the People's Republic of China, 1983.

[22] Convention for the Unification of Certain Rules with Respect to Collision between Vessels, 1910, arts. 1, 3.

[23] CMC 1992, art. 165.

[24] CMC 1992, art. 170.

[25] Supreme People's Court of China (2017).

[26] See Yuzhuo (1998), p. 256.

[27] 1992 CMC, art. 170.

[28] Wuhan Maritime Court (2018).

result, the court determined that an indirect collision had occurred, and both ships bore tort liability based on their respective faults.[29]

Proportional Liability for Ship Collisions

Maritime judges face significant challenges in determining the proportion of liability in ship collision cases, given the complexity of such incidents and the often limited legal provisions. The lack of detailed rules for apportioning collision liability in China has led to inconsistent and, at times, arbitrary decisions. The basis for fault classification in ship collisions typically follows the 1972 COLREG, along with local navigational rules applicable to the location of the collision. As British judge Wright observed in the MacGregor case, the apportionment of liability in ship collisions is highly dependent on the specific facts of each case, including the navigational environment at the time of the collision.[30]

Liability Under General Tort Law

Under Chinese tort law, liability for torts is generally categorized into fault-based liability, presumption of fault liability, and no-fault liability.[31] In the absence of specific legal provisions to the contrary, fault-based liability serves as the default principle in tort cases. The principles of presumption of fault and no-fault liability are considered exceptions and are governed by explicit legal provisions, primarily under the Tort Liability Law. The provisions on presumption of fault and no-fault liability all use the term 'legal provisions'.[32] From the perspective of literal interpretation, the legal provisions mainly refer to the provisions of the Tort Liability Law; that is, the imputation principle is only applicable to the provisions of the Tort Liability Law. In the absence of special provisions in the law, the imputation principle cannot be applied.

(a) Fault-based Liability: This principle holds that the actor is liable for infringing upon another's civil rights due to fault, where fault forms the basis for establishing responsibility and the scope of liability.[33]
(b) Presumption of Fault Liability: Under this rule, if an offending act occurs, the law presumes fault on the part of the actor, though the actor can rebut this

[29] Ibid.

[30] *The McGregor* [1943] A.C. 197 (H.L.)

[31] Tort Liability Law of the People's Republic of China, Chapter II, arts. 6–7.

[32] Tort Liability Law, art 6 and art 7.

[33] Ibid.

presumption by proving that they were not at fault.[34] The purpose is to alleviate the victim's burden of proof in fault-based liability cases.

(c) No-fault Liability: In this instance, the actor is held liable regardless of fault, provided that their actions or those of someone under their management have caused harm to another party.[35] This principle prioritizes the protection of victims' rights and ensures timely relief.

The development of China's tort liability system reflects its unique legal traditions and national conditions. It aims to balance competing interests and has significantly contributed to the construction of China's legal framework while aligning with global civil legal cultures.

Principle of Proportional Liability

The 1992 CMC, like the 1910 Collision Convention, generally attributes collision damage liability based on fault. The Convention establishes three key scenarios for liability apportionment: First, If the collision is entirely the fault of one ship, that ship bears full responsibility.[36] Second, if both ships are at fault, the liability is divided in proportion to each ship's fault. Third, if fault is equal or indeterminate, the liability is equally divided between the ships involved. Liability for damage to ships, goods, and property is apportioned according to the above principles. If the collision results in personal injury or loss of life to a third party, the ships involved are jointly and severally liable for compensation.[37] Additionally, a ship that has paid compensation exceeding its prescribed share may seek recourse from the other ships involved.[38]

In the case of *Xinhua Company v. Xinda Company (2002),*[39] the Guangzhou Maritime Court applied the 1972 COLREG to determine the liability ratio based on the parties' failure to maintain a proper lookout. The M/V Fudong was found to be 40% responsible for the collision, while the other vessel, which violated the COLREG more significantly, bore 60% of the liability.

Similarly, in *Orient Overseas Container Line Limited v. BeiHai Honghai Shipping (The Orient Overseas Europe),*[40] the Supreme Court ruled that, in a crossing situation, the give-way vessel (M/V Xinghai 668) was primarily at fault for failing to take appropriate action. Compared with direct sailing ships, give-way ships have a greater obligation to avoid collisions. If the give-way ship fails to fulfil the obligation to give way as soon as possible, this may lead to the occurrence of an

[34] Ibid.

[35] Ibid

[36] CMC 1992, art. 168.

[37] CMC 1992, art. 168 and art. 169.

[38] Ibid.

[39] Guangzhou Maritime Court (2002).

[40] (2012)Min Ti Zi No.142 (SPC) (Retrial).

urgent situation, and the give-way ship shall bear the main responsibility for the collision accident. Therefore, the Orient Overseas Europe can independently take manoeuvring actions to avoid collision, but the ship on the port side should not turn to the left in any circumstance. Thus, in a final retrial the SPC held that, according to the first paragraph of Article 169 of the Maritime Law of the People's Republic of China, the two ships in the collision were at fault, and each ship was liable for compensation in proportion to the degree of fault. The liability was apportioned with Xinghai 668 bearing 60% of the responsibility and Orient Overseas Europe bearing 40%.[41]

Non-attributable Causes and Force Majeure in Collision Accidents

Article 167 of the 1992 CMC addresses collisions caused by force majeure or other factors not attributable to either party, providing that neither party shall be liable under such circumstances.[42] According to Article 6 of the Tort Law, a party is liable if it negligently infringes upon the civil rights of another, unless they can prove that the harm was caused by an unforeseeable or unavoidable event.[43]Nevertheless, if the parties involved in the collision can prove that the loss of the third party was due to force majeure or the victim's own fault, the liability will be exempted.[44]

In the Contract Law 1999, force majeure means that the objective situations cannot be foreseen, avoided or overcome. In judicial practice, the courts assess the collision disputes involving force majeure using the same principle. Article 118 of the Contract Law stipulates that the obligator should notify the counterparty in a timely manner to mitigate the loss that occurs to the counterparty. The obligator should provide evidence to prove that they are unable to perform the contractual obligation within a reasonable period. Once a party successfully establishes the argument of force majeure, the principle of fairness shall be used to determine whether liability should be exempted wholly or partially and how the two parties should share the costs incurred, provided that the contract is silent on these matters. The legal consequences of a force majeure event in China include termination of contract and exemption from contractual liability.

In *Hudong Shipbuilding v. Dongfang Dredging,*[45] the Shanghai High Court ruled that the defendant was not liable for a collision caused by a gale force 10 wind, which broke the cables anchoring the ship. The court found that the gale was unforeseeable and that the defendant had taken appropriate precautions.

---

[41] The SPC overturned the decision by the Guangzhou High Court that the 'Orient Overseas Europe' bears 60% of the responsibility.

[42] CMC 1992, art 167.

[43] Tort law of China, art 6.

[44] Tort law of China, art 26–31.

[45] Shanghai High Court (1999) (C.A.).

Quantification of Liability Proportions

Quantifying liability for ship collisions remains a complex and contentious issue, as courts are required to fairly assess the fault ratio of each party. Unfortunately, China has yet to adopt a standardized method for calculating fault ratios in such cases. In practice, maritime judges often base their decisions on the claims made by the parties involved, without a universally accepted standard or guidance on how to assess fault proportions. Maritime judges assign the proportion case by case based on the parties' claims. Meanwhile, it is noteworthy that neither judicial practice nor theoretical research has yet created a specific standard that is universally recognised and provides guidance for maritime judges to calculate the proportion of liability in various situations.[46] The accurate calculation of the collision liability ratio requires not only good legal knowledge, but also proficiency in navigation technologies. Related navigational rules can be international rules or other collision-avoidance rules that are valid locally at the place of the incident.[47]

The Korea Marine Safety Tribunal (KMST)[48] provides a model for China in this regard. Although the fault ratio determined by the KMST differs from that of civil courts, it is widely respected and accepted by the maritime community. Since 2007, the KMST has issued guidelines for determining fault in collision cases, which have contributed to more consistent and predictable rulings.[49]

While some scholars advocate for the use of complex mathematical models to quantify fault, these models are not yet practical for judicial use in China.[50] The evaluation of collision fault should be based on certain standards, such as collision avoidance rules or other route rules. In addition, it should be affected by multiple factors and investigated in the specific collision environment. It is suggested that fault should be evaluated using established collision-avoidance rules and navigational standards, considering the specific circumstances of each case. Fortunately, scholars from both South Korea[51] and China[52] have begun to call for the development of quantitative measures to unify the standards for assessing the fault ratio, particularly among the East Asian countries whose vessels frequently meet in the Yellow Sea and the East China Sea. In the future, the development of a unified, quantitative standard for assessing fault in ship collision cases, particularly in East Asia where cross-border maritime traffic is common, would enhance legal clarity and promote safer navigation.

---

[46] Chen (2014), pp. 35–47.

[47] Shanghai Maritime Court (2010).

[48] Korea Marine Safety Tribunal, "Accident Investigation Reports." Available at: https://www.kmst.go.kr.

[49] InHyeon (2011), p. 11.

[50] Hongkai (2019), p. 196.

[51] See InHyeon(2011), p. 11.

[52] See Hongkai (2019), p. 196.

Compensation for Damages

Property Damage

Damages for property loss arising from ship collisions encompass compensation for physical damage to the vessel and other property, expenses incurred, and environmental harm.[53] A claimant involved in a collision dispute may seek compensation for the following categories: (a) Property damage resulting from the collision; (b) Consequential losses and expenses arising from the collision; (c) Reasonable expenses or losses incurred in efforts to avoid or mitigate further damage; and (d) Loss of anticipated profit.

The general principle for property damage compensation is to restore the property to its original condition, or, if restoration is not feasible, to reimburse its estimated value.[54] Notably, no compensation is awarded for losses attributable to the claimant's fault, particularly where such losses involve aggravated damage.

In the event of total loss of a ship, compensation includes not only the value of the ship itself but also losses associated with onboard supplies such as fuel, materials, spare parts, and other items not part of the vessel's base value (e.g., fishing gear or equipment on a fishing vessel). Additionally, expenses like crew wages, repatriation fees, and other reasonable costs are compensable. In the case of The Orient Overseas Europe, the Supreme People's Court (SPC) ruled that fuel loss caused by leakage was not directly related to the collision, as the leakage occurred over a prolonged period after the incident. The court held that, had the vessel (OOCL Europe) inspected the hull and identified the fuel leak promptly, the damage could have been mitigated. As OOCL Europe failed to act quickly, and the leak was not discovered until 24 hours after the collision, the court denied compensation for fuel losses.[55]

The value of the ship is typically determined by the market price of similar vessels at the time of the collision. In cases where no comparable market prices exist at the location of the collision, the price of similar ships at the port of registry or the average market price in other regions may be used. If such market data is unavailable, the original construction or purchase price, adjusted for depreciation, is employed.[56] In The Orient Overseas Europe, OOCL UK sought to reassess the vessel's purchase and modification costs based on investigation records from the competent authorities. However, the evidence presented by Beihai Shipping Company was deemed more probative,[57] and the SPC determined the ship's value based on the original purchase price, applying an 8% annual depreciation rate.

The calculation of time loss is restricted to the reasonable period required to secure a replacement vessel, with a maximum duration of 2 months. The loss of hire

[53] Provisions on Compensation for Vessel Collision (1995), arts. 1–3, 8, 10.

[54] Ibid, art 1. art 2.

[55] The Orient Oversea Europe, Ibid.

[56] Provisions on Compensation for Vessel Collision 1995, art 8.

[57] Several Provisions on Evidence in Civil Litigation, art. 77.

is generally assessed based on the average net profit of voyages immediately before and after the collision. In the absence of such voyages, the average net profit from other comparable voyages is used.[58]

Compensation for partial damage to the ship includes reasonable costs for temporary repairs, permanent repairs, auxiliary services, and maintenance. However, the following conditions apply: (a) The ship should be repaired locally, unless the claimant can demonstrate that repairing the ship elsewhere would reduce losses or save costs; If the ship can continue to operate after temporary repairs, the requester is responsible for the temporary repairs. (b) Compensation is limited to the repair costs directly associated with the collision damage, excluding losses from other accidents or routine maintenance.[59]

Additional compensation includes reasonable salvage fees, costs for surveys, wreck removal, and the establishment of wreck signs, as well as expenses related to towage, freight loss, and other reasonable costs incurred during the voyage.[60] Compensation for time lost due to partial damage is limited to the reasonable period required for actual repairs, including time for docking, inspection, and other necessary procedures.[61]

If a ship causes damage to a third party's property through collision, compensation is required.[62] In addition to the principal damages, any interest losses must also be reimbursed. If the ship retains residual value after salvage, this amount must be deducted from the total compensation.[63]

Property Damage

The compensation for goods damaged or lost in a ship collision is calculated based on the value of the goods at the time of shipment. In cases of total loss, the claimant may also recover the freight and insurance premiums paid, minus any saved expenses.[64] In cases of damage to goods, compensation is based on repair costs or the salvage value of the goods, with any saved costs deducted from the actual value of the goods. If the collision delays the delivery of goods, the compensation should include the actual value of the goods, plus the difference between the expected profit and the market price at the time of delivery. However, the expected profit may not exceed 10% of the actual value of the goods.[65]

---

[58] Provisions on Compensation for Vessel Collision 1995, art 10.

[59] Ibid, art 3.(2).

[60] Ibid, art 3.

[61] Ibid, art 10.

[62] Supreme People's Court of China (2005), art. 131.

[63] Provisions on Compensation for Vessel Collision 1995, art 6.

[64] Beijing High Court (2019) (C.A.).

[65] *Interpretation on Compensation for Personal Injury* (2003), arts. 17, 25.

Freight Loss

In instances where a collision leads to off-hire of a time-chartered vessel, or the charterer refuses to pay hire due to the collision, the hire loss is calculated based on the off-hire period or non-payment, deducting any expenses saved due to the off-hire or non-payment.[66] Similarly, in cases where the loss or damage to goods results in freight loss, the amount of uncollected freight is calculated, deducting any saved expenses.[67]

Personal Injury

Under the Interpretation on Compensation for Personal Injury (2003), claims for personal injury may include medical expenses and lost income due to absence from work.[68] Specifically, compensation covers medical costs, loss of income, nursing care expenses, transportation, accommodation, and necessary nutrition. In cases of disability, compensation is determined based on the degree of incapacity and the average per capita income in the court's jurisdiction, with compensation provided for up to 20 years from the date of the injury.[69] In the event of death due to a ship collision, compensation includes funeral expenses and death benefits, along with claims for mental distress.[70]

The Interpretation on Compensation for Mental Distress (2001) allows claims for mental distress, but the claimant must prove that the distress is severe. If the claimant fails to provide sufficient evidence of the severity of the distress, the claim may be rejected.[71] Relatives of the deceased are also allowed to file claims for mental distress compensation, with the amount determined by factors such as the fault of the responsible party, their economic capacity, and the consequences of the infringement.[72]

Liable Persons

Pursuant to Article 4 of the Provision on Vessel Collision (2008), the owner of the vessel is liable for compensation arising from a ship collision. During the period of bareboat charter, the bareboat charterer assumes liability for the collision, provided

[66] Ibid, art.11.

[67] Ibid.

[68] Ibid, art.17.

[69] Ibid, art. 25.

[70] Ibid, art 17.

[71] Qingdao Maritime Court (2015).

[72] Ibid, art.10.

the bareboat charter is registered.[73] Under the Regulations on the Registration of Ships (2014), both the owner and the bareboat charterer must register the vessel.[74] A ship that is not registered is not permitted to fly the Chinese flag,[75] and China reserves the right to board and inspect vessels suspected of lacking proper nationality registration.[76] Unregistered vessels are subject to punitive measures, including fines, revocation of nationality certificates, and confiscation.[77]

In China, the acquisition, transfer, and termination of ship ownership and bareboat charter must be formally registered; otherwise, such transactions cannot be invoked against bona fide third parties.[78] This registration requirement is based on the principle of property rights publicity, which seeks to protect the interests of third parties acting in good faith. If the ownership of a vessel changes but the registration is not updated, it can hinder the identification of the liable party in the event of an infringement. Therefore, the registered shipowner is considered liable.

The rationale behind holding the registered shipowner liable is rooted in the concept of fairness: those who benefit from the operation of a ship should bear the responsibility for any infringements. This ensures that victims are not unfairly burdened with the task of distinguishing between the registered shipowner and other parties who may have actual control over the vessel.[79] Another reason that the registered shipowner should be liable is that the registered shipowner should be the interested party in the ship's operation: if the ship's property rights change, or the ship is bareboat chartered, but it is not registered, this means that the registered shipowner has a close relationship with the new owner or bareboat charterer in terms of economic interests. According to the concepts of equity and fairness, those who benefit from the operation of the property should bear the liability for its property infringement.[80]

The bareboat charterer is also required to register their rights with the relevant authority, including the establishment, transfer, and termination of the bareboat charter.[81] Failure to do so renders the charter agreement ineffective against third parties. In such cases, the shipowner remains liable for the collision damages, although the bareboat charterer may be held jointly and severally liable under certain circumstances.[82]

---

[73] *Provisions on Vessel Collisions (2008), art. 4.*

[74] Regulations on the Registration of Ships (2014), arts. 4–6, 50–51.

[75] Ibid, art.4.

[76] See Jiancuo and Pengfei (2022), p. 18.

[77] Regulations on the Registration of Ships 2014, art 50,51.

[78] Property law of People Republic of China, 2007. Art 24. Similar provision can also be found in 1992 CMC, and, Regulations on the Registration of Ships 2014.

[79] See Yuzhuo and Zhiwen (2009), p. 926.

[80] Ibid.

[81] Regulations on the Registration of Ships 2014, art 6. 1992 CMC also made similar requirements.

[82] Shanghai High Court (2010).

In The Orient Overseas Europe case, Beihai Shipping Company filed a lawsuit against OOCL (the operator), OOCL UK (the bareboat charterer), and Swan (the registered shipowner), seeking joint and several liability for the collision. The court held that only the bareboat charterer, OOCL UK, should bear the responsibility for the collision, and neither OOCL nor Swan was liable.[83]

The manager or operator of the ship, if authorized to deal with ship collisions, may be held jointly liable with the shipowner or bareboat charterer if it is proven that their actions contributed to the collision.[84] Given the diversity of ship operators in modern maritime practice, it is challenging to standardize the legal status of ship operators and managers. Therefore, it is recommended that ship operators and managers not be classified as liable parties in ship collision cases under current legislation.

Hull Insurance and Indirect Collisions

The liability for collision under hull insurance is typically compensated by the insurer who underwrites the associated risks. The PICC 86 hull clauses incorporate collision liability arising from the insured vessel. However, there is significant ambiguity regarding the interpretation of 'collision' in Chinese maritime law. According to Article 165(2) of the 1992 CMC, a ship collision refers to a direct collision between two ships. Meanwhile, Article 170 of the same Code extends the application of Chapter VIII (ship collision)[85] to cases involving indirect collisions, even when no physical contact occurs. This distinction between direct and indirect collisions raises an important issue: whether hull insurance covers liability arising from indirect collisions. The scope of collision liability in hull insurance remains contentious in China, with court precedents diverging on the matter. The critical issue lies in defining the term 'collision' within the context of hull insurance. If indirect collisions are included under this definition, the hull insurer would be obligated to cover the damages resulting from such collisions. However, the concept of indirect contact remains vague, with various legal authorities offering conflicting interpretations.

On one hand, the ITC 83 (Institute Time Clauses) clearly excludes liability for collisions that do not involve physical contact. Additionally, the 1992 CMC[86] explicitly differentiates between direct and indirect collisions, suggesting that the latter should be treated separately from 'collisions'. Professor Philip Yang, for instance, contends that the term 'collision' does not encompass indirect contact between

---

[83] The Orient Oversea Europe, Ibid.

[84] Minutes of the second National Working Conference 2005, art.130.

[85] CMC1992, Chapter VIII.

[86] Ibid, art. 170.

vessels, thereby implying that hull insurers should not be liable for losses stemming from non-physical collisions.[87]

On the other hand, Professor Chu and Dr. Wang from Dalian Maritime University argue that the 1992 CMC does include indirect collisions as a form of collision under Article 170. They emphasize that marine insurance should align with the provisions of the CMC, which takes precedence over other regulations.[88] Furthermore, they advocate for an interpretation that favors the insured party when the insurance wording is ambiguous. According to this view, it is the insurer's responsibility to explicitly exclude indirect collision from the insurance coverage if such risks are to be excluded at all. Failure to make such exclusions clear in the policy could result in a waiver of the insurer's rights.[89] This approach also aims to prevent market distortions, as insured parties might otherwise pursue claims for direct collisions after experiencing indirect collisions, expecting to be compensated under the hull insurance.[90] The writer supports the latter viewpoint, as industry practices show a tendency for hull insurers, including those under PICC, to compensate for damages arising from indirect collisions in certain cases.

Burden of Proof in Ship Collisions

Liability for ship collisions is determined based on facts and evidence. The legal presumption of fault, previously a standard in collision liability, has been abolished in China under Article 5 of the 1910 Collision Convention. In accordance with this, relevant authorities must investigate the facts surrounding a collision. The facts, as agreed upon by the parties, serve as evidence in court, unless contradicted by sufficient evidence. The burden of proof rests with the party disputing the facts, requiring them to present adequate evidence to the contrary.[91]

In the Orient Overseas Europe case, the OOCL UK submitted a notarized Maritime Investigation Report by the Hong Kong Maritime Department during retrial. The report aimed to demonstrate that the Xinghai 668 vessel was unseaworthy at the time of the collision. The court acknowledged the authenticity of the report, noting that it was publicly available for inspection. However, the report did not include crew investigation data, as it relied on the crew findings by the China Maritime Safety Administration. As such, the report could not conclusively prove the unfitness of the Xinghai 668's crew. OOCL UK subsequently applied to obtain further accident investigation materials from the Guangdong Maritime Safety Administration. The Supreme People's Court (SPC) delegated the Guangzhou

[87] Philip (2008), pp. 27–73.

[88] Pengnan (2004), p. 288.

[89] Ibid.

[90] Haiping (2006).

[91] Provisions on Vessel Collision 2008, art 11.

Maritime Court to retrieve relevant materials, including ship certification, crew certification, and interview transcripts.[92]

However, the investigation materials, which primarily consisted of witness testimonies, lacked verification from Beihai Shipping Company, and the individuals involved in the investigation did not testify in court. Furthermore, the competent authority did not issue a formal accident investigation report or establish the crew's unseaworthiness. As such, the SPC ruled that the investigation materials did not qualify as evidence for determining the facts of the case, in accordance with Article 11 of the Provisions on Vessel Collision (2008). Consequently, the SPC did not accept the evidence submitted by OOCL UK regarding the unseaworthiness of the Xinghai 668.[93]

Conclusion

The formulation and implementation of the Tort Liability Law constitutes a fundamental pillar of Chinese civil and commercial legislation, regulating property and personal relationships between equal parties. This law also serves as a critical framework within the broader structure of the Civil Code, providing the legal basis for its further application. The codification of civil law in China marks a significant step forward in its legal development, signaling the country's ongoing efforts to establish a comprehensive legal order that underpins its market economy.

The collision liability system in Chinese maritime law shares a similar goal with the exemption and liability limitation framework in the 1992 CMC: both aim to protect the shipping industry through legal mechanisms. Although the Supreme Court has issued relevant judicial interpretations concerning the principle of liability for ship collisions and the scope of damage compensation, there remains a need for further refinement of China's tort liability framework.

Encouragingly, many Chinese scholars have recognized the limitations of the current law and have called for the compilation of a comprehensive maritime code. Learning from international best practices, such a code would better protect and promote shipping trade and the maritime economy. In fact, the revision of China's Maritime Law has already been placed on the legislative agenda, with preparations underway. The goal of this revision is to make the Maritime Law more systematic and adaptable, improving the regulation of maritime transport relations and safeguarding the rights and interests of all parties involved. This process also aims to provide a more robust framework to support the social and economic development of China's shipping industry. The revised law is expected to be finalized by 2023.

---

[92] *Several Provisions on Evidence in Civil Litigation*, Supreme People's Court of China, art. 17.

[93] The Orient Oversea Europe, Ibid.

References

Aleka M-S (2013) Modern maritime law and risk management. Informa Law, London
Beijing High Court (2019) China Huadian Engineering Co Ltd v CONTI JORK Shipping Ltd Jin Gao Min Si Zhong Zi No. 369. (C.A.)
Chen L (2014) Studies on ship collision liability in Chinese law. Shanghai Maritime University Press, Shanghai
China Maritime Code. The Maritime Code of the People's Republic of China. Adopted November 7, 1992, entered into force July 1, 1993
Guangzhou Maritime Court (2002) Guang Hai Fa Chu Zi No. 139
Haiping Z (2006) Judicial practice of ship collision in China. China Maritime Law J 23
Hongkai Z (2019) Maritime collision and liability. Maritime Law Press, Beijing
InHyeon K (2011) Ship collision law. Maritime Law Institute, Seoul
Interpretation on Compensation for Personal Injury (2003) Supreme People's Court of China
James (2013) The challenges and implications of removing shipwrecks in the 21st century. Lloyd's, London. https://www.lloyds.com/~/media/lloyds/reports/emerging%20risk%20reports/wreck%20report%20final%20version%20aw.pdf
Jiancuo Q, Pengfei Z (2022) Enforcement failures and remedies: review on state jurisdiction over ships at sea. J East Asia Int Law 14(1)
Korea Marine Safety Tribunal. "Accident Investigation Reports." Available at: https://www.kmst.go.kr
Minghua W (2019) Notification of Ship Collision Case Trial and Navigation Safety Status Was Released for the First Time in Shanghai. Navigation: 3
Nicholas JH. "Maritime Law." Encyclopædia Britannica.Available at: https://www.britannica.com/topic/maritime-law
Patent Law of the People's Republic of China, 1984 (amended 1992, 2000, 2008)
Pengnan L (2004) Comparative maritime collision law. Ocean Press, Beijing
Philip Y (2008) Collision liability under ITC 1983. Maritime Law Rev 17:27–73
Qingdao Maritime Court (2015) Zhu Xindong v Shen Zhouhang and Others, Qing Hai Fa Shi Chu Zi No. 116
Shanghai High Court (1999) Hu Gao Jing Zhong Zi No. 423 (C.A.)
Shanghai High Court (2010) Hongkong Changxin Shipping Service Co Ltd v Hachiuma Steamship Co Ltd, Hu Gao Min Si (Hai) Zhong Zi No. 74
Shanghai Maritime Court (2010) Jiangsu Weilun Shipping Co Ltd v Miranda Rose Co Ltd, Hu Hai Fa Shang Chu Zi No. 24, Guiding Case No 31
Supreme People's Court of China (2005) Minutes of the Second National Working Conference on Civil and Commercial Trials
Supreme People's Court of China (2017) M/V MIN NAN PING HUO 4572, Min Min Xia No. 71
Supreme People's Court of China. Several Provisions on Evidence in Civil Litigation
The Esso Brussels (1972) 1 Lloyd's Rep. 286
The McGregor [1943] A.C. 197
Tort Liability Law of the People's Republic of China
Trademark Law of the People's Republic of China, 1982 (amended 1993, 2001, 2013, 2019)
Wuhan Maritime Court. Yue 72 Min Te No. 50 (2018)
Yuzhuo S (1998) The maritime law dictionary. Peking University Press, Beijing
Yuzhuo S (2015) Maritime Law, 3rd edn. Law Press, Beijing
Yuzhuo S, Zhiwen L (2009) Special research on basic principles of maritime law in China. Maritime Law Press, Beijing

Chapter 8
Legal Framework for Marine Garbage and Plastic Waste Management in South Korea

Hojeong Dan

Introduction

The ocean covers approximately 70% of the Earth's surface, and hundreds of millions of diverse species are estimated to inhabit the marine environment. The ocean plays a crucial role in mitigating climate change by regulating climate and temperature, decomposing pollutants, and absorbing significant amounts of carbon dioxide. Furthermore, the ocean is a source of abundant resources and provides the foundation for various marine industries, including fishing, marine tourism, resource exploration, offshore plant construction, and artificial island construction. Thus, the ocean holds a crucial value for human life.

However, due to indiscriminate development and increased marine use, the ocean is becoming the final destination for various pollutants. It is estimated that eight million pieces of plastic enter the ocean every day, resulting in an annual influx of approximately 6.4 million tons.[1] Studies show that 5 to 12 million tons of plastic enter the ocean each year, equivalent to the equivalent of 2000 garbage trucks per day.[2] More than 800 marine species are directly affected by plastic entanglement or

Academic Research Professor at Korea Maritime & Ocean University, PhD in Law (University of Exeter, UK).

[1] Cefas (28 February 2019).

[2] Jambeck et.al. (2015), p. 769.

H. Dan (✉)
Korea Maritime & Ocean University, Busan, Republic of Korea
e-mail: danhojeong@kmou.ac.kr

J. Choi (ed.), *Public Maritime Law in Asia*, International Law in Asia,
https://doi.org/10.1007/978-981-95-7037-9_8

ingestion.[3] Marine plastics impede legitimate ocean use, including shipping, fishing, and tourism, and also impact marine safety, resulting in economic losses.

To address the negative impacts of marine plastics on the marine environment and our lives, the United Nations Environment Assembly (UNEA) agreed to establish a binding international agreement to directly regulate marine plastics. A total of five INC meetings have been held; the fifth was held in Busan, Korea, from November 25 to December 1, 2024. Unfortunately, the Plastics Convention failed to reach a conclusion, and the INC 5-2 meeting is scheduled to be held in Geneva, Switzerland, from August 5 to 14, 2025.[4]

Although no agreement was reached, the official INC-5 meeting was held in South Korea, and given the high expectations of the international community, Korea's role remains crucial. Therefore, this article introduces the current status of marine plastic pollution in South Korea and the current laws and regulations related to marine garbage,[5] and describes Korea's position and response to the International Plastics Convention.

Marine Garbage and Plastic Pollution in South Korea: Impact and Current Status

Impacts of Marine Garbage and Plastics

Just as many other oceans are facing serious threats from plastic pollution, Korea's marine environment is no exception. Plastic waste continues to enter Korea's coastal waters and oceans through various channels, including marine activities, land-based garbage, and the fishing and shipping industries. This causes serious damage to marine ecosystems, fisheries resources, and marine landscapes.

---

[3] Harding (2016), p. 9.

[4] UNEP (2025).

[5] The South Korean legislation uses the term *pyegimul*. The most representative law regarding waste in Korea is the 'Wastes Control Act.' This law aims to contribute to environmental conservation and the improvement of the quality of life of citizens by minimizing waste generation and disposing of generated waste in an environmentally friendly manner. The most representative law regarding the marine environment is the Marine Environment Management Act. This law aims to establish a legal basis for establishing a national comprehensive plan, integrated management of pollution sources, and policy implementation to ensure the sustainable use of environmentally friendly marine resources and effective conservation of the marine environment. The definition of waste under this act is adopted by the 'Management of Marine Garbage and Contaminated Marine Sediment Act.' While the Wastes Control Act, which governs general household waste, uses the term *waste*, marine environment-related laws use the term *garbage*. Therefore, this article will primarily use the term *garbage*. However, in cases where alternative terms such as litter or debris appear in the original text, those terms will be retained. Additionally, when compound terms like plastic waste or wastewater are more appropriate, waste will be used instead of garbage.

The damage to the marine ecosystem caused by marine plastic pollution in Korea has been clearly revealed through various studies and observations. A survey conducted by related organizations including the Korea Institute of Ocean Science and Technology (KIOST) from 2017 to 2023 found a total of 1280 pieces of plastic in 28 of the 34 dead sea turtles caught or stranded along the coast of Korea, which is 82%. In particular, loggerhead and green sea turtles were found to have a high incidence of plastic ingestion and entanglement, with an average of 38 pieces of plastic in their bodies per turtle.[6]

In addition, according to a 20-year data analysis from 2003 to 2023, a total of 428 marine organisms were damaged by marine plastic and marine garbage along the coast of Korea, and 77 species were damaged. There have been many reports of seabirds, especially black-tailed gulls, becoming entangled in fishing lines and hooks, and marine mammals, including sea turtles and dolphins, frequently becoming entangled in discarded fishing gear (abandoned, lost and wasted gear, hereafter referred to as ALDFG) and dying.[7] Such entanglement damage has been on the rise. Wildlife rescues and citizen reports include cases of sea swans with their beaks entangled in recreational fishing gear, sea swans caught in discarded gillnets, and plastic found in the intestines of sea turtles and whales.[8] Major sources of pollution include ALDFG, plastic bags, and single-use plastic packaging, which pose a serious threat to marine biodiversity and ecosystem health.[9] Plastic pollution also has a negative impact on marine ecosystems with high biodiversity, such as coral reefs and mangroves, and there are also research reports that more than 90% of organisms throughout the marine food chain are under the influence of plastic.[10] Moreover, 1902 microplastics were detected in the digestive organs of 12 large marine animals, including finless porpoises, right whales, and southern right whales, found dead on domestic beaches from 2019 to 2021, confirming that microplastic pollution is being introduced into marine organisms in large quantities.[11]

In addition, marine garbage poses a serious threat to the safety of ships internationally, as it can become entangled or clogged in ships' propellers, engines, and cooling water pipes, causing accidents such as drifting, engine failure, and fire.[12] Marine garbage also causes various secondary damages and is identified as a major cause of ship accidents internationally.[13] Ship accidents caused by marine garbage are also serious in South Korea. It is estimated that accidents caused by marine garbage such as ALDFG, ropes, and vinyl account for about 10% of all ship

---

[6] Yoon (30 Jun 2022).

[7] KIOST (12 Mar 2025).

[8] Ibid.

[9] Ibid.

[10] Mine et al. (2022), p. 7.

[11] Hong (12 Apr 2023).

[12] McIlgorm et al. (2022), p. 2.

[13] Werner et al. (2016), p. 7.

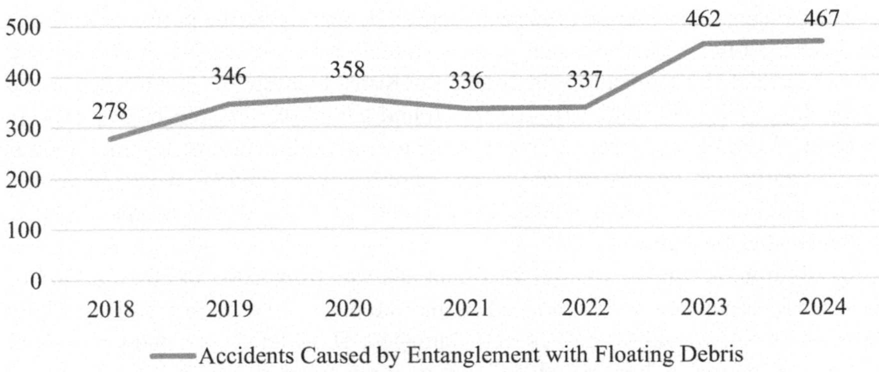

Fig. 8.1 Statistics of Accidents Caused by Entanglement with Floating Garbage *(Marine Accident Statistics Report, 2024)* (Marine Accident Statistics Report (2024) Ministry of Oceans and Fisheries, Korea Maritime Safety Tribunal, p. 18.)

accidents.[14] In particular, in the past 3 years (2022-2024), approximately 180 ship accidents caused by marine garbage occurred in the Gyeonggi Province alone,[15] and a total of 1120 accidents were reported nationwide during the same period.[16] These statistics clearly show the impact of marine garbage on ship safety and maritime traffic (Fig. 8.1).

In this way, South Korea's marine environment and ecosystem are suffering due to plastic. Furthermore, the possibility that microplastics accumulated in marine products will be ingested by humans is gradually increasing, and it is reported that the amount of microplastics consumed by Koreans is at a high level worldwide.[17]

The Current Status of Marine Garbage and Plastic Pollution in South Korea

The annual marine garbage generation in South Korea is estimated at about 145,000 tons, of which about 65.3% is generated on land and flows into the ocean through rivers, and the remaining 34.7% is directly generated in the ocean, such as from fishing activities.[18] Excluding vegetation (broken trees, grass, etc.) that temporarily flows in large quantities during the flood season, about 84,000 tons of marine

[14] Kim (8 Jul 2022).

[15] Choi (31 May 2024).

[16] Ministry of Oceans and Fisheries (2019), p. 40.

[17] Kim (02 Nov 2023).

[18] Policy Briefing of the Republic of Korea (25 Feb 2025).

Table 8.1 Estimated Annual Generation of Marine Plastics and Garbage in South Korea, 2018 (Policy Briefing of the Republic of Korea 2025)

		Estimated Amount (Excluding Vegetation)			Estimated Amount (Including Vegetation)	
Category	Sub—category	Marine Garbage	Marine Plastic	Ratio (%)	Marine Garbage	Ratio (%)
Land-based	River inflow	26,108	20,886	31	26,108	17.9
	Coastline	7554	6043	9	7554	5.2
	Flood-season vegetation	–	–	–	61,152	42.1
	Subtotal	33,662	26,930	40	94,814	65.3
Ocean-based	Fishing vessel operations	38,616	30,893	45.9	38,616	26.6
	Aquaculture	6462	5170	7.7	6462	4.4
	Port	5366	4293	6.4	5366	3.7
	Subtotal	50,444	40,355	60	50,555	34.7
Total		84,106	67,285	100	145,258	100

garbage is generated annually, of which 40% is of terrestrial origin and 60% is of marine origin (Table 8.1).[19]

About 88.9% of marine garbage collected from the coast of South Korea is plastic, which is a very high level of pollution even by international standards.[20] In particular, the west coast of Incheon and Gyeonggi Province and the Nakdong River Estuary are reported to have the highest concentration of microplastics on a global scale (Fig. 8.2).[21]

To address the serious problem of marine garbage, the Korean government, before the establishment of the Ministry of Oceans and Fisheries in 1996, local governments focused on collecting floating garbage from beaches and the ocean, and implemented activities such as operating port and fishing port cleaning ships once a month, coastal clean-up activities, and 'ocean cleaning campaigns' once a year. After the Ministry was established, more systematic management at the central government level began, and policy interventions such as collecting sediment garbage and purchasing marine garbage salvaged by fishermen during fishing operations were strengthened. In particular, since 2008, the 1st (2009), 2nd (2014), and 3rd (2019) master plans for marine garbage management have been established in order to establish a national response system for marine garbage management, and a comprehensive national management system has been transitioned from the prevention of marine garbage generation to collection and processing.[22]

[19] Ibid.

[20] Coastal garbage monitoring statistics, Ministry of Oceans and Fisheries, Marine Environment Information Portal. https://www.meis.go.kr/mli/monitoringInfo/stat.do.

[21] Ibid.

[22] Policy Briefing of the Republic of Korea, op. cit.

Fig. 8.2 Map of South Korea

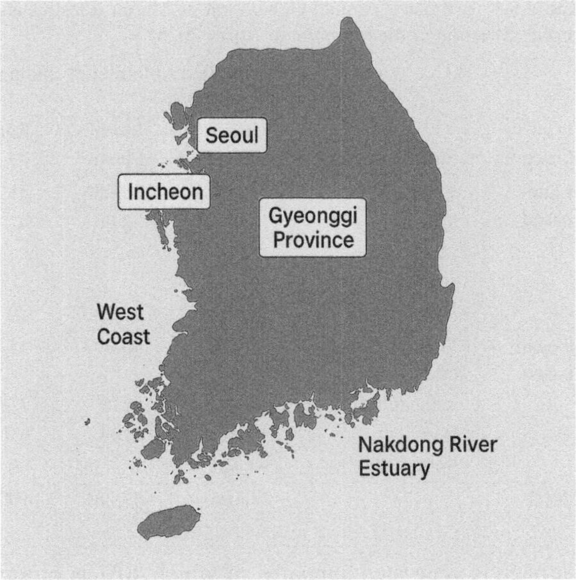

South Korea is making various policy efforts to reduce marine garbage, and the coastal garbage monitoring statistical survey conducted as part of this effort provides important data for quantitatively analyzing changes in the amount of plastic waste generated. In the second survey (since 2018), the weight of plastic waste accumulated on the coast in 100 m sections at 60 coastal locations nationwide was measured. The survey has been conducted regularly every 2 months since the survey area was expanded (Figs. 8.3, 8.4, 8.5 and 8.6).[23]

According to the results of a survey conducted in 2022 and 2023, about 88.9% of marine garbage collected from the coast is composed of plastic, indicating the seriousness of plastic pollution. Examining the origin of the garbage, 98.1% of all coastal waste originated domestically, while only 1.9% came from foreign sources. However, when viewed in terms of weight ratio, foreign-origin garbage accounts for 18.4%, which is not negligible.

According to coastal garbage monitoring statistics released by the Marine Environment Information Portal operated by the Ministry of Oceans and Fisheries, coastal garbage has shown a steady and stable trend since 2023.These results suggest that the generation of plastic marine garbage in domestic coastal areas is decreasing in the short term and has recently shown a stagnant trend at a certain level. This can be interpreted as being due to complex factors such as the effect of policy intervention and improved public awareness.

[23] Coastal garbage monitoring statistics, op. cit.

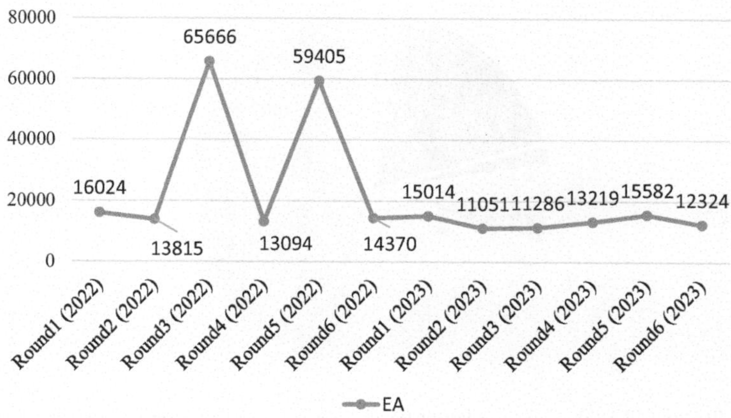

Fig. 8.3 Coastal Garbage Monitoring Statistics (EA) *(Coastal garbage monitoring statistics)*

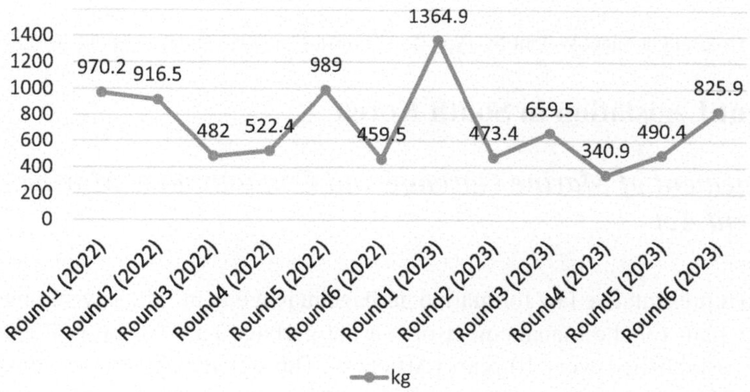

Fig. 8.4 Coastal Garbage Monitoring Statistics (kg) *(Coastal garbage monitoring statistics)*

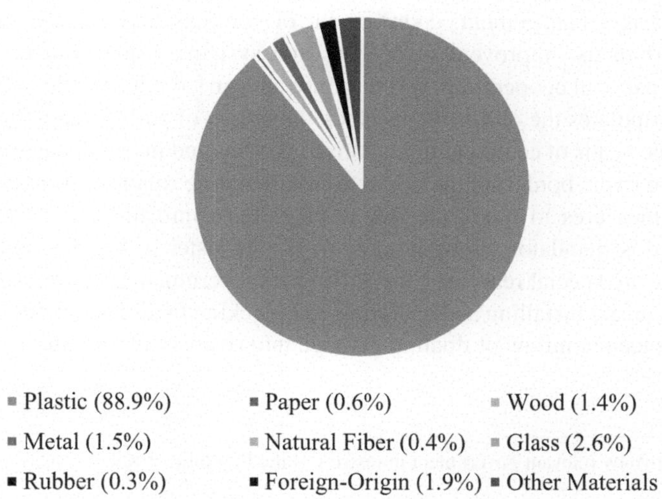

Fig. 8.5 Coastal Garbage: Number of Type (EA) *(Coastal garbage monitoring statistics)*

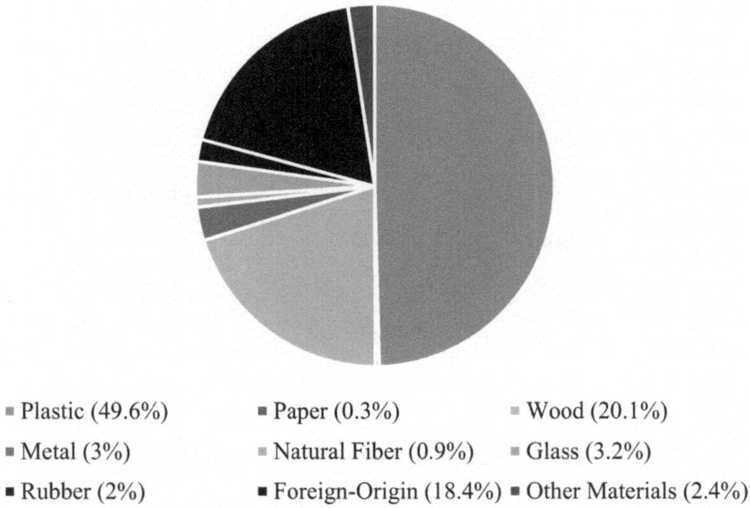

Fig. 8.6 Coastal Garbage: Weight by Type (kg) *(Coastal garbage monitoring statistics)*

Current Legislation in South Korea

Management of Marine Garbage and Contaminated Marine Sediment Act

This is a representative law for marine garbage management. The law stipulates that a master plan for the management of marine garbage and marine pollutant sediments be established every 10 years (Article 5). Through the operation of the Marine Garbage Management Committee, various agenda items and measures for reducing marine garbage are deliberated, coordinated, and mutually cooperated with by relevant ministries, public institutions, and experts. In addition, important policies on marine garbage management, coordination of conflicts between the central and local governments, improvement of laws and systems, establishment of master plans, international cooperation, and response are carried out (Article 5-2). The law explicitly stipulates the obligation to block the inflow of garbage into the ocean by requiring the heads of central administrative agencies and master local governments that manage rivers bordering the ocean to install marine runoff prevention facilities and other measures to block the inflow of garbage into the ocean (Article 11). Compliance is mandatory upon request by the Minister of Oceans and Fisheries unless there are special reasons. Currently, local governments, water resources corporations, etc. are installing and operating 132 blocking facilities (19,408 m) nationwide to reduce the inflow of floating garbage into rivers or the ocean.[24]

[24] Joint initiative by relevant government ministries of the Republic of Korea (2023), p. 4.

Through the marine garbage collection order system, collection orders are issued to those who have caused beach, floating, and sediment garbage. (Articles 12-14) In addition, as a measure to identify the cause of generation, monitoring of habitual occurrence areas (regions) and monitoring of dumping are conducted and regular surveillance activities are conducted.

This Act requires the designation of a specialized marine garbage investigation agency (Article 25) and the establishment and operation of a marine garbage and marine pollutant sediment management center (Article 27). The center regularly investigates and analyzes the current status, distribution, and types of marine garbage, and carries out related research, technology development, and policy support.

Necessary financial support must be provided to corporations or organizations involved in surveillance activities, damage prevention projects, and other related efforts to prevent the generation of marine garbage (Article 29). Institutional support mechanisms should be established to encourage private sector participation and to strengthen the cooperative framework between local communities and related organizations. In addition, an electronic information processing system for marine garbage must be established and operated (Article 30).

Act on the Promotion of Recycling of Fisheries By-Products

Fishery by-products[25] are by-products generated from the catching, harvesting, farming, processing, and selling of fishery products, and the amount of by-products discarded is relatively large compared to other agricultural and livestock products. However, since recycling[26] is not done properly, most of them are disposed of as business waste, which increases the burden on fishermen. In addition, in the process, they cause various environmental problems such as illegal dumping, landfilling, abandonment, wastewater, and foul odors, which pollute the surrounding landscape and environment.

Fishery by-products contain a large amount of useful ingredients such as calcium and protein, and thus have a high recycling value, making them highly recyclable as raw materials for food, fertilizer, feed, medicine, and cosmetics. Therefore, the relevant law was enacted to process fishery by-products in an environmentally friendly

---

[25] "Fisheries by-products" refers to bones, fins, entrails, skins, etc. that are produced incidentally in addition to the primary products during the process of catching, harvesting, cultivating, processing, and selling fishery products. (Article 2, Paragraph 2)

[26] "Recycling of fishery by-products" refers to manufacturing or processing fishery by-products into raw materials for finished products such as food, fertilizer, feed, cosmetics, and medicine, public water surface reclamation materials, building materials, desulfurization agents, and slaked lime, etc. (Article 2, Paragraph 3).

and sanitary manner and to promote their recycling, thereby efficiently utilizing fishery resources.[27]

The Master Plan for Recycling Fishery By-products is established based on the relevant law. (Article 5) The master plan sets out the basic goals and directions for promoting the recycling of fishery by-products. In addition, the Act mandates to research and develop environmentally friendly and hygienic treatment technologies and disseminate them, and install, operate and support resource recycling facilities.

Fisheries Act

This law establishes a legal basis for the use of biodegradable fishing gear and the real-name system for fishing gear, which can be a fundamental solution to the problem of ALDFG, in order to systematically manage fishing gear. Currently, regulations related to fishing gear are being developed to clarify the "fishing gear recovery system," which restricts fishing in specific areas for a certain period of time and then issues a gear recovery order to intensively collect ALDFG.

To promote the recovery of fishing gear and buoys, a "fishing gear deposit system" will be introduced to promote the full-cycle management of fishing gear and buoys and the voluntary recovery of marine garbage, thereby reducing marine garbage. (Article 81) Fishing gear deposits will be returned to purchasers of fishing gear, and any remaining deposits will be managed. (Article 82).

The system is an economic incentive-based system to prevent unauthorized dumping and loss of ALDFG, which are one of the main causes of marine garbage. In addition, since the installation of new fishing gear requires high costs, fishermen continue to use old fishing gear, which increases the risk of loss, so awareness of the importance of fishing gear management is also increased. To this end, the operation of the Fishing Gear Deposit Management Center (Article 83) and matters related to financial and technical support necessary for the management and operation of the national fishing gear deposit system are stipulated. (Article 84).

[27] The rationale for enacting the Act on the Promotion of Recycling of Fishery By-products was referenced, based on information from the Ministry of Government Legislation of the Republic of Korea.

National Plans and Policies

National Plans: Master Plan for Marine Garbage and Marine Pollutant Sediment Management

Management was further strengthened when the Management of Marine Garbage and Contaminated Marine Sediment Act was enacted in 2019 and the first Master Plan for Managing Marine Garbage and Contaminated Marine Sediments was established in 2021. Marine garbage disposal, which has shifted from passive collection centered on local governments to active collection at the central government level, is now managed in a planned and preventive manner.

The management direction is (i) shifting from marine garbage collection to the stage of preventing occurrence and reducing impacts, (ii) promoting decarbonization of marine garbage through a resource circulation approach, (iii) enhancing management capacity through science-based policy establishment and smart technology application, and (iv) realizing participatory policies that link with regions and cooperate with citizens.

To this end, the Ministry of Oceans and Fisheries announced the Master Plan for Managing Marine Garbage and Contaminated Marine Sediments in May 2021. This is a statutory plan pursuant to Article 5 of the Management of Marine Garbage and Contaminated Marine Sediment Act, and presents the basic direction of government policies on marine garbage, etc. for 10 years from 2021 to 2030. With the vision of 'A healthy future we all enjoy by creating a clean ocean environment' (Clean Ocean, Healthy Future), South Korea aims to reduce the amount of marine plastic waste by 60% by 2030 and to zero by 2050. The government have established a strategy to promote management of the full lifecycle of marine garbage, including prevention of generation, improvement of collection and transportation systems, promotion of processing and recycling, strengthening of management, and raising of public awareness.[28]

Strategies to Activate Marine Garbage Recycling

The 'Marine Garbage Recycling Activation Measures' were established by the government to improve the overall marine garbage collection, transportation, collection, and recycling system in line with the rapid growth of the domestic and international recycling market and the movement toward a circular economy society, and to increase the recycling of high value-added materials. This measure consists of four major strategies[29] and 11 promotion tasks, and aims to establish a raw

[28] Policy Briefing of the Republic of Korea, op. cit.

[29] The main tasks to be promoted include (i) strengthening fishing gear management, (ii) establishing a stable supply system for recycled raw materials, (iii) supporting companies participating in recycling, and (iv) forming and operating a public-private-research council.

material supply system that can be stably connected from marine garbage preprocessing to intermediate raw material production, final recycled material production, and demand supply by 2024, and to recycle more than 20% of the marine garbage collected by 2027.[30] A representative example is a plan to recycle a significant amount of plastic water bottles generated from ships. Previously, plastic water bottles discharged from ships were treated as port waste, but Yeosu Gwangyang Port Authority selectively collects them and recycles them to make branded clothing, and this revitalization measure will be expanded and applied to all ports. In addition, it includes a plan to promote the 'Bring Our Water Bottles Back and Circulate Them as Resources' campaign[31] to fishermen, which brings back plastic water bottles from fishing boats and recycles them.

Additionally, public institutions such as the Ministry of Oceans and Fisheries, the Navy, and the Coast Guard collect and recycle discarded ropes and illegal fishing gear confiscated through crackdowns. Furthermore, the plan includes easing regulations related to pretreatment and fostering pretreatment and recycling companies to facilitate the recycling of high-salinity marine garbage. Regulations will be improved by establishing new water quality standards for wastewater discharged directly from marine garbage pretreatment facilities, and companies participating in recycling will be given bonus points in marine garbage treatment bids. Furthermore, a public certification system for recycled marine garbage products will be introduced, along with the development of joint brands for recycled products, preferential treatment for entry into environmental industrial complexes, and support for technology start-ups.[32]

However, due to the lack of preprocessing facilities for marine garbage and the lack of establishment of separation and sorting, it is necessary to establish a marine garbage recycling ecosystem. Moreover, the government's role in promoting the consumption of recycled materials and products is important. In fact, the factor hindering the recycling of marine garbage is pointed out as economic feasibility. Among the annual collection amount, only 10% (annual collection amount of 120,000 tons) is suitable for recycling, and the reasons are pointed out as a lack of recycled materials, manual work in the preprocessing process, absence of preprocessing facilities for highly polluted sedimentary waste, and lack of establishment of basin sorting practices. Establishing a marine garbage recycling ecosystem is key, and for this, marine garbage collection, information on raw materials for recyclable waste, and installation and automation of highly polluted preprocessing

[30] "Material recycling" refers to the technology of regenerating a material into a usable state while maintaining its chemical structure. In addition to material recycling, there are other technologies, such as "chemical recycling," which transforms the chemical structure of a material to recycle it into a raw material, and "thermal recycling," which converts it into thermal energy.; Ministry of Oceans and Fisheries (12 Dec 2022b).

[31] Through the campaign, 250,000 used plastic water bottles from fishing vessels were collected.; Korea Coast Guard (18 Mar 2025). https://www.kcg.go.kr/kcg/na/ntt/selectNttInfo.do?nttSn=59795.

[32] Ministry of Oceans and Fisheries, op. cit.

facilities are necessary. Ultimately, the government's bridging role is important for promoting the consumption of recycled materials and products and coexistence.

Innovative Strategies for Marine Garbage Reduction

The plan aims to realize a clean ocean through zero marine garbage and aims to collect more marine garbage than the annual amount generated.

To strengthen the permanent collection system spatially, various measures are being implemented, including the establishment of permanent collection points along coastal areas such as tourist sites, rapid response systems for floating garbage, expanded collection of sedimentary pollutants, and the development of a sustained cooperation framework with the private sector. Additionally, to address marine litter in vulnerable areas, management and clean-up efforts are being enhanced on uninhabited islands and small inhabited islands, with joint operations involving the military and police to ensure the simultaneous collection of garbage in blind spots. Infrastructure for collection is also being expanded, and systems for recycling marine litter are being established. Finally, source management strategies are being implemented to block the inflow of land- and river-based garbage, and to strengthen governance mechanisms. Facilities designed to intercept land-based waste before it enters the marine environment are being expanded through intensive source management. Furthermore, the management of fishing gear is being reinforced, and the installation of new Styrofoam buoys in fish farms has been prohibited since 2023.

Master Plan for Fishery By-Product Recycling

This is the first statutory master plan related to fishery by-products established in accordance with the Act on Promotion of Recycling of Fishery By-products. Fishery by-products contain a large amount of useful ingredients such as calcium and collagen, so they have high value as recyclable resources.[33] However, recycling has been difficult due to management systems that have not considered the characteristics of fishery by-products and the need to handle large amounts of moisture and salt. The plan is to increase the recycling rate of fishery by-products to 30% (currently 19.5%) by 2027 and invest a total of KRW 100 billion to foster related industries that can utilize fishery by-products as high value-added resources. The plan strives to establish a full lifecycle fishery by-product resource circulation foundation in order to establish a circulation system for fishery resources. In addition, it develops high value-added recycling technology and fosters a fishery by-product recycling ecosystem.

[33] see the Act on the Promotion of Recycling of Fisheries By-products.

Main Policies on Marine Garbage: Aquaculture[34]

Currently, most Styrofoam buoys[35] used in aquaculture farms are easily broken by waves and dispersed into fine particles, which accounts for a large proportion of marine plastic waste,[36] but are very difficult to collect or remove. The Ministry of Oceans and Fisheries introduced an eco-friendly buoy distribution project in 2015 and has been working to replace 50% of the buoys with eco-friendly buoys by 2022 by reflecting related content in the "Comprehensive Plan to Reduce Marine Plastics (May 2019)". However, aquaculture sites have raised issues such as eco-friendly buoys being more expensive than existing Styrofoam buoys, as well as being heavy and hard, which rapidly lose buoyancy when water seeps in, making distribution difficult. Accordingly, the Ministry of Oceans and Fisheries determined that in order to fundamentally solve the problem of Styrofoam buoys in aquaculture farms, quality improvement is necessary along with the participation of aquaculture fishermen, and has prepared an improvement plan that reflects the voices of the field as much as possible.

First, in order to encourage the participation of aquaculture farmers, the government held an 'Open Communication Forum' three times at the fishing site to verify the quality of eco-friendly buoys with civil society groups such as environmental groups and consumer groups, and led the active participation of aquaculture farmers. In addition, South Korea are continuing research to improve the quality of eco-friendly buoys and are also promoting the development of materials that completely replace plastic materials in the mid- to long-term. Korea government are also making efforts to promote recycling and material improvement. The government produce styrofoam buoys (EPS buoys) used in aquaculture farms annually as ingots and sell them to the private sector, and operate a pre-suitability examination system for new certified buoys to replace EPS buoys to evaluate their eco-friendliness, recyclability, durability, and usability.

Main Policies on Marine Garbage: Recycling

In order to increase the recycling rate of marine garbage and respond to the national resource circulation policy and international trends, a system is being established and operated to collect, transport, and collect recyclable waste among marine

[34] The contents announced by the Ministry of Oceans and Fisheries has been summarized; Ministry of Oceans and Fisheries (26 May 2020).

[35] As of 2019, 41 million (75%) of the 55 million buoys in fish farms nationwide are made of Styrofoam. This refers to buoys that do not use Styrofoam or have a significantly lower risk of generating Styrofoam pellets.; ibid.

[36] According to the 2015 Marine Garbage Survey, plastic waste accounts for 55% of marine debris along the Korean coast.; ibid.

garbage. Efforts are being made to operate a wide-area marine garbage treatment facility by expanding the installation of collection facilities that can collect garbage generated from the fishing industry. In Korea, a total of 5.29 tons of marine garbage was recycled in collection facilities installed in ports nationwide in 2023, and the figure increased significantly to 135.49 tons in 2024.[37] This is a growth rate of approximately 25.6 times compared to the previous year, which can be said to be the result of a combination of factors such as expanding recycling collection facility infrastructure, expanding marine garbage collection business, and improving the operating system.

In addition, as part of support for recycling companies, a marine garbage recycling product certification system is being introduced and the marine garbage recycling industry is being fostered and product development and consumption of recycled products or raw materials are being promoted.

Main Policies on Marine Garbage: New Technology[38]

South Korea is developing eco-friendly ship technology that collects and processes marine garbage on board, along with a system that enables one-stop processing of marine garbage on the vessel. In addition, the government is supporting the development of equipment for collecting marine garbage in areas that are difficult to access, and for collecting microplastics on the coast.

Main Policies on Marine Garbage: Fishing Gear, Nets, etc.

The goal is to establish a recycling base from the source of garbage fishing gear[39] to the regional level in order to strengthen the proper treatment and recycling of ALDFG. The Korean government reports that, despite the fact that it has been carrying out a project to collect ALDFG in the sea, the amount of ALDFG still exceeds the amount collected. In order to fundamentally solve the problem, it was determined that compliance with fishing gear usage, proper disposal of ALDFG, strengthening crackdowns on lost fishing gear management and illegally ALDFG, and incentives to encourage voluntary participation by fishermen are necessary. Accordingly, fisheries with high usage of fishing gear such as nets and traps will be

[37] Coastal garbage monitoring statistics, op. cit.

[38] The contents announced by the Ministry of Oceans and Fisheries has been summarized; Ministry of Oceans and Fisheries (23 May 2022a).

[39] Among the 145,000 tons of marine garbage generated annually in Korea, approximately 95,000 tons originate from land-based sources and 50,000 tons from sea-based sources. Of the sea-based debris, an estimated 38,000 tons are believed to be discarded fishing gear.; Ministry of Oceans and Fisheries (26 Sep 2024).

strengthened in management responsibility and fines will be imposed for violations. In addition, a system to immediately remove illegally ALDFG will be introduced. Moreover, in order to encourage fishermen to participate by returning ALDFG in cash in addition to the deposit, a system is established to encourage them to dispose of it properly.

In order to strengthen the disposal and recycling of ALDFG, it is essential to implement carbon waste through proper disposal of marine garbage in fishing villages and island areas, strengthen management through efficient storage and transportation of marine garbage accumulated on land, build infrastructure that can recycle and turn marine garbage materials into fuel, and improve the resource circulation of waste resources. Additionally, efforts should be made to recycle marine garbage in fishing villages and island areas to return the profits to local communities and contribute to economic development such as creating local jobs.

However, despite these institutional efforts, the amount of ALDFG is still high, with approximately 5000 tons abandoned in the ocean every year, and the actual reduction results are limited. In terms of fishermen's perception, there are frequent cases of excessive use of fishing gear such as traps and gillnets beyond the legal allowance, and there is a lack of sense of responsibility, such as dumping ALDFG into the ocean after use. In reality, the annual appropriate fishing gear usage is 82,000 tons, but the actual usage is estimated to be 2–3 times more than this.

In addition, crackdowns on illegal activities at sea are limited, and infrastructure such as collection facilities for recovering ALDFG is insufficient. There are approximately 2000 ports nationwide, but there are only 133 onshore collection sites that can process marine garbage, and voluntary recovery activities by fishermen are also limited due to the burden of transportation and processing costs and lack of incentives.

In particular, discarded fishing gear abandoned far out at sea compared to coastal fishing grounds remains a blind spot in management because there are no dedicated vessels to recover it. Between 2019 and 2023, 32,646 tons of fishing gear waste—representing 97.9% of the total 33,346 tons—were collected in coastal waters. In contrast, only 700 tons (2.1%) were collected in remote waters, highlighting the continued inadequacy of waste management in those areas.[40]

South Korea's Efforts to Respond to the Plastics Convention

South Korea's Stance on the Plastic Convention

South Korea is securing global competitiveness in various industries such as automobiles, electronics, and batteries through plastics, so the Plastics Convention will inevitably have a wide-ranging impact not only on South Korea's industrial

[40] Ibid.

competitiveness but also on the daily lives of citizens who consume plastics. South Korea has officially stated its position in the discussions on the International Plastics Convention that it "actively contributes to the drafting of the agreement as a global pivotal country." As the key discussions on the 2024–2025 agreement were held in Busan (INC-5), the South Korean government took on the role of mediator and facilitator for resolving global plastic pollution, emphasizing the importance of successfully holding the meeting and concluding the agreement.[41] However, during the actual negotiation process, South Korea's stance is evaluated as somewhat cautious or ambiguous.[42] In particular, it did not clearly agree with binding provisions such as reducing the production of primary plastic polymers, and showed a passive attitude even in the early signing of related agreements (e.g., the "Bridge to Busan" Declaration). Until the middle of the meeting, the government maintained a conservative stance on setting plastic production reduction targets, but joined the joint statement of position stating the need for production reduction in the final stage.

In responding to plastic pollution, the Korean government emphasizes the downstream approach such as recycling, waste management, and technological innovation rather than production reduction, and focuses on sharing established resource circulation systems (e.g., extended producer responsibility, advanced recycling technology, waste-to-energy technology, etc.) with the international community.[43] In addition, it maintains the position that gradual and realistic transition and strengthening of the resource circulation system should be carried out in parallel rather than radical production regulations due to concerns about weakening industrial competitiveness and economic shock.[44] This can be seen as considering the domestic industrial structure, which is the world's fourth largest producer and consumer of plastics and has a high proportion of petrochemical-based industries.

Meanwhile, South Korea actively participates in the activities of the High Ambition Coalition to End Plastic Pollution (HAC) during the negotiation process, and as the host country of the meeting, it continuously demonstrates its will to contribute internationally through mediation and platform roles and recycling and technology sharing. However, domestic and international civil society groups and some experts are raising their voices calling for clearer and bolder production reduction targets and policy implementation as the main responsible country.

---

[41] Ministry of Foreign Affairs (2 Dec 2024).

[42] Moon Doun (23 Nov 2024).

[43] Ibid.

[44] Kalinova (2 Dec 2024).

South Korea's Efforts to Address Plastic Pollution

In 2020, the Ministry of Environment set a goal of reducing 20% of household plastics by 2025 in the 'Plastic-Free Measures for Living Waste'.[45] Then, in 2022, the reduction target was expanded in the 'Full Lifecycle Plastic-Free Strategy' to set a goal of reducing all waste plastics by 20% by 2025.[46] In addition, the 2025 and 2030 goals were set for the rate of use of recycled raw materials, material recycling rate, and bioplastic technology level. In the long term, in conjunction with the 2050 carbon neutrality, the goal was set to replace 100% with pure bioplastics by 2050.[47] This was linked to the 'Korean (K)-Circular Economy Implementation Plan' and was adjusted to 100% household plastics and 45% workplace plastics.[48]

In addition, a policy roadmap for managing the full lifecycle of plastics was prepared. According to the 'Full Lifecycle Plastic-Free Strategy' jointly prepared by relevant ministries in 2022, South Korea is a country that consumes a lot of plastic, with the demand for and garbage of plastic continuously increasing. In particular, it emphasized the seriousness of the problem of packaging and container garbage with a short use cycle after COVID-19. Accordingly, in order to prepare for the post-plastic era and establish a plastic-free foundation, a promotion task consisting of four main tasks and 14 detailed tasks was presented.

First, to reduce the use of disposable products, the government plans to strengthen the foundation for alternative services by introducing a certification system for reusable containers and rental/cleaning services, and by establishing related cost subsidies and shared-use models. South Korea is also striving to reduce their use through nudge-based measures, such as setting kiosks and delivery apps to default to not provide disposable products. The government further encourages consumers to use reusable containers through economic incentives and information on eco-friendly stores. In addition, it is establishing a management system for excessive packaging and standardize standards for the thickness, material, and color of plastic delivery containers to enhance recyclability.

Second, to ensure the stable management of waste resources, South Korea establishes a high-quality supply system across the entire process—from discharge to sorting—and puts in place an early warning system to respond to changes in the recycling market. The government develops a household waste information management system and diagnostic criteria for the recycling market. Furthermore, recycling will shift from incineration to material recycling and pyrolysis recycling, and the recycling subsidy rate and unit price will be increased. To expand recycling demand, manufacturers of end products such as PET bottles will be required to use recycled materials, and a certification system for recycled materials based on international standards will be established.

---

[45] Ministry of Environment (24 Dec 2020).

[46] Ibid.

[47] Ibid.

[48] Ministry of Trade, Industry and Energy (30 Dec 2021), p. 1.

Moreover, to promote the transition to bioplastics, the government gradually strengthens biomass content standards and revamps the biodegradable plastic certification system to include criteria for biodegradation under various environmental conditions. It supports overseas expansion by establishing collection and processing infrastructure for separately disposable biodegradable products and through international cooperation programs. The government also eases the regulatory burden on industry by utilizing regulatory sandboxes and circular resource recognition systems. Furthermore, it strengthens industrial capacity by supporting small businesses, launching circular economy R&D starting in 2024, and creating a plastics industry cluster.

Lastly, to respond to the Plastics Convention, the government develops a strategy that reflects both domestic and international industrial and policy conditions and establishes a negotiation community. Furthermore, to implement international cooperation tasks aligned with the 2022 OECD Recommendations, it installs deposit systems for fishing gear and buoys, as well as estuary barriers to prevent plastic inflow into vulnerable areas such as coastal and rural regions, while also strengthening waste collection and disposal capacities.

To strengthen the domestic implementation system, the government improves statistics on waste plastics and establishes a system to calculate actual recycling rates based on processing volume and residual information. Furthermore, it operates a pan-societal consultative body focused on key tasks such as plastic reduction, advanced recycling, and the development of alternative material industries to enhance policy effectiveness. In addition, the government establishes a close cooperative framework among relevant ministries and agencies to ensure active participation in international discussions.

Conclusion

Just as oceans around the world suffer from plastic pollution, Korea's oceans are no exception. South Korea's annual marine waste generation is considered a very high level of pollution by international standards. Accordingly, the central government is strengthening and operating a marine waste collection and disposal system, and coastal waste volume has stabilized and has shown a moderate decline since 2023. Furthermore, Korea is actively participating in international discussions on solving plastic pollution issues. Through diplomatic contributions, such as hosting the INC-5 conference and acting as a mediator, Korea is strengthening its image as a responsible nation.

Considering Korea's heavy reliance on the petrochemical industry and the resulting national interests, Korea has maintained a somewhat ambiguous stance on plastic lifecycle regulations during international agreement negotiations. This reflects the current state of the domestic industrial structure and concerns about weakening global competitiveness. Nevertheless, Korea is establishing systematic policies for plastic reduction and resource recycling through the "Full Lifecycle Plastic-Free

Strategy." The country is developing a mid- to long-term plan aimed at reducing plastic waste by 20% by 2025 and transitioning to 100% bioplastics by 2050. Furthermore, the country is pursuing a transition to a plastic-free society through specific implementation tasks, including reducing disposable items, establishing a high-quality recycling system, fostering the bioplastics industry, and establishing a foundation for international cooperation and agreement implementation. Meanwhile, civil society and experts are demanding that the Korean government present clearer and bolder plastic production reduction targets consistent with its international responsibilities. For substantive implementation after signing an international agreement, institutional reform and policy implementation remain key challenges.

Although Korea's regulatory response may not fully meet the expectations of the international community and environmental groups, it is gradually establishing a legal and institutional foundation for plastic lifecycle regulation based on detailed national plans. If these policies and plans are successfully implemented, Korea is expected to play a leading role in the international community in addressing plastic and marine plastic pollution. Going forward, Korea is expected to maintain a balance between industrial competitiveness and environmental responsibility, demonstrating substantial leadership in addressing the global plastic pollution problem.

References

Centre for Environment, Fisheries and Aquaculture Science (Cefas) (2019) South Pacific region Commonwealth Litter Programme conference to discuss marine litter research, monitoring and solutions to reduce plastic pollution. Retrieved from https://www.cefas.co.uk/news/south-pacific-region-commonwealth-litter-programme-conference-to-discuss-marine-litter-research-monitoring-and-solutions-to-reduce-plastic-pollution

Choi JS (2024) An average of 140,000 tons of marine debris... also causes accidents. KBS News. Retrieved from https://news.kbs.co.kr/news/pc/view/view.do?ncd=7977550

Coastal Garbage Monitoring Statistics. Ministry of Oceans and Fisheries, Marine Environment Information Portal. Retrieved from https://www.meis.go.kr/mli/monitoringInfo/stat.do

Harding S (2016) Marine debris: understanding, preventing and mitigating the significant adverse impacts on marine and coastal biodiversity. Secretariat of the Convention on Biological Diversity

Hong JS (2023) Microplastics found in finless porpoises and right whales off Korean beaches. Yonhap News. Retrieved from https://www.yna.co.kr/view/AKR20230411147000530

Jambeck JR, Geyer R, Wilcox C, Siegler TR, Perryman M, Andrady A, Narayan R, Law KL (2015) Plastic waste inputs from land into the ocean. Science 347(6223):768–771

Joint Initiative by Relevant Government Ministries of the Republic of Korea (2023) Measures to reduce river debris flowing into the ocean

Kalinova K (2024) INC-5 Busan fails to secure a global plastics treaty—Can South Korea still seize momentum for leadership? Climate Solution. Retrieved from https://forourclimate.org/newsroom/1009

Kim HG (2022) Marine waste policy and coastal debris issues. Emedia

Kim JS (2023) Our oceans are polluted with microplastics... The threat to marine life is reaching the limit. Hankyoreh. Retrieved from https://www.hani.co.kr/arti/society/environment/1114728.html

Korea Institute of Ocean Science and Technology (KIOST) (2025) A serious threat to the marine ecosystem: Marine debris entanglement damage has increased annually for 20 years. Retrieved from https://www.kiost.ac.kr/synap/skin/doc.html?fn=BBS_202503121035255560.hwp&rs=/viewer/result/BBSMSTR_000000000075/

Korea Coast Guard (2025). Retrieved from https://www.kcg.go.kr/kcg/na/ntt/selectNttInfo.do?nttSn=59795

McIlgorm A, Campbell HF, Rule MJ (2022) The cost of marine litter damage to the global marine economy: insights from the Asia-Pacific into prevention and the cost of inaction. Mar Pollut Bull 174:113168

Mine B, Tekman MB, Gutow L (2022) Impacts of plastic pollution in the oceans on marine species, biodiversity and ecosystems. WWF, Alfred-Wegener Institute

Ministry of Environment (2020) Establishment of measures for plastic life-cycle reduction and recycling. Retrieved from https://www.korea.kr/briefing/pressReleaseView.do?newsId=156429057

Ministry of Foreign Affairs (2024) The Fifth Intergovernmental Negotiating Committee (INC-5) on the UN Convention on Plastics closed. Retrieved from https://www.mofa.go.kr/www/brd/m_4080/view.do?seq=375703

Ministry of Oceans and Fisheries (2019) The Third National Master Plan for Marine Debris Management (2019–2023)

Ministry of Oceans and Fisheries (2020) Promoting zero Styrofoam buoys in aquaculture farms by 2025. Retrieved from https://www.mof.go.kr/doc/ko/selectDoc.do?docSeq=32551&menuSeq=971&bbsSeq=10

Ministry of Oceans and Fisheries (2022a) Developing an eco-friendly vessel for one-stop marine waste disposal. Retrieved from https://www.mof.go.kr/doc/ko/selectDoc.do?docSeq=46181&menuSeq=971&bbsSeq=10

Ministry of Oceans and Fisheries (2022b) Establishing a foundation for promoting high-value recycling of marine debris. Retrieved from https://www.mof.go.kr/doc/ko/selectDoc.do?docSeq=48189&menuSeq=971&bbsSeq=10

Ministry of Oceans and Fisheries (2024) Reduce discarded fishing gear and maximize retrieval: By 2027, aim for "Discarded Gear ≤ Retrieved Gear" in the ocean. Retrieved from https://www.mof.go.kr/doc/ko/selectDoc.do?docSeq=58765&bbsSeq=10&menuSeq=971

Ministry of Trade, Industry and Energy (2021) Formulation of Korea's circular economy implementation plan for achieving net-zero

Moon D (2024) Why South Korea's leadership is critical for a successful global plastics treaty. The Diplomat. Retrieved from https://thediplomat.com/2024/11/why-south-koreas-leadership-is-critical-for-a-successful-global-plastics-treaty/

Policy Briefing of the Republic of Korea (2025) Marine litter reduction measures. Retrieved from https://www.korea.kr/special/policyCurationView.do?newsId=148899381

United Nations Environment Programme (UNEP) (2025) Second part of the fifth session (INC-5.2). Retrieved from https://www.unep.org/inc-plastic-pollution/session-5.2

Werner S, Budziak A, van Franeker JA, Galgani F, Hanke G, Maes T, Matiddi M, Nilsson P, Oosterbaan L, Priestland E, Thompson R, Veiga J, Vlachogianni T (2016) Harm caused by marine litter. JRC Technical Reports, European Commission

Yoon YB (2022) Eight out of ten sea turtles eat plastic discarded by humans. HelloDD.com. Retrieved from https://www.hellodd.com/news/articleView.html?idxno=97381

Chapter 9
Marine Protected Area in the Waters Surrounding Dokdo

Junghwan Choi and SangSeop Lim

Introduction

Many countries have increasingly established certain zones as marine protected areas to sustainably protect and preserve marine ecosystems and fisheries resources. The first marine protected area was considered an annexed region of national-sovereignty governed land, and the subsequent ones tended to be coastal or land-adjacent areas. Such areas are controlled via different management systems and laws per country. South Korea has established 15 areas of protected marine ecosystems, 14 areas of protected wetlands, two areas of protected marine organisms, and one area of protected marine landscape in compliance with the Conservation and Management

This is an updated and revised version of the author's article "Establishing a Marine Protected Area in the Waters Surrounding Dokdo: Necessity and Legality" published at Sustainability (Vol.16 No.2, 2024) under the official permission of Publication company and Co-Author.

Junghwan Choi Xinghai Associate Professor at The School of Law of Dalian Maritime University, China. LL.M. in Maritime Law (Korea Maritime & Ocean Uni.), LL.M. in International Maritime Law with Merit (Swansea Uni., UK), Ph.D. in Maritime Law (Exeter Uni., UK).

SangSeop Lim Professor at the Division of Navigation Convergence Studies, Korea Maritime and Ocean University, Busan, Korea. B.Eng. in Navigation Science (KMOU); M.Sc. and Ph.D. in Shipping Management (KMOU).

J. Choi
Law School, Dalian Maritime University, Dalian, P.R. China
e-mail: junghwanchoi@dlmu.edu.cn

S. Lim (✉)
Division of Navigation Convergence Studies, Korea Maritime & Ocean University, Busan, Republic of Korea
e-mail: limsangseop@kmou.ac.kr

J. Choi (ed.), *Public Maritime Law in Asia*, International Law in Asia,
https://doi.org/10.1007/978-981-95-7037-9_9

of Marine Ecosystems Act and the Wetlands Conservation Act.[1] Such areas can increase the cultural, ecological, and social values of regions and encourage regional development when associated with regional tourism policies. Designated marine protected areas can receive support from management projects to conserve, protect, and manage marine ecosystems effectively, per the aforementioned acts.[2] On December 24, 2014, the Ministry of Oceans and Fisheries (MOF) designated 39.44 km^2 of water near Ulleungdo in the East Sea for marine ecosystem protection. Gyeongsangbuk-do set the surrounding waters as marine protected areas to protect habitats and spawning areas for protected marine organisms and conserve the submarine landscape, including coral reefs and seaweeds.[3]

This study emphasizes the need to conserve Dokdo's marine ecosystem by establishing the surrounding waters of Ulleungdo and Dokdo as marine protected areas. It addresses the following research questions: Is there a need to establish marine protected areas to conserve and protect Dokdo's marine ecosystem? Can South Korea establish marine protected areas in overlapping sea areas? Do issues from territorial sovereignty disputes and the absence of maritime boundary delimitation affect such establishment? What are the legal grounds for the establishment of marine protected areas in Dokdo and the legitimacy of these grounds in South Korea? Should South Korea cooperate with Japan to establish marine protected areas in Dokdo?

Dokdo, an indigenous land of South Korea, is effectively administered by South Korea. Under these circumstances, Japan's territorial sovereignty claims over Dokdo have aggravated diplomatic and cooperative relations between Japan and South Korea. In response, Korean researchers have investigated the territorial sovereignty over Dokdo. However, none proposes measures that enable South Korea, a coastal state, to exercise its sovereignty and exclusive jurisdiction over Dokdo by establishing marine protected areas to protect Dokdo's marine ecosystem. Bridging this gap, this study verifies the legitimacy and appropriateness of such establishments as marine protection measures for conserving Dokdo's marine ecosystem, which benefits South Korea and Japan. The study examines Korean and international laws as grounds for the necessity of establishing marine protected areas and the legal validity of such establishment to protect Dokdo's marine ecosystem and increase the island's social, cultural, and educational perspectives and marine tourism value. It facilitates socio-political discussions on the establishment of Dokdo and its surrounding waters as marine protected areas.

---

[1] KOEM, 'Designation and Management of Marine protected areas' available at https://www.koem.or.kr/site/eng/02/10201040000002019071509.jsp; accessed 25 August 2022.

[2] KOEM, 'Marine protected area' available at https://www.koem.or.kr/common/board/getPdf.do?bcIdx=29681&cbIdx=508&fileNo=1.

[3] MOF, 'Notice of Designation of Marine protected area in Ulleungdo Island', Notice of Ministry of Oceans and Fisheries No. 2014–139.

Marine Protected Areas in South Korea

Concept of Marine Protected Area

A protected area is a special-purpose area designated to protect a specified space. In natural resource management, spatial use of a protected area is restricted to protect biodiversity in the area and various created values.[4] As a protected area conceptually targets a certain space, this area should contribute to protecting organisms, populations, and colonies that live and breed within it, the habitat of these organisms, and the corresponding area ecosystem. The designation of a protected area somewhat restricts actions of collecting or hunting organisms living and growing in a certain area, protecting endangered organisms and minimizing the reduction of rare organisms.[5]

The first World Conference on National Parks in 1962 provided an international forum to discuss the use of marine protected areas as a measure for region-based management.[6] There have been international efforts to develop effective regulations for protecting marine environments and managing marine resources since the 1950s and 1960s. Subsequently, the Ramsar Convention, the first international treaty for the conservation of wetland resources, was concluded in 1971, and the Regional Seas Programme of the United Nations Environment Program was established in 1972. Such measures have introduced detailed region-based management measures, providing bases for further measures.[7]

In 1988, the International Union for the Conservation of Nature and Natural Resources (IUCN) defined a marine protected area as a clearly defined geographical space, recognized, dedicated, and managed via legal or other valid means to achieve the long-term conservation of nature with associated ecosystem services and cultural values.[8] As per the Convention on Biological Diversity, a protected area is a geographically defined area designated to achieve conservation objectives.[9] In Article 2(14) of the Conservation and Management of Marine Ecosystems Act, established in South Korea, "marine protected areas" are conservation worthy, as their diverse marine organisms and assets, including marine landscapes, determined by the Ordinance of the MOF under Article 25, makes them ecologically important.[10]

A marine protected area is a zone preserved by laws or other effective measures to keep a certain part of the ocean from harm. Marine protected area types include those for marine preservation, fisheries resource protection, valuable heritage conservation, and provision of opportunities for tourism, leisure, and education

[4] Agardy (1997), p. 103.

[5] Ibid., 109.

[6] Humphreys and Clark (2019), p. 11.

[7] Kelleher and Kenchington (1992), p. 3.

[8] IUCN (1988).

[9] CBD, Art. 2.

[10] Conservation And Management of Marine Ecosystems Act, Art 2(14).

activities. These types vary per designation purposes and each country's degree of regulation for protection. Indeed, marine protected areas are established for various purposes, including protection of the marine environment, marine ecosystems, fisheries resources, marine cultural heritage and conservation of wetlands, marine tourism, and education.[11]

Roberts and Hawkins note that biodiversity and productivity in the sea can be significantly recovered if networks of marine protected areas ensure ecological consistency and if 30% of each marine habitat is protected.[12] The expansion of marine protected areas can reduce poverty, strengthen food security, create jobs, and protect coastal villages. In 2014, the IUCN World Parks Congress presented its goal to achieve at least 30% of marine protected area coverage worldwide.[13] Since the Royal National Park in Australia was established as the world's first marine protected area in 1879, 248 countries have designated marine protected areas as of 2022. They manage 17,742 marine protected areas that cover 29,452,490 km^2 area. This gross area accounts for 8.13% of the oceans worldwide.[14] For spatial range, marine protected areas comprise areas under the jurisdiction of coastal states and areas beyond national jurisdiction (61% of the oceans). Only 1.18% of the areas are marine protected areas.[15]

Legal Basis for Marine Protected Areas

United Nations Convention on the Law of the Sea (UNCLOS) provides legal bases for applying region-based management measures, such as the establishment of marine protected areas, to conserve the marine environment despite the absence of specified regulations. Coastal states can establish marine protected areas in waters in their jurisdiction and regulate marine activities in such areas per the responsibility to protect and preserve the marine environment stated by Article 192 of UNCLOS.[16] Paragraph 5 of Article 194 of UNCLOS indicates that coastal states must take necessary measures "to protect and preserve rare or fragile ecosystems as well as the habitat of depleted, threatened, or endangered species and other forms of marine life".[17] Thus, establishing marine protected areas is a measure coastal states can adopt to safeguard their marine environment. Paragraph 1 of Article 2 of

---

[11] Ibid.

[12] Roberts and Hawkins (2000), p. 5.

[13] Brander et al. (2015), p. 5.

[14] Protected Planet, 'Marine protected areas' available at https://www.protectedplanet.net/en/thematic-areas/marine-protected-areas.

[15] Ibid.

[16] Scott (2019), p. 164.

[17] Ibid.

UNCLOS affirms that coastal state sovereignty extends to territorial seas.[18] Coastal states can exercise their complete and exclusive jurisdiction (e.g., prescriptive and enforcement jurisdiction) over territorial seas, thus establishing marine protected areas to protect the marine ecosystem of territorial seas.

Korean laws that provide grounds for establishing marine protected areas include the Conservation and Management of Marine Ecosystems Act, which presents regulations on protected areas for marine organisms, ecosystems, and landscapes. The Wetlands Conservation Act provides regulations on areas for protecting wetlands. Article 27 of the Conservation and Management of Marine Ecosystems Act prohibits new construction or extensions of buildings or other artificial structures, changes to the structure of public waters, any increase or decrease in the water level or seawater quantity, and any collection of sea sand, quartz sand, soil, and stones from public waters in marine protected areas. Furthermore, local governments that have established marine protected areas can apply for projects on collecting marine wastes, installing marine pollution reduction facilities, and providing support for marine protected areas and residents living near such areas, as per Article 34 of the Conservation and Management of Marine Ecosystems Act and Article 14 of the Enforcement Ordinance Act.[19]

Establishment Procedure

Paragraph 1 of Article 25 of the Conservation and Management of Marine Ecosystems Act specifies standards for the designation of marine protected areas: (1) sea areas where marine ecosystems maintain primitiveness or sea areas worthy of conservation and academic research for their diverse marine organisms; (2) academic research or conservation worthy areas for their unusual topography, geological features, or ecology; (3) sea areas worthy of conservation for their high primary production capacity or function as the habitat or spawning areas of marine organisms under protection; (4) sea areas that may represent diverse marine ecosystems or are equivalent to examples thereof; (5) sea areas worthy of special conservation for their beautiful marine or submarine landscape, including coral reefs and seaweeds; (6) areas worthy of conservation to maintain or improve their function as marine ecosystem carbon sinks; and (7) other sea areas prescribed by presidential decree, which are especially necessary for the effective conservation and management of marine ecosystems.[20]

Procedures for such designation include stages of preliminary preparation, designation preparation, and designation. In the first stage, the central government recommends a marine protected area and undergoes advance consultations with the

[18] Spadi (2000), p. 289.

[19] Park and Lee (2020), pp. 19–36; Nam et al. (2010), pp. 703–710.

[20] Conservation And Management of Marine Ecosystems Act, Art. 25(1).

corresponding local government. Further, it conducts a detailed survey on the target area to determine the appropriateness of the area as a marine protected area.[21] In the second stage, the central government prepares a designation plan based on the results of the detailed survey. It then holds a public hearing and a presentation for relevant local residents to emphasize the necessity and expected effects of establishing the target area as a marine protected area and form a sufficient consensus among them.[22] Subsequently, it formulates, designates, and announces the target area as a marine protected area via the review of the Marine Fishery Development Committee, as per relevant laws. Accordingly, the Korean government has designated 32 marine protected areas, covering a 1798.692 km^2 area (Fig. 9.1).[23] The Korea Marine Environment Management Corporation operates the marine protected area center to enhance its management system and reinforce the foundation for regional autonomous management of marine protected areas.[24]

Necessity of Establishing Marine Protected Areas in Dokdo

Before the establishment of Dokdo and its surrounding waters as marine protected areas, the Korean government designated the surrounding waters of Ulleungdo as the first protected area for marine ecosystems in the East Sea on December 24, 2014 (Fig. 9.2). The surrounding waters of Ulleungdo are target areas for protecting the habitat and spawning areas of marine organisms that provide excellent submarine landscapes, including coral reefs and seaweeds. The Korean government had long discussed the necessity of such an establishment. The main marine resources of the surrounding waters include invertebrates (e.g., *Dendrophyllia cribrosa*, species of *Antipathes japonica*, *Axinella copiosa Thiele*, species of *Haliclona [Reniera] cinerea*, *Corynactis viridis*, *Metridium senile*, and *Melithaea flabellifera Kukenthal*) and seaweeds (*Undaria pinnatifida*, *Ecklonia cava*, *Myagropsis myagroides*, *Dictyopteris undulata Holmes*, and *Cladophora sakaii Abott*).[25] Figure 9.2 shows the surrounding waters of the northern and western parts of Ulleungdo as a marine protected area. The local government with jurisdiction over the island (Gyeongsangbuk-do) has operated the Visitor Centre to inform the public about the value and importance of the marine protected area and increase the public consensus on the establishment of Dokdo and its surrounding waters as marine protected areas.[26]

In the surrounding seas of Dokdo, cold and warm currents ensure the diversity of marine organisms. Approximately 250 (520) species of seaweed (marine

---

[21] Ibid., Art. 26.

[22] Ibid.

[23] Ibid.

[24] KOEM, supra note 1.

[25] Song et al. (2017), p. 163; Kim and Yu (2021), p. 1310.

[26] MOF, supra note 3.

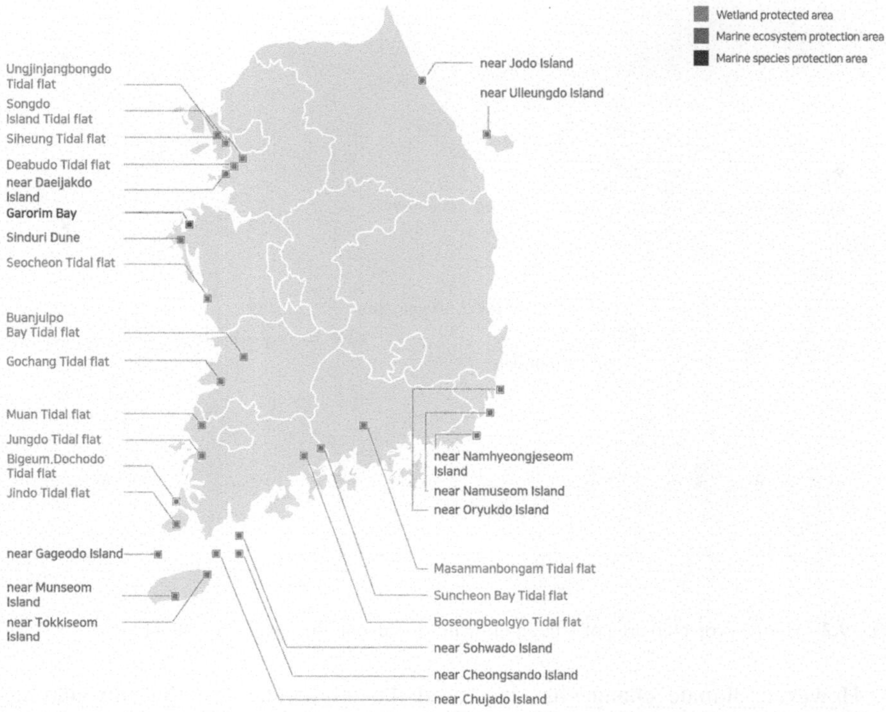

Fig. 9.1 Designated marine protected areas in South Korea; South Korea has designated 14 wetland protected areas (Green), 13 marine ecosystem protected areas (Sky-Blue), and one marine species protected area (Dark Blue) as marine protected areas

invertebrates) live in Dokdo.[27] Seodo is home to the largest colony of *Dendrophyllia cribrosa*, a marine organism that has been designated a protected marine species by the MOF and Class II endangered wildlife by the Ministry of Environment given the contraction of its habitat.[28] Fishers can catch squid (*Doryteuthis bleekeri Kefer*), Alaska pollock (*Gadus chalcogrammus*), cod (*Gadus*), octopus (*Octopoda*), and shrimp (*Caridea*) in Dokdo's fishing grounds. Its rocky areas provide abundant fisheries resources, including Asian sheepshead wrasse (*Semicossyphus reticulatus*), striped beakfish (*Oplegnathus fasciatus*), *Sebastes pachycephalus*, Korean rockfish (*Sebastes schlegelii*), largescale blackfish (*Girella punctata*), marbled rockfish (*Sebastes inermis*), *Sebastes thompsoni*, and Pearl-spot chromis (*Chromis notata*).[29] Additionally, Dokdo is Korea's representative marine tourist attraction; tourists visit to appreciate its beautiful landscape and experience its historical, cultural, and educational values.

[27] SW Jung et al., supra note 14.

[28] K-Dokdo, supra note 11.

[29] J Cho, HM Kim and JY Choi, supra note 11.

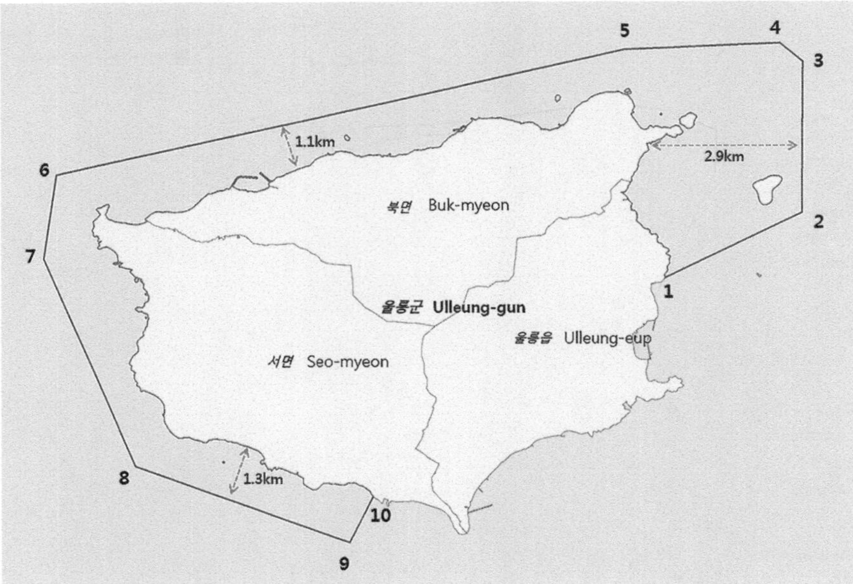

Fig. 9.2 Marine protected area of Ulleungdo with its surrounding sea areas (39.44 km)

However, climate change has increased the temperature of the surrounding waters, worsening albinism and damaging the marine ecosystem balance.[30] The Korean government should designate Dokdo and its surrounding waters as marine protected areas to overcome this problem. The marine ecosystem of Dokdo's surrounding waters warrants conservation and protection. As noted, several laws verify the significance of conserving and protecting it. Thus, though the Korean government has implemented projects on restoring the diversity of marine organisms to prevent albinism, the designation of Dokdo's surrounding waters as marine protected areas will maximize the efficiency of such projects.

Expected Effects of Marine Protected Area on Dokdo

The effects of a marine protected area are as follows. First, from a financial perspective, it increases the cultural, ecological, and social value of the relevant regions. It can also help develop local communities based on an increase in tourists in association with local tourism policies.[31] By designating a marine protected area, the government can conserve and restore the marine ecosystem of the target area, manage

[30] Chung et al. (2020), p. 701.

[31] Australian Government Department of Climate Change, Energy, the Environment and Water, 'The Benefits of Marine protected areas' available at https://www.dcceew.gov.au/sites/default/

it as a sustainable tourism resource, and use the area to promote ocean ecology experience and education on marine organisms. Moreover, protected area designation can strengthen the sustainability of local communities. Second, it can bring positive environmental effects. A marine protected area provides approximately four times more fish species than a commercial fishing region. Furthermore, the reduced influence of human activities and enhanced management of marine protected areas help restore the marine ecosystem and protect the marine environment.[32] Third, it induces positive political effects. When a certain region is designated as a marine protected area per Korean laws, the relevant local community responsible for its management can receive support for management projects and systematically implement conservation plans.[33] Establishing Dokdo as a marine protected area will enable South Korea to promote the value of Dokdo's marine ecosystem globally and invigorate marine tourism. This move will benefit South Korea and Japan while serving as a measure for actively countering the territorial sovereignty claims of Japan, helping South Korea reinforce its effective control and sovereignty over Dokdo.

General Characteristics of Dokdo

Geographical Features

Dokdo comprises east and west volcanic islands—Dongdo and Seodo, respectively—and 89 surrounding rocks (Fig. 9.3).[34] It is located 87.4 km southeast of Ulleungdo and 157.5 km northwest of Oki Island, Japan, with an area of 187,554 m^2.[35] Dokdo is called Takeshima in Japanese and Liancourt Rocks in English.[36] Dongdo (Seodo) is 98.6 (168.5) m above sea level, with a surface area of 73,297 (88,740) m^2. The distance between them is 151 m.[37] Dongdo has a manned lighthouse, marine and fishery facilities, and accommodations for the Dokdo Security Police (DSP). At its center is a vertical hole reaching sea level.[38] Seodo has a rough cone-shaped peak that is challenging to reach. Jongdeok Choi was registered as the first resident of Dokdo in March 1965. Since then, 14 Koreans, including Kim Sung-do and his wife, Kim Shin-yeol, have been registered.

files/documents/benefits-mpas.pdf; KOEM, 'Marine protected area' available at https://www.koem.or.kr/common/board/getPdf.do?bcIdx=29681&cbIdx=508&fileNo=1.

[32] Davies et al. (2021), p. 2463.

[33] YK Park and S Lee, supra note 42.

[34] MOFA, 'Dokdo' available at https://dokdo.mofa.go.kr/eng/introduce/residence.jsp.

[35] Akimoto (2020), p. 52.

[36] Ibid.

[37] Park and Kim (2017), p. 9892.

[38] MOFA, supra note 4.

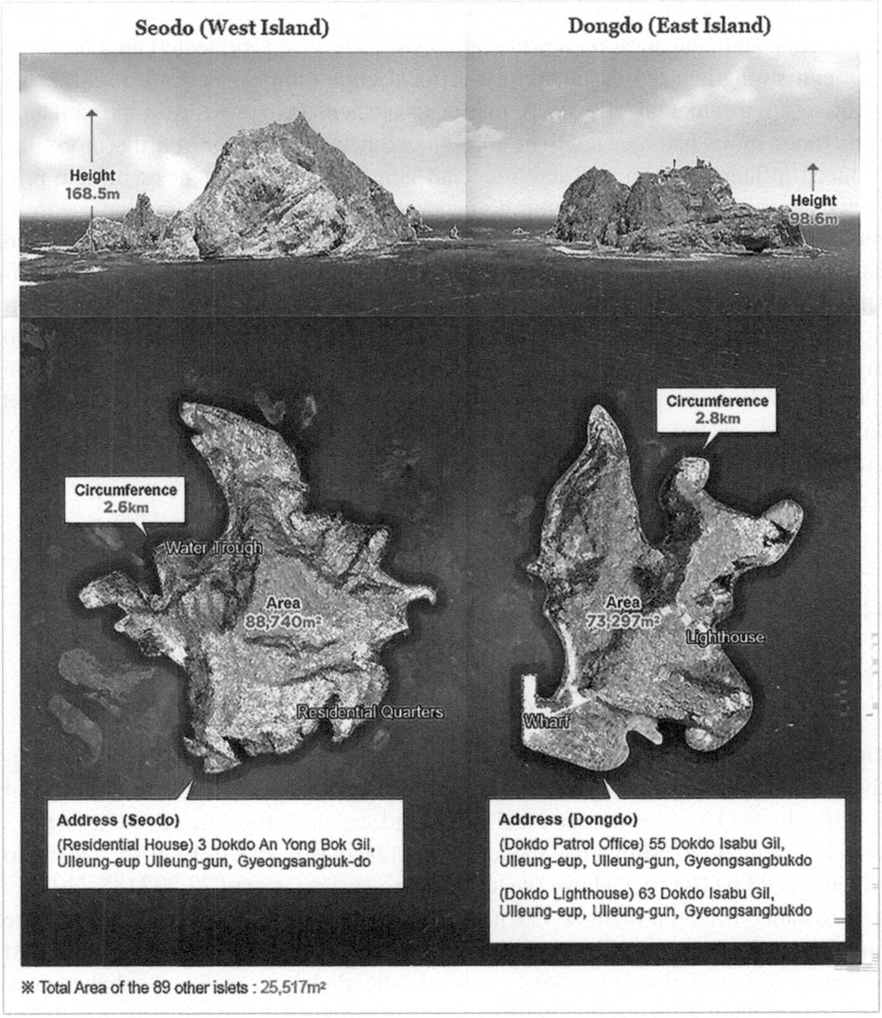

Fig. 9.3 Two main islands of Dokdo; Dongdo (Right) and Seodo (Left)

Dokdo has approximately 40 officers from the DSP, three Dokdo lighthouse keepers from the Pohang Regional Office of Oceans and Fisheries, and two members of the Dokdo Administration Office from the Ulleung-gun Office.[39]

[39] MOFA, supra note 4.

Ecologically Significant Marine Area

Dokdo has a mild oceanic climate influenced by warm currents. Its annual average temperature is 12 °C, with average temperatures of 1 °C and 23 °C in January and August, respectively.[40] In the surrounding seas of Dokdo, the nutrient-rich water is blended by the complex influence of cold and warm seasonal currents. Thus, various types of plankton, which prefer abundant nutrition, thrive. Indeed, climate change affects ecosystem change, the marine environment, and the flourishing of plankton, which many fishes depend on for food. Dokdo's surrounding waters provide fishing grounds with abundant diadromous fishes.[41]

Such seas are the main fishing ground in South Korea given the various types of fish, shellfish, and seaweeds therein. The National Marine Ecosystem Monitoring Program's 2020 evaluation result show that 345 species of marine organisms live in areas adjacent to Dokdo, including 215 species of invertebrates in rocky areas, 94 species of seaweeds, 21 species of coral reefs, and 15 species of fish.[42] Approximately 180 species of fish are in Dokdo's surrounding waters, varying per current and water temperature changes. Rocky areas have the following: Pearl-spot chromis (*Chromis notata*), Asian sheepshead wrasse (*Semicossyphus reticulatus*), Pacific saury (*Cololabis saira*), Japanese amberjack (*Seriola quinqueradiataz*), black scraper (*Thamnaconus modestus*), *Hyperoglyphe japonica*, wrasse (*Labridae*), blowfish (*Tetraodontiformes*), dotted gizzard shad (*Konosirus punctatus*), yellowtail amberjack (*Seriola lalandi*), righteye flounder (*Pleuronectidae*), and sandfish (*Arctoscopus japonicus*). Young sedentary fishes, such as largescale blackfish (*Girella punctata*), striped beakfish (*Oplegnathus fasciatus*), and marbled rockfish (*Sebastes inermis*) live in forest areas with low water levels between Dongdo and Seodo. Japanese sea lions (*Zalophus japonicus*), a marine mammal species, were frequently observed there but are now extinct from overhunting by Japanese fishers. Currently, spotted seals (*Phoca largha*), Steller sea lions (*Eumetopias jubatus*), and fur seals (*Arctocephalinae*) inhabit these areas.[43] Indeed, diverse marine organisms live in Dokdo's surrounding waters, where cold and warm currents meet.[44] However, such waters have recently suffered albinism, a process where rocky areas become white given calcareous algae and the loss of seaweeds.[45] This phenomenon has been worsened by a rapid rise in the water temperature and sea urchins that eat up seaweeds,

[40] K-Dokdo, 'Climate' available at https://kdokdo.com/english/index.do?menu_id=00000130&servletPath=%2Fenglish.

[41] Cho et al. (2009), p. 366; K-Dokdo, 'Marine life' available at https://k-dokdo.com/english/index.do?menu_id=00000139.

[42] MOF, 'National Marine ecosystem Monitoring Program' available at https://www.meis.go.kr/mes/data/1/board.do.

[43] Ibid.

[44] Jung et al. (2020), pp. 537–538.

[45] Ibid.

heightening concerns over the imbalance of the marine ecosystem.[46] The MOF has aimed to restore the diversity of marine organisms in Dokdo since 2015, conducting comprehensive marine ecosystem enhancement programs, including diagnosing and observing albinism, removing sea urchins and calcareous algae and releasing their natural predators, and transplanting seaweeds.[47]

Marine Tourism in Dokdo

Dokdo was designated as Korea's Natural Monument No. 336 in 1982, and its entire area has been treated as a restricted zone. However, since 2005, the Korean government has allowed the public to visit certain areas of Dongdo to increase accessibility to Dokdo and attract visitors in response to growing public interest.[48] Visitors can take a tour around permitted areas of Dokdo from 8:00 to 19:00 to prevent potential damage. The viewing time per session cannot exceed an hour, except in special cases or as approved by the governor.[49] Only up to 470 tourists can visit the berthing facilities located in permitted areas of Dongdo per session. A passenger ship can enter Dokdo less than 10 times per day in May and June, the breeding period of seabirds, as per a regulation implemented in 2015. From April to June, people can visit for relief and rescue missions on a helicopter.[50] Dokdo is a marine tourist attraction for special purposes given its natural history and socio-cultural value. Marine tourists to Dokdo tend to broadly understand and be interested in its history, culture, and land.[51] Thus, the behaviors of Korean tourists who visit Dokdo are affected by the general image of Dokdo as a marine tourism destination, as reflected by its territorial protection, resistance to Japan, clean zone, and ecological tourism. Moreover, such behaviors reflect unique cultural characteristics.[52] From Table 9.1, the number of visitors to Dokdo gradually increased from approximately 40,000 persons in 2005 to 250,000 persons in 2013. Despite decreasing sharply in 2014, it rose steadily again, exceeding 200,000 persons in 2018. Thus, the number of visitors has constantly increased, except for the rapid decrease in 2014 and 2020, when the COVID-19 pandemic started. The number is significantly low in winter given frequent ship cancellations because of the rough weather of the East Sea. Meanwhile, the ratio of ships that turn around Dokdo to outgoing ships is high in spring. Additionally, May and September record the highest number of visitors.

---

[46] Kim et al. (2012), p. 969.

[47] Lim et al. (2017), p. 968.

[48] MOFA, 'Residents and Visitors' available at https://dokdo.mofa.go.kr/eng/introduce/residence.jsp.

[49] Ibid.

[50] Ibid.

[51] Nam and Lee (2021), p. 44.

[52] Ibid.

Table 9.1 Number of visitors in Dokdo

Year	Number of visitors	Variation	Ratio of increase or decrease from the previous year
2010	111,808	−20,750	−16%
2011	176,822	65,014	58%
2012	202,098	25,276	14%
2013	251,734	49,636	25%
2014	136,438	−115,296	−46%
2015	173,870	37,432	27%
2016	202,050	28,180	16%
2017	200,728	−1322	−1%
2018	221,722	20,994	10%
2019	252,821	31,099	14%
2020	86,839	−165,982	−66%
Total	2,016,930		

South Korean Laws and Regulations Regarding Dokdo

Korean laws on the status of Dokdo are as follows. First, Dokdo is an administrative property of the Ministry of Land, Infrastructure, and Transport, as per Article 6 of the State Property Act.[53] Second, the Cultural Heritage Administration (CHA) designated Dokdo as Korea's Natural Monument No. 336 on November 16, 1982, as per Article 25 of the Cultural Heritage Protection Act, after considering Dokdo's historical features and natural science and academic value. Its title was revised to "natural reserve" on December 10, 1999.[54] Third, the Ministry of Environment designated Dokdo as a specified island on September 5, 2000, to conserve its natural environment and ecosystem, as per the Special Act on the Conservation of the Ecosystems in Island Areas Including Dokdo. Dokdo is a natural environment conservation area, as per the National Land Planning and Utilization Act.[55]

The task management conditions on the use of Dokdo, performed by the administrative departments of Korea, are as follows. As Dokdo belongs to Ulleung-gun in Gyeongsangbuk-do, based on the administrative district system, the Ulleung-gun Office conducts projects on preparing solutions for issues on the territory of Dokdo and providing support for residents. The Korean Coast Guard patrols the surrounding waters and manages the safety of passenger ships that enter Dokdo. The Gyeongbuk Provincial Police operates the DSP. The MOF has established comprehensive plans for the protection of ecosystems and development of fisheries resources to encourage sustainability by implementing surrounding ecosystem conservation, using fisheries resources, and researching ocean science in balance, as per the Act on the Sustainable Use of Dokdo. The Ministry of Environment and CHA

[53] K-Dokdo, 'Conservation Management' available at https://dokdo.mofa.go.kr/eng/introduce/management.jsp.

[54] Kang et al. (2013), p. 157.

[55] K-Dokdo, supra note 23.

have set management programs to protect Dokdo, including its natural environment, as per relevant laws.[56]

Factors Behind Hampering the Establishment of Dokdo MPA

Disputes Over Dokdo Sovereignty

Since the Peace Line (a South Korean marine boundary line) was declared in 1952, South Korea and Japan have faced political and diplomatic issues concerning sovereignty over Dokdo. Japan lodged an official diplomatic complaint against South Korea after the declaration of the Peace Line; both countries exchanged diplomatic documents four times.[57] Arguments about Dokdo-related issues hinged on legal justifications for the historical sovereignty over Dokdo and the effective right to its control. Japan has attempted to register this island as an internationally disputed region based on constant provocation. Indeed, the local parliament of Shimane Prefecture passed an ordinance designating February 22 as Takeshima Day in 2005. Japan's Ministry of Education, Science, Sports, and Culture has included distorted content on Dokdo in school textbooks. Moreover, marine exploration ships of the Japan Coast Guard (JCG) approached Dokdo to conduct a hydrographical survey.[58] Japan has claimed its territorial sovereignty over Dokdo to increase its jurisdiction over the oceans and ultimately reinforce military strategies and gain practical economic benefits.[59] The decades-long territorial sovereignty over Dokdo issue between South Korea and Japan has been actively examined in various fields, from history to international law, geography, and ecology. South Korea and Japan have investigated the Dokdo issue to academically justify securing territorial sovereignty. Findings from the history and international law perspectives are used as territorial sovereignty justifications. Claimant countries must hold a dominant position for their claims for territorial sovereignty in international law to receive international approval for their claims. That is, South Korea and Japan should provide historically clear grounds for their territorial sovereignty.

Japan has called on international observers to recognize Dokdo as a disputed region and prepared judicial measures to solve the issue of territorial sovereignty per the International Court of Justice (ICJ), especially after Japan could not successfully negotiate with South Korea.[60] Currently, Japan takes a passive attitude toward

---

56 K-Dokdo, supra note 23.

57 Van Dyke (2007), p. 158; D Akimoto, supra note 5, at p. 67; R Pedrozo, 'Sovereignty Claims over the Liancourt Rocks (Dokdo/Takeshima)' (year) 28 Chinese (Taiwan) Yearbook of International Law and Affairs 78-97, at p. 78; Lee and Lee (2011), p. 1.

58 S Lee and HE Lee (eds), ibid., at p. 320.

59 Lee (2007), p. 374.

60 Schrijver and Prislan (2015), p. 219; JM Van Dyke, 'Addressing and Resolving the Dokdo Matter' in S Lee and HE Lee, (eds) *Dokdo*, 29–40, at p. 30.

the judicial management of its disputes over the Kuril and Senkaku Islands based on the intervention of the ICJ. However, it is actively urging judicial management of the Dokdo issue. Japan recognizes that it will not suffer a loss even if it loses against South Korea, which exercises effective control over Dokdo. Japan's actions also conceal its strategic intention to lead the ICJ to deliver favorable trial results by demonstrating its political and diplomatic capabilities.[61] South Korea has actively opposed Japan's claim for territorial sovereignty over Dokdo. It has verified grounds for legitimacy in claiming territorial sovereignty over Dokdo via history, geography, and international law.[62] Thus, reviewing the accuracy of data on Dokdo may help relieve the enraged sentiments of the public on the Dokdo issue in South Korea and Japan and enhance state partnership.

Undelimited Maritime Boundary in the East Sea

After the UNCLOS was adopted, South Korea and Japan declared their respective 200-nautical mile exclusive economic zones (EEZs) in 1996 (see Fig. 9.4). The distance between the shores of Korea, China, and Japan cannot exceed 400 nautical miles in most cases, and the EEZs and continental shelves of such countries overlap in certain waters.[63] Therefore, the maritime boundary for the surrounding waters of the Korean peninsula has not been delimited, which is associated with disputes on territorial sovereignty over Dokdo. International law notes that the Dokdo's possessor can claim the waters under its sovereignty, including the territorial sea, contiguous zone, EEZ, continental shelf, and adjacent resources. Hence, Japan has claimed its territorial sovereignty over Dokdo to extend its jurisdiction over the oceans. The tense conflict about Dokdo between South Korea and Japan has hindered the maritime boundary delimitation for the waters of this island.[64] Per the UNCLOS, a coastal state has sovereign rights for exploring, exploiting, conserving, and managing the natural resources, whether living or non-living, of the waters overlying the seabed and the seabed and its subsoil and rights to other activities for the economic exploitation and exploration of the zone, such as the production of energy from the water, currents, and winds in the EEZ.[65] Moreover, the coastal state can exercise exclusive jurisdiction as provided for in the relevant provisions of the Convention regarding the establishment and use of artificial islands, installments, and structures for marine scientific research. The coastal state also has general duties and prescriptive and enforcement jurisdiction to protect the marine environ-

[61] Lee (2016), p. 111; MOFA, 'The Government's Basic Position' available at https://dokdo.mofa.go.kr/eng/dokdo/government_position.jsp.

[62] MOFA, Ibid.

[63] Van Dyke (2003), p. 509; Kim (2017), p. 70.

[64] Van Dyke (2007), p. 158.

[65] UNCLOS, Art. 56(1)(a).

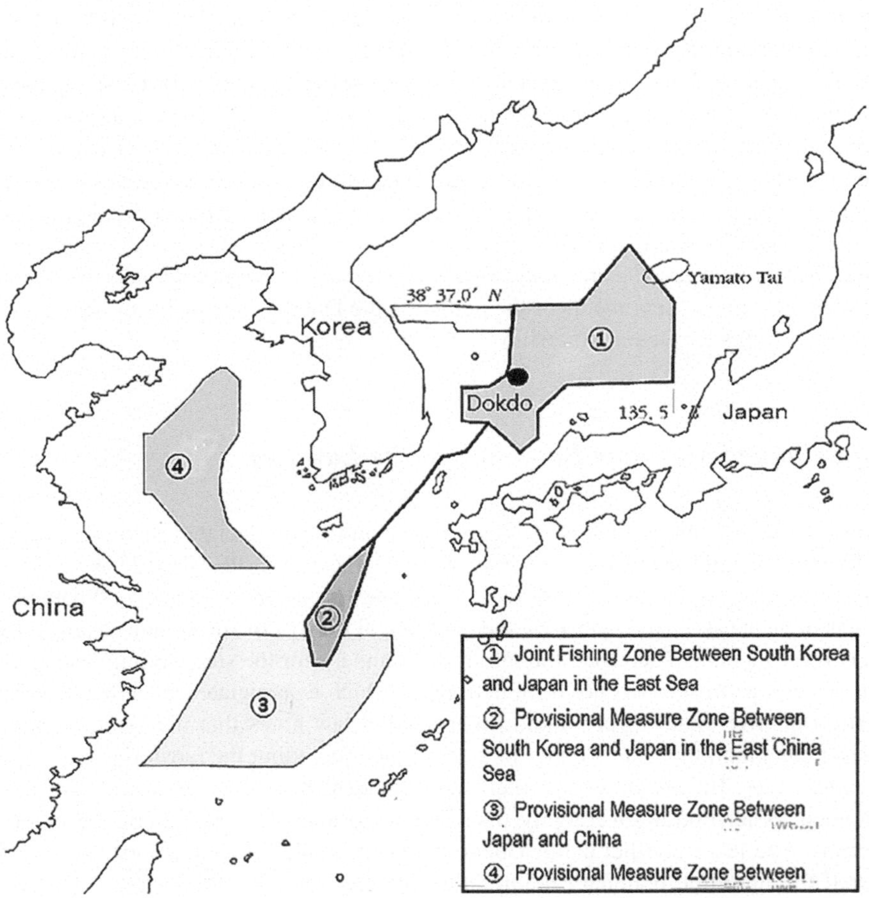

Fig. 9.4 Provisional measure zones Between South Korea, Japan, and China (Source: International Institute for Law of the Sea Studies)

ment.[66] Though coastal states with overlapping waters eventually fail to delimit a maritime boundary for such waters, the states have the rights and duties specified by this Convention. Nevertheless, this Convention notes that coastal states that face overlapping water issues must enter into provisional arrangements of a particular nature and avoid jeopardizing or hampering the final agreement during this transitional period.[67]

This article serves as a regulation that restricts the application of rights of coastal states to overlapping waters. Coastal states may clash in the exercise of rights over overlapping waters.[68] For example, the JCG informed the International Hydrographic

---

[66] UNCLOS, Art. 56(1)(b), (c).

[67] UNCLOS, Art.74(3).

[68] Valencia (2007), p. 127; Anderson and Van Logchem (2014), pp. 192–193.

Organization of its plan to conduct a hydrographic survey and marine scientific research in Dokdo's surrounding waters on April 14, 2006.[69] Although Dokdo's surrounding waters are overlapping waters, South Korea exercises effective control over Dokdo and jurisdiction over the EEZ, as per Korean and international laws. Therefore, Japan's one-sided action of performing "marine scientific research on waters without a delimited maritime boundary" violates South Korea's right as a coastal state and its strategy to refer issues on territorial sovereignty over Dokdo and relevant marine jurisdiction to the international community. Effective provisional agreements on the overlapping waters between South Korea and Japan include the 1974 Agreement on the Joint Development of the Southern Part of the Continental Shelf adjacent to the Two Countries[70] and the 1998 Agreement on fisheries,[71] concluded to conserve living resources.

South Korea-Japan Fisheries Agreement

Regarding fishery issues in the EEZ, including overlapping waters, the 1998 Agreement between Japan and the Republic of Korea concerning fisheries notes that both countries should annually inform their counterpart on conditions allowed to the public, including fishers, in their EEZs, such as catchable species of fish, fishing quota, and fishing zones.[72] Moreover, they should quickly release counterpart ships and crews arrested or detained after appropriate guarantees or other equivalent documents are submitted. They must comply with international laws on navigation, maintain fishing safety and order by fishing vessels, and implement the right measures to manage marine accidents smoothly and swiftly.[73] The EEZ in the East Sea comprises overlapping waters with issues on territorial sovereignty over Dokdo. This zone is open to the fishing vessels of both countries; they can exercise jurisdiction for fishing in this zone.[74] As this agreement applies only to the fishing field, it is not relevant to territorial sovereignty over Dokdo issues, maritime boundary delimitation in the EEZ, and control over the continental shelf. First, the agreement does not apply to territorial seas because it targets the EEZ. The agreement intends to regulate fishing-related issues before the final maritime boundary delimitation in

[69] Wiegand (2015), p. 348; Bong (2013), p. 191; S Lee and HE Lee (eds), *Dokdo*, page; A Kanehara, 'A Possible Practical Solution For The Dispute Over The Dokdo/Takeshima Islands From The Perspective Of The Law Of The Sea' in S Lee and HE Lee, (eds) *Dokdo*, 71–89, at p. 71.

[70] Agreement between the Republic of Korea and Japan concerning the Joint Development of the Southern Part of the Continental Shelf adjacent to the Two Countries, 2 September 1977, available at https://www.law.go.kr/LSW/trtyBInfoP.do?chrClsCd=010202&trtySeq=1747.

[71] Agreement between Japan and the Republic of Korea concerning fisheries, Kagoshima 28 November 1998, available at https://www.un-ilibrary.org/content/books/9789210565592s002-c008.

[72] Ibid., Art. 1.

[73] Ibid., Art. 11.

[74] Ibid., Art. 6.

the EEZ. As in the Minquiers and Ecrehos Case decided by the ICJ in 1953, the UK and France agreed to establish a joint fishing zone in the surrounding waters of the islet groups in the Minquiers and Ecrehos. Despite this agreement, the ICJ decided that it does not affect territorial sovereignty over the target islets.[75] On March 1, 2001, the Constitutional Court of Korea published a decision on a constitutional appeal that the fisheries agreement does not affect territorial sovereignty over Dokdo, despite the location of this island in middle waters where fishers from South Korea and Japan can freely catch fish. It also decreed that the agreement is irrelevant to the territorial sea issue.[76] In another maritime dispute between El Salvador and Honduras, a Special Chamber of the ICJ decided that the joint water system established by the corresponding countries, which succeeded the prior countries that historically possessed the target waters, is separate from territorial sovereignty over islands located in joint waters (Fig. 9.5).[77] The precedent indicates that an agreement on a maritime boundary between countries does not affect their territorial sovereignty.

Effect on Formulating a Marine Protected Area in Dokdo

Dokdo is located in the overlapping sea area of EEZ between South Korea and Japan. Waters without a delimited maritime boundary can induce sovereignty and jurisdiction disputes between the countries concerned. Such countries have duplicated rights to possess the EEZ and continental shelf and legal grounds for somewhat justifying their rights in this zone. UNCLOS specifies that coastal countries should not hamper the fulfillment of duties for negotiations based on trust and good faith to conclude provisional agreements with countries adjacent to overlapping waters and the reaching of the final agreement on maritime boundary delimitation. Hence, South Korea and Japan signed the Agreement between Japan and the Republic of Korea concerning fisheries in 1998 and established middle waters in the

---

[75] The Minquiers and Ecrelzos case, Judgment of 17 November 1953: ICJ Report, p. 58, '…even if it be held that these groups lie within this common fishery zone, the Court cannot admit that such an agreed common fishery zone in these waters would involve a regime of common user of land territory of the islets and rocks, since the Articles relied on refer to fishery only to any kind of user of land territory'.

[76] New Agreement on Fisheries between the Republic of Korea and Japan Case [13–1 KCCR 676, 99Hun-Ma139, etc., (consolidated), 21 March 2001], 'The Agreement in this case is a fisheries agreement, and is not directly related to the territorial rights within the exclusive eco- nomic zones. Although the Agreement distinguishes an exclusive eco- nomic zone from a neutral zone, the neutral zone is formed between the two countries by yielding a proportion of EEZ to their coastal lines from a median line that would have to be drawn in case a mutual argument on the EEZ is not made. In this light, it can be concluded that interests of both countries have been duly reflected in the instant Fisheries Agreement', available at https://search.ccourt.go.kr/ths/pr/ths_pr0101_P1.do.

[77] Land, Island and Maritime Frontier Dispute, El Salvador and Nicaragua (intervening) v Honduras, Judgment, Merits, ICJ Rep 35, 11 September 1992.

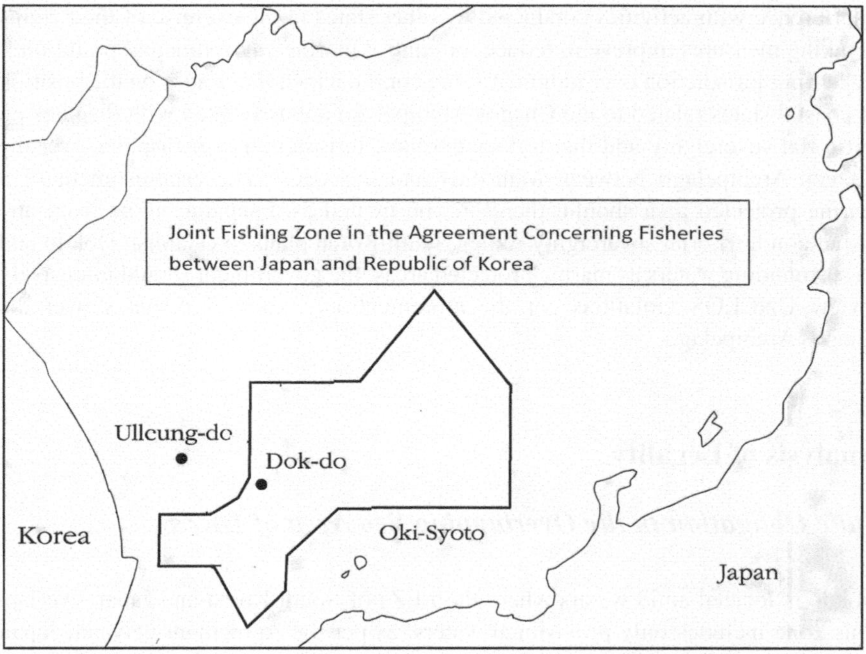

Fig. 9.5 Dokdo in Joint Fishing Zone Between Japan and South Korea (Source: International Institute for Law of the Sea Studies); Dokdo is located in the Provisional Measure Zone, as per the 1998 Agreement between Japan and the Republic of Korea Concerning Fisheries

East Sea, where fishing vessels of both countries can catch fish. In such waters, each country can exercise jurisdiction over fishing. The agreement regulates only fishing-related issues and is separate from disputes about territorial sovereignty over Dokdo; thus, it does not affect the exercise of sovereignty and exclusive jurisdiction of coastal states over Dokdo, except for fishing. Indeed, Mauritius initiated arbitral proceedings against the UK in December 2010, arguing that the UK declared a marine protected area near the Chagos Archipelago unilaterally and that the UK's action of prohibiting fishing in the marine protected area violated the UNCLOS. Permanent Court of Arbitration (PCA) decided that the UK violated the UNCLOS based on its action of setting a marine protected area one-sidedly without discussions with Mauritius.[78] PCA notes that the UK violated the following: Paragraph 3, Article 2 of the UNCLOS, which indicates that coastal states should exercise sovereignty over the territorial sea per the Convention; Paragraph 2, Article 56, which indicates that coastal states should properly consider the rights and duties of other states in the process of exercising their rights in the EEZ; and Paragraph 4, Article 194, which notes that coastal states should refrain from unjustifiable

[78] In the Matter of the Chagos Marine protected area Arbitration between The Republic of Mauritius and The United Kingdom of Great Britain and Northern Ireland, Award of the Arbitral Tribunal (18 March 2015).

interference with activities conducted by other states in the exercise of their rights in taking measures to prevent, reduce, or control marine environmental pollution.[79] Regarding jurisdiction over judgments, the court decided that issues on the position of coastal states related to the Chagos Archipelago are associated with disputes on territorial sovereignty and that it does not have jurisdiction over disputes over the Chagos Archipelago between Mauritius and the UK.[80] The establishment of a marine protected area should, therefore, be treated as a separate issue from any dispute on territorial sovereignty. When South Korea plans to establish Dokdo and its surrounding waters as marine protected areas, the government should intensively review UNCLOS violations per the aforementioned case of disputes over the Chagos Archipelago.

Analysis of Legality

State Obligation in the Overlapping Sea Area of EEZs

Dokdo is located amid waters where the EEZs of South Korea and Japan overlap. This zone includes only provisional waters, as per the Agreement between Japan and the Republic of Korea concerning fisheries, without a delimited maritime boundary. The issue of territorial sovereignty over Dokdo hinders the agreement between South Korea and Japan on the final maritime boundary delimitation in this zone and disturbs their cooperation, such as on marine environment protection. Article 74 of the UNCLOS mentions the rights and duties of coastal states in waters without a delimited maritime boundary. Paragraph 1 notes that delimitation of the EEZ between neighboring states should be made by agreement based on international law. Paragraph 3 stipulates the duties of coastal states as follows:

> Pending agreement as provided for in Paragraph 1, the States concerned, in a spirit of understanding and cooperation, shall make every effort to enter into provisional arrangements of a practical nature and, during this transitional period, not to jeopardize or hamper the reaching of the final agreement. Such arrangements shall be without prejudice to the final delimitation.[81]

South Korea and Japan have established provisional waters based on the UNCLOS and the Agreement between Japan and the Republic of Korea concerning fisheries. One-sided actions of coastal states in overlapping waters occasionally threaten neighboring states, thereby violating Paragraph 3, Article 74 of the UNCLOS. Such coastal state behaviors are clearly highlighted in international precedents represented by the Aegean Sea Continental Shelf case between Greece and Turkey in 1976, the Guyana and Suriname arbitration in 2007, and the dispute

[79] Ibid., para. 543.

[80] Ibid., para. 223–225.

[81] UNCLOS, Art. 74(3).

concerning the delimitation of the maritime boundary between Ghana and the Ivory Coast in 2017.

In the aforementioned case between Greece and Turkey, the Turkish State Petroleum Company gained approval for oil exploration on a continental shelf in the overlapping waters of Greece and Turkey and launched seismic wave exploration without discussions with Greece.[82] Greece requested the ICJ to conduct provisional measures, stating that Turkey's actions of unilateral exploration and scientific research brought irreparable damage to the overlapping waters of both countries, which did not include a delimited maritime boundary, and that these actions will obstruct their favorable relations. The ICJ noted that Turkey's exploration actions did not cause irreparable damage to the rights of Greece based on the following grounds: (1) no complaint has been made that this form of seismic exploration involves any risk of physical damage to the seabed or subsoil or their natural resources; (2) seismic exploration activities undertaken by Turkey are all transitory and do not involve the establishment of installations on or above the seabed of the continental shelf; (3) no suggestion has been made that Turkey has embarked upon any operations involving the actual appropriation or other use of the natural resources of the areas of the continental shelf in dispute.[83] As for the arbitration case of Guyana and Suriname in 2007, the Tribunal presented standards for decisions based on the irreparable damage from the one-sided actions of a coastal state in overlapping waters.[84] Guyana allowed CGX Resources Inc., a Canadian company, to perform oil exploration and development in overlapping waters of Guyana and Suriname. When CGX vessels conducted oil exploration in the overlapping waters on June 3, 2000, they were ordered by vessels of the Navy of Suriname to leave the zone immediately; armed conflict ensued. Guyana initiated arbitral proceedings accordingly, and the Tribunal decided that Guyana and Suriname violated their obligations under Articles 74(3) and 83(3) of the UNCLOS.[85] The Tribunal mentioned the Aegean Sea Continental Shelf case between Greece and Turkey in 1976 as a precedent and stated that the ICJ's decision in the cited case distinguishes between activities of a transitory character and those that risk irreparable prejudice to the position of the other party.[86]

Accordingly, the Tribunal regarded seismic wave exploration as an allowed activity in overlapping waters and drilling as an action that can cause permanent physical change to the marine environment, thus requiring an agreement or discussion with neighboring states.[87] As noted, a coastal state should review the status of violation against obligations indicated in Paragraph 3, Article 74 of the UNCLOS

[82] Aegean Sea Continental Shelf (Greece/Turkey), Judgment, ICJ Reports 1978, para. 16.

[83] Ibid., para. 30.

[84] In the Matter of an Arbitration between Guyana and Suriname, Award of the Arbitral Tribunal (17 September 2007), para. 156.

[85] Ibid., para. 488.

[86] Ibid., para. 468.

[87] Ibid., para. 468 and 478.

when it plans to exercise its rights unilaterally in overlapping waters. However, the establishment of a marine protected area is a measure that a coastal state can implement to protect the marine environment and marine ecosystems. As this action benefits coastal and neighboring states, it is recommended not to prohibit neighboring states excessively from exercising their rights, such as fishing and navigation rights.

Coastal States' Rights and Exclusive Jurisdiction

UNCLOS guarantees the exclusive sovereignty of coastal states over territorial seas. Exclusive sovereignty refers to independent and exclusive rights of coastal states, including fishing rights, obligations of protection and preservation of the marine environment, marine scientific research, rights to develop and explore natural resources, and legal execution rights. Per Article 56 of the UNCLOS, in EEZs, the coastal state has sovereign rights for exploring and exploiting, conserving, and managing the natural resources, whether living or non-living, of the waters overlying the seabed and the seabed and its subsoil. It includes rights for other activities for the economic exploitation and exploration of the zone, such as the production of energy from the water, currents, and winds. Coastal states can also exercise jurisdiction as provided for in the relevant provisions regarding the establishment and use of artificial islands, installations, and structures, marine scientific research, and protection and preservation of the marine environment.[88] The Territorial Sea and Contiguous Zone Act notes that Dokdo belongs to the territorial sea of South Korea, and South Korea exercises exclusive sovereignty over this island. Korean laws indicate the status of Dokdo as the sovereign territory of South Korea.[89]

Regarding the exercise of coastal state rights to conserve the marine environment indicated in the UNCLOS, South Korea designated and announced Dokdo as Korea's Natural Monument No. 336 to conserve the natural environment and ecosystem of Dokdo, as per the Cultural Heritage Protection Act. It also formulated the Special Act on the Conservation of the Ecosystems in Island Areas Including Dokdo to designate and manage Dokdo as a specified island. Additionally, Dokdo is designated as a natural conservation area per the National Land Planning and Utilization Act. The laws specify that Dokdo is the national territory of South Korea. Hence, Korea has exclusive and active rights as a coastal state to establish Dokdo's surrounding waters as a marine protected area to protect the marine ecosystem and environment of this zone actively, as per the Conservation and Management of Marine Ecosystems Act. However, Dokdo is located amid a provisional zone in overlapping waters of South Korea and Japan, established per the Agreement between Japan and the Republic of Korea concerning fisheries. Thus, South Korea can establish Dokdo's surrounding waters as a marine protected area without

[88] UNCLOS, Art. 211.

[89] Territorial Sea and Contiguous Zone Act, Art. 1.

excessively extending the range of establishment of this area and provoking Japan based on actions such as the restriction of fishing rights. The establishment of Dokdo as a marine protected area would protect the marine ecosystem of its surrounding waters, benefiting South Korea and Japan.

Effective Control Over Dokdo and Domestic Laws

Discussions on the issue of territorial sovereignty over Dokdo have emphasized that South Korea exerts effective control over Dokdo. South Korea's argument for sovereignty over Dokdo is based on historical, geographical, and international law legitimacy.[90] The grounds are as follows: (1) operation of the Korean police stationed in Dokdo to defend the island; (2) operation of the Korean military to defend Dokdo's territorial sea and airspace; (3) application of various laws to Dokdo; (4) installation and operation of different facilities, including the lighthouse, in Dokdo; (5) Korean residents in Dokdo. These grounds are based on an ancient claim. South Korea argues that it implemented a series of measures after the Second World War and recovered its exercise of effective sovereignty over Dokdo, which was severed during the Japanese colonization, based on the applied measures. South Korea also asserts that it has constantly exercised effective control over Dokdo since the re-exercise of sovereignty over Dokdo.[91] The country also adopts the geographical unity of Dokdo with Ulleungdo or the principle of adjacency based on geographical proximity as grounds for its claim to the territory. South Korea's claims of effective control over Dokdo closely relate to its historical claim on the territory of Dokdo via international law. South Korea has exercised effective control over Dokdo based on legislative and administrative power per the Special Act on the Conservation of the Ecosystems in Island Areas Including Dokdo and the Act on the Sustainable Use of Dokdo. That is, given the constant, peaceful application of legislative, administrative, and judicial functions, Dokdo is the sovereign territory of South Korea. South Korea's effective sovereignty is also backed by its residents and members of the DSP on the island.[92] Given that South Korea currently exercises territorial sovereignty over Dokdo based on effective control, it can legitimately establish the surrounding waters of Dokdo as a marine protected area to protect the marine ecosystem and environment of this island, according to Korean laws.

---

[90] Lee (2013), pp. 319–320.

[91] Wiegand and Choi (2017), p. 235.

[92] YH Lee, supra note 90.

The Need for Regional Cooperation Regime of Marine Environmental Protection

South Korea and Japan have encountered challenges in developing cooperation systems in fields that require partnership, such as in the protection of the marine environment. A coastal state has prescriptive and enforcement jurisdiction in its EEZ regarding pollution caused by ocean dumping and vessels. Therefore, the exercise of enforcement jurisdiction by one or all the coastal states in overlapping waters can yield conflicts among the states concerned. For example, in the case of the South China Sea Arbitration between the Philippines and China in 2016, the Tribunal admitted that China's actions of reclaiming land and rocks and constructing artificial islands in the Spratly Islands had caused serious and irreparable damage to the marine ecosystem surrounding the islands. Moreover, harmful fishing activities of Chinese fishers and catching endangered fish violated regulations on marine environment protection described in the UNCLOS.[93] Thus, coastal states should focus on violations against their obligations of protecting the marine environment when they perform resource development, such as oil exploration and drilling, and facility construction.

The issue of territorial sovereignty over Dokdo can be expected to delay maritime boundary delimitation considerably in the EEZ between South Korea and Japan. Under this assumption, South Korea should implement measures for protecting and conserving the marine environment and ecosystem of Dokdo's surrounding waters to prevent conflicts by the exercise of jurisdiction in overlapping waters. Cooperation between South Korea and Japan is required to establish Dokdo's marine protected areas. Accordingly, we propose the establishment of marine protected areas as a measure for enhancing cooperation between South Korea and Japan. The establishment will reduce the tension between South Korea and Japan caused by the issue of territorial sovereignty. This measure will also help form and advance collaborative relations between South Korea and Japan toward achieving global values associated with marine environment protection and marine ecosystem conservation.

Conclusion

Dokdo is known for its considerable diversity of marine organisms. However, climate change has increased water temperatures in its surrounding waters, significantly threatening the balance of the marine ecosystem in this zone. Thus, South Korea should designate and manage Dokdo as a marine protected area to protect and conserve its marine ecosystem. On December 19, 2014, the MOF designated

[93] In the Matter of the South China Sea Arbitration (The Republic of the Philippines v. The People's Republic of China), Award of the Arbitral Tribunal (12 July 2016), para. 815.

the surrounding waters of Ulleungdo as a marine protected area. The range of the designation includes the surrounding waters of the northern and western parts of Ulleungdo, extending three nautical miles. Gyeongsangbuk-do, the administrative district responsible for the management of Dokdo, announced that it will expand its marine protected areas for ecological reasons. Indeed, there has constantly been a demand for establishing Dokdo as a marine protected area like Ulleungdo to protect the habitats and spawning areas of protected marine organisms and conserve the excellent submarine landscape, including coral reefs and seaweeds.

This study examined the necessity of establishing Dokdo as a marine protected area and reviewed the legal grounds for justifying South Korea's action of establishing Dokdo and its surrounding waters as marine protected areas. Recently, albinism aggravated by climate change has induced significant damage to the marine ecosystem of Dokdo. The establishment of Dokdo and its surrounding waters as marine protected areas will, thus, serve as a crucial legal measure for effectively conserving and protecting the marine ecosystem of this island.

Regarding the social, cultural, and historical values of Dokdo, the establishment of Dokdo as a marine protected area will contribute to protecting the marine ecosystem of Dokdo, advancing local communities, globally promoting Dokdo in association with marine tourism, and reinforcing South Korea's sovereignty over Dokdo and relevant marine areas based on the active exercise of sovereignty as a coastal state. Furthermore, the protection of overlapping waters will benefit South Korea and Japan. Thus, this action can serve as an opportunity for relieving diplomatic tension between these countries and enhancing their cooperation.

Unlike the case of disputes over the Chagos Archipelago, South Korea clearly exercises effective control over Dokdo as a coastal state. Specifically, it has effective sovereignty over Dokdo per various Korean laws and its related legislative and administrative rights. Despite the location of Dokdo in overlapping waters without a delimited maritime boundary and the constant claims of Japan for its territorial sovereignty, South Korea's action of establishing Dokdo as a marine protected area per the Conservation and Management of Marine Ecosystems Act is equivalent to its exercise of exclusive sovereignty over Dokdo. Nevertheless, South Korea should thoroughly review violations against regulations on the establishment of a marine protected area described in the UNCLOS to minimize diplomatic conflicts with Japan. South Korea may need to reach an agreement or exchange information with Japan. In the case of disputes over the Chagos Archipelago, the Tribunal concluded that coastal states should discuss and exchange information with the other party before establishing a marine protected area. Furthermore, in establishing Dokdo and its surrounding waters as marine protected areas, South Korea must analyze and consider various factors, such as legitimacy, validity, the possibility of conflicts, and measures for managing conflicts.

References

Agardy TS (1997) Marine protected areas and ocean conservation. Academic Press, Cambridge
Akimoto D (2020) Takeshima or Dokdo? Toward conflict transformation of the Japan-Korea territorial dispute. Asian-Pacific Law Policy J 22:51–53
Anderson D, Van Logchem Y (2014) Rights and obligations in areas of overlapping maritime claims. In: The South China Sea disputes and law of the sea. Edward Elgar Publishing
Australian Government Department of Climate Change, Energy, the Environment and Water, *The Benefits of Marine Protected Areas*, available at: https://www.dcceew.gov.au/sites/default/files/documents/benefits-mpas.pdf (accessed 30 Sept 2025)
Bong YD (2013) Built to last: The Dokdo territorial controversy. The baseline conditions in domestic politics and international security of Japan and South Korea. *Memory Studies* 6(2):191–203
Brander L et al (2015) The benefits to people of expanding marine protected areas. Institute for Environmental Studies, VU University Amsterdam; WWF
Cho J, Kim HM, Choi JY (2009) The Dokdo/Takeshima dispute between Korea and Japan: understanding the whole picture. Pac Focus 24(3):365–378
Chung JM, Shin J-K, Kim H-M (2020) Diversity of vascular plants native to the Ulleungdo and Dokdo Islands in Korea. J Asia-Pacific Biodiversity 13(4):701–708
Davies B et al (2021) Ecosystem approach to fisheries management works: how switching from Mobile to static fishing gear improves populations of fished and non-fished species inside a marine-protected area. J Appl Ecol 58, 11:2463–2478
Humphreys J, Clark R (eds) (2019) Marine protected areas: science, policy and management. Elsevier, Amsterdam
IUCN (1988) *General Assembly Resolution 17.38, Protection of the Coastal and Marine Environment*, https://portals.iucn.org/library/sites/library/files/resrecfiles/GA_17_REC_038_Protection_of_the_Coastal_and_Marine.pdf. Accessed 30 Sept 2025
Jung SW et al (2020) Subtidal marine algal community and endangered species in Dokdo and Ulleungdo, two Oceanic Islands in the East Sea of Korea. Ocean Sci J 55(4):537–547
Kang DW et al (2013) Diversity of intertidal benthic invertebrate of Dokdo and Ulleung-Do Island from Korea. J Asia-Pacific Biodiversity 6(1):157–164
K-Dokdo, *Climate*, available at: https://kdokdo.com/english/index.do?menu_id=00000130&servletPath=%2Fenglish (accessed 30 Sept 2025)
K-Dokdo, *Conservation Management*, available at: https://dokdo.mofa.go.kr/eng/introduce/management.jsp (accessed 30 Sept 2025)
K-Dokdo, *Marine Life*, available at: https://k-dokdo.com/english/index.do?menu_id=00000139 (accessed 30 Sept 2025)
Kelleher G, Kenchington R (1992) Guidelines for establishing marine protected areas. IUCN
Kim SK (2017) Maritime boundary negotiations between China and Korea: the factors at stake. Int J Marine Coastal Law 31(1):69–94
Kim SL, Yu OH (2021) Understanding the spatial and temporal distribution and environmental characteristics of Polychaete assemblages in the coastal waters of Ulleungdo, East Sea of Korea. J Mar Sci Eng 9(11):1310
Kim YD et al (2012) Studies on Technology for Seaweed Forest Construction and Transplanted Ecklonia Cava Growth for an artificial seaweed reef. J Environ Biol 33(5):969
KOEM, *Designation and Management of Marine Protected Areas*, available at: https://www.koem.or.kr/site/eng/02/10201040000002019071509.jsp (accessed 25 Aug 2022)
KOEM, *Marine Protected Area*, available at: https://www.koem.or.kr/common/board/getPdf.do?bcIdx=29681&cbIdx=508&fileNo=1 (accessed 30 Sept 2025)
Lee CW (2007) Implication of Dokdo issue under the Korea-Japan fisheries agreement and maritime boundary delimitation in Northeast Asia: an evaluation from the perspective of Korea. Korean J Int Law 52(2):373–397
Lee YH (2013) Reviews on the concept of effective control in international legal cases and with regard to Dokdo. *Ocean and Polar Research* 35(4):313–322

Lee MC (2016) The similarities and differences between tensions over the Senkaku Islands and Dokdo Island. In: Ishihara M, Hoshino E, Fujita Y (eds) Self-determinable development of Small Islands. Springer, Singapore, pp 101–113
Lee S, Lee HE (eds) (2011) Dokdo: historical appraisal and international justice. BRILL
Lim SY, Jin SJ, Yoo SH (2017) The economic benefits of the Dokdo seals restoration project in Korea: a contingent valuation study. Sustainability 9(6):968
Ministry of Oceans and Fisheries (MOF), *Notice of Designation of Marine Protected Area in Ulleungdo Island*, Notice No. 2014-139
MOF, *National Marine Ecosystem Monitoring Program*, available at: https://www.meis.go.kr/mes/data/1/board.do (accessed 30 Sept 2025)
MOFA, *Dokdo*, available at: https://dokdo.mofa.go.kr/eng/introduce/residence.jsp (accessed 30 Sept 2025)
MOFA, *The Government's Basic Position*, available at: https://dokdo.mofa.go.kr/eng/dokdo/government_position.jsp (accessed 30 Sept 2025)
Nam SM, Lee MS (2021) A study on determinants of Dokdo's tourism demand. J Korean Island 33(2):41–55
Nam J et al (2010) Designation processes for marine protected areas in the coastal wetlands of South Korea. Ocean & Coastal Management 53(11):703–710
Park SH, Kim KH (2017) Analysis of the Dokdo museum Seoul as a virtual experience place. Adv Sci Lett 23(10):9891–9894
Park YK, Lee S (2020) Marine protected areas in South Korea. Asia-Pacific J Ocean Law Policy 5(1):19–36
Pedrozo R (year) Sovereignty claims over the Liancourt rocks (Dokdo/Takeshima). Chin (Taiwan) Yearb Int Law Aff 28: 78–97
Protected Planet, *Marine Protected Areas*, available at: https://www.protectedplanet.net/en/thematic-areas/marine-protected-areas (accessed 30 Sept 2025)
Roberts SM, Hawkins JP (2000) Fully-protected marine reserves: a guide. WWF Endangered Seas Campaign, Washington
Schrijver NJ, Prislan V (2015) Cases concerning sovereignty over islands before the international court of justice and the Dokdo/Takeshima issue. Ocean Dev Int Law 46(4):281–314
Scott KN (2019) Area-based protection beyond National Jurisdiction: opportunities and obstacles. Asia-Pacific J Ocean Law Policy 4:158–180
Song SJ et al (2017) Biodiversity hotspot for marine invertebrates around the Dokdo, East Sea, Korea: ecological checklist revisited. Mar Pollut Bull 119(2):162–170
Spadi F (2000) Navigation in marine protected areas: national and international law. Ocean Dev Int Law 31(3):285–302
Valencia MJ (2007) The East China Sea dispute: context, claims, issues, and possible solutions. Asian Perspect 31(1):127–167
Van Dyke JM (2003) the Republic of Korea's maritime boundaries. Int J Marine Coastal Law 18:509
Van Dyke JM (2007) Legal issues related to sovereignty over Dokdo and its maritime boundary. Ocean Dev Int Law 38(1–2):157–224
Van Dyke JM Addressing and resolving the Dokdo matter. In: Lee S, Lee HE (eds) Dokdo, pp 29–40
Wiegand KE (2015) The South Korean–Japanese security relationship and the Dokdo/Takeshima islets dispute. *The Pacific Review* 28(3):347–366
Wiegand KE, Choi A (2017) Nationalism, public opinion, and dispute resolution: The Dokdo/Takeshima dispute. *Journal of Asian Pacific Communication* 27(2):232–245

Chapter 10
The Need for Designating the Yellow Sea as a Particularly Sensitive Sea Area (PSSA)

Junghwan Choi

Introduction

With the rapid economic growth and increasing interdependence between China and South Korea, the issues relevant to marine pollution in the Yellow Sea have been in the global spotlight. Industrialisation, the high population density of the coastal areas bordering the Yellow Sea, and the exploitation of oil and natural resources for economic development were indicated as primary causes behind the deterioration of all sources of marine pollution. Furthermore, the Yellow Sea has physical features that make it more vulnerable to marine pollution than other sea areas, as a semi-enclosed sea.[1] Vukas states 'every sea connected to another sea or the ocean by a narrow outlet, even when of considerable size, is due to its poor connection to such other sea or ocean particularly vulnerable and deserves special protection'.[2] Narrow outlets result in the slow exchange of waters. Geographical features of semi-enclosed sea make the Yellow Sea difficult to recover the marine environment if its sea area becomes contaminated. The damage to the marine ecosystem and the

This is an updated and revised version of the author's article "Assessing the need for the designation of the Yellow Sea Particularly Sensitive Sea Area (PSSA)" published at Marine Policy (Vol. 137, 2022) under the official permission of publication company and co-author.
Junghwan Choi: Xinghai Associate Professor at The School of Law of Dalian Maritime University, China. LL.M. in Maritime Law (Korea Maritime & Ocean Uni.), LL.M. in International Maritime Law with Merit (Swansea Uni., UK), Ph.D. in Maritime Law (Exeter Uni., UK).

[1] Teng et al. (2012), p. 16.

[2] Vukas (2004), p. 283.

J. Choi (✉)
Law School, Dalian Maritime University, Dalian, P.R. China
e-mail: junghwanchoi@dlmu.edu.cn

J. Choi (ed.), *Public Maritime Law in Asia*, International Law in Asia,
https://doi.org/10.1007/978-981-95-7037-9_10

pollution from South Korea adjacent to the Yellow Sea inevitably have effects on neighbouring states that have a common interest in the Yellow Sea. For instance, the Hebei Spirit spilt approximately 12,500 tonnes of crude oil due to a collision with the barge boat in Taean on the Yellow Sea in 2007. Over 300 km of the coastline of South Korea and EEZ of the Yellow Sea was contaminated.[3] The oil spill greatly influenced fishing activities, agriculture, and marine living resources of the Yellow Sea.[4]

Vessel-source pollution, which is classified operational and accidental discharges, is recognised as one of the contributors to the worsening of the marine environment in the Yellow Sea. South Korea has the highest degree of dependence on sea trade with foreign countries, accounting for 99.7% of all trade freight.[5] Approximately 90% of the total volume of international trade is conducted by shipping in China.[6] China exerts a strong influence on the shipping industry as the largest importer and exporter in the world. The North Korean foreign trade policy is highly reliant on China (approximately 91% of total foreign trade). According to the 2024 edition of *Lloyd's List One Hundred Ports*, six of the world's ten container ports are in China.[7] Of these, two ports (Qingdao and Tianjin) are situated at the coastal waters of the Yellow Sea. Similarly, the significant ports or offshore terminals of South Korea and North Korea are densely located in the Yellow Sea. The Yellow Sea has the busiest shipping routes, and it is potentially exposed to the risks of vessel-source pollution. In relation to this, oil pollution incidents that have happened in the coastal waters of the Yellow Sea (e.g. the Sea Prince, the Honam Sapphire, and the Hebei Spirit) devastated the marine environment and human life.[8] Enormous recovery costs and compensation against the claims for civil liability were incurred. Due to their nature, ships also generate operational discharges (e.g. bilge waters, ballast waters, grey waters, and garbage, etc.) Such operational discharges from ships have negative consequences for the marine environment to some extent in cases where there are no proper discharge restriction measures of a coastal state. The Yellow Sea has long been exposed to such pollutants from ships. Recently, the air quality of the Yellow Sea states has worsened because of ships' emissions.

The Yellow Sea has a strong possibility of becoming contaminated by various types of vessel-source pollutants unless the Yellow Sea states continue to make regulatory efforts to combat vessel-source pollution. Since China, South Korea, and North Korea have a common interest in the Yellow Sea, marine pollution incidents that occur in maritime zone of one state may inevitably affect another state. As vessel-source pollution results in transboundary pollution, and accidental discharges

[3] Cedre (2007, 2008).

[4] Ibid.

[5] Korea Shipowners' Association (2020).

[6] Jiang et al. (2018), p. 84.

[7] Lloyd's List (2024).

[8] Over the past few decades, there have been tragic oil pollution incidents, such as The Sea Prince incident (1995), the Honam Sapphire (1995), and the Hebei Spirit (2007) in the coastal waters of the Yellow Sea.

from ships can occur anywhere and anytime, regional cooperation between the states bordering semi-enclosed seas is needed to prevent vessel-source pollution beforehand or to minimise pollution incidents. However, the dispute of maritime boundary delimitation of the EEZ in the Yellow Sea is becoming a major obstacle to regional cooperation. For this reason, there is no useful, effective regulatory instrument to deal with the prevention of vessel-source pollution in the Yellow Sea so far. As a practical and feasible approach, the International Maritime Organisation (IMO) introduced PSSA concept at the global level to protect a certain sea area that is vulnerable to the risks of international shipping activities. The IMO allows a coastal state to adopt various associated protective measures (APMs) under PSSA resolution.

Against these backgrounds, this study suggests the need for the designation of a PSSA in the Yellow Sea. To achieve the goal of this study, the following are discussed. The first section conducts essentially a review of the geographical and environmental significance of the Yellow Sea, the complexities in management of pollution, and maritime activities. In the next sections, this paper introduces PSSA review with case studies, discuss palpability to the Yellow Sea, and present recommendations with discussion of methods that may work or steps to achieving the Yellow Sea PSSA.

Characteristics of the Yellow Sea

Geographical Features

Semi-enclosed or enclosed seas have long been recognised as vulnerable to marine pollution because of their geographical disadvantages. As a semi-enclosed sea, the Yellow Sea has had a great deal of exposure to various marine pollutants for a long time. The Yellow Sea is a marginal sea of the Western Pacific Ocean. It is surrounded by the Chinese mainland to the west, the Korean Peninsula to the east, and a line running from just north of the Changjiang River mouth to Jeju Island.[9] The innermost of the northern gulf of the Yellow Sea is named Bohai Bay, which entirely consists of Chinese internal waters and territorial waters.[10] The Yellow Sea is unable to properly exert assimilative capacity because there is little water exchange with open seas.[11] As a result, the Yellow Sea is considerably vulnerable to various marine pollutants.

The total area of the Yellow Sea is about 400,000 km^2, and its average depth is 44 m with a maximum depth of 100 m.[12] Bohai Bay ranges from an average depth

[9] Valencia (1988), p. 385.

[10] Auer (1991), p. 164.

[11] GEF/UNDP (2010).

[12] Valencia (1988).

of 21 m to the maximum depth of 72 m.[13] The Han River, Datung River, Yalu River, Guanhe River, and Sheyang River flow into the Yellow Sea. Approximately 1.6 billion tonnes of sediment arising from China's Huanghai River and Changjiang River are deposited in the Yellow Sea annually, eventually making large deltas in the centre of the Yellow Sea. The fresh waters of the Yellow River and Yangtze River flow across the continental shelf, and large volumes of sediments are discharged to the Okinawa Trough.[14] The volume of fresh water discharged from the Yellow River and the Yangtze River to the Yellow Sea peaks in the summer, which has a considerable impact on the salt concentration of the Yellow Sea. Besides, the Yellow Sea is prominently influenced by the monsoon season, which results in changes of biomass in the Yellow Sea.[15] The drift of tidal currents in the Yellow Sea is stronger than in other sea areas, which may lead to pollutant dispersion. Tidal currents reach 4–8 m in the port of Incheon, South Korea. The average tidal current in Bohai Bay is 5 m in the spring season.[16] Strong tidal currents make it difficult to promptly conduct clean-up and preventive operations in the event of oil pollution incidents.[17]

Marine Environmental Characteristics

Marine Ecosystem

A total of 64 large marine ecosystems exist in the world, and the Global Environment Facility (GEF) has designated the Yellow Sea as containing a large marine ecosystem.[18] The marine ecosystems in the Yellow Sea have long been threatened by pollution from land-based sources and vessel-source pollution. To restore and conserve the marine ecosystems in the Yellow Sea, in 2000, China and South Korea launched the Yellow Sea Large Marine Ecosystem (YSLME) Project under the financial auspices of United Nations Development Programme and GEF.[19] According to the YSLME Project, there are total 17 species of whales and dolphins, as well as 4 species of seals and sea lions in the Yellow Sea. The Yellow Sea provides a comfortable habitat for the Eurasian otter (*Lutra lutra*) and the finless porpoise (*Neophocaena*

---

[13] GEF/UNDP (2010).

[14] Teng et al. (2012).

[15] Ibid.

[16] Murray et al. (2015), p. 477.

[17] YSLME, YSLME PROJECT. http://www.yslmep.org/?page_id=43 (assessed 28 December 2021).

[18] The Global Environment Facility (GEF) was established on the eve of the 1992 Rio Earth Summit to help tackle our planet's most pressing environmental problems. Since then, the GEF has provided over $17 billion in grants and mobilized an additional $88 billion in financing for more than 4000 projects in 170 countries. Today, the GEF is an international partnership of 183 countries, international institutions, civil society organisations, and the private sector that addresses global environmental issues.

[19] Teague et al. (1998), p. 27788.

phocaenoides). Largha seals (*Phoca largha*) migrate to the northern Yellow Sea each winter to breed. According to the YSLME, eight species of marine mammal in this region are endangered. To conserve these species, three sea areas have been designated as Mammal Ecologically Important Areas (MEIA) within the Yellow Sea.[20]

The Yellow Sea also offers an essential habitat for algae. Algae generate more than 50% of the world's oxygen through photosynthesis.[21] As the bottom of the food chain, these plants provide the fundamental sources of food and energy to other organisms and top predators. There are 42 species of red algae, 22 species of brown algae, and 11 species of green algae in the northern Yellow Sea; 15 species of green algae, 15 species of brown algae, and 28 species of red algae are observed in the southern Yellow Sea. About 43 species of blue-green algae, 45 species of green algae, 90 species of brown algae, and 217 species of red algae species live exclusively in South Korea.[22]

In recent years, various marine pollutants have come to threaten the marine ecosystem of the Yellow Sea. For example, oil pollution and hazardous and noxious substances (HNS) pollution incidents have caused reproductive issues and the failure of the immune systems of marine mammals, marine life habitat destruction, the toxic contamination of molluscs, and productivity of algae.[23]

Wetlands

Wetlands are water areas that provide habitats for the plant and animal life. These areas help to conserve the marine ecosystem and protect the marine environment by maintaining wet conditions, either permanently or temporarily.[24] Due to the interaction of the physical, biological, and chemical characteristics of wetlands, we can protect areas from storms, mitigate floods, stabilise shorelines, and control erosion. Wetlands have a high economic value in terms of the water supply, agricultural timber and other building materials, energy resources, and wildlife resources for tourism and leisure activities.[25] Wetlands also provide a billion people with livelihoods worldwide in modern society.

However, over 50% of wetlands around the world have been destroyed in the past.[26] Of these, more than 60% of Asian wetlands have been lost [23]. Wetlands in the Yellow Sea have been rapidly destroyed as well. Over the past five decades, about 65% of intertidal wetlands have been lost—more than 28% of them between

---

[20] KORDI and WWF (2006).

[21] Chapman (2013), p. 5.

[22] Ibid.

[23] Ibid.

[24] Ramsar Convention Secretariat (2016), p. 9.

[25] Ramsar (2015), p. 4.

[26] Ibid.

the 1980s and the 2000s.[27] Conservationists have estimated that, every year, wetlands will continue to disappear at a rate of 1.5% on average, mainly due to reclamation.[28] Another cause involves habitat modifications, which have led to changes in wetlands' ecological function. Approximately 60% of the coastal wetlands in China have been altered for use for other purposes or reclamation.[29] Jiangsu Province's wetlands disappeared due to their conversion into salt ponds, and others were modified for use in agriculture and aquaculture.

A wide array of wetlands that need the protection and conservation are distributed all over the Yellow Sea. There are four designated Ramsar sites in the Chinese coastal regions, including the Dalian National Spotted Seal Nature Reserve, the Shandong Yellow River Delta Wetland, the Dafeng (*Elaphurus davidianus*) National Nature Reserve, and the Shuangtai Estuary.[30] In South Korea, there are 17 Ramsar sites in total throughout the Yellow Sea. This figure accounts for about two-thirds of total Ramsar sites.[31]

Fisheries

The Yellow Sea provides an abundant fishing ground for the Yellow Sea states. Fish represent an essential food source, and fisheries contribute to economic growth. According to the Korea Ocean Research and Development Institute and the Korea Environment Institute, 276 different species of fish live in the Yellow Sea. Of these, only 100 species of fish are used commercially.[32] Over the past few years, overfishing has become recognised as a serious problem in the Yellow Sea, and the exhaustion of the fish stock has emerged as an issue. Overfishing led to the reduction of the populations of red sea bream (*Pagrosomus major*), jewfish (*Otolithoides mijuy*), yellow croaker (*Nibea albiflora*), and white croaker (*Argyrosomus argentatus*).[33] The trend of commercially catchable fish species has shifted from commercially valuable and large fish to the small-sized, unmarketable fish.[34] Experts have identified marine pollution and reclamation as another cause behind the decrease in fishery biomass and changes in the trends of catch pattern.[35]

---

[27] MacKinnon et al. (2016).

[28] Murray et al. (2014), p. 267.

[29] Walton (2010), pp. 336–337.

[30] Ramsar (2016).

[31] Ganghwa Maehwamareum Habitat, Du-ung Wetland Ramsar Site, Jangdo Wetland, 1100 Altitude Wetland, Han River-Bamseom Islets, Mulyeongari-oreum Ramsar Site, Dongbaekdongsan, Muljangori-oreum wetland, Sumeunmulbaengdui Ramsar Site, Ungok Wetland, Dongcheon Estuary, Songdo Tidal Flat, Seocheon Tidal Flat Jeungdo Tidal Flat, Suncheon Bay, Muan Tidal Flat, Gochang and Buan Tidal Flats.

[32] KORDI and WWF (2006).

[33] KORDI and WWF (2006).

[34] KORDI and KEI (2017).

[35] WWF (2017).

The Importance of Maritime Transport

The Yellow Sea significantly contributes to economic growth by providing various fishing grounds and natural resources to the Yellow Sea states. Along with these roles, the Yellow Sea serves as major international shipping route.[36] The Yellow Sea states have a high degree of dependence on seaborne trade compared to other countries, and the shipping industry is irreplaceable in terms of expanding their economic production. Since the significant ports are situated at the Yellow Sea, many vessels pass through the Yellow Sea daily.

With the growth of seaborne trade over the world, the number of vessels navigating the Yellow Sea will continue to increase. The shipping industry plays a core role in boosting Chinese economic growth. For example, about 36% of the oil products imported from western Asia are consumed in the Asia-Pacific region, including China and South Korea. In relation to this fact, UNCTAD stated that the countries with the most crude oil imports are China and India.[37] In dry cargoes, China is the largest steel producer (53% of the world total) and steel user (51% of the world total) in the world. China is also the largest importer of a variety of products, ranging from iron ore (72% of the world total) and coal (19% of the world total) to grain (46% of world total).[6]

Moreover, approximately 33% of the world container volume is handled in South Korea and China [6]. The world-leading container ports are densely distributed over the Chinese coastal regions on the Yellow Sea, such as Qingdao, Tianjin, Dalian, Yingkou, and Lianyungang. According to *Lloyd's List One Hundred Ports*, the container throughput of these ports stood at 21 million 20-foot equivalent units (TEUs) (Port of Qingdao), 17.2 million TEUs (Port of Tianjin), 8.7 million TEUs (Port of Dalian), 5.4 million TEUs (Port of Yingkou), and 4.7 million TEUs (Port of Lianyungang) in 2019. The Chinese container throughput located in the coastal regions of the Yellow Sea amounts to approximately 8% of the world total.[38] Remarkably, six of the top ten container ports are concentrated in China. Amongst them, the ports of Qingdao and Tianjin are situated on the Yellow Sea. It is widely presumed that North Korea relies on foreign trade through shipping.[39] Officially, North Korea has a total of eight port terminals, including Chongjin, Haeju, Dancheon, Nampo, Hyungnam, Songnim, Sonbong, and Wonsan. Amongst them, Nampo, Haeju, and Songnim are situated on the Yellow Sea.[40] Nampo is the biggest port of North Korea with a total port cargo handling capability of 1.3 million tonnes.

---

[36] Zhang et al. (2016), p. e0166640.5.

[37] UNCTAD, Review of Maritime Transport 2024.

[38] According to UNCTAD STAT, world total container port throughput recorded at 811 million TEUs in 2019. About 270 million TEUs of container port throughput handled by China and South Korea.

[39] Lee et al. (2020).

[40] Chung and Jeon (2021), p. 340.

Nampo deals mainly with cement, coal, and general cargoes.[41] The proportion of foreign trade handled through the port of Nampo is estimated at about 29%.[42] Such cargoes largely depend on trade with Shanghai and Dalian (China), Southeast Asia, the Middle East, and Africa. Cargo throughput in Haeju and Songnim accounts for 9.8% and 2.9% of trade in the country, respectively.[43] These ports play a significant role as export ports to China.[44] The volume of seaborne trade in North Korea is relatively lower than that in China and South Korea. North Korea has shown a high level of dependence on trade with China via ships (Fig. 10.1).

The Benefits of a PSSA in Preventing Vessel-Source Pollution

The Concept of a PSSA

The PSSA concept arises from the IMO Resolution A.982(24). A PSSA is defined as 'an area that needs special protection through action by IMO because of its significance for recognised ecological, socio-economic, or scientific attributes where such attributes may be vulnerable to damage by international shipping activities'.[45] The PSSA concept was first introduced by the Swedish delegation at the International *Conference* on Tanker Safety and Pollution Prevention (TSPP conference) in 1978.[46] Sweden called for special protection for areas of particular value to prevent oil discharges in these places because of their renewable natural resources or their scientific importance.[47] The Swedish proposal was adopted as Resolution 9 at the TSPP conference.[48] While NGOs (e.g. the Friends of the Earth International and the International Union for Conservation of Nature) had urged the IMO to take proper action for the development of PSSAs based on the Swedish proposal adopted in the

[41] Jeong (2008), pp. 11–14.

[42] Ibid.

[43] Ibid.

[44] Ministry of Unification (2018).

[45] IMO Resolution A.982(24), Revised Guidelines for the Identification and Designation of Particularly Sensitive Sea Areas, 2006.

[46] United States Senate Committee on Commerce (1979), p. 159.

[47] Roberts (2006), pp. 88, 112, 192, 258, 512.

[48] IMCO TSPP Resolution 9, 'Protection of Particularly Sensitive Sea Areas' (1978) '1) making an inventory of sea areas around the world which are in special need of protection against marine pollution from ships and dumping, on account of the area's particular sensitivity in respect of their renewable resources or in respect of their importance for scientific purposes; 2) assessing as far as possible, the extent of the need for protection, as well as the measures which might to be considered appropriate, in order to achieve a reasonable degree of protection, taking into account also other legitimate uses of the seas; and 3) on the basis of this work, action should be taken with a view to incorporate any necessary revisions within the framework of relevant conventions'.

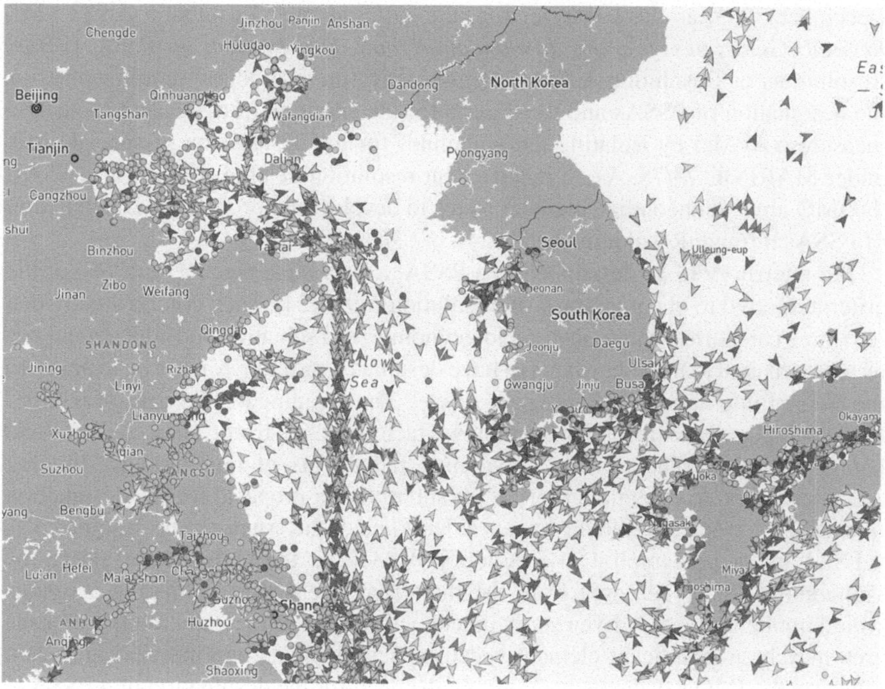

Fig. 10.1 Ship tracking in the Yellow Sea on 20th August 2025 (Source: vesselfinder.com)

TSPP conference, there was not any progress until the mid-1980s.[49] At the 22nd meeting of the Marine Environment Protection Committee (*MEPC*) in 1986, the IMO began discussing the concept of PSSAs through MEPC/Circ.171 in earnest.[50] After extended discussions, the IMO eventually decided to develop the criteria for the designation of PSSAs and separate guidelines for the member states that wish to have areas in their territories designated as PSSAs. In 1990, Australia submitted to the MEPC the proposal for the identification of the Great Barrier Reef as a PSSA for the first time.[51] In response to the Australian proposal, the MEPC adopted two resolutions (i.e. the identification of Great Barrier Reef as a PSSA and compliance with Australia's pilotage requirements for foreign vessels operating in the Inner Route of the Great Barrier Reef).[52] At the 17th IMO Assembly in November 1991, the IMO adopted Resolution A.720 (17), *Guidelines for the Designation of Special Areas and the Identification of Particularly Sensitive Sea Areas* (the 1991 guidelines). In

[49] IMO MEPC 23/16/1, Identification of Particularly Sensitive Areas: note by Friends of the Earth International. Submitted by Friends of the Earth International, 1986.

[50] IMO MEPC/Circ.171, MEPC Circular on Particularly Sensitive Sea Areas, 1986.

[51] IMO MEPC 30/19/4, Identification of particularly sensitive sea areas, including development of guidelines for designating special areas under Annex I, II, and V, submitted by Australia, 1990.

[52] IMO Resolution MEPC.44(30), Identification of the Great Barrier Reef region as a particularly sensitive sea area, 1990.

December 2005, as the latest version, the IMO adopted Resolution A.982 (24), *Revised Guidelines for the Identification and Designation of PSSA* (PSSA Resolutions or Resolution A.982 [24]), to clarify the procedural requirements for the designation of PSSAs and the criteria for the adoption of associated protective measures (APMs) by isolating the guidelines for the designation of special areas under MARPOL 73/78. As an independent resolution dealing solely with PSSAs, the IMO aims to encourage member states to develop and promote the designation of PSSAs through Resolution A.982(24).

For a territory to be designated as a PSSA, a state must meet at least one of the criteria referred to in paragraph 4 of Resolution A.982(24). Such criteria are divided into three categories: ecological, socio-economic, and scientific and educational criteria. A sea area that a state wants to have designated as a PSSA must be exposed to the risks of international shipping activities.[53] The meaning of 'the risks of international shipping activities' must contain two factors: vessel traffic characteristics and natural elements. The element concerning the threats of international shipping activities is not an essential criterion for submitting a proposal for the designation of a PSSA. If a sea area already meets at least one of the criteria to be designated as a PSSA under paragraph 4 of Resolution A.982(24), the obligation to prove the vulnerability of its sea area from the threats of international shipping activities would not be imposed.[54] Even so, in practice, the proof of the vulnerability of a sea area may be a significant element because such elements may have a significant effect on the IMO's decision in assessing the need for the designation of a PSSA.[55]

Associated Protective Measures as an Effective Mechanism

Resolution A.982 (24) allows a state to establish APMs in order to prevent various pollutants from ships effectively within sea areas to be designated as PSSAs. In the literature, APMs are defined as 'specific regulatory methods' that enable states to protect their sea areas against the risks or the threats posed by international shipping activities.[56] Resolution A.982 (24) requires a state to adopt APMs under existing IMO instruments or general accepted international rules and standards for the prevention of vessel-source pollution or Article 211(6) of UNCLOS. The term 'existing IMO instruments' encompasses IMO conventions, codes, guidelines, and resolutions.[57] Whether existing IMO instruments have a legally binding effect over foreign vessels must be prudently decided by a state when formulating a proposal for the adoption of APMs in a proposed special sea area. Moreover, APMs play a

[53] IMO Resolution A.982(24),

[54] Sage (2006), p. 374.

[55] Kachel (2008), pp. 166, 190, 222, 252.

[56] Ibid.

[57] Molenaar (1998), p. 438.

crucial role in the PSSA concept to combat pollution arising from shipping activities. However, PSSAs without APMs are unable to exert their effect properly. Unlike existing IMO instruments, the IMO has been encouraging the prevention of vessel-source pollution in designated PSSAs by allowing states to adopt various APMs.

APMs are divided two categories such as measures for the safety of navigation and special discharge restriction measures. Firstly, there are current adopted APMs related to the safety of navigation, such as the vessel traffic service (VTS) and pilotage regimes. The IMO first adopted Resolution A.572 (14) *General Provisions on Ships' Routeing* in 1985 to provide procedures and guidelines for the criteria of the adoption of ships' routeing measures.[58] Resolution A.572 (14) aims at preventing and reducing the risk of pollution or other damage to the marine environment caused by ships colliding or grounding in or near environmentally sensitive areas.[59] The legal basis for ships' routeing measures is underpinned by Regulation 10, Chapter V of the International Convention for the *Safety of Life at Sea* (SOLAS) and Rule 1(d) and Rule 10 of Convention on the International Regulations for Preventing Collisions at Sea (COLREG). Ship's routeing measures are concretely comprised of traffic separation scheme (TSS), two-way routes, recommended tracks, areas to be avoided, inshore traffic zones, precautionary areas, and deep-water routes.[60] Amongst ships' routeing measures, TSS is the most notable APM; its legal source arises from Rule 10 of COLREG and is based on various IMO resolutions—such as A.572 (14), MSC.71 (69), and MSC.165 (78).

Concerning the second category of APMs, paragraph 6.1.1 of Resolution A.982 (24) allows a state to cite the concept of 'special areas' and 'emission control areas' under the International Convention for the Prevention of Pollution from Ships, 1973, as modified by the Protocol of 1978 (MARPOL 73/78) in order to protect the marine environment of PSSAs from vessel-source pollution.[61] In that case, a state may apply stringent discharge standards to foreign vessels navigating in designated PSSAs. To do so, a sea area where a state wishes to propose the designation of a PSSA should be preferentially designated as a special area or emission control area by the IMO. The procedures and criteria for the designation of 'special areas' and 'emission control areas' are stipulated in Resolution A. 927(22) and Appendix 3 to Annex VI of MAPROL 73/78. Besides the citation for special areas or emission control areas, a state can prevent foreign vessels from discharging ballast waters within proposed PSSAs based on the International Convention for the Control and Management of Ships' Ballast Water and Sediments (BWM).

[58] IMO Resolution A.572(14), General Provisions on Ships' Routeing, 1985.

[59] IMO Resolution A.572(14) Annexe 1.1.

[60] Roberts (2005), p. 135.

[61] IMO Resolution A.982(24) para 6.1.1.

Current Status of PSSAs

As seen in Table 10.1, a total of 19 PSSAs have been designated so far since the Great Barrier Reef was first declared a PSSA in 1990. These designated PSSAs are adopted and implemented by each MEPC resolution. Of these, six PSSAs are in European waters, and five PSSAs are situated in Central America, South America, and the USA.[62] The EU and the USA are actively and practically striving to protect of their coastal waters from the threats of various pollutants from ships through existing IMO instruments based on regional cooperation. Unfortunately, there are no designated PSSAs in East Asian seas to date despite the need for special measures to combat vessel-source pollution because of its significance to the marine environmental, marine traffic, economic and historical characterises, and natural resources.

Implications

The PSSA concept has played a notable role in preventing vessel-source pollution compared to other existing IMO instruments since the concept of PSSA was introduced in 1992. A PSSA is a very useful method to prevent marine pollution from ships in a particular sea area that is vulnerable to marine pollution in its functional aspects. A PSSA has a unique advantage that a coastal state can apply discharge regulations for particular pollution substances through complementary regulatory relation with MAPROL 73/78 as well as various protective measures. A PSSA is called 'a comprehensive regulatory mechanism' protecting the marine environment from the threats of international shipping activities.[63] A coastal state vulnerable to vessel-source pollution is able to protect its sea areas from various vessel-source pollutants by adopting effective and practical APMs. Unlike other regulatory instruments over vessel-source pollution, the IMO allows a coastal state to adopt various APMs, including (but not limited to) measures for the safety of navigation and measures for discharge restrictions under existing IMO instruments, such as conventions, codes, and resolutions.[64] As a core role in the PSSA concept, the application of APMs over foreign vessels makes it possible for a coastal state to prevent operational or accidental discharges from ships in a particular sea area that requires special attention. The most important benefit of the establishment of a PSSA is to grant discretionary authority for the adoption of wider protective measures based on existing IMO instruments or UNCLOS to a coastal state.[65] For instance, protective measures for the safety of navigation such as TSS, VTS, ship reporting system, and

---

[62] IMO (2021).

[63] Beckman (2007), p. 350.

[64] Ibid.

[65] Gjerde and Freestone (1994), p. 431.

Table 10.1 Current status of designated PSSAs and APMs by the IMO

No.	Designated PSSA	Year	Location/countries	Adopted APMs
1	Great Barrier Reef	1990	Australia	Compulsory pilotage (inner), recommended pilotage, mandatory ship reporting system
2	Sabana-Camagüey Archipelago	1997	Cuba	MARPOL Annex V special area, area to be avoided, traffic separation scheme (TSS)
3	Malpelo Island	2002	Colombia	Area to be avoided
4	Sea around the Florida Keys	2002	The USA	Four areas to be avoided, three mandatory no-anchoring areas
5	Wadden Sea	2002	Denmark, Germany, the Netherlands	MARPOL Annex I and V special area, recommended TSSs, mandatory deep-water route, mandatory ship reporting system
6	Paracas National Reserve	2003	Peru	Four recommended TSSs, area to be avoided
7	Western European Waters	2004	Portugal, Spain, France, Belgium, the UK, Ireland	Recommended TSSs, mandatory ship reporting system, area to be avoided, recommended deep-water route
8	Extension of Great Barrier Reef to Torres Strait	2005	Australia, Papua New Guinea	Recommended pilotage, recommended two-way route, mandatory ship reporting system
9	Canary Islands	2005	Spain	Five areas to be avoided, three recommended TSSs, mandatory ship reporting system
10	Galapagos Archipelago	2005	Ecuador	Mandatory ship reporting system, mandatory TSSs, area to be avoided
11	Baltic Sea area	2005	Denmark, Estonia, Finland, Germany, Latvia, Lithuania, Poland, Sweden	MARPOL Annex I, II, V, VI special area, mandatory ship reporting system, localised compulsory pilotage, recommended TSSs, deep-water route between TSSs, two areas to be avoided
12	Papahānaumokuākea Marine National Monument	2007	The USA	Mandatory ship reporting system, area to be avoided
13	Strait of Bonifacio	2011	France, Italy	Mandatory ship reporting system, recommended pilotage, recommended two-way route
14	Saba Bank	2012	North-eastern Caribbean, Kingdom of the Netherlands	Mandatory no-anchoring areas, area to be avoided

(continued)

Table 10.1 (continued)

No.	Designated PSSA	Year	Location/countries	Adopted APMs
15	Extension of the Great Barrier Reef and Torres Strait	2015	Australia	Ships' routing systems (SOLAS V), recommended two-way route
16	Jomard Entrance	2016	Papua New Guinea	Recommended two-way route
17	Tubbataha Reefs Natural Park	2017	Sulu Sea, Philippines	Recommended pilotage, area to be avoided
18	North-Western Mediterranean Sea	2023	France, Italy, Monaco, Spain	Measures to reduce ship strikes with cetaceans
19	Nusa Penida and Gili Matra Islands	2024	Lombok Strait, Indonesia	Measures to protect marine biodiversity

Source: IMO website

pilotage system are helpful to combat accidental discharges from ships by enhancing safe and efficient navigation within a PSSA. The APMs regarding special discharge restrictions strictly prohibit the ship from discharging any pollutants. Such measures are directly and greatly contributing to protect a particular sea area that needs a special attention for the protection the marine environment from vessel-source pollution.

Another advantage is that a PSSA promotes global awareness of the need for the protection of the marine environment from various vessel-source pollutants within designated PSSAs due to its significance in the ecological, socio-economic, and marine environmental aspects. In particular, officials in a PSSA can alert foreign vessels to the dangers of the violations of discharge standards while travelling in the PSSA. The promulgation of the designation of PSSAs can help coastal states to protect sea areas by raising public awareness of the need for special attention to the protection of the marine environment.[66] The master or the shipowner must pay more attention in order ensure that the vessel does not violate the adopted APMs in a designated PSSA than in other sea areas. Besides, the simple and concise PSSA designation procedures may facilitate the submission of the application to the IMO and the final designation of a PSSA than 'special areas' under MARPOL 73/78. In this light, the expansion of a PSSA may be conducive to the acceleration of the achievement of common or global pursuits to prevent and reduce vessel-source pollution.

[66] Prylipko (2014), p. 23.

Analysis of the Yellow Sea PSSA

Case Studies for the Way Forward on the Yellow Sea PSSA: The Need for Governing Body

To attain the designation of the proposed Yellow Sea PSSA, the Yellow Sea states need to set up a phased, strategic approach. The analysis of the environmental, geographical, and maritime traffic characteristics and the study of the impact of vessel-source pollution on the marine environment and potential risks of shipping activities in the Yellow Sea should take precedence in order to highlight the need for a comprehensive regulatory instrument at the regional level.[67] Such scientific certainty would help the Yellow Sea states to determine the geographical scope and APMs. After the PSSA is established, the matter how the Yellow Sea states can faithfully and practically implement the adopted APMs becomes important. Thus, the Yellow Sea states need to consider establishing an administrative governing body (e.g. a commission) responsible for cooperation and coordination in regional activities with respect to the prevention of vessel-source pollution in the Yellow Sea to push ahead with a proposal and deal with overall matters related to the Yellow Sea PSSA. The commission can play various roles in formulating the proposal.[68] Firstly, the commission can play a role as a policymaker in establishing the institutional strategy at the regional level and implementing the IMO instruments. As there is no regional convention on the prevention of marine pollution from ships in the Yellow Sea, the Yellow Sea states should make an effort to create a regional convention or agreement through the commission. Secondly, the commission should be able to act as a coordinator in negotiating the decisions regarding APMs, the geographical scope, and procedural matters.

In addition, the commission can play a significant role in coordinating and carrying out the designation of a special area under MARPOL 73/78. While the Northwest Pacific Action Plan (NOWPAP) and the Coordinating Body on the Seas of East Asia (CORSEA) administered by United Nations Environment Programme (UNEP) play a role as the governing bodies of each action plan under regional sea programmes covering the Yellow Sea, these do not concentrate on the prevention of marine pollution from ships.[69] Since the geographical scope of the proposed PSSA is too vague, the NOWPAP and the CORSEA may have difficulty establishing a regional legal framework for the prevention of marine pollution from ships in the Yellow Sea.[70] Despite North Korea's observer status, the country was not involved in the NOWPAP or the CORSEA.[71] For these reasons, the establishment of an

[67] Cho and Ju (2013), p. 192.

[68] Ibid.

[69] NOWPAP (2020).

[70] NOWPAP (2007).

[71] Valencia (1994), p. 28.

administrative governing body to deal with the prevention of vessel-source pollution in the Yellow Sea is needed to forge an agreement for the designation of the proposed Yellow Sea PSSA amongst the Yellow Sea states. The following case studies can guide the discussion of which aspects would be applicable to the Yellow Sea and then the Yellow Sea recommendations. Case studies insight the significance of the role of a governing body when formulating a proposal for the designation of a PSSA.

The Baltic Sea PSSA Case

The first case involves the Baltic Sea PSSA, which was first proposed by the Baltic Marine Environment Protection Commission (HELCOM), which is the governing body of the Helsinki convention, in 2001 and 2003.[72] This organisation plays various roles: It is a marine environmental policymaker; an environmental focal point providing information about the state of and trends in the marine environment, as well as the efficiency of measures to protect it; a supervisory body that dedicated to ensuring that all parties fully implement HELCOM environmental standards throughout the Baltic Sea; and a coordinating body.[73] The Baltic Sea was designated as a PSSA in 2005 through the efforts of HELCOM. The organisation still provides an important platform for dealing with matters related to the Baltic Sea PSSA and the coordination of regional activities.

The Wadden Sea PSSA Case

In a second example, Denmark, Germany, and the Netherlands agreed to submit a proposal for the designation of the Wadden Sea PSSA to the IMO at the Ministerial Declaration of the 9th Trilateral Governmental Conference in 2001.[74] The trilateral application for the designation of the Wadden Sea PSSA was mainly coordinated through the Common Wadden Sea Secretariat.[75] This organisation was established in 1987 according to an administrative agreement concluded between the Danish Ministry of the Environment, the German Federal Ministry for the Environment, Nature Conservation, Building, and Nuclear Safety, and the Dutch Ministry of Economic Affairs.[76] The Secretariat coordinates the activities of the cooperation and reviews evaluation reports. The members have also attempted to raise awareness of relevant issues, held discussions on risk management as a central aspect of

[72] HELCOM (2021).

[73] Ibid.

[74] Common Wadden Sea Secretariat (2021).

[75] Ibid.

[76] Ibid.

navigational safety, and promoted the implementation of the adopted APMs ever since the Wadden Sea was designated as a PSSA in 2002.[77]

The Regional Marine Pollution Emergency Response Centre for the Mediterranean Sea (REMPEC)

The third example is the Regional Marine Pollution Emergency Response Centre for the Mediterranean Sea (REMPEC). This organisation's members have consistently suggested the need for designation of a Mediterranean Sea PSSA due to its geographical disadvantages and the environmental, socio-economic, and cultural significance, as well as the intense maritime traffic congestion.[78] Eventually, REMPEC decided to develop an implementation strategy for the designation of a Mediterranean Sea PSSA at the 14th Ordinary Meeting of the Contracting Parties to the Barcelona Convention in 2005.[79] Although the parties involved have not yet submitted the final application for the designation of the Mediterranean Sea PSSA to the IMO, they agreed to continue to initiate the process of identification of those areas which, after examination according to the REMPEC focal points, could be proposed for designation as a PSSA based on the publication *Regional Strategy for Prevention of and Response to Marine Pollution from Ships (2016–2021)*.[80] Recently, REMPEC released a statement indicating that an assessment of the benefits, costs, and feasibility of implementing an ECA to limit SOx from ships in the Mediterranean Sea has begun.[81] Moreover, REMPEC is dedicated to coordinating and cooperating on regional activities in an attempt to identify a sea area in which two or more states have common interests as a PSSA or an ECA.

---

[77] Ibid.

[78] The REMPEC, which is administered by the IMO and UNEP, is the governing body of the Protocol Concerning Cooperation in Preventing Pollution from Ships and, in Cases of Emergency, Combating Pollution of the Mediterranean Sea to the Barcelona Convention ("the 2002 Prevention and Emergency Protocol"). The primary objective of REMPC encourages the Contracting Parties to the Barcelona Convention to ratify, implement, and enforce the IMO instruments so as to prevent vessel-source pollution in the Mediterranean Sea. REMPEC, The Regional Marine Pollution Emergency Response Centre for the Mediterranean Sea. https://www.rempec.org/en, 2021 (accessed 3 May 2021).

[79] UNEP(DEPI)/MED IG.16/13, ANNEX III -Recommendation for 2006-2007. https://wedocs.unep.org/bitstream/handle/20.500.11822/7271/05ig16_13_ann3_recommendations_eng.pdf?sequence=1&isAllowed=y, 2006 (accessed 3 May 2021).

[80] REMPEC/WG.36/6/Corr.1, Regional Strategy for Prevention of and Response to Marine Pollution from Ships 2016-2021. https://www.rempec.org/en/knowledge-centre/online-catalogue/wg-36-6-corr_1.pdf, 2015 (accessed 4 May 2021).

[81] IMO, IMO helps assess further sulphur reductions in the Mediterranean. https://imo.org/en/MediaCentre/Pages/WhatsNew-1172.aspx, 2018 (accessed 4 May, 2021).

Recommendations for the Yellow Sea Management

Likewise, the Yellow Sea states need to consider establishing a governing body with administrative responsibility to deal actively and directly with regional cooperation and coordination on the designation of the proposed Yellow Sea PSSA. The governing body can continue to play the central role in devising a strategic approach for the prevention of marine pollution from ships in the Yellow Sea even after as the designation of the PSSA. To do so, the conclusion of an administrative agreement on the establishment of the governing body is needed. It is also worth discussing this agenda in more in depth at South Korea's annual maritime safety policy meeting. After determining a strategic direction to establish an administrative governing body for promoting the designation of the proposed Yellow Sea PSSA, South Korea and China should ask North Korea to participate in an administrative agreement.

Review of the Need for Designation of the Yellow Sea PSSA

As regards why the Yellow Sea needs to be designated as a PSSA, first, the Yellow Sea has been recognised as one of polluted sea areas in the world since the report entitled Dying Sea was released by the Worldwatch Institute in 1992.[82] As one of the semi-enclosed seas in the world, the Yellow Sea features some geographical disadvantages that result in the worsening of the marine environment and the marine ecosystems.[83] For example, the Yellow Sea is shallow, and the movement of the ocean current is more prominent than in other sea areas. Such geographical disadvantages make it more difficult for the Yellow Sea to circulate compared with open seas. Sediments from major rivers in South Korea and China pour into the Yellow Sea. In addition, industrial and domestic wastewaters from the coastal regions of the Yellow Sea result in severe pollution in the Yellow Sea.

Although industrialisation and urbanisation in the coastal waters of the Yellow Sea constitute the primary cause exacerbating the situation in the marine environment, policymakers should not overlook the fact that vessel-source pollution has also accelerated the deterioration of the marine environment of the Yellow Sea. The Yellow Sea has long played a vital role as an international shipping route. In particular, the major ports are densely situated at the coastal regions of the Yellow Sea. Since the Yellow Sea states depend highly on seaborne trade with foreign countries, the Yellow Sea is still exposed to the risks of operational or accidental discharges from ships. Besides, as significant fishing grounds between the Yellow Sea states, the Yellow Sea provides abundant food and contributes to the economic growth of the Yellow Sea states. Due to severe marine pollution, some fish stocks are threatened with exhaustion. The Yellow Sea is a sea area that needs particular protective

[82] Platt (1995), p. 599.

[83] Cho (2003), p. 205.

measures and intensive regional cooperation to protect and preserve the coastal sea area and the resources from vessel-source pollution because of its environmental, socio-economic, and scientific significance.

The second factor concerns the necessity of a comprehensive legal instrument to deal specifically with the matters for the prevention of vessel-source pollution. The IMO has long acted as a global rule-making organisation to protect and preserve the marine environment from the threats of international shipping activities. The IMO provides a wide range of global regulatory instruments, ranging from the prevention of accidental and operational discharges from ships, the control of ballast waters, and the establishment of an international cooperation framework for pollution incidents to international civil liability regimes for pollution damage. The fundamental limitation in applying the IMO instruments is that the implementation wholly relies on member states. The status of ratification by the Yellow Sea states is closely associated with the profit of their marine industries and economic levels. The Yellow Sea states have somewhat different attitudes towards the implementation of the IMO conventions at the domestic level.[84] Moreover, there are still ongoing disputes regarding the maritime boundary delimitation between China and South Korea and the status of Northern Limit Line (NLL) on the Korean peninsula.[85] Due to these issues, fundamental limitations exist, along with a legal vacuum in exercising enforcement jurisdiction over the IMO instruments. While the Yellow Sea is contained in the Coordinating Body on the Seas of East Asia (CORSEA) and in the Action Plan for the Protection, Management and Development of the Marine and Coastal Environment of the Northwest Pacific Region (NOWPAP), which are administered by United Nations Environment Programme (UNEP), these sea programmes do not provide an effective regional instrument for the prevention of vessel-source pollution. The absence of the participation of North Korea in regional sea programmes is one factor weakening the effectiveness of regional regimes in dealing with the protection of the marine environment in the Yellow Sea.[86] Given that North Korea does not often cooperate with the international community in the marine environment field, except for the IMO diplomatic conference, the designation of a PSSA may become a significant motivation to improve regional cooperation by encouraging North Korea without any administrative burden.

Thirdly, designating the Yellow Sea as a PSSA is imperative because the Yellow Sea has not been granted a special status at the IMO level so far. The Yellow Sea PSSA can raise public awareness about the significance of protection of the marine environment of the Yellow Sea and can contribute to combating vessel-source pollution effectively by imposing strict discharge standards and the navigational safety measures on foreign vessels. The Yellow Sea has been exposed to the threats of various marine pollutants from ships for a long time. Given the environmental and geographical significance of the Yellow Sea and its maritime traffic characteristics, the

---

[84] Choi (2021), p. 225.

[85] Van et al. (2003), p. 149.

[86] Olsen (2009), pp. 10–11.

Yellow Sea should be given a special status under the IMO regulatory framework to actively and effectively prevent operational and accidental discharges from ships.

In the future, the proposed Yellow Sea PSSA may play a crucial role as a comprehensive management tool in preventing vessel-source pollution by providing effective and useful APMs against foreign vessels. The Yellow Sea states can also overcome current legal issues concerning the exercise of the enforcement jurisdiction over foreign vessels in an overlapping area of the EEZ through the proposed Yellow Sea PSSA by offering a unified and harmonised enforcement procedure for APMs. A Yellow Sea PSSA would strengthen regional cooperation for dealing with the prevention of vessel-source pollution, and it could serve as a valid legal instrument by encouraging the participation of North Korea.

Adoption of Effective APMs in the Yellow Sea PSSA

Measures for the Safety of Navigation

The most serious oil pollution incidents are related to accidental discharges from ships (e.g. collisions, groundings, bad weather, etc.). The international community has been striving to eliminate maritime accidents by providing practical navigational safety measures at the global level.[87] Based on the IMO instruments, a coastal state can apply more strict navigational safety measures than global standards considering their marine traffic characteristics and marine environmental characteristics. The IMO allows a coastal state to take various navigational safety measures within a PSSA under existing IMO instruments, including (but not limited to) SOLAS, COLREG, and non-binding documents (e.g. Resolutions, Codes, and Guidelines). A coastal state can enjoy regulatory shopping to improve the safety of navigation in PSSAs if approved by the IMO. Currently, all PSSAs have established navigational safety measures as APMs (i.e. TSSs, areas to be avoided, pilotage schemes, and ship-reporting systems).

To determine which navigational safety measures are effective as APMs in the Yellow Sea, an analysis for maritime traffic characteristics and risk assessment of the Yellow Sea should take precedence. In addition to such an analysis, this paper strongly recommends the necessity of introducing the transnational Vessel Traffic Management and Information System (VTMIS) in the Yellow Sea. The transnational VTMIS can considerably contribute to decreasing numbers of maritime accidents that may happen beyond territorial seas or in overlapping EEZ areas. The transnational VTMIS is a practical application of the coastal states' precautionary jurisdiction. For instance, the British and French maritime authorities jointly operate the transnational VTMIS and the Dover Strait Channel Navigation Information Service to improve maritime safety and the efficiency of navigation.[88] Another

[87] Anyanova (2012), p. 34.

[88] Anderson (2007), p. 169.

reason for the necessity of the introduction of the transnational VTMIS as an APM in the Yellow Sea PSSA is that China and South Korea may be unable to properly exercise enforcement jurisdiction over vessel-source pollution due to the overlapping area of the EEZs in the Yellow Sea. Taking prior measures is of paramount significant to prevent marine pollution from ships beforehand in disputed areas. The introduction of the transnational VTMIS may help to prevent accidental discharges beforehand by enhancing navigational safety and monitoring illegal discharges that have happened beyond the territorial sea. The Chinese and South Korea maritime authorities can also provide a comprehensive and systematic maritime traffic service with vessels passing through the Yellow Sea in consideration of its marine traffic congestion. The transnational VTMIS may play a crucial role as clear grounds that foreign vessels have violated discharge standards in the Yellow Sea. Based on such evidence, the Yellow Sea states may conduct a physical inspection or institute legal proceedings if foreign vessels' activities have resulted in marine pollution in the EEZs.

Special Discharge Restrictions

To invoke the strict discharge standards of MARPOL 73/78 as APMs, the Yellow Sea must be preferentially designated as a special area. Despite the need, the Yellow Sea has not yet been designated as a special area. Considering the geographical vulnerability, marine environmental and socio-economic significance, and maritime traffic characteristics, the Yellow Sea needs to be designated as a special area under Annex I (oil), Annex V (garbage), and Annex VI (ECA) of MARPOL 73/78.[89] In that case, the Yellow Sea states may apply strict discharge standards against foreign vessels navigating the Yellow Sea PSSA by citing special area regimes of MARPOL 73/78. The Yellow Sea can be also granted a dual special status as both a special area and a PSSA by the IMO. Moreover, since 1 January 2016, China has implemented a domestic emission control area (DECA) to reduce SOx emission from ships within the Pearl River Delta, the Yangtze River Delta, and the Bohai Sea.[90] Given that air pollution is becoming a critical issue all over the world, the Chinese efforts to reduce sulphur at the domestic level may become a significant motivation to extend the ECA to the Yellow Sea through designation of an ECA under Annex VI of MARPOL 73/78. The more stringent SOx emission limit (compared to the global level) can be applied to the Yellow Sea PSSA.

In addition, the Yellow Sea states need to establish prohibition measures for the discharge of ballast waters as APMs in the Yellow Sea PSSA. Article 2(3) of the BWM stipulates that a state may take more stringent measures individually or jointly with other parties with respect to the prevention, reduction, or elimination of the transfer of harmful aquatic organisms consistent with international law. Based

---

[89] Tan (2005), p. 133.

[90] Wang et al. (2021), pp. 1–37.2.

on this provision, the Yellow Sea states would be able to take joint special discharge measures with respect to the control of ballast waters as APMs in the Yellow Sea as necessary.

Surveillance System

As another appropriate measure, the Yellow Sea states need to introduce a comprehensive surveillance system to monitor oil spills and illegal discharges within the Yellow Sea PSSA. For example, the EU provides a wide range of surveillance mechanisms using military surveillance, the Sistema Integrado de Vigilancia Exterior, and the coastal VTS.[91] To monitor any kinds of vessel-source pollution in European waters, the EMSA established a satellite-based surveillance system for illegal oil discharges (i.e. 'CleanSeaNet').[92] The EMSA provides member states with radar satellite images obtained from a commercial satellite provider. Such surveillance systems not only play a crucial role as ex post facto evidence concerning the violation of discharge standards, but they can also result in a precautionary effect by alerting vessels of oil spills or illegal discharges when they pass through particular sea areas.[93] The establishment of a comprehensive surveillance system can considerably help the Yellow Sea states to control and monitor illegal discharges and oil pollution that may occur beyond the coastal state's jurisdiction.

Conclusion

While the total volume and the frequency of contamination by pollutants from vessels are comparatively low compared to land-based sources, the negative influence of various pollutants from ships on the marine environment and the marine ecosystem should not be overlooked. Oil and HNS spill incidents have more a fatal effect on the marine environment than those from land-based sources.[94] Vessel-source pollution may occur anywhere and anytime. Namely, the geographical range of marine pollution from ships is very extensive and not limited to a particular sea area. The Yellow Sea has suffered a number of tragic oil and HNS pollution incidents (e.g. the

---

[91] European Commission, Legal Aspects of Maritime Monitoring & Surveillance Data – Summary Report. https://op.europa.eu/en/publication-detail/-/publication/a6551ad5-ecd1-4b3c-b95f-d3d6a097e54d, 2008 (accessed 2 May 2021).

[92] EMSA, Addressing Illegal Discharges in the Marine Environment. http://www.emsa.europa.eu/csn-menu/items.html?cid=122&id=1879, 2008 (assessed 28 December 2021).

[93] Ibid.

[94] ITOPF, Response to Marine Chemical Incidents, Technical Information Paper No.17. https://www.itopf.org/fileadmin/uploads/itopf/data/Documents/TIPS_TAPS_new/TIP_17_Response_to_Marine_Chemical_Incidents.pdf, 2014.

Sea Prince, the Honam Sapphire, and the Hebei Spirit).[95] Vessels inevitably produce operational discharges because many ships now use the Yellow Sea to enter the coastal ports of South Korea and China. These operational pollutants include harmful substances that threaten marine life and the marine environment in the Yellow Sea. In addition, with increasing numbers of vessels passing through the Yellow Sea, ship emissions are accelerating air pollution along with land-based sources. A high level of regional cooperation is required to exercise unified, harmonised enforcement and legislative jurisdiction over foreign vessels within the Yellow Sea. Considering that maritime boundary disputes are impeding regional cooperation, there is a need to devise a way for regulatory instruments to prevent vessel-source pollution beforehand by overcoming the issues of maritime boundaries. If countries do not cooperate, the Yellow Sea's marine environment may become worse.

The PSSA Resolution stipulates that a state must meet at least one requirement for the designation of a PSSA amongst a total of 17 criteria, which are compartmentalised into ecological, socio-economic, and scientific elements. The IMO provides member states with minimum criteria to use the PSSA concept, compared with the criteria for the designation of special areas under MARPOL 73/78. The Yellow Sea is eligible to become a PSSA in consideration of the significance of its environmental, socio-economic, and marine traffic characteristics. The Yellow Sea PSSA can combat various marine pollutants from ships both effectively and actively. In the PSSA concept, APMs play a core role. The most important factor in establishing a PSSA is to determine APMs. Concerning what APMs will be effective in the Yellow Sea PSSA, this paper proposes not only special discharge restrictions and the introduction of the transnational VTMIS but also the establishment of a comprehensive surveillance system.

The PSSA may prove significantly helpful in increasing public awareness about the significance of the protection of the marine environment of the Yellow Sea. Since the Yellow Sea has not yet been conferred a special status at the IMO level, the Yellow Sea PSSA may become the first step towards directly dealing with the prevention of vessel-source pollution based on regional cooperation and coordination. The Yellow Sea states should start to discuss a proposal for the designation of a PSSA as soon as possible. When formulating a proposal, the Yellow Sea states have to make every effort in good faith to attain the final goal: designating a PSSA through the establishment of a commission that plays a role as the coordinator and policymaker in cooperating and coordinating for the project. Without a doubt, it can be said that the proposed Yellow Sea PSSA may pave the way for a cleaner Yellow Sea by preventing vessel-source pollution.

[95] Cho (2010), p. 448.

References

Anderson D (2007) Modern law of the sea: selected essays. Brill, Leiden, p 169
Anyanova E (2012) Oil pollution and international marine environmental law. In: Curkovic S (ed) Sustainable development–authoritative and leading edge content for environmental management. Intechopen, London, p 34
Auer MR (1991) Prospects for environmental cooperation in the Yellow Sea. Emory Int Law Rev 5:163–208
Beckman RC (2007) PSSAs and transit passage—Australia's pilotage system in the Torres Strait challenges the IMO and UNCLOS. Ocean Dev Int Law 38:325–357
Cedre (2007, 2008) The Hebei Spirit. https://wwz.cedre.fr/en/Resources/Spills/Spills/Hebei-Spirit. Accessed 10 Jan 2021
Chapman RL (2013) Algae: the world's most important 'plants'—an introduction. Mitig Adapt Strateg Global Change 18(1):5–12
Cho KK (2003) Building an environmental regime in the Yellow Sea sphere. Korean J Int Stud 1(1):203–226
Cho DO (2010) Limitations of 1992CLC/FC and enactment of the Special Law on M/V Hebei Spirit incident in Korea. Mar Policy 34(3):447–452
Cho DO, Ju HH (2013) A consideration on Yellow Sea governance of Korea and China. J Korean Soc Mar Environ Safety 19(2):186–192
Choi JH (2021) Domestic legal system of the Yellow Sea states for the prevention of vessel-source pollution under the UNCLOS: a comparative legal study. J East Asia Int Law 14(2):219–244
Chung TW, Jeon JW (2021) System dynamics-based prediction of North Korean Port Volumes. Asian J Shipp Logist 37(4):337–344
Common Wadden Sea Secretariat (2021) Common Wadden Sea Secretariat. https://www.waddensea-worldheritage.org/common-wadden-sea-secretariat. Accessed 3 May 2021
GEF/UNDP (2010) Analysis. https://iwlearn.net/resolveuid/d066663c6e3935d55e93d15b1061e7ca. Accessed 20 Mar 2021
Gjerde KM, Freestone D (1994) Particularly sensitive sea areas—an important environmental concept at a turning-point. Int J Mar Coast Law 9:425–468
HELCOM (2021) HELCOM. https://helcom.fi/about-us/. Accessed 2 May 2021
IMCO TSPP Resolution 9, Protection of Particularly Sensitive Sea Areas, 1978
IMO (2021) Particularly sensitive sea areas help protect fragile environments from the risks posed by shipping. http://pssa.imo.org/#/intro. Accessed 22 Apr 2021
IMO MEPC 23/16/1, Identification of Particularly Sensitive Areas: Note by Friends of the Earth International, 1986
IMO MEPC 30/19/4, Identification of Particularly Sensitive Sea Areas, Including Development of Guidelines for Designating Special Areas Under Annex I, II and V, submitted by Australia, 1990
IMO MEPC/Circ.171, MEPC Circular on Particularly Sensitive Sea Areas, 1986
IMO Resolution A.572(14), General Provisions on Ships' Routeing, 1985
IMO Resolution A.982(24), Revised Guidelines for the Identification and Designation of Particularly Sensitive Sea Areas, 2006
IMO Resolution MEPC.44(30), Identification of the Great Barrier Reef Region as a Particularly Sensitive Sea Area, 1990
Jeong BM (2008) Integration plan of the shipping and logistics system between North Korea and South Korea. Korea Maritime Institute
Jiang B, Li J, Gong C (2018) Maritime shipping and export trade on 'Maritime Silk Road'. Asian J Shipp Logist 34(2):83–90
Kachel MJ (2008) Particularly sensitive sea areas: the IMO's role in protecting vulnerable marine areas. Springer, Berlin
KORDI and KEI (2017) Fish of the Yellow Sea ecoregion and their habitats. https://www.wwf.or.jp/activities/data/200710y-seamap04e.pdf. Accessed 28 Dec 2021

KORDI and WWF (2006) Yellow Sea ecoregion: a global treasure, a global responsibility. https://www.wwf.or.jp/activities/lib/pdf/%5BENG%5DYellowSea_Ecoregion-A_global_treasure_a_global_responsibility(Fact%20sheet).pdf. Accessed 20 Mar 2021

Korea Shipowners' Association (2020) The importance of shipping industry. http://www.shipowners.or.kr/eng/ks_industry/ks_industry1.php. Accessed 14 Jan 2021

Lee SW, Seo JW, Kauppila J, Martinez L, Okamoto N (2020) 2019-2020 KOTI-ITF-EASTS special research report on transport connectivity in East Asia. The Korea Transport Institute

Lloyd's List (2024) The 2024 edition of Lloyd's list one hundred ports. https://lloydslist.maritimeintelligence.informa.com/one-hundred-container-ports-2020. Accessed 1 May 2025

MacKinnon J, Verkuil YI, Murray NJ (2016) IUCN situation analysis on east and southeast Asian intertidal habitats, with particular reference to the Yellow Sea (including the Bohai Sea). https://www.iucn.org/content/iucn-situation-analysis-east-and-southeast-asian-intertidal-habitats-particular-reference-yellow-sea-including-bohai-sea-0. Accessed 6 Apr 2021

Ministry of Unification (2018) North Korea's Economic. http://nkinfo.unikorea.go.kr/nkp/overview/nkOverview.do?sumryMenuId=EC210. Accessed 10 Apr 2021

Molenaar EJ (1998) Coastal state jurisdiction over vessel-source pollution. Kluwer Law International BV, Alphen an den Rijn

Murray NJ, Clemens RS, Phinn SR, Possingham HP, Fuller RA (2014) Tracking the rapid loss of tidal wetlands in the Yellow Sea. Front Ecol Environ 12:267–272

Murray NJ, Ma Z, Fuller RA (2015) Tidal flats of the Yellow Sea: a review of ecosystem status and anthropogenic threats. Austral Ecol 40(4):472–481

NOWPAP (2007) State of the marine environment in the NOWPAP region, https://www.unep.org/nowpap/zh-hans/node/104. Accessed 2 May 2021

NOWPAP (2020) Northwest Pacific Action Plan (NOWPAP). https://www.unep.org/nowpap/. Accessed 2 May 2021

Olsen EA (2009) Marine environmental cooperation in Northeast Asia. Korean J Def Anal 7:7–28

Platt AE (1995) Dying seas. Oceanogr Lit Rev 7:599

Prylipko A (2014) PSSA in the Baltic Sea: protection on paper or potential progress. World Maritime University, Malmo

Ramsar (2015) State of the world's wetlands and their services to people. https://www.ramsar.org/sites/default/files/documents/library/strp19_4_bn7_e.pdf. Accessed 2 Apr 2021

Ramsar (2016) The Ramsar Sites Information Service in China. https://www.ramsar.org/wetland/china. Accessed 10 Apr 2021

Ramsar Convention Secretariat (2016) Ramsar handbook: an introduction to the Ramsar Convention on Wetlands. https://www.ramsar.org/sites/default/files/documents/library/handbook1_5ed_introductiontoconvention_e.pdf. Accessed 2 Apr 2021

Roberts J (2005) Protecting sensitive marine environments: the role and application of Ships' routeing measures. Int J Mar Coast Law 20(1):135–159

Roberts J (2006) Marine environment protection and biodiversity conservation: the application and future development of the IMO's particularly sensitive sea area concept. Springer, Berlin

Sage B (2006) Precautionary coastal states' jurisdiction. Ocean Dev Int Law 37(3):359–387

Tan AKJ (2005) Vessel-source marine pollution: the law and politics of international regulation. Cambridge University Press, Cambridge, p 133

Teague WJ, Perkins HT, Hallock ZR, Jacobs GA (1998) Current and tide observations in the Southern Yellow Sea. J Geophys Res: Oceans 103:27783–27793

Teng SK, Yu H, Tong L, Choi CI, Kang D, Liu H, Chun Y, Juliano RO, Rautalahti-Miettinen E, Daler D (2012) Yellow Sea, Global International Waters Assessment, GIWA, Regional Assessment 34

UNCTAD, Review of Maritime Transport 2024

United States Senate Committee on Commerce, Science, and Transportation, 1978 IMCO Protocols: Hearing Before the Committee on Commerce, Science, and Transportation, Journal of Travel Research (1979)

Valencia MJ (1988) The Yellow Sea: transnational marine resource management issues. Mar Policy 12:382–395

Valencia MJ (1994) Involving the DPRK in Northeast Asia: regional economic and environmental cooperation. NAPSNet Special Reports

Van JMD, Jon M, Valencia MJ, Jenny MG (2003) The North/South Korea Boundary Dispute in the Yellow (West) Sea. Mar Policy 27(2):143–158

Vukas B (2004) Enclosed or semi-enclosed seas. In: Vukas B (ed) The law of the sea: selected writings. Martinus Nijhoff Publishers, Leiden

Walton M (2010) Biodiversity conservation and the Yellow Sea large marine ecosystem project. J Korean Soc Mar Environ Energy 13:335–340

Wang XT, Yi W, Lv ZF, Deng FY, Zheng SX, Xu HL, Zhao JC, Liu H, He K (2021) Annual changes of ship emissions around China under gradually promoted control policies from 2016 to 2019. Atmos Chem Phys Discuss 21:1–37. https://doi.org/10.5194/acp-21-13835-2021

WWF (2017) The Yellow Sea Ecoregion. https://en.wwfchina.org/en/what_we_do/marine/yellow_sea_ecoregion/threats/. Accessed 28 Dec 2021

YSLME, YSLME Project, http://www.yslmep.org/?page_id=43. Accessed 28 Dec 2021

Zhang S, Jin S, Zhang H, Fan W, Tang F, Yang S (2016) Distribution of bottom trawling effort in the Yellow Sea and East China Sea. PLoS ONE 11(11):e0166640

Chapter 11
Developments in Crew Management and the Protection of Rights and Interests in China

Xingguo Cao, Runze Wu, Yuxuan Jiang, and Jing Zhang

Introduction

Maritime crews play a central role in the development of waterborne transport and have made significant contributions to the construction of maritime power, the Belt and Road Initiative, and broader economic and social development. As such, they constitute a vital strategic resource for the state. Globally, crews are increasingly recognized as key workers in many countries and regions, reflecting their importance to both national and international maritime operations. In line with China's strategy to enhance its maritime influence, the development, management, and protection of the crew workforce have received substantial attention.

According to the China Crew Development Report 2023, China had 1,982,163 registered crew members by the end of 2023, marking a 4.5% year-on-year increase. The number of crew members dispatched abroad also rose by 13.3%, reaching 143,582. The growing international deployment of Chinese crew members supports the stability of the global maritime logistics supply chain and strengthens both domestic and international economic circulation. These figures underscore China's status as a major global provider of professional maritime crews. However, despite significant progress in crew management and protection, several challenges persist. These include a declining influx of new entrants into the profession, concerns

Xingguo Cao: Professor of Law at the School of Law of DMU, China. Ph.D. in Maritime Law (DMU, China), Postdoctoral Research (CUPL), Visiting Scholar (Center for Maritime Law Studies, Tulane University, USA).

X. Cao (✉) · R. Wu · Y. Jiang · J. Zhang
Law School, Dalian Maritime University, Dalian, P.R. China
e-mail: caoxingguo@dlmu.edu.cn; wrz15004560604@dlmu.edu.cn; jyxrenee29@dlmu.edu.cn; jasmine0688@dlmu.edu.cn

J. Choi (ed.), *Public Maritime Law in Asia*, International Law in Asia,
https://doi.org/10.1007/978-981-95-7037-9_11

regarding overall crew competency, and issues related to sustainable workforce development. Furthermore, maritime operations inherently involve risks that can threaten human life, port security, and the marine environment.

This study examines China's legal and institutional framework for crew management, focusing on both legislative structure and practical implementation. Particular attention is given to the role of judicial interpretations, official replies, letters, and other guidance issued by the Supreme People's Court, which have increasingly shaped the resolution of crew-related disputes in Chinese courts. Of particular significance is the "Provisions on the Trial of Certain Issues Concerning Disputes Involving Seamen", promulgated in 2020. This instrument, comprising 21 articles, addresses critical issues including the definition and resolution of legal relationships involving seamen, recognition and exercise of maritime priorities, protection of remuneration, legal status of wages in cases of unlawful conduct, tort liability in labour conditions, the interface between work-related injury insurance and civil compensation, and the application of law in international labour contracts. Clarification of these issues is essential for enhancing the understanding and practical application of judicial interpretations in maritime dispute resolution.

Overview of Crew Legislation in China

Before discussing the legislation, it is important to clarify the distinction between the terms "crew" and "seafarer". While both refer to individuals working on board ships, "crew" is a broader term encompassing all persons on a vessel, including the master, officers, engineers, and other personnel. In contrast, "seafarer" generally refers to individuals professionally employed on a ship and specifically recognized under international conventions such as the STCW Convention and the Maritime Labour Convention (MLC 2006). In practice, all seafarers are crew members, but not all crew members qualify as seafarers under legal and international standards. This distinction is critical in understanding the scope of legislation, rights, duties, and protections provided under Chinese law.

Crew-related legislation in China spans multiple legal domains and regulatory levels. From a departmental law perspective, it includes administrative law, civil law, economic law, labour and social security law, and others. From a legislative effectiveness perspective, it involves laws, administrative regulations, departmental rules, and normative documents. Additionally, the legal system incorporates both domestic and international legislation.

Key Legislations

To date, China has not formulated a unified crew law; its domestic legislation on crews is scattered across many laws, regulations, and rules. At the legal level, Article 34 and Article 35 of the Maritime Law and Article 13 of the Maritime Traffic Safety Law provide fundamental provisions for crew management. Other laws, such as the Labour Law and the Contract Part of the Civil Code, play key roles in safeguarding crew rights and interests. In terms of administrative laws and regulations, the Regulations on Seamen offer comprehensive provisions for the registration, employment, training, and job security of crews, as well as the services provided to them, forming a legal foundation for crew management and protection in China. At the regulatory level, further rules and provisions have refined China's crew-related system and regulations, including the Provisions on the Administration of Overseas Assignment of Seamen, the Rules for the Administration of Seamen Training, the Rules for the Competency Examination and Certification of Seafarers Serving in Seagoing Ships, the Rules on the Competency Examination and Certification of Inland Vessel Crew, the Rules on the Minimum Safe Manning of Ships, and the Measures for Administering the Working and Living Conditions of Seafarers on Board Vessels.

Concurrently, the international treaties involving seafarers, to which China is a party, are also an important component of its seafarer legislation. Among them, the International Convention on Standards of Training, Certification and Watchkeeping for Seafarers, 1978 (STCW Convention), to which China acceded in 1980, and the Maritime Labour Convention, 2006 (MLC 2006), acceded to in 2015, have played a positive role in upgrading seafarers' quality and strengthening the protection of their rights.[1] Regarding their quality, the principles and standards for the examination of seafarers set out in the Measures for the Examination and Certification of Ship's Crew Examinations, which were formulated in 1979, essentially align with the STCW Convention. The Measures brought an end to the disorderly state of China's seafarer management, transitioning the management of education, training, examination, and certification of seafarer members from institutions and state-owned shipping companies to government-led management during the Cultural Revolution. In October 1997, China further completed the transformation of domestic law into the STCW 78/95 Convention, forming a set of domestic compliance regulations comprising the Rules for the Competency Examination and Certification of Seafarers Serving in Seagoing Ships, as well as a series of normative documents. The MLC 2006 addresses seafarers' employment and social rights, stipulating the minimum requirements for seafarers to work on board ships, including those relating to employment conditions, living quarters, recreational facilities, health protection, and medical treatment. These provisions are crucial for helping to ensure that China's seafarers achieve decent working and living conditions, enhancing the level of protection of their rights and interests. The 2022 Amendment to the MLC 2006,

---

[1] Li et al. (2022), pp. 22–29.

which is binding on China, entered into force on 23 December 2024. The amendments include revisions to areas related to recruitment and placement, repatriation, accommodation and recreational facilities, meals, and emergency medical care, to safeguard the rights of seafarers and provide them with a fair and safe working environment.

Specific Contents of China's Legislation on Crews

Crew Registration and Qualifications

The new revised Article 34 of the Maritime Law (amended on 28th October 2025) stipulates that "Chinese national crew shall obtain the corresponding certificate of competency and medical certificate in accordance with the provisions of relevant laws and administrative regulations governing crew matters. The provisions of relevant laws and administrative regulations governing crew matters shall apply to foreign crew serving on Chinese-flagged ships". Article 13 of the Maritime Traffic Safety Law stipulates that "Chinese crew members and staff members working on offshore installations shall receive professional education and training on maritime traffic safety and corresponding positions. A Chinese crew member shall, according to the provisions of the laws and administrative regulations on the management of crews, apply to the maritime safety administration for a certificate of competency and obtain a health certificate. A foreign crew member working on a vessel of Chinese nationality shall be governed by the laws and administrative regulations on the management of crews. A crew member working on a vessel shall comply with the scope of the vessel, navigation area, and duties specified in his certificate of competency".

The above two laws establish principal provisions for the qualifications of crew members. Building upon this, Chapter 2 of the Regulations on Seamen provides details on the registration and qualification of crews, including the conditions that should be met in order to apply for the certificate of crew competency, including the content of this certificate, and to apply for the seafarer's certificate, and so forth. The relevant provisions of the Regulations promote the alignment of China's crew management standards with the international standards and have positive impacts on the crews, the education and training institutions, the crew's service organizations, and society as a whole.

In practice, China has also made a breakthrough in issuing a Certificate of Competency for Foreign Seafarers. On 15 April 2022, the Shenzhen Maritime Safety Administration issued the Certificate of Competency for Seafarers of the People's Republic of China to Croatian seafarer Sivio Jodovic. This is the first certificate of competency issued to a foreign crew member in China, marking a new breakthrough in facilitating the practice of foreign professionals.

Crew Member Duties

As mentioned previously, the provisions concerning the duties of crew members are clearly stipulated in the Maritime Law, the Maritime Traffic Safety Law, and the Regulations on Seamen, as well as in other laws and regulations. In particular, the newly amended Maritime Traffic Safety Law in 2021 has upgraded some of the crew duties stipulated in the Regulations on Seamen into legislative provisions, playing an important role in improving the legislative system for crew duties in China. Among these provisions, those relating to the authority and duties of the master are particularly crucial.

The master is the highest commanding officer on board and is usually the most experienced pilot on board. Therefore, like other national legislation, Article 37(1) of the Maritime Law stipulates that "The Master shall be responsible for the management and command of the ship". Article 38 of the Maritime Traffic Safety Law further stipulates that "A master shall have the right to make independent decisions on the protection of life safety at sea, vessel security, and prevention and control of vessel pollution". This is the first time that China has explicitly given the captain the right to make independent decisions in the above respects at the legal level, which is significantly valuable in ensuring the captain's independent decision-making and ability to maintain the safety of maritime navigation. Meanwhile, Article 40 of the Safety of Maritime Traffic Law also stipulates that "Where a person on board suffers or is suspected of suffering from an infectious disease that seriously threatens the health of others, the master shall immediately launch the corresponding contingency plan, take necessary isolation measures against the relevant persons within the scope of his functions, and report to the relevant competent department in a timely manner". In the context of the COVID-19 epidemic, this provision is of great significance in clarifying the procedures and responsibilities of a ship's master in dealing with an epidemic outbreak at sea. In addition, Article 38 of the Maritime Law and Article 39 of the Maritime Traffic Safety Law stipulate that the master has the right to confine or take other necessary measures against those who carry out illegal and criminal activities on board the ship. This connects to the legal application of Article 4 of the Public Security Administration Punishments Law for the violation of public security administration on board ships of the People's Republic of China, and Article 39 of the Maritime Law also stipulates the right of the master to notarize under special circumstances.

In addition to the above powers, Article 41 of the Maritime Law also stipulates that "The duty of the Master in the management and navigation of the ship shall not be absolved even with the presence of a pilot piloting the ship". Meanwhile, Article 183 of the Maritime Law and Article 112 of the Maritime Traffic Safety Law also clearly stipulate the master's duty to carry out rescues at sea, as well as outlining their responsibility for violating the duty to rescue.

Protection of the Rights and Interests of Crews

China has long prioritized crew welfare. As early as 1953, the Interim Measures for Crew Public Holidays were issued by the Ministry of Communications of the Central People's Government; in 1955, the Ministry of Foreign Trade, the Ministry of Health, the Ministry of Communications, and the General Staff Department of the People's Liberation Army jointly issued the Measures for the Administration of Landing of Crews. The Regulations on Seamen, which came into force in 2007, made more comprehensive provisions for the occupational security of crews during their work on board ships and included principal or convergent provisions for the principles and core contents stipulated in the MLC 2006. These principles and core contents were stipulated either in principle or in connection with each other. Given that China was still considering whether to accede to the MLC 2006, it was an innovative and forward-looking move in the history of China's domestic legislation that reflected the main spirit and principles of the Convention. The Regulations on Seamen also laid the legal foundation for the entry into force and implementation of the MLC 2006 in China.[2] In terms of specific content, Chapter 4 of the Regulations on Seamen, "Professional Safeguard for Seamen", provides for the social insurance of crews; the protection, hygiene, and medical care on board and in the workplace; the conclusion of the labour contract; the protection of trade unions; crew wages and benefits; the prevention of fatigue duty; special paid annual leave; and the repatriation of crews, and so on. More systematic provisions have been made, which play an important role in safeguarding the legitimate rights and interests of seafarers. Also, in the newly amended Maritime Law, a new article (article 36) is introduced for the protection of crew welfare, which states that: Crew employers shall enter into employment contracts with crew in accordance with the provisions of relevant laws, administrative regulations and international treaties on crew labor and social security concluded or acceded to by the People's Republic of China. In the absence of specific provisions in this Code regarding the employment of crew and their rights and obligations in relation to labor and social security, the provisions of relevant laws and administrative regulations shall apply.

With China's formal ratification of and accession to the MLC 2006 in 2015, the protection of the rights and interests of crews has a more comprehensive legal basis under China's policy of active compliance. Crews' rights have become clearer, such as the right to fair employment, remuneration for labour, rest and leave, medical treatment on board and ashore, and the right to social security. The new Article 6 of the Maritime Traffic Safety Law stipulates that "The state shall protect the labour safety and occupational health of crews in accordance with the law, and safeguard the lawful rights and interests of crews", which for the first time incorporates the protection of the rights and interests of crews into the national law and provides legal protection for maintaining labour safety and crew occupational health. With China's continuous improvement of legal provisions related to the rights and

[2] Maritime Bureau of the Ministry of Transportation and Communications (2019), p. 267.

interests of crews, a more stable legislation has gradually formed. This includes, first, laws and regulations, such as the Regulations on Seamen, the Labour Law, and the Labour Contract Law; second, international conventions, such as the STCW Convention and the MLC 2006; third, collective agreements, mainly including the National Committee of the Chinese Seamen and Construction Workers' Union and the China Shipowners' Association signing of the Collective Bargaining Agreement For Chinese Crews on an annual basis; fourth, national policies, including the Announcement of the Ministry of Finance and the State Taxation Administration on the Individual Income Tax Policies for Oceangoing Seafarers; and fifth, judicial interpretations, which are primarily Provisions of the Supreme People's Court on Several Issues Concerning Trial of Cases Involving Seafarer-Related Disputes.

Crew Training

The transport authorities in China have always assigned great importance to the task of crew training. As early as April 1950, the General Administration of Maritime Affairs of the Ministry of Transport instructed the Shanghai Harbor Authority to establish a crew examination committee, followed by Dalian, Tianjin, and other places.[3] In April 1982, at the "Symposium on Crew Examination Work" held in Beijing, the China Water Supervision Bureau decided to take the lead in training Hong Kong crews concerning the "four small certificates" (i.e. fire-fighting on board ships, operation of lifeboats and rafts, life-saving at sea, and rescue at sea in case of emergencies). Huangpu Port Supervision proposed a draft method and took responsibility for the training, examination, and issuance of certificates.[4] Between 1984 and 1985, Huangpu Port Supervision issued a total of 25,629 "four small certificates", marking the first time China fully complied with the STCW Convention's requirements for professional training of international seafarers. On 6 September 1982, the Ministry of Transport approved the "Report on Four Individual Certificates for Seafarers" by the Water Safety Supervision Bureau, agreeing that the port supervision of Dalian, Shanghai, Tianjin, Qingdao, and Huangpu should handle the issuance of certificates for four individual training courses for seafarers dispatched by other countries.[5] On 7 January 2025, the Maritime Safety Administration of China (MSAC) issued the Measures for the Implementation of the Rules of the People's Republic of China for the Administration of Seamen Training, which specifically added a chapter on "Teaching Personnel", placing greater emphasis on enhancing the skills of teaching personnel and further refining the rules related to seafarer training.

---

[3] Ibid, 30.

[4] Ibid, 172.

[5] Ibid, 173.

In 1997, China formally promulgated the Rules for the Competency Examination and Certification of Seafarers Serving in Seagoing Ships. These rules were used in the revision of the provisions of the Regulations on Seamen, upon which the Rules for the Administration of Seamen Training were based, promulgated on 22 June 2009 by the Ministry of Transport. In 2010, the China Maritime Safety Administration issued three documents to further clarify matters related to the training of crew members as well as the responsibilities of the maritime agencies: the Measures for the Supervision and Inspection of Seamen Training, On-site Verification of Training Institutions, and the Authority for the Administration of Certification for the Crew Training Examination.[6] Article 14 of the newly amended Maritime Traffic Safety Law also clarifies the conditions that Chinese ships on international voyages must meet in order to obtain a maritime labour certificate. This institutional arrangement is necessary for China to fulfil the MLC 2006 by obtaining maritime labour certificates for ships on international voyages, thereby satisfying the Convention's requirement that member states stipulate by law that ships on international voyages must hold maritime labour certificates. Meanwhile, in order to strengthen the competence of seafarers and the management of fitness assessments, the Maritime Safety Administration of the Ministry of Transport promulgated the revised Code of the People's Republic of China for the Fitness Assessment of Seafarers (2024 Edition) on 23 December 2024, which has led to the standardization of seafarer training, and lays the foundation for the further construction of a high-quality seafarers' team.

China's seafarer-related laws, rules, and regulations have thus been improving with practice, manifested in the complementarity of domestic legislation and international conventions; clearer and more systematic regulations on the qualifications, duties, and training of seafarers; and more comprehensive legal protection of seafarers' rights and interests. Seafarers play an irreplaceable role in the construction of a strong maritime nation, the Belt and Road, and international trade. The improvement and development of the crew-related legislation will also play a positive role in promoting and safeguarding the layout and implementation of the relevant strategies.

[6] Ibid, 232–233.

Development of Law Enforcement Relating to Seafarers

Authorities Responsible for Seafarer-Related Law Enforcement

China Maritime Safety Administration (MSA)

The China Maritime Safety Administration and its affiliated maritime agencies are the primary enforcement and regulatory bodies for crew management in China. To effectively conduct crew management, the MSA has established a Crew Management Division, whose primary responsibilities include the following:

- Organizing the drafting of laws, regulations, rules, and normative documents related to crew management and supervising their implementation
- Being responsible for organizing the establishment, operation, and management of the crew management quality system
- Being responsible for formulating qualification standards for seafarers (including pilots) and magnetic compass adjusters and supervising their implementation
- Being responsible for the training, examination, and certification management of seafarers (including pilots) and magnetic compass adjusters
- Being responsible for the management of crew development and professional safeguards, for inspections and certification management related to maritime labour conditions, for undertaking the work of the National Maritime Labour Tripartite Coordination Mechanism Office, and safeguarding the overall rights and interests of seafarers; participating in relevant work on comprehensive governance and stability maintenance in the transportation industry of the Ministry of Transport
- Being responsible for the qualification management of training institutions engaged in crew (including pilots) training, as well as the audit and supervision of their quality management systems
- Being responsible for the management of agencies engaged in seafarer outsourcing business and for the management of seafarer certificates
- Being responsible for organizing the formulation of standards for the minimum safe manning of ships and the management of manning certificates[7]

In the "14th Five-Year Development Plan for the Maritime System", improving crew management and promoting the sustainable and healthy development of the crew team are listed as an essential task, including strengthening the construction of a high-quality crew team, optimizing the crew development environment, broadening crew training channels, enhancing crew professionalism, safeguarding crew rights and interests, improving the tripartite coordination mechanism for maritime

[7] Internal Departments, "Article" MSA Website https://www.msa.gov.cn/page/article.do?articleId=45AF5734-8B5D-429C-BAB3-F8EFD079E1AC&channelId=7B1BBBD5-BBF4-438F-8CDA-B026A8B5003F (accessed 22 September 2025).

labour relations, building a public service system for crew professional safeguards, fully implementing the MLC 2006, and continuously promoting the mutual recognition of crew certificates with global shipping countries.[8]

Other Agencies and Organizations Related to Seafarer Management

Ministry of Human Resources and Social Security (MOHRSS). The Ministry of Human Resources and Social Security is the state authority responsible for the overall management of personnel in government agencies, enterprises, and institutions, as well as for coordinating urban and rural employment and social security policies. Regarding crew management, MOHRSS is responsible for direct communication and coordination with the International Labour Organization. During inspections related to maritime labour certificates, the MSA is responsible for supervising and inspecting the minimum age, wage payment, working hours, labour contracts, leave, social insurance, and other aspects stipulated by the Convention. MOHRSS is responsible for supervising and inspecting the implementation of national labour security laws, regulations, and other relevant provisions of the Labour Law and Labour Contract Law.

China Shipowners' Association (CSA) and China Maritime Trade Union (CMTU). The China Shipowners' Association is an industry association voluntarily formed by the owners, operators, and managers of merchant ships registered in the People's Republic of China and engaged in water transportation, as well as units and organizations related to shipping. The association serves as a bridge between the government and enterprises. The China Maritime Trade Union National Committee is a national industrial trade union organization under the leadership of the All-China Federation of Trade Unions, representing and safeguarding the legitimate rights and interests of seafarers. In the tripartite coordination mechanism stipulated by the MLC 2006, the China Shipowners' Association and the China Maritime Trade Union hold collective negotiation meetings every year to discuss the minimum standard wage, minimum board allowance, and overtime allowance for crew members and evaluate the provisions of the China Seafarers' Collective Agreement.

Ministry of Agriculture and Rural Affairs (MOA). According to the Measures for the Administration of Fishery Crews in the People's Republic of China, the Ministry of Agriculture and Rural Affairs is responsible for the management of fishery crews nationwide. Local competent fishery departments at or above the county level and their affiliated fishery and port supervision and management agencies are responsible for the management of fishery crews following their respective functions and responsibilities. To strengthen the management of fishery crews, safeguard their legitimate rights and interests, and ensure the safety of life and property of the fishery vessels and the personnel on board, the MOA manages various aspects such as the qualification and certification of fishery crew, crew manning and

[8] Ministry of Transport of the People's Republic of China (2021a), p. 14.

responsibilities, crew training and services, crew professional management and safeguards, supervision and management, and penalty provisions.

Law Enforcement and Supervision of Seafarers

Maritime Labour Inspections

To fulfil the MLC 2006 and protect the legitimate rights and interests of crew members, the Ministry of Transport and the Ministry of Human Resources and Social Security jointly issued the Measures for the Inspection of Maritime Labour Conditions (hereinafter referred to as the Measures), which were implemented starting on 1 January 2017. From pilot projects for inspections of maritime labour conditions in Shanghai, Shandong, Zhejiang, Guangdong, and Shenzhen jurisdictions in 2018 to the official establishment of the first maritime labour condition inspection workstation in the country in 2022, China's implementation mechanism for the MLC 2006 has entered a standard track. In December 2024, the 2022 Amendment to the Maritime Labour Convention officially entered into force, making major revisions in areas such as recruitment and placement, repatriation, accommodation and recreational facilities, food and catering services, medical care on board and ashore, the protection of health and safety, and accident prevention, which will further enhance the protection of seafarer rights and interests. China will conduct further inspections of labour conditions covering the scope of the amendment to ensure its effective implementation.

The inspection of maritime labour conditions nationwide is supervised by the Ministry of Transport and the Ministry of Human Resources and Social Security, with local maritime agencies and local human resources and social security administrative departments responsible for its implementation. There are three main types of inspections: regular, additional, and temporary inspections. The inspection content is divided into two parts: the first is the inspection of the physical environment related to the crew's workplace and catering; the second is the inspection of the management and operational aspects that constitute decent work. Maritime labour inspections can be conducted using document verification, facility inspections, and interviews with crew members. Shipowners of vessels that pass the temporary/regular inspection of maritime labour conditions can provide relevant proof materials to the maritime administrative authority where the company is registered, and the competent authority will issue a temporary/maritime labour certificate.

Port State Control

The Port State Control (PSC) mechanism is implemented by port authorities to ensure that foreign ships entering their ports comply with domestic conventions and laws, and inspections related to crew training and job performance are important components of PSC inspections. China began pilot PSC projects in Tianjin and Dalian as early as 1986 and became a signatory to the Memorandum of Understanding on Port State Control in the Asia-Pacific Region (Tokyo MOU) in 1994. Since then, maritime administrative authorities at all levels have conducted inspections on ship manning and related statutory certificates and documents, as well as crew members' performance of their job responsibilities, under relevant provisions such as the Maritime Traffic Safety Law and the Tokyo MOU.[9] On 4 January 2024, the PSC Data Research Laboratory for the Asia-Pacific Region was established at Liaoning Maritime Safety Administration, becoming the first research laboratory based on PSC defect data analysis within the maritime system. In the future, under the guidance of the PSC Research Subcommittee, international exchanges and cooperation will be carried out to fulfil convention obligations research, cultivate international convention fulfilment talents, and improve China's leadership in PSC inspections in the Asia-Pacific region, and China will continue to promote development and innovation in areas such as the regulatory and policy environment, supervision and technical means, talent training, and team building, to promote the sustained and healthy development of the country's port industry.

Supervision and Management of Seafarers' Service Organizations

To strengthen the management of seafarer services and standardize the conduct of seafarer service agencies, as well as safeguard the legitimate rights and interests of both seafarers and seafarer service agencies, the Ministry of Transport, referring to the provisions of the MLC 2006, issued the "Regulations on the Administration of Seafarer Services" in 2008. These regulations stipulate that the Ministry of Transport is responsible for overseeing seafarer service work, and the Maritime Safety Administration of the People's Republic of China is responsible for uniformly implementing the management of seafarer services.[10] In May 2010, to promote the healthy development of the seafarer outsourcing business and regulate the management of the seafarer outsourcing market, the Ministry of Commerce transferred the management of labour personnel in the category of seafarer outsourcing to the Ministry of Transport. Concurrently, the Ministry of Transport issued the "Regulations on the Administration of Seafarer Outsourcing", which clarify the entry thresholds for seafarer outsourcing agencies. The regulations establish four central systems: a qualification system, an annual review system, an exit system, and an emergency management system. These systems regulate the conduct of market entities such as seafarer outsourcing agencies and foreign shipowners at all stages, as well as clarify related responsibilities.[11] In February 2015, the Maritime Safety Administration of the People's Republic of China issued the "Notice of the

[9] Ministry of Transport of the People's Republic of China (2018), p. 138.

[10] Ministry of Transport of the People's Republic of China (2008).

[11] Ministry of Transport of the People's Republic of China (2011).

Maritime Safety Administration of the People's Republic of China on Further Regulating the Management of Seafarer Service Agencies", requiring seafarer service agencies to establish relevant management systems, such as quality management systems for seafarer services and personnel as well as resource guarantee systems. The notice also emphasized the supervisory responsibilities of maritime administrative authorities over seafarer service agencies.[12] In 2023, the Maritime Safety Administration of the People's Republic of China aimed to further optimize the management of seafarer service operations, enhance the quality of seafarer services, clarify the scope of seafarer service activities, strengthen the administration of filings for seafarer service operations, increase the transparency of information disclosure by service agencies, standardize the professional activities of these agencies, and strictly supervise the quality of services provided by them.[13]

Protection of Crews' Rights and Interests

Establishing Seafarer Service Platforms

To better serve seafarers and safeguard their rights and interests, China's maritime law enforcement agencies have innovated in establishing platforms for seafarers' material support and dispute resolution. For example, since 2021, Nanjing Maritime Safety Administration, in collaboration with multiple departments, has established the country's first cluster of comprehensive green service areas on the water, integrating ten functions, including floating supermarkets, courier service points, clinics, and pharmacies. It has also set up a 24-h maritime government service self-service station, providing comprehensive material support for seafarers. In November 2022, China's first provincial-level seafarer protection agency, the Jiangsu Seafarer Rights and Interests Protection Centre, was established in Nanjing, linking five workstations to provide services such as training, career planning, legal assistance, and dispute mediation, forming a comprehensive seafarer protection system. In 2024, China's first maritime and commercial legal public service centre was also established in Nanjing, with a professional team providing legal consultation and dispute resolution services to comprehensively safeguard seafarers' rights and interests and contribute to the development of the port and shipping economy.

Maritime bureaus in coastal provinces such as Guangdong, Shandong, Jiangsu, Zhejiang, and Fujian have also established various seafarer service platforms that cover seafarers' living supplies, leisure and entertainment, education and training, and labour management, realizing the protection of seafarers' rights and interests.

---

[12] China Maritime Bureau (2015).

[13] China Maritime Bureau (2023).

Organizing Various Activities

To celebrate "World Seafarers' Day", in 2023, the Maritime Safety Administration of the Ministry of Transport and the China Seafarer Construction and Trade Union National Committee led the sixth China Seafarer Skills Competition. The competition involved 48 teams and 504 contestants from national shipping enterprises and nautical colleges, stimulating seafarers' enthusiasm for learning and competitive spirit. Furthermore, maritime bureaus organize activities, such as legal publicity and education, as well as evacuation and escape drills, to enhance seafarers' legal awareness and professional practical skills, providing powerful talent support for the construction of marine and transportation power.

Promoting Seafarer Employment Development

To thoroughly implement the "Outline of Building a Powerful Transportation Country", in 2021, the Ministry of Transport, Ministry of Education, Ministry of Finance, Ministry of Human Resources and Social Security, Ministry of Veterans Affairs, and the All-China Federation of Trade Unions jointly issued the "Guiding Opinions on Strengthening the Construction of a High-Quality Seafarer Workforce".[14] The guidance explicitly expands channels for seafarer training to broaden employment opportunities for seafarers. It includes incorporating nautical-related majors into the category of talents in short supply, optimizing physical examination conditions for nautical colleges, and scientifically formulating recruitment plans. It also supports enterprises and institutions in central and western provinces to engage in the seafarer training business. It encourages graduates of non-nautical colleges and universities to participate in vocational skills training for seafarers. Furthermore, it promotes school-enterprise cooperation in training veterans for careers in the seafaring industry, connecting with quality resources to ensure their smooth employment.

Operating Seafarer Complaint Procedures

The seafarer complaint procedure aims to protect seafarers' rights and interests as well as to address complaints against violations of conventions, laws, and regulations that infringe upon seafarers' rights and interests. Following the MLC 2006 and its amendments, as well as relevant regulations of the China Maritime Safety Administration, ships should establish and operate seafarer complaint procedures while paying special attention to issues of harassment and bullying. In 2018, the

[14] Ministry of Transport of the People's Republic of China (2021b).

China Maritime Safety Administration published the "Working Procedures for Handling Complaints from Seafarers on Board",[15] clarifying complaint methods, handling processes, boarding procedures, and handling deadlines. The aim is to encourage seafarers and the public to participate in the supervision of water transportation safety, thereby maintaining order.

With the China Maritime Safety Administration serving as the backbone of law enforcement for seafarers, multiple agencies collaborate and coordinate in the law enforcement and management of seafarer affairs, providing good organizational support for related law enforcement work involving Chinese seafarers. To continuously and effectively fulfil the requirements of international conventions such as the STCW Convention and the MLC 2006, as well as domestic laws such as the Maritime Traffic Safety Law, China has established a comprehensive inspection system for seafarer law enforcement, which is thorough in content and diverse in form. It covers inspections of maritime labour conditions, port state control, the supervision and management of seafarer service agencies, seafarer training management, the issuance of seafarer certificates, and the inspection of seafarers' duty performance. This better safeguards seafarer's fundamental rights and interests and stabilizes the development of the seafarer market.

Development of Seafarers' Judicature

Since the establishment of six maritime courts on 14 November 1984, China's maritime judicial system has undergone 40 years of transformation, evolving from nonexistent to strong, with continuous improvement in its functions and mechanisms. Currently, China has 11 maritime courts and 42 branch courts, making it the country with the most maritime judicial institutions in the world. The role of the maritime judicial system in resolving disputes among crew members and protecting their rights and interests has also been continuously improved. As a maritime power, the proportion of maritime disputes involving crew members in China's maritime judicial practice has always been relatively high. In the annual maritime judicial white papers released by various maritime courts, disputes over crew labour contracts have consistently ranked among the top five cases; from 2016 to 2020, the proportion of cases involving crew labour contract and personal injury compensation disputes handled by national maritime courts were 30.98%, 21.78%, 17%, 17.95%, and 29% respectively;[16] from 2018 to 2021, the distribution of causes of maritime cases in the national maritime courts showed that there were a total of 9970 disputes over crew labour contracts, accounting for 13.73%, and 3417 cases of maritime and inland waterway personal injury liability disputes, accounting for 4.71%.[17] It is evi-

[15] China Maritime Bureau (2021).

[16] Jiang (2020), p. 30.

[17] Supreme People's Court of China, *China's Maritime Judicial Review (2018–2021)*.

dent that as one of the critical channels for the relief of crew members' rights and interests, the importance of the maritime judicial system in safeguarding crew members' rights is indubitable.

Based on the summaries of maritime judicial white papers from various maritime courts, disputes involving crew members typically involve disputes over labour contracts and disputes relating to compensation for personal injuries in maritime and navigable waters. Disputes over crew labour contracts are the primary category; in a broad sense, this also includes related special procedure cases, such as applications for enforcement, evidence preservation, ship seizure, registration, compensation of maritime claims, and confirmation of people's mediation agreements. Disputes involving crew members primarily concern crew members requesting payment of overdue wages, repatriation fees, social insurance fees, or compensation for expenses involving industrial injuries, disabilities, and deaths, which relate to maritime civil cases related to people's livelihood. Maritime judicial practice should prioritize the protection of crew members' rights and interests and implement the judicial concept of serving the people. At the same time, the occurrence of crew labour disputes and labour contract disputes is sometimes closely related to the shipping market situation, and the resolution of disputes must ensure the realization of crew members' interests while also reasonably considering the interests of shipowners. For example, in times of market downturn, when enterprises are unable to pay wages and remunerations due to difficulties in capital turnover, the enforcement of cases must take into account the enterprise's operating conditions. In addition, due to the special nature of crew work and flexible employment methods, disputes often involve foreign factors, and the identification and handling of relevant legal relationships and the timely resolution of disputes put higher requirements on maritime judicial work.

The Implementation of the Judicial Service Mechanism for Crew Members Embodies the Concept of Judicial Service for the People

The "Fengqiao experience" of the new era, which resolves grassroots contradictions and problems through the thinking and methods of the rule of law, involves meeting the people's diverse demands, promoting the legalization of grassroots social governance, and providing a basic outline and rich material for the overall structure of China's diversified dispute resolution mechanism.[18] It also provides an important work path for the protection of seafarers' rights and interests in maritime judicial practice. Chinese maritime courts have established judicial service mechanisms for seafarers at various stages, promoting the resolution of disputes among seafarers and practicing the "Fengqiao experience" at sea. At the pre-litigation stage, the

[18] Peng (2023), p. 23.

mediation room expands from the litigation service centre to shipping centres, fishing area townships, and judicial offices, utilizing an online and offline one-stop dispute resolution platform, to carry out pre-litigation mediation and reconciliation close to the source of the disputes. In this way, it can facilitate improved performance of pre-litigation mediation for seafarers. At the same time, some courts establish characteristic mediation teams, building them with professional mediators and people from various sea-related industries. For example, the Ningbo Maritime Court has established the maritime "Lao Niangjiu" judicial mediation team, which employs experienced fishermen and ship captains. These mediators have a natural advantage in resolving disputes involving seafarers. At the trial stage, maritime courts in various places have also established "green channels" for resolving seafarer disputes, enabling the fast establishment, trial, and enforcement of cases to conclude them as soon as possible and ensure that judgement results are promptly executed. For example, the Nanjing Maritime Court has opened a "green channel" for filing and mediation, successfully mediating a 5-year international shipbuilding contract dispute online in 27 days.[19] At the enforcement stage, innovative enforcement models are adopted, such as the Qingdao Maritime Court's innovative "Internet+" ship seizure and auction model, which independently designed and developed a ship seizure and auction management platform and command platform for the timely location and tracking of involved ships, meeting the urgent needs of seized ships to the maximum extent. In addition, the Xiamen Maritime Court's handling of a 2024 international maritime personal injury liability dispute demonstrated the wisdom of diversified maritime judicial dispute resolution. In this case, the presiding judge learned that H Company had insured Zhao for accidents, but the claim application was rejected due to incomplete materials. The judge actively communicated, prompting H Company to assist in providing the necessary materials and guiding the family to claim from the insurance company. Finally, they successfully helped the complainant obtain 500,000 yuan in insurance compensation within just 1 month. This case highlights the innovative ability of the maritime judicial system in solving foreign-related disputes, reflecting the professionalism and care of the court for the people, and promoting the realization of fairness and justice.[20]

Judicial Guidance on Crew Disputes

The judicial interpretations, replies, letters, and other documents issued by the Supreme People's Court, as well as the minutes of meetings, play an important guiding role in the trial of crew-related cases by various courts. Relevant documents and content are presented in Table 11.1.

---

[19] Supreme People's Court of China (n 17).

[20] Wang (2024), p. 23.

Table 11.1 Interpretative judgments on crew disputes

Nature	Name	Implementation time	Regarding crew aspects
Judicial interpretation	"Regulations of the Supreme People's Court on Property Damage Compensation for Cases of Ship Collision and Contact"	1995.10.18 (revised on 2020.12.23)	Regarding the calculation of compensation for property loss on board; the loss of the crew's personal necessities shall be compensated appropriately according to the actual loss; the loss of currency, gold, silver, jewellry, securities, or other valuable items carried by the crew shall not be recognized. Maintenance expenses refer to the daily consumption costs of the vessel and crew during the period of vessel repair, including the consumption of fuel, materials, fresh water, and supplies, as well as the crew's wages
	"Judicial Interpretation of the Supreme People's Court of Guangdong Province on Whether Maritime Courts Should Handle Disputes over Seamen's Remuneration Involving maritime lien ([2001] Guangdong High People's Court Civil Case No. 1)"	2002.04.15	Captain, crew, and other personnel on board involved in cases concerning maritime priorities are not subject to the mandatory arbitration requirement
	"Interpretation of the Supreme People's Court on Certain Issues Concerning the Application of the Special Procedures Law of the People's Republic of China on Maritime Civil Procedures"	2003.01.06 (amended on 2018.12.31)	Direct litigation to the maritime court due to disputes over crew labour contracts shall be accepted by the maritime court
	"Provisions of the Supreme People's Court on the Application of Law in Seizure and Auction of Vessels"	2015.03.01	Where there is an application for the detention of a vessel due to disputes over crew labour contracts, maritime and inland waterway personal injury compensation, and the facts are clear and the rights and obligations are clearly defined, it is not necessary to require a guarantee
	"Provisions of the Supreme People's Court on the Scope of Cases Accepted by Maritime Courts (2016)"	2016.03.01	Seafarer employment contracts, labour contracts (including seafarer dispatch agreements), and disputes related to compensation for remuneration and personal injury compensation for seafarers boarding, serving on board, and being repatriated are within the jurisdiction of maritime courts

	"Provisions of the Supreme People's Court on Several Issues Concerning the Trial of Disputes Involving Seamen"	2020.09.29	Specific provisions are made regarding the scope of acceptance, determination of legal relationships, confirmation of maritime priorities, whether illegal wages are protected, wage compensation, and the determination of work-related injury insurance
	"Reply of the Supreme People's Court on the Issue of Whether a Seafarer Convicted of Imprisonment with Suspended Execution Can Retain His Original Position and Enjoy Political Rights (Document No. 2043 of the Legal and Administrative Department)"	1954.03.23	1. A suspended sentence of imprisonment is generally applicable to defendants who pose a minor social harm, have been sentenced to lighter penalties, or for whom temporary suspension of sentence execution is deemed appropriate due to specific circumstances. During the probation period of the suspended sentence, defendants who have not been adjudicated to be deprived of political rights nor placed under public surveillance shall retain their political rights 2. The official's criminal conviction results in a suspended sentence, which does not necessarily preclude the ability to retain the original position or to be promoted. If they continue working at the original unit, enhanced education and supervision are required. The defendant in this case committed a crime of negligence while performing the duties of a chief officer, and whether they should succeed as the chief officer should be carefully considered
	"Reply of the Supreme People's Court on Whether the Civil Liability for the Private Contracting of Transportation and Unauthorized Sailing by Seamen Should Be Borne by the Steamship Company (Legal Letter No. [1995] 43)"	1995.04.21	In accordance with relevant regulations and the practical operations of transportation enterprises, there has been no authorization granted to crew members (including the captain) to enter into contracts for transportation business on behalf of the company. Violating the aforementioned regulations, crew members' unauthorized undertaking of transportation and unauthorized departure are acts exceeding their authority. The steamship company should not be held civilly liable for the personal actions of the crew members

(continued)

Table 11.1 (continued)

Nature	Name	Implementation time	Regarding crew aspects
	"Supreme People's Court's Reply to the Inquiry Regarding Whether There Is an Employment Contract Relationship Between Yang Haishui and Beijing Xinyusheng Ship Management Co., Ltd. ([2011] Min Si Ta Zhi No. 4)"	2011.05.03	Pursuant to the "Regulations on Crew Service Administration" promulgated by the Ministry of Transport, crew service agencies shall provide crew service business to crew members and shall enter into crew service agreements with them. In this case, Xin Yu Sheng Company is a crew dispatch service agency with qualifications for engaging in foreign labour cooperation operations and is not an employer of labourers. Therefore, the "Crew Employment Contract" signed by Yang Hai Shui and Xin Yu Sheng Company is a crew service contract, not a crew labour contract, nor a crew labour contract
Guidance documents for trial	"Minutes of the Symposium of Presidents of National Maritime Courts"	2001.09.11	To protect the legitimate rights and interests of crew members with maritime lien, where a lawsuit is directly filed with the maritime court due to disputes over labour contracts of crew members, the maritime court shall accept the case
	"Second National Conference on Maritime Commercial Judicial Work Minutes"	2005.12.26	Article 169, second paragraph of the "Maritime Code of the People's Republic of China" defines third-party property loss as other property losses directly caused by ship collision accidents, excluding goods or items carried by vessels with mutual fault, as well as the property of crew, passengers, or other persons on board; the third paragraph defines third-party personal injuries, including personal injuries to crew, passengers, and other persons on the colliding vessels
	"National People's Court Symposium on Foreign-related Commercial and Maritime Judicial Work Minutes"	2021.12.31	The regulations stipulate that it is a statutory obligation for the shipowner to purchase work injury insurance and the burden of proof for labour contract disputes (the shipowner's presumption of fault and mitigation of liability)

The Supreme People's Court promulgated the "Provisions on the Trial of Certain Issues Concerning Disputes Involving Seamen" (hereinafter referred to as the "Provisions on the Trial of Disputes Involving Seamen") in 2020, which is worthy of special attention. The provisions comprise 21 articles, which make clear provisions for the identification and resolution methods of various legal relationships such as the labour and service contracts of seamen involved in disputes; the confirmation, exercise, and transfer of maritime priorities; the composition and legal protection of seamen's remuneration; whether wages should be protected under circumstances where seamen have conducted illegal operations; the assumption of tort liability under labour conditions; the mutual relationship between work-related injury insurance benefits and civil compensation in circumstances involving industrial accidents; and the application of law in international labour contracts, etc. These are urgent issues to be solved in maritime judicial practice.[21] Clarifying the following important issues will enable us to better understand and apply this judicial interpretation.

Jurisdiction Issue

The principal issue in crew-related cases is that the court should first consider the handling of disputes over crew labour contracts. Before 2020, judicial practice in China exhibited inconsistent approaches to determining whether claims filed by seafarers—excluding those related to boarding, on-board service, or disembarkation and repatriation—should be subject to mandatory arbitration as a prerequisite or directly adjudicated by maritime courts. Article 1 of the "Regulations on the Trial of Disputes Involving Crew Members" regulates the latter issue: for disputes over crew labour contracts, if they are unrelated to boarding, on-board work, or disembarkation repatriation, as they do not involve the issue of maritime priorities, they are general labour disputes and should be handled according to the provisions of the "Labour Dispute Mediation and Arbitration Law", following the procedure of "arbitration first, then trial". For disputes over crew labour contracts and labour disputes related to boarding, on-board work, and disembarkation repatriation, as they often involve the strong professional issue of maritime priorities, they should still be handled per Article 2 of the judicial interpretation, by the maritime court with jurisdiction. This aligns with the concept of establishing a maritime court, which should concentrate professional resources on handling special maritime cases that are different from other civil and commercial cases, and general courts can handle such disputes unrelated to on-board work.

[21] Wang and Guo (2023), p. 30.

Conclusion

China's legal and institutional framework for crew management has undergone significant transformation, evolving into a comprehensive and multi-level system that supports both the expansion of its maritime ambitions and the protection of crew members' rights. Through an intricate array of domestic laws, administrative regulations, departmental rules, and international conventions, most notably the STCW Convention and the MLC 2006, China has built a substantive foundation for the regulation, training, and welfare of its maritime workforce.

Despite these advances, the legislative landscape remains fragmented, with relevant provisions dispersed across various statutes and regulatory instruments. Recent developments, particularly the growing reliance on judicial interpretations and guidance provided by the Supreme People's Court, such as the "Provisions on the Trial of Certain Issues Concerning Disputes Involving Seamen", have played a pivotal role in standardizing dispute resolution, clarifying the application of law, and improving the predictability of judicial outcomes for crew related cases.

These judicial instruments address urgent and complex issues in the sector, including the recognition of labour relationships, the exercise of maritime lien, the safeguarding of remuneration, the relationship between tort liability and labour contracts, and the proper handling of work-related injuries and foreign related disputes. The existence of specialized maritime courts and increasingly sophisticated pre-litigation and enforcement mechanisms further ensures that crew members' rights are protected in a manner consistent with the principles of access to justice and fairness.

Nonetheless, the system faces persistent challenges, such as the declining influx of new seafarers, concerns regarding overall competency, and the imperative of creating a sustainable workforce to support China's leadership in global shipping. Continuous legislative refinement, enhanced cross-sectoral coordination, and sustained emphasis on both the practical and judicial protection of crew members' rights will be crucial to overcoming these obstacles.

Overall, China's approach serves as both a model and a work in progress for the integrated management and legal protection of maritime crews in a rapidly changing international environment. Future efforts should focus on unifying legislation, strengthening law enforcement, promoting professional development, and deepening the practical synergy between legislative and judicial measures to fully realize the rights and interests of crew members.

References

China Maritime Bureau (2015) Notice of the Maritime Safety Administration of the People's Republic of China on Further Regulating the Management of Seafarer Service Agencies

China Maritime Bureau (2021) Working Procedures for Handling Complaints from Seafarers on Board

China Maritime Bureau (2023) Notice of the Maritime Safety Administration of the People's Republic of China on Measures to Further Improve Quality of Seafarer Service Operations
Internal Departments, "Article" MSA Website https://www.msa.gov.cn/page/article.do?articleId=45AF5734-8B5D-429C-BAB3-F8EFD079E1AC&channelId=7B1BBBD5-BBF4-438F-8CDA-B026A8B5003F. Accessed 22 Sep 2025
Jiang P (2020) Unify Judicial Standards, Safeguard the Rights and Interests of Crew Members, and Standardize the Guidance of the Shipping Market Order — The Head of the Civil Division of the Supreme People's Court Answers Questions from Journalists about The Supreme People's Court on Several Issues Concerning the Trial of Disputes Involving Crew Members. In: China Maritime Bureau (ed) China Maritime. China Maritime, Tianjin, p 30
Li Y, Meichao T, Ma R, Li X (2022) The implications of the typical system of foreign seafarers for China's seafarer legislation. In: Academy of Sciences Ministry of Transport (ed) Transportation Research. People's Transportation, Beijing, pp 22–29
Maritime Bureau of the Ministry of Transportation and Communications, History of Chinese Seafarers (Modern Part) (People's Transportation, Beijing 2019)
Ministry of Transport of the People's Republic of China (2008) Interpretation of the Regulations on the Administration of Seafarer Services of the People's Republic of China
Ministry of Transport of the People's Republic of China (2011) Interpretation of the Regulations on the Administration of Seafarer Outsourcing of the People's Republic of China
Ministry of Transport of the People's Republic of China (2018) List of Powers and Responsibilities of the Direct Maritime System
Ministry of Transport of the People's Republic of China (2021a) 14th Five-Year Plan for the Maritime System
Ministry of Transport of the People's Republic of China (2021b) Guiding Opinions on Strengthening the Construction of a High-Quality Seafarer Workforce
Peng X (2023) The Fengqiao experience and the structural change of dispute resolution mechanisms in contemporary China. In: China Law Society (ed) China Legal Science. China Law Magazine, Beijing, p 23
Supreme People's Court of China, China's Maritime Judicial Review (2018–2021)
Wang Y (2024) Xiamen Solution for International Maritime Dispute. In: Ministry of Transport of the People's Republic of China (ed) China Water Transport Daily. China Water Transport Daily, Wuhan, p 23
Wang S, Guo Z (2023) Interpretation and Application of the Provisions on the Handling of Certain Issues in Dispute Cases Involving Seamen. In: Supreme People's Court of China (ed) People's Justice. People's Court, Beijing, p 30

Chapter 12
Overview of the Japanese Seafarers' Act and Its Recent Reform

Kengo Minami

Introduction

This article aims to provide a structural overview of the Japanese Seafarers' Act for foreign maritime law researchers and readers, along with an examination of its recent reforms aimed at improving the occupational environment on board and reduce the workload for seafarers.

In Japan, the main labour laws govern labour contracts, labour unions, and the labour market.[1] Labour laws relating to labour contracts include the Labour Contracts Act and the Labour Standards Act; ones relating to labour unions include the Trade Union Act; and ones regulating the broader labour market include the Employment Security Act. However, these laws were designed primarily for land-based labour. Therefore, not all of these laws apply to seafarers.[2] Maritime labour is

Kengo Minami: Professor at the Faculty of Law of Keio University, Ph.D. in Corporate Law (Hokkaido Uni., Japan).

[1] Sugeno and Yamakawa (2024), p. 1.

[2] However, it should be noted that these laws are not entirely inapplicable to seafarers. For example, the Labour Contracts Act applies to seafarers, except for certain provisions relating to rules of employment and labour contracts with a definite term (Labour Contracts Act, Art. 20). Additionally, regarding, the general provisions concerning working conditions in the Labour Standards Act also apply to seafarers. For example, shipowners must not discriminate against seafarers on the basis of their nationality, beliefs, or other such grounds (Labour Standards Act, Art. 3) nor may they discriminate against female seafarers in terms of wages on the basis of their gender (Labour Standards Act, Art. 4). Furthermore, shipowners must not compel seafarers to work through violence or threats (Labour Standards Act, Art. 5). See Seafarers' Act, Art. 6.

The Trade Union Act also applies to the seafarers' trade union, known as the All Japan Seamen's Union. See, available at <https://www.jsu.or.jp/eng/> (Last access 6/30/2025).

K. Minami (✉)
Faculty of Law, Keio University, Tokyo, Japan
e-mail: minami-.kengo@keio.jp

J. Choi (ed.), *Public Maritime Law in Asia*, International Law in Asia,
https://doi.org/10.1007/978-981-95-7037-9_12

subject to a legal system different from that governing land-based labour because of its unique characteristics. In Japan, a special law called the Seafarers' Act governs the relationship between shipowners as employers and seafarers engaged in maritime labour separately from the laws governing land-based labour.[3]

History[4]

The Japanese Seafarers' Act is said to have originated in 1879. At the time of the Meiji Restoration, Japan's maritime transport was carried out using traditional Japanese ships known as "wasen". Subsequently, Japanese companies began to use Western-style merchant ships to establish several international shipping routes. At that time, the quality of Japanese seafarers serving on Western-style merchant ships became a concern, while issues such as shipping companies failing to pay seafarers' wages arose. Consequently, the Meiji government was compelled to establish regulations to govern seafaring. This led the Meiji government to the establish the Western-style Merchant Ship Crew Employment and Dismissal Regulations of 1879. These regulations are said to have been modelled after the 1854 British Merchant Shipping Act.[5] The regulations were revised in 1899 as the Seafarers' Act. However, while the Act contained many provisions regarding the management of seafarers, provisions regarding the contractual relationships between seafarers and shipowners were regulated by the 1899 Commercial Code.

In the early twentieth century, criticism emerged that the 1899 Seafarers' Act and the Commercial Code were no longer suitable for the shipping industry's development, leading to growing demands for reform. In response, the Special Committee on the Revision of the Seafarers' Act was established in 1929 to consider revisions, leading to a revision of the Seafarers' Act in 1937. The reform consisted in transferring the provisions of the 1899 Commercial Code relating to seafarers to the Seafarers' Act. The Act was amended further in 1947 following the adoption of the Japanese Constitution at the end of World War II. The new constitution necessitated the enactment of laws to protect workers, resulting in laws such as the Labour Standards Act in addition to the amendment of the Seafarers' Act. Subsequently, the Seafarers' Act was amended in 1982 to implement the STCW Convention domestically; in 1988, to reduce seafarers' working hours; and in 2008, to implement the MLC 2006 domestically.

[3] There is a special law for the maritime labour market, known as the Seafarers Employment Security Act.

[4] Nemoto (2020), p. 63.

[5] Sasaki (1962), p. 54; Hemmi (2018), p. 259.

Overview of the Japanese Seafarers Act

Characteristics of Seafarers' Workload

Japanese textbooks on the Seafarers' Act highlight five distinctive characteristics of seafarers' work.[6] First, seafarers on rocking ships are forced to work in confined spaces with a limited number of crew members. Second, seafarers are separated from society and their families for long periods. Third, it is difficult for seafarers to call for timely rescues from land. Fourth, all crew members are exposed to maritime risks, and the negligence of one crew member can place the entire crew at risk.[7] Fifth, seafarers have to work and live in the same space. Taking these characteristics into account, the Japanese labour law governing seafarers, the Seafarer's Act, was enacted separately from the laws concerning land-based work.

Structure of the Seafarers' Act

The Japanese Seafarers' Act consists of 14 chapters and contains provisions for protecting seafarers' rights, as well as ones for maintaining order on board ships and occupational safety.

- Chapter 1: General Provisions (Articles 1–6)
- Chapter 2: Duties and Powers of the Shipmaster (Articles 7–20)
- Chapter 3: Discipline (Articles 21–30)
- Chapter 4: Employment Contracts, etc. (Articles 31–51)
- Chapter 5: Wages and Other Remuneration (Articles 52–59)
- Chapter 6: Working Hours, Days Off, and Crew Strength (Articles 60–73)
- Chapter 7: Paid Leave (Articles 74–79-2)
- Chapter 8: Food, Safety, and Hygiene (Articles 80–83)
- Chapter 9: Minors on Board (Articles 84–86)
- Chapter 9-2: Women on Board (Articles 87–88-8)
- Chapter 10: Compensation for Accidents (Articles 89–96)
- Chapter 11: Employment Rules (Articles 97–100)
- Chapter 11-2: Inspection of Seafarers' Working Conditions, etc. (Articles 100-2–100-11)
- Chapter 11-3: Registered Inspection Bodies (Articles 100-12–100-28)
- Chapter 12: Supervision (Articles 101–112)
- Chapter 13: Miscellaneous Provisions (Articles 113–121-4)
- Chapter 14: Penal Provisions (Articles 122–136)

---

[6] Kiyota et al. (2023), p. 21.

[7] See Ishii (1940), pp. 4–5.

Although this article cannot explain all provisions of the Japanese Seafarers' Act, it illustrates some significant legal schemes regarding maritime labour in Japan based on the Seafarers' Act. Specifically, this paper introduces the following topics: the scope of application of the Seafarers' Act, provisions concerning the maintenance of order on board and the shipmaster's authority, contracts between shipowners (as employers) and seafarers, and seafarers' working conditions.

Scope of Application of the Seafarers' Act: What Is a Ship, and Who Is a "Seafarer" Under This Act?

The Japanese Seafarers' Act defines "seafarer", in principle, as the shipmaster and other seafarers who are on board Japanese ships and ships other than Japanese ships specified by the Ministry of Land, Infrastructure, Transport, and Tourism (MLIT) ordinances and reserve seafarers (Seafarers' Act, Article 1).

To define the scope of this Act, the definition of seafarers and ships to which it applies must first be introduced. "Seafarer" includes three types of seafarers, namely, the shipmaster, other seafarers, and the reserve seafarers under the Act. This article specifically focuses on reserve seafarer. Reserve seafarers are seafarers who have been hired to work on a ship but have not yet boarded the ship (Seafarers' Act, Article 2, paragraph 2). As explained in detail later, those who want to become seafarers must first enter into a "contract of employment" with the shipowner (as an employer) to become reserve seafarers. After being employed, they then enter into "articles of agreement" with the shipowner when they are assigned to a specific vessel, at which point they become seafarers.

In this Act, Japanese ships include ships owned by Japanese government agencies, ships owned by Japanese citizens, ships owned by companies established under Japanese law in which all representatives and two-thirds or more of the executive officers are Japanese citizens, and ships owned by companies other than those mentioned above in which all representatives are Japanese citizens (Seafarers' Act, Article 1, paragraph 1 and the Ship Act, Article 1). Furthermore, even non-Japanese ships, such as those chartered by persons who own Japanese ships, ships on which the Japanese government assigns seafarers, and ships that only navigate between ports within Japan are subject to the Seafarers' Act (Seafarers' Act Enforcement Regulation, Article 1). However, this Act does not apply to ships with a gross tonnage of less than 5 tons, ships navigating only in ports, rivers, or harbours, fishing ships with a gross tonnage of less than 30 tons, and small boats used for sports or recreation. Seafarers on board these ships perform work similar to that of land-based workers from the perspectives of hours of work and work style.[8]

The Seafarers' Act regulates labour management relations between seafarers as workers and shipowners as employers. A shipowner is generally understood as a

[8] Nemoto (2020), p. 74.

person who employs seafarers and owns and operates a ship.[9] Bareboat charterers and ship managers who employ seafarers in the case of ships owned by two or more partner owners are also included in the definition of shipowners (Seafarers' Act, Article 5).

Shipmaster's Duties and Authority and Discipline on Board

In Japan, the private law authority of a shipmaster (e.g. the authority to enter into contracts as an agent of the shipowner outside the port of registry or the authority to issue bills of lading) is stipulated in the Commercial Code (Articles 708 and 757). By contrast, the public law authority ensuring the safety of seafarers and passengers on board ships, or navigation safety, is stipulated in the Seafarers' Act. The shipmaster must be on the ship (Seafarers' Act, Article 11) and have the authority to command and supervise other seafarers and other persons on board (Seafarers' Act, Article 7). Additionally, the shipmaster is obligated to inspect the seaworthiness of the ship before its departure (Seafarers' Act, Article 8) and take necessary measures to rescue human life or cargo when the ship is in imminent danger (Seafarers' Act, Article 12). In the event of a collision, the shipmaster must assist in rescuing human life and vessels and notify the other party of the ship's name, owner, port of registry, port of departure, and port of destination (Seafarers' Act, Article 13). Furthermore, the shipmaster is granted disciplinary authority over seafarers to maintain order on board. Article 21 of the Seafarers' Act lists the following prohibited acts for crew members, for which the shipmaster may discipline them, though without abusing this authority.

1. Failing to comply with the shipmaster's orders in the performance of their duties
2. Neglecting their duties or obstructing the duties of other crew members
3. Failing to board the ship by the time designated by the shipmaster
4. Not leaving the ship without the shipmaster's permission
5. Not using lifeboats or other necessary equipment without the shipmaster's permission
6. Not wasting food or fresh water on board
7. Not using electricity or fire without the shipmaster's permission or smoking in prohibited areas
8. Not bringing items other than personal necessities onto the ship or removing them from the ship without the shipmaster's permission
9. Not engaging in fights, drunkenness, or other violent behaviour on board the vessel
10. Not engaging in any other acts that disrupt order on board the vessel

[9] Fujisaki (1975), p. 75.

The shipmaster's powers have traditionally been interpreted as being exercised to maintain order on board the vessel, as ships were historically regarded as an extension of national territory.[10] However, these powers are better regarded as necessary for shipmasters to fulfil their obligation to ensure the safety of the vessel under labour or passenger transport contracts.[11] The shipmaster has additional powers under the Seafarers' Act and the Household Registration Act to handle a birth or death on board. In the event of a death on board, the shipmaster may, in accordance with MLIT regulations, dispose of the remains by sea (Seafarers' Act, Article 15) and is obligated to take appropriate measures regarding personal belongings (Seafarers' Act, Article 16). Conversely, in the event of a birth on board, the shipmaster must, in accordance with the Household Registration Act, record the birth in the ship's log within 24 hours. Furthermore, the shipmaster must notify the mayor of the municipality where the deceased's household is registered if someone dies on board (Household Registration Act, Article 55).

Contract Between Shipowner and Seafarer

Dual Contract Structure

Seafarers enter into contracts with shipowners to provide labour, for which shipowners agree to pay them wages. The contract between seafarers and shipowners is a type of employment contract. However, the relationship between seafarers and shipowners under the Japanese Seafarers' Act is more complex than regular land-based labour relations. For instance, Article 31 of the Seafarers' Act provides for the following:

> Any articles of agreement (for reserve seafarers, contract of employment) that establish working conditions that do not meet the standards outlined in this law shall be deemed invalid to the extent that they fail to meet such standards. In such cases, the articles of agreement shall be deemed to have established working conditions that meet the standards outlined in this law to the extent that it is invalid.

This provision stipulates that if the working conditions established by a contract between a seafarer and shipowner are inferior to those prescribed by the Seafarers' Act, such working conditions are invalid, and the seafarer is subject to the working conditions stipulated by the Seafarers' Act. However, what is noteworthy here is that this provision uses the two terms: "articles of agreement" and "contract of employment". This implies that the Seafarers' Act treats articles of agreement and contracts of employment as separate contracts.[12] A question then arises regarding the relationship between the articles of agreement and the contract of employment.

[10] Fujisaki (1975), p. 79.

[11] Minami (2018), p. 362.

[12] See MLC2006, Article II, Paragraph 1 (g).

Japanese case law[13] and some researchers[14] explain that the labour contract of a seafarer has a dual contract structure. Specifically, when a seafarer is hired by a shipowner, they enter into a "contract of employment" and become a reserve seafarer. Then, when they board the ship in accordance with the shipowner's boarding order, they enter into "articles of agreement" with the shipowner. Upon disembarking the vessel at the end of the voyage, the articles of agreement are terminated, and the seafarer returns to the status of a reserve seafarer based on the contract of employment.[15]

Procedures Regarding the Seafarers' Employment Agreement

When a shipowner intends to enter into articles of agreement with a seafarer, the shipowner must provide the prospective seafarer with a written document detailing the shipowner's name, address, and the terms and conditions of employment, including wages and working hours (Seafarers' Act, Article 32, paragraph 1). Furthermore, the written document must state the name, address, and date of birth of the prospective seafarer and the place and date of the contract (Seafarers' Act, Article 36, paragraph 1). In addition, the shipowner must promptly notify the Minister of Land, Infrastructure, Transport, and Tourism of the conclusion, termination, renewal, or amendment of the articles of agreement (Seafarers' Act, Article 37). The Minister confirms whether the articles of agreement comply with the provisions of laws and regulations concerning the safety of navigation or the labour relations of seafarers and whether the agreement between the parties is adequate (Article 38). As such, shipowners must provide seafarers with detailed explanations of the articles of agreement between them. Even after a contract is concluded, its contents are subject to verification by the administrative authorities. These procedures are in accordance with the MLC 2006.[16]

The Seafarers' Act lists the following cases in which articles of agreement may be terminated: when the vessel sinks, the shipowner or seafarer terminates the contract, or the shipowner changes (Seafarers' Act, Articles 39–43). The shipowner may terminate the contract, for example, if the seafarer is grossly unfit for duty, the seafarer seriously disrupts order on board, the seafarer is unable to perform duties due to injury or illness, or for other unavoidable reasons (Seafarers' Act, Article 40). On the other hand, cases in which a seafarer may terminate the contract include, for example, when the vessel has lost its registry at the time of contract conclusion, there is a significant discrepancy between the working conditions stipulated in the contract and the actual conditions, or the seafarer is unable to perform their duties

[13] Nagasaki Chiho Saibansho [Nagasaki Dist. Ct.] October 14, 1955, Sho 30 (yo) no. 87, no. 94, RODO KANKEI MINJI HANREI SHU [ROMINSHU] vol. 6, No. 5, p. 721 (Japan).

[14] Ishii (1964), p. 180, Tanaka (1985), p. 208, Kobayashi (2022), p. 158.

[15] More detailed discussion on this issue, see Minami (2019a), p. 80.

[16] See MLC (2006) Regulation 2.1, Standard A2.1.

due to injury or illness (Seafarers' Act, Article 41). A change in the shipowner refers to a case in which the shipowner transfers all its business to another company. This provision aims to protect seafarers from unemployment.[17] In such a case, the contract between the seafarer and the shipowner is terminated, but articles of agreement under the same terms are concluded between the seafarer and the new shipowner.[18] Seafarers may terminate articles of agreement with the new shipowner (Seafarers' Act, Article 43).

Working Conditions

First, seafarers' wages must be determined based on the special nature of the seafaring work, considering the seafarer's experience, ability, and the nature of their duties (Seafarers' Act, Article 52). Additionally, shipowners must pay wages directly in currency to seafarers and provide them with written documents detailing the payment terms (Seafarers' Act, Article 53).[19] Furthermore, seafarers may claim wages and other benefits during the employment period even if they are unable to perform their duties because of injury or illness (Seafarers' Act, Article 57). The minimum standards for seafarers' wages were established by the Minimum Wage Act and are similar to the standards for land-based labour (Seafarers' Act, Article 59).

Second, the daily work hours of seafarers should not exceed 8 hours, and the weekly working hours should not exceed an average of 40 hours per week, based on the standard working period (Seafarers' Act, Article 60, paragraphs 1 and 2). The standard working period refers to the period determined within 1 year or less, considering the navigation area and route of the vessel in accordance with the classification of vessels specified by the MLIT (Seafarers' Act, Article 60, paragraph 3). This refers to the average working hours when seafarers are on and off the vessel. Shipowners are obligated to provide seafarers with at least one rest day per week, on average, during the standard working period (Seafarers' Act, Article 61). However, the shipowner may, by written agreement with a labour union organised by a majority of the seafarers or their representative, require seafarers to work more than 8 hours per day and more than 40 hours per week based on the standard working period (Seafarers' Act, Article 64-2). However, this limit shall not exceed 14 hours per day or 72 hours per week, excluding cases in which the shipmaster is working (Seafarers' Act, Article 65-2, paragraph 2).[20] Shipowners are prohibited from dividing hours of rest into three or more segments per day, and if hours of rest are divided into two segments, the length of the two segments must be at least 6

[17] Minami (2019b), p. 340.

[18] Tokyo Koto Saibansho [Tokyo High Ct.] April 25, 2018, Hei 29 (ne) no. 3951, no. 5299, no. 5333, Rodo Hanrei [ROHAN] No. 1193, p. 5.

[19] See MLC (2006) Regulation 2.2, vol 2, Standard A2.2.2.

[20] There is no legal limit on the hours of work of the shipmaster under the agreement between the shipowner and the labour union or the representative of a majority of the seafarers.

hours (Seafarers' Act, Article 65-3). However, if there is a labour union organised by a majority of the seafarers or their representative, the shipowner may, by written agreement with them, divide the hours of rest into three or more parts or grant the longer hours of rest for less than 6 hours (Seafarers' Act, Article 65-3, paragraph 3).

Third, shipowners must grant paid leave to seafarers who have worked continuously for 6 months on vessels belonging to the same business (Seafarers' Act, Article 74). In principle, there should be 15 days of paid leave for every six consecutive months of service, with an additional 5 days for every additional 3 months of consecutive service (Seafarers' Act, Article 75). Shipowners must pay seafarers on paid leave their regular wages as well as certain allowances and meal expenses (Seafarers' Act, Article 78).

Fourth, workers on board ships are exposed to accidents. Therefore, shipowners must comply with MLIT measures targeted at preventing harm and maintaining hygiene on board ships (Seafarers' Act, Article 81). In Japan, in addition to the Seafarers' Act, regulations such as the Regulations for Labour Safety and Health of Seafarers have been established to prevent accidents involving seafarers.[21] Shipowners must provide food to seafarers (Seafarers' Act, Article 81).

Recent Reform for the Improvement of the Working Conditions in 2021

Background

In 2021, the Seafarers' Act and the Coastal Shipping Business Act were amended. These amendments aimed to improve the working conditions of seafarers. This initiative is referred to as the "seafarer's work-style reform". Before introducing the details of the legal amendments, this paper explains the shortage of seafarers in Japan that precipitated this reform. As shown in Table 12.1 and Fig. 12.1, the number of seafarers in Japan has remained relatively stable, with a slight decrease. The effective job vacancy rate for seafarers in 2023 stands at 3.95. According to another

Table 12.1 Number of seafarers in Japan from 2014 to 2023[a]

	2018	2019	2020	2021	2022	2023
Foreign shipping seafarers	2093	2174	2200	2165	2062	2017
Coastal shipping seafarers	28,142	28,435	28,595	28,625	28,097	28,549
Fishing ship seafarers	17,940	17,469	16,866	15,999	15,432	15,159
Others	15,678	15,718	16,373	16,586	16,523	16,854

[a] This table is cited from MLIT (2025), p. 50

[21] Minami (2025).

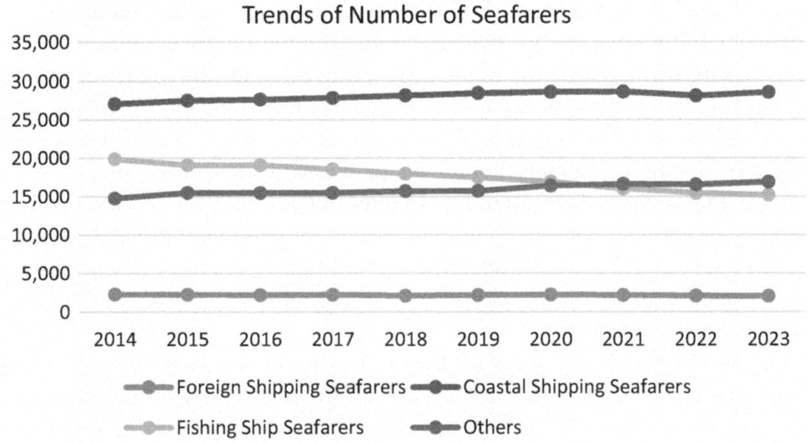

Fig. 12.1 Trends in the number of seafarers in Japan based on Table 12.1

statistic, approximately 40% of domestic seafarers are aged 50 years or older, indicating an ageing workforce.[22] Consequently, the number of seafarers is expected to decline. Under these circumstances, the MLIT decided to hold a meeting to discuss ways to improve seafarers' working conditions and make maritime work more attractive.

Additionally, at the time of revising labour laws related to seafarers, several labour laws on the working conditions for land-based workers had already been revised in 2018. The purpose of these revisions was to prevent "karoshi" (death from overwork) by addressing excessive working hours for land-based workers and improving the treatment of non-regular workers. However, those labour law reforms did not apply to seafarers. In response, in September 2020, the MLIT published a report titled "Toward the Realisation of Work Style Reform for Seafarers"[23] outlining the direction for work reform for seafarers. It is essential to recognise that the background of work reform among seafarers differs from that of land-based workers. This is because there are fewer deaths due to overwork among seafarers than among land-based workers and because regulations limiting overtime work to address long working hours for land-based workers already existed under the Seafarers' Act. Furthermore, the work-style reform for land-based workers adopted the policy of equal pay for equal work, but such issues were not taken into consideration for seafarers.[24] Instead, the work-style reform for seafarers aimed to make the occupational environment more attractive for existing and prospective seafarers.[25]

[22] This explanation is based on the statistics shown by the MLIT (2025), p. 50.

[23] The Ministry of Land, Infrastructure, Transport and Tourism (2020), p. 1.

[24] Shinobu (2021), p. 71.

[25] MLIT, supra note 4, p. 1.

Overview of "Work-Style Reform" for Seafarers

As mentioned in Sect. 3.1, to make ships more attractive workplaces, especially for young people and women, the MLIT has considered various measures, including revisions to laws such as the Seafarers' Act. To realise this objective, the MLIT then surveyed the current working and living conditions of seafarers to inform them of what measures and reforms to undertake.

The surveys include the following:

- Working conditions of seafarers on board
- Management of working hours on board
- Living conditions of seafarers on board
- Maritime students' awareness of seafarers' labour
- Health of seafarers

First, regarding the working conditions of seafarers, it was found that the total monthly working hours of cargo ship crew members tended to be long (238.06 hours per month) and that longer cargo handling operations tended to result in longer working hours. Second, regarding the management of working hours, it was found that the most common method for tracking working hours was recording in logbooks due to a lack of machines for this purpose. In addition, it was found that fixed overtime pay was paid, although overtime premiums were not calculated. Third, it was found that when watchkeeping and port entry/departure operations were conducted consecutively, working hours tended to become longer. Consequently, crew members who perform watchkeeping in the morning tended to have fragmented sleep. However, securing a temporary berth once a week could keep working hours within 72 hours. Fourth, according to a questionnaire given to maritime students, the reasons for seafarers changing jobs included poor interpersonal relationships. Furthermore, the questionnaire made it clear that the students desire to understand working hours, salaries, and work-life balance before accepting seafarer positions. Fifth, regarding health, crew members have a higher incidence of illness than land-based workers and suffer more from stress due to the dangers of the workplace, poor interpersonal relationships on board, and a shortage of rest.

To achieve the above purposes, excluding changes to working conditions, the MLIT considered measures and reforms of laws concerning seafarers, including the Seafarers' Act and the Coastal Shipping Act based on the above surveys. It should be noted that none of the measures considered by the MLIT based on results of the surveys required revisions to the laws for implementation.[26] For example, the

[26] According to the "Minutes of the Meeting of the Seafarers' Division of the Maritime Subcommittee of the Transportation Policy Council" (2/20/2020), in fact, at a meeting of the MLIT, Professor Tomotaka Fujita said that matters requiring amendment to laws and regulations should be distinguished from those that can be addressed without such amendments. <Available at https://www.mlit.go.jp/common/001292277.pdf> (Last access 6/30/2025).

following measures have been proposed: First, employers should establish short-term sailing cycles and create an environment that allows seafarers to take planned holidays in accordance with their individual preferences to make it easier for them to take leave. Second, managers and human resources personnel should adopt a mindset that is accepting of diverse work styles and human resources, including understanding childcare leave systems that enable a balance between work and family life.[27] Third, many shipowners record crew working hours using paper logbooks, but they are now encouraged to consider software-based recording methods. This method of managing seafarers' working hours is not unique to Japan. The issue was also addressed in a 2020 report on seafarers' working hours and rest periods compiled by the World Maritime University (WMU) in collaboration with the International Transport Workers' Federation (ITF). According to the report, recording working hours was time-consuming for crew members and contributed to an increased workload.[28] Consequently, proposals were made to utilise software that automatically records working hours. However, new systems must consider the privacy of crew members and monitor who makes changes to the system.[29]

However, several amendments to the laws were necessary to implement reforms in seafarers' working conditions. The following section introduces and examines the 2021 amendments to the Seafarers' Act and the Coastal Shipping Act.

Prevention of Long Working Hours for Seafarers

Work Hours of Seafarers Under the Seafarers' Act

Before the 2021 amendment to the Seafarers' Act, there were cases in which the time spent by seafarers performing their work did not have to be counted as working hours. The following are some examples: first, when performing life-saving operations; second, when conducting fire drills or lifeboat drills; and third, when performing watch-change operations during navigation.[30] Therefore, crew members could not claim wages from shipowners for these tasks. The purpose of the original provision was explained as follows: orders issued by the shipmaster for the safety of navigation are absolute, and therefore, to ensure such safety, the rights and obligations established in modern labour management relations must be sacrificed, thereby permitting the enforcement of compulsory unpaid labour.[31] Furthermore, to ensure the safe operation of ships, this work was viewed as an inherent duty of crew members and, therefore, could be required of them with no guarantee of overtime pay.[32]

---

[27] The MLIT, supra note 4, pp. 14–15.

[28] World Maritime University (2020), pp. 33–34.

[29] WMU (2020), pp. 36–37.

[30] Former Article 68, Paragraph 1 of the Seafarers' Act.

[31] Terui (1998), p. 111.

[32] Saburo (1973), p. 8.

However, this reasoning is no longer appropriate today and has been subject to intense criticism. Therefore, under the policy of reviewing, to the extent possible, work that may be considered as working hours, amendments were made to include fire drills, lifeboat drills, and work related to the handover of watchkeeping as working hours. However, life-saving work was still not included in working hours. In relation to this point, MLC2006 provides the following clarifying statement:

> Nothing in this Standard shall be deemed to impair the right of the master of a ship to require a seafarer to perform any hours of work necessary for the immediate safety of the ship, persons on board or cargo, or for the purpose of giving assistance to other ships or persons in distress at sea. Accordingly, the master may suspend the schedule of hours of work or hours of rest and require a seafarer to perform any hours of work necessary until the normal situation has been restored.[33]

The rest of the hours which do count as working hours are defined under Article 4, paragraph 2, as mentioned in previous sections. This definition aligns with the definition provided in MLC 2006. However, there are some issues regarding the definition of working hours under Japanese labour laws. According to Japanese case law regarding land-based workers, working hours are defined as the time during which workers are under the direction and control of their employers.[34] The term "under the direction and control" refers to the time during which workers are both physically and temporally constrained. In addition, regarding the working hours of seafarers, the MLIT has established guidelines to clarify the periods that constitute working hours for seafarers.

Management of Work Hours of Seafarers

Prior to the amendment, the Seafarers' Act required the shipmaster to maintain a ship's logbook on board the vessel to manage the working hours of seafarers (former Seafarers' Act, Article 67). The shipmaster was obligated to record in the ship's logbook matters related to working hours, compensatory rest days, rest periods, and seafarers' overtime allowances (former Seafarers' Act, Article 67, paragraph 1). Additionally, the shipmaster was required to provide seafarers with a copy of the logbook (former Seafarers' Act, Article 67, paragraph 2). However, recent amendments have clarified that the responsibility of managing working hours lies with the shipowner as the employer. Accordingly, the logbook must be kept at the main office on the shore rather than on board the vessel. Furthermore, the shipowner must appoint a labour management officer at the land-based office to oversee the creation of the record book and other related matters, as well as to manage the crew's labour affairs (former Seafarers' Act, Article 67, paragraphs 1 and 2). In other words, the shipowner, as the employer, is now held responsible for the overall management of

[33] MLC 2006, Standard 2.3, Regulation 14.

[34] Saiko Saibansho [Sup. Ct.] March 9, 2000, Hei 7 (o) no. 2029, 54 Saiko Saibansho Minji Hanreishu [Minshu] 801 (Japan).

the seafarers' working hours. This aligns with the explanation provided by the International Labour Office regarding the MLC 2006.[35] In addition, shipowners are expected to keep track of their crew members' working hours in accordance with the methods specified in the Seafarers' Act Enforcement Regulations (Seafarers' Act, Article 67, paragraph 3).[36] The amendment recognising shipowners as employers of seafarers brings the labour laws governing seafarers in line with those already governing land-based labour where employers were always required to keep track of their employees' working hours (Labour Safety and Health Act, Article 66-8-2).[37]

In addition to maintaining records of seafarers' working hours and managing their labour matters (Seafarers Act, Article 67-2), the labour management officer must provide the shipowner with opinions regarding the reduction of seafarers' working hours, granting days off or paid leave, or the need to change the vessel on which seafarers are assigned (Seafarers' Act, Article 67-2, paragraph 2). Upon receiving such opinions, the shipowner shall take them into consideration and, if necessary, take appropriate measures (Seafarers' Act, Article 67-2, paragraph 3). Furthermore, the shipowner must request that the coastal shipping operator responsible for the operational management of the vessel make any changes deemed necessary regarding the preparation and implementation of the voyage plan (Seafarers' Act, Article 67-2, paragraph 4).

Cooperation with Stakeholders

One of the causes of seafarers' long working hours is the unreasonable shipping schedules imposed by cargo owners (also known as shippers) or operators. In Japan, cargo owners (shippers) not only directly commission shipowners to transport cargo but may also charter vessels from shipowners to transport cargo. Additionally, cargo owners (shippers) may enter into a prime transportation contract with a specific operator, who then subcontracts the transportation to a subcontractor. In such cases, the operational schedules are often determined not by the shipowner but by the cargo owner (shipper) or operator. In reality, there is a disparity in bargaining power between the shipowner (as the employer) and the cargo owner (shipper) or operator in the actual cargo handling and navigation, and it is often necessary for the shipowner to align with the intentions of the cargo owner (shipper) or operator.[38] As a result, seafarers' working hours are influenced not by the shipowner but by the cargo owner (shipper) or operator. In response, the amended Seafarers' Act and the

[35] International Labour Office (2008), p. 136.

[36] Article 45-2 of the Seafarers' Act Enforcement Regulation provides that the methods to track of the working hours are an object method such as recoding the start and end times of work using a personal computer or other electronic computer, recording using a time card, or other appropriate methods.

[37] In the case of a land-based labour, see Kagoshima Chiho Saibansho [Kagoshima Dist. Ct.] February 16, 2010, Hei 19 (wa) no. 335, 2078 Hanrei Jiho [Hanji] 89 (Japan).

[38] Hatamoto (2021), p. 41.

Coastal Shipping Business Act of 2021 seek cooperation from cargo owners (shippers) and transport operators regarding seafarers' working hours. Specifically, Article 12, paragraph 1, of the Coastal Shipping Business Act stipulates the following:

> Operators engaged in inland waterway transport must establish appropriate voyage plans (meaning plans concerning operational schedules and other matters related to the operation of vessels; the same applies in Article 20, paragraph 1) that take into account the working hours of crew members, and must take other necessary measures to prevent crew members from becoming overworked.

Furthermore, paragraph 2 of the same article stipulates the following: "In taking the measures referred to in the preceding paragraph, the operator engaged in coastal shipping shall respect the opinions of shipowners as provided for in Article 67-2, paragraph 4 of the Seafarers' Act".

As a corollary mentioned above, in response to the requirement that shipowners must communicate their opinions to coastal shipping operators when changes to the operation plan are necessary, coastal shipping operators are obligated to respect such opinions. However, from the perspective of effectiveness, there is concern that coastal shipping operators will only be required to "respect" the opinions of shipowners, with no enforcement power. To prevent this, if a coastal shipping operator is found to obstruct transport safety by ignoring the opinions of the shipowner, the Minister of Land, Infrastructure, Transport, and Tourism may order the operator to take necessary measures, such as improving the operation plan to ensure transport safety (Coastal Shipping Business Act, Article 20, paragraph 1). When the primary cause of acts that hinder the safety of transport by coastal shipping operators is the conduct of cargo owners (shippers), and when orders to coastal shipping operators alone are insufficient to prevent the recurrence of such violations, the Minister may recommend that cargo owners (shippers) take appropriate measures to prevent the recurrence of such violations by the operators (Coastal Shipping Business Act 30, paragraph 1). In addition, the Minister of Land, Infrastructure, Transport, and Tourism must make the above recommendation publicly (Coastal Shipping Business Act 30, paragraph 2). Regulations similar to those now being introduced for coastal shipping operators and cargo owners (shippers) have already been adopted for trucking businesses.[39] It should be further noted that revisions to the Seafarers' Act and the Coastal Shipping Business Act are likely to impact the contractual relationship between time charters[40] and the bargaining power among shipowners, cargo owners, and coastal shipping operators.

---

[39] See Moriyama (2020), p. 212.

[40] Sasaoka (2022), p. 353.

Prevention of Harassment and Bullying on Board

This section outlines Japanese law regarding the prevention of harassment and bullying on board vessels, although it was not included in recent amendments to the Seafarers' Act. Discussions on the work-style reform of seafarers have also focused on preventing harassment on board vessels. As seafarers live and work on the ships, when interpersonal problems arise, it can be more difficult to relieve stress than on land.[41] Therefore, preventing harassment among maritime workers is more critical than among land-based workers. In Japan, two laws are already in place to prevent sexual harassment and bullying, and these laws also apply to seafarers. One is the "Act on Equal Opportunity and Treatment between Men and Women in Employment", and the other is the "Act on Comprehensively Advancing Labour Measures, and Stabilising the Employment of Workers, and Enriching Workers' Vocational Lives". Article 11, paragraph 1, of the former law provides the following measure:

> Employers must take necessary measures for employment management, such as developing a necessary system for providing consultations to workers and appropriately handling the matters, so that the workers they employ do not suffer any disadvantageous working conditions on the grounds of that workers' response to sexual harassment in the workplace, nor suffer any damage to the work environment due to sexual harassment.

Article 30-2 of the latter law stipulates the following:

> [I]n order for an employer to preclude any behavior that constitutes bullying in the workplace and exceeds the scope necessary and reasonable in the course of business, preventing it from damaging the work environment, the employer must provide consultation to those workers and take necessary measures in terms of employment management to develop necessary systems for appropriately handling such behavior.

Because these laws also apply to maritime labour, shipowners, as employers, must comply with these articles and establish a system for preventing sexual harassment and bullying within the company, including on board their vessels, based on the "Guidelines for Measures to Be Taken by Employers Regarding Issues Arising from Sexual Conduct in the Workplace Concerning Seafarers"[42] and the "Guidelines for Measures to Be Taken by Employers Regarding Issues Arising from Conduct Based on a Superior Relationship in the Workplace Concerning Seafarers".[43] To assist shipowners in this regard, the Maritime Human Resource Institute published a handbook on the prevention of bullying in maritime labour, named the *Harassment*

[41] "Minutes of the Meeting of the Seafarers' Division of the Maritime Subcommittee of the Transportation Policy Council" (5/24/2020) <available at https://www.mlit.go.jp/policy/shingikai/content/001309813.pdf (Last access 6/30/2025)>, p. 12.

[42] Available at <https://www.mhlw.go.jp/web/t_doc?dataId=00005170&dataType=0&pageNo=1> (Last access 6/30/2025).

[43] Available at <https://www.mhlw.go.jp/web/t_doc?dataId=00011940&dataType=0&pageNo=1> (Last access 6/30/2025).

Prevention Handbook for Seafarers.[44] However, crew members are encouraged to be mindful of their words and actions towards other crew members and must make efforts to maintain a good working environment at sea.

In addition, the discussion regarding the work-style reforms for seafarers also touched upon the policy for female seafarers. The discussion highlighted the importance of shipowners being flexible in accepting female seafarers. It has been said that male norms and values in the workplace and on board vessels are one of the reasons why the number of female seafarers has not increased.[45] Therefore, it is essential to continue efforts to remove barriers for female seafarers by adopting the above systems to prevent harassment and bullying.

Conclusion

Japan is currently facing a severe shortage of seafarers. The Japanese Seafarers' Act not only complies with the MLC 2006 but also aims to make a seafarer's job more attractive by creating better working conditions on board. One such effort was the 2021 amendment to the Seafarers' Act. However, real change requires more than legal amendments. Therefore, shipowners must continue to make efforts to improve working conditions without neglecting their responsibilities.

References

Fujisaki M (Revised ed. 1975) Senin ho soron (General principles of Seafarers' Act), Seizando Shuppan, Tokyo

Hatamoto I (2021) Naiko senin no hatarakikata ni tsuite (About work style of coastal shipping seafarers). Nihon Rodo Kenkyu Zasshi (Jpn J Labour Stud) 728:38–46

Hemmi S (2018) Sencho shoku no shoso (Various aspects of shipmaster's responsibilities). Yamagata Kinen Zaidan, Tokyo

International Labour Office (2008) Compendium of maritime labour instruments. ILO Publications, Geneva

Ishii T (1940) Kaijo rodo ni kansuru hoteki kisei no hattatsu (The development of legal regulations for maritime labour). Horitsu Jiho (Law J) 13(1):5–10

Ishii T (1964) Kaisho ho (Maritime commercial law). Yuhikaku, Tokyo

Kitada M (2021) Women seafarers: an analysis of barriers to their employment. In: The World of Seafarer. Springer, Cham, pp 65–76

[44] Available at <https://www.maritime-forum.jp/et/pdf/power_harassment.pdf> (Last access 6/30/2025). Furthermore, the Maritime Human Resource Institute shows some movies about the prevention of bullying on board ships on YouTube in both Japanese and English (Available at <https://youtube.com/channel/UCRwLvVaEKVxZo0ZnxCP1Tdg?si=Bz_2eXnCIx0SJOAa> (Last access 6/30/2025)).

[45] Kitada (2021), pp. 70–71.

Kiyota K, Kobayashi G, Kaneko H (2023) Senin ho (Seafarers' Act). In: Kaiji ho (maritime law). Kaibundo Shuppan, Tokyo
Kobayashi N (2022) Shin kaisho ho (New maritime commercial law). Shinzansha, Tokyo
Minami K (2018) Senin ho no seishitsu (The characteristics of Seafarers' Act). Nihon Hogaku (J Law) 84(3):343–369
Minami K (2019a) Kaijo rodo keiyaku no kozo (Structure of maritime labour contract). In: Rodo keiyaku ron no saikosei (Reconstruction of labour contract theory). Horitsu Bunkasha, Kyoto
Minami K (2019b) Senpaku shoyusha no jigyo joto kaisha bunkatsu to kaijo rodo keiyaku no kisu (Business transfers or company splits by shipowners and maritime labour contracts: the significance of Article 43 of the Seafarers' Act). Nihon Hogaku (J Law) 85(2):453–506
Minami K (2025) The legal systems for the prevention of seafarers accidents in Japan. J Work Health Saf Regul 4(1):1–19. https://doi.org/10.57523/jaohlev.cr.25-003. Accessed 30 June 2025
Moriyama M (2020) Torakku unso no kadai seisaku to hatarakikata kaikaku (The issues in the trucking businesses and the policy of work style reform). Taisei Shuppansha, Tokyo
Nemoto I (2020) Senin ho (Seafarers' Act). In: Gaisetsu kaiji hoki (The overview of maritime law), 2nd edn. Seizando Shoten, Tokyo
Saburo M (1973) Senin no jikangai rodo to senin ho 67 jo no kaishaku (Overtime work of seafarers and interpretation of Article 67). Rodo Horitsu Junpo (Labour Law Weekly) 837:4–11
Sasaki H (1962) Senin seisaku to kaiin kumiai (Seafarer policy and seamen's union). Seizando Shoten, Tokyo
Sasaoka M (2022) Maritime law in Japan: responding to today's and future maritime industries. Yokohama Hogaku (Yokohama Law Rev) 30(3):343–359
Shinobu N (2021) Naiko senin no hatarakikata kaikaku ni mukete (Toward the work style reform for coastal shipping seafarers). Nihon Rodo Kenkyu Zasshi (Jpn J Labour Stud) 728:65–75
Sugeno K, Yamakawa R (2024) Rodo ho (Labour law), 13th edn. Kobundo Tokyo
Tanaka S (1985) Kaisho ho Shoron (Detailed discussion of maritime commercial law). Keiso Shobo, Tokyo
Terui T (1998) Senin ho ga wakaru hon (Textbook of the Seafarers' Act). Seizando Shoten, Tokyo
The Ministry of Land, Infrastructure, Transport and Tourism (2020) Toward the realisation of work style reform for seafarers. https://www.mlit.go.jp/report/press/content/001363752.pdf. Accessed 6 June 2025
The Ministry of Land, Infrastructure, Transport and Tourism (2025) Suji de miru kaiji (Maritime industry from the viewpoint of numbers). https://www.mlit.go.jp/maritime/content/001753380.pdf. Accessed 30 June 2025
World Maritime University (2020) A culture of adjustment, evaluating the implementation of the current maritime regulatory framework on rest and work hours. https://commons.wmu.se/cgi/viewcontent.cgi?article=1079&context=lib_reports. Accessed 6 June 2025

Chapter 13
Regulations of Seafarers' Employment Agreements: Vietnam and Korea in Comparison

Hoang Thi Hong Hanh and Sungho Park

Introduction

Seafarers constitute a vital segment of the maritime labour force supporting international seaborne trade. With over 80% of global trade by volume transported by sea,[1] the world heavily depends on maritime shipping for the delivery of essential goods. However, seafaring remains a stressful and hazardous profession due to the peculiarity of working at sea, including isolation, excessive workload, and exposure tremendous risks. Protecting the rights and welfare of seafarers is therefore a fundamental responsibility shared by the international community, national governments, and other stakeholders in the maritime industry. For this purpose, the Maritime Labour Convention (the MLC or Convention) was adopted by the ILO in

[1] UNCTAD (2022), p. xv.

Hoang Thi Hong Hanh: Lecturer in Maritime Law at Vietnam Maritime University. LL.M. in International Law (School of Law, Vietnam National University, Hanoi), MSc in Maritime and Law Policy (World Maritime Uni., Sweden), Ph.D. in Maritime Law (Korea Maritime & Ocean Uni).

Sungho Park is Professor in the Division of Navigation Convergence Studies at Korea Maritime and Ocean University (KMOU). He received his B.Eng. and M.Eng. in Navigation System Engineering, and his LL.M. and Ph.D. in Maritime Law from KMOU. His research specialties include Public International Law (Law of the Sea), Maritime Law, and Maritime Traffic Law.

H. T. H. Hanh (✉)
Navigation Faculty, Vietnam Maritime University, Hai Phong, Vietnam
e-mail: hanhhth.hh@vimaru.edu.vn

S. Park
Division of Navigation Convergence Science, Korea Maritime & Ocean University, Busan, Republic of Korea

J. Choi (ed.), *Public Maritime Law in Asia*, International Law in Asia,
https://doi.org/10.1007/978-981-95-7037-9_13

2006 and entered into force in 2013 as a global achievement in protecting the human rights of seafarers with 104 Member States equating to 96.6% of the world's gross tonnage of ships.[2] To ensure the Convention brings about meaningful change and tangible, effective national implementation in good faith is a prerequisite.[3] Each Member State is therefore obliged to implement the Convention with the highest responsibility across three perspectives: (i) the promulgation of national laws and regulations; (ii) the enforcement of those laws and regulations; and (iii) the provision of adequate infrastructure to support implementation.[4] Among these, promulgating the national the adoption of national laws and regulations that fully align with the mandatory provisions of the MLC is the requisite step in ensuring the Convention's effective application at the national level.

The regulations concerning "seafarers' employment agreements" (SEAs), which aim to ensure decent working and living conditions for seafarers, are regarded as "the heart" of the MLC.[5] However, the incorporation of these regulations into the national legal systems of numerous Member States has not fully satisfied the Convention's requirements, particularly in developing countries with a relatively insignificant seafaring workforce, such as Vietnam.

Vietnam has 34,590 seafarers, accounting for approximately 1.83% of the total number of the global total.[6] This country ratified the MLC in 2013, becoming the 37th Member State, and has since accepted all four amendments to the Convention. Over the past decade, Vietnam has made effort to implement the MLC; however, significant shortcomings remain in establishing a comprehensive legal framework to protect the rights and benefits of seafarers reveals several shortcomings. Notably, gaps persist in the national legal system when compared to the Convention's requirements, particularly regarding fundamental areas such as SEAs. Vietnam currently lacks a dedicated legal instrument specifically designed to protect seafarers' rights in general and to regulate SEAs in particular. Instead, SEAs are governed by the general provisions of the Labour Code, despite the fact that the contractual relationship of employment between seafarers and shipowners is markedly different from that of onshore workers. In contrast, other maritime nations in Asia, such as Japan, South Korea, and the Philippines, have enacted specialized legislation, such as a Seafarers Act, to address the unique nature of seafaring labour. As Vietnam continues to improve its legislative framework for seafarers, drawing on the experiences of countries with well-established and robust maritime industries represents an effective approach to developing and strengthening its national maritime legal system.

[2] ILO (2014a).

[3] Moira et al. (2011), p. vii.

[4] Resolution A.1070(28) on 4 December 2013 on the IMO Instruments Implementation Code (III Code), Objective, paragraph 1.

[5] Moira et al., op. cit., p. 291.

[6] UNCTAD (2023a).

The primary objective of this article is to examine the gaps in Vietnam's legal system regarding the regulation of seafarers' employment agreements (SEAs), in comparison with the Seafarers Act of the Republic of Korea, by evaluating both against the standards set by the MLC and proposing measures to address these deficiencies in Vietnam's legal framework. The Seafarers Act of the Republic of Korea is adopted as a model for how the MLC can be effectively incorporated into a national legal system.

Regarding methodology, this article employs an applied legal research approach[7] to review and analyse Vietnam's legal documents in order to identify gaps in the current legal framework concerning SEAs. In addition, a comparative legal research method is adopted to examine Vietnam's legal provisions against the relevant regulations of Seafarers Act of the Republic of Korea and the MLC, with the aim of proposing suitable legal reforms. Descriptive statistical analysis is also used to examine data from the reports of the ILO's Committee of Experts on the Application of Conventions and Recommendations (CEACR), focusing on how SEAs are incorporated into the legal systems of Member States. Following the introduction, this chapter is structured into three main parts: (i) an overview of seafarers' employment agreements; (ii) an analysis of Vietnam's regulations on SEAs in comparison with the Seafarers Act of Korea and the MLC; and (iii) implications and conclusions.

Seafarers Employment Agreements (SEAs)

A seafarer's employment agreement (SEA) serves as the fundamental legal instrument establishing the contractual relationship between a seafarer (as employee) and a shipowner (as employer). It outlines the rights and obligations of both parties in accordance with national laws and the MLC. Upon execution of the SEA, both the seafarer and the shipowner become legally bound not only to each other but also in relation to third parties, administrative authorities, and courts. Specifically, the SEA stipulates the scope of work, working and living conditions, seafarers' entitlements, and the shipowner's responsibilities. Additionally, it serves as key evidence in legal proceedings for resolving disputes between the two parties. For administrative purposes, the SEA is a critical document used by Flag State inspectors and Port State Control (PSC) officers to verify compliance with national legislation and the MLC. The SEA constitutes one of the 16 general areas subject to inspection by both Flag and Port State authorities.[8] For Member States, the SEA also functions as an essential criterion in evaluating the effectiveness of national implementation of the MLC.

[7] Chynoweth (2008), p. 31.

[8] Appendix A5-I and Appendix A5-2, MLC, 2006.

From a practical perspective, the maritime industry is expected to face a significant workforce shortage in the coming decades.[9] Since the MLC was negotiated on an international tripartite basis, relevant stakeholders have recognized that declining interest in seafaring as a profession requires a strong commitment from shipowners to improve employment conditions as a means of attracting and retaining seafarers.[10] Accordingly, the SEA serves as the best guarantee[11] to protect seafarers' rights and benefits in compliance with both national laws and international standards. However, the most frequently observed deficiencies concerned the absence of signed SEAs (16%) and the lack of access by seafarers to information regarding their employment conditions (28%) as reported by Tokyo MoU in its 2024 Concentrated Inspection Campaign on crew wages and SEAs.[12] Therefore, the establishment of comprehensive regulations governing SEAs is essential for all States Parties, including Vietnam. This section examines the SEA from the perspective of employment contract law, addressing its definition, parties, form, and substantive content.

Definition of the Seafarers' Employment Agreement

Article 2.1 paragraph (g) of the MLC provides an inclusive definition: "seafarers' employment agreement includes both a contract of employment and articles of agreement".[13] According to this definition, the SEA encompasses two distinct forms: the "contract of employment" and the "articles of agreement", both of which are recognized as SEAs under the MLC. The term "articles of agreement" originates from the Seamen's Articles of Agreement Convention, 1926 (Convention No. 22), which was the first international instrument to regulate the contractual employment relationship between seafarers and shipowners. The MLC's inheritance of the term "articles of agreement" aligns with the legal traditions and practices of countries that had previously ratified Convention No. 22.[14]

According to Regulation 2.1, a SEA is defined as a written contract of employment signed by both the seafarer and the shipowner.[15] To ensure that seafarers are afforded fair employment terms,[16] the SEA must contain clear, legally enforceable

[9] ICS (2023).

[10] Moira (2017).

[11] ITF. Before You Board. n.d. ITF Seafarers. https://www.itfseafarers.org/en/resources/you-board. Accessed 30 July 2025.

[12] Tokyo MoU (2024), p. 3.

[13] ILO (2014b), p. 18.

[14] Moira et al. (2011), op. cit., p. 281.

[15] Regulation 2.1, paragraph 1, MLC, 2006.

[16] Article 4.2 and Regulation 2.1, MLC, 2006.

provisions that are consistent with the regulations and standards of the MLC.[17] Moreover, the seafarer must be given the opportunity to review the agreement, seek advice regarding its terms and conditions, and freely consent to them prior to signing.[18] In addition, a collective bargaining agreement could be incorporated into the SEA as a part of its terms.[19]

As a form of employment agreement, the SEA possesses distinct features that differentiate it from other types of contracts. Firstly, in accordance with the exchange principle of employment contracts, the SEA embodies "an exchange or a series of exchanges of work and remuneration" between the seafarer and the shipowner.[20] This essential feature of an employment relationship also has been held by a judge that "for a certain period of time a person performs service for and under the direction of another person in return for which he receives remuneration".[21]

Secondly, fairness in employment term is a crucial peculiarity of the SEA. Historically, seafarers have frequently been subjected to unfair treatment with different forms of coercion and abuse while embarking upon vessels.[22] In response, the Seaman's Articles of Agreement Convention, 1926, established a mechanism to protect seafarers through standardized articles of agreement. Under this framework, seamen and their advisers were granted the right to examine the agreement and were provided with reasonable facilities to do so before signing. The terms and conditions had to comply with national laws and were subject to oversight by competent public authorities. This protective spirit is inherited in the MLC, which explicitly upholds "fair terms and conditions of employment" in Regulation 2.1 and Article 4.2. These provisions ensure that seafarers freely enter into the contract with sufficient understanding of their rights and responsibilities and without any coercion or deception.

The fair employment relationship between seafarers and shipowners also reflects "integration principle" and the "reciprocity principle" in employment law. The integration principle posits that "the worker should be regarded and treated as being integrated into the organization of the employer"[23], while the reciprocity principle emphasizes that "the employer and the worker should be regarded and treated as being committed to reciprocal cooperation in the conduct of the contractual relationship".[24] In the maritime context, SEA regulations must uphold all three principles. Given the stressful and hazardous nature of seafaring work, essential to the protection of ships, cargo, and passengers, seafarers should be fully recognized as

---

[17] Regulation 2.1, paragraph 1, MLC, 2006.

[18] Regulation 2.1, paragraph 2, MLC, 2006.

[19] Regulation 2.1, paragraph 3, MLC, 2006.

[20] Freedland (2016), p. 43.

[21] See case 66/85 Lawrie-Blum v Land Baden-Württemberg [1986] ecr 2121, [17]. See also case 197/86 Brown v The Secretary of State for Scotland [1988] ecr 3205 and case c-3/90 Bernini v Minister van Onderwijs en Wetenschappen [1992] ecr i-1071, as cited in Lavelle (2014), p. 188.

[22] ILO (2014), op. cit, p. 18.

[23] Freedland (2016), op. cit, p. 43.

[24] Freedland (2016), op. cit, p. 44.

integral members of the shipowner's enterprise. Accordingly, they are entitled to decent working and living conditions and to the full protection of their rights and benefits, arguably to a greater extent than general onshore workers.

Parties of the Seafarers' Employment Agreement

According to the MLC, a SEA must be signed by both the seafarer and the shipowner or a representative of the shipowner.[25] Therefore, it can be affirmed that the principal parties to the SEA are the shipowner and the seafarer.

Article 2.1(f) of the MLC provides a broad definition of seafarer as "any person who is employed or engaged or works in any capacity on board a ship to which this Convention applies". This definition is notably more inclusive than "seaman" in Convention No. 22, which excluded categories such as "masters, pilots, cadets and pupils on training ships, duly indentured apprentices, naval ratings, and other persons in the permanent service of a government". In contrast, the terminology of seafarer under the MLC encompasses a wider range of maritime personnel.

With the exception of individuals working on vessels to which the MLC does not apply, such as ships engaged in fishing or similar pursuits, ships of traditional build (e.g. dhows and junks), and warships or naval auxiliaries,[26] the Convention applies to all persons employed, engaged, or working in any capacity on board a ship, including masters, cadets, and self-employed seafarers.[27] From the standpoint of the MLC's definitions and scope of application, cadets and self-employed individuals qualify as seafarers. However, from a legal perspective concerning employment contracts, they are not considered employees if they do not have a formal employment relationship with the shipowner. Accordingly, they do not constitute contractual parties to the SEA.

With regard to the employer as a party to the SEA, Article 2.1(j) of the MLC defines shipowner as "the owner of the ship or another organization or person, such as the manager, agent, or bareboat charterer, who has assumed the responsibility for the operation of the ship from the owner and who, on assuming such responsibility, has agreed to take over the duties and responsibilities imposed on shipowners in accordance with this Convention, regardless of whether any other organization or persons fulfil certain of the duties or responsibilities on behalf of the shipowner".

This comprehensive definition is derived from the Recruitment and Placement of Seafarers Convention, 1996 (Convention No. 179)[28], and is also consistent with the definition of "Company" under the International Safety Management Code (ISM

[25] Standard A 2.1 paragraph 1(a), MLC, 2006.

[26] Article II paragraph 4, MLC, 2006.

[27] Article II paragraph 2, MLC, 2006.

[28] Article 1(c), C179 - Recruitment and Placement of Seafarers Convention, 1996 (No. 179).

Code).[29] It reflects the contractual complexity of the maritime industry, where entities such as bareboat charterers, ship managers, or manning agents may assume the responsibilities of the shipowner under law or contractual agreement. In practice, it is critically important to identify the party who is directly and ultimately responsible under the SEA, particularly in cases where a third-party employer, such as a crew manning agency, breaches contractual obligations.

Form of the Seafarers' Employment Agreement

The SEA shall be drafted and concluded in the form of a written document.[30] It must be signed by both the seafarer and the shipowner or by a duly authorized representative of the shipowner.[31] Each party shall retain an original signed copy of the SEA.[32] Additionally, a copy of the SEA must be kept on board the vessel to ensure that seafarers, as well as officers of the competent authority, can readily access and review it.[33]

Contents of the Seafarers' Employment Agreement

A SEA sets out the rights and obligations of both the seafarer and the shipowner in a manner consistent with the Code of the MLC.[34] The fundamental requirement of the SEA is to ensure that seafarers are provided with decent working and living conditions on board, as mandated by the Convention.[35] The MLC obliges Member States to adopt laws and/or regulations addressing the issues specified under Regulation 2.1 and Standard A2.1. These include the basic principles and minimum requirements of SEAs, encompassing (i) general requirements for SEAs; (ii) collective bargaining agreements (CBAs); (iii) records of employment; (iv) minimum contents of the SEA; (v) termination of the SEA; (vi) termination with shorter notice; and (vii) the validity of SEAs in situations involving piracy and armed robbery.

[29] Regulation 1.2, The International Safety Management (ISM) Code.

[30] Regulation 2.1 paragraph 1, MLC, 2006.

[31] Standard A2.1 paragraph 1(a), MLC, 2006.

[32] Standard A2.1 paragraph 1(c), MLC, 2006.

[33] Standard A2.1 paragraph 1(d), MLC, 2006.

[34] Regulation 2.1 paragraph 1, MLC, 2006.

[35] Standard A2.1 paragraph 1(a), MLC, 2006.

Promulgating the Regulations of the SEAs in Member States' Legal Systems

On 24 August 2013, the MLC officially entered into force after achieving the required number of ratifications. Since this historical milestone, the implementation and application of the Convention by Member States have been monitored by the Committee of Experts on the Application of Conventions and Recommendations (CEACR), an independent body of ILO.[36] The CEACR's annual reports include expert legal commentary on the national legislation of each Member State, assessing whether such laws have been promptly and effectively aligned with the provisions of the MLC. This section provides an overview of how the regulations concerning SEAs have been incorporated into Member States' legal frameworks, based on the CEACR's observations over several years. The CEACR examines the national reports submitted in accordance with Article 22 of the MLC, identifying gaps and inconsistencies between national laws and the Convention, and offers recommendations to guide Member States toward full compliance.

As of November 2023, 104 countries and 9 territories are members of the MLC. Figure 13.1 illustrates that 19% of these members, equivalent to 21 countries, do not yet have reports from the CEACR. These countries, including Brazil, Iraq, and Madagascar, have ratified the MLC within the past 1–5 years and may require additional time to review and align their national legal frameworks with the Convention. Another 19%, equivalent to 22 countries, proportion which is equivalent to 22 countries have not received any CEACR comments specifically related to the regulation of SEAs in their national legislation. These are typically developed nations with advanced legal systems or major contributors to the global seafaring workforce, such as the United Kingdom, Germany, and the Philippines. The largest

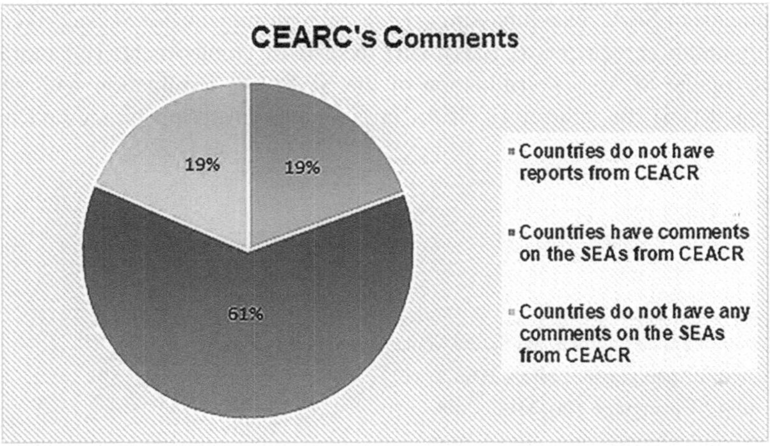

Fig. 13.1 CEACR's comments on the SEA regulations to the Member States

[36]Article 19, 22, 35 of the ILO's Constitution.

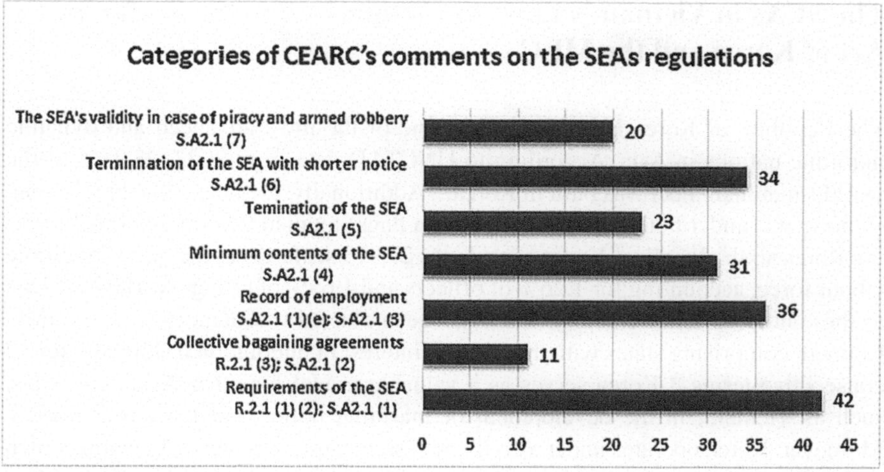

Fig. 13.2 Categories of CEARC's comments on the SEA regulations of 70 Member States

group, accounting for 61% or 70 countries, has received CEACR comments regarding the incorporation of SEA-related provisions of the MLC into their national legal systems. This data indicates that a substantial number of Member States are required to enact new legislation or amend existing laws to ensure full compliance with the Convention's requirements on SEAs. It may be concluded that, in numerous States Parties, the current legal provisions on SEAs still fall short of meeting the full standards set by the MLC.

Figure 13.2 illustrates the number of CEACR comments across different categories of existing SEA regulations among 70 Member States. A total of 114 comments are distributed across 7 aspects of the SEA, reflecting two main types of shortcomings: (i) failure by Member States to adopt laws, regulations, or other measures required by the MLC and (ii) existing national provisions that are insufficient or inconsistent with the MLC. The category with the highest number of deficiencies, 42 comments, relates to the "Requirements of the SEA", as stipulated in Regulation 2.1, paragraphs 1 and 2, and Standard A2.1, paragraph 2. This is followed by the "Record of Employment" category, under Standard A2.1, paragraph 1(e) and paragraph 3, which received 36 comments. The "Minimum Contents of the SEA", set out in Standard A2.1, paragraph 4, ranks third with 31 comments. Meanwhile, "Termination of the SEA", as specified in Standard A2.1, paragraph 5, and "Termination of the SEA with Shorter Notice", under paragraph 6, received 23 and 34 comments, respectively. The category with the fewest comments, 20 in total, concerns the validity of the SEA in cases of piracy and armed robbery.

Based on these statistics, it is evident that shortcomings exist across all aspects of SEAs within the national legal systems of the 70 Member States. Although SEAs play a critical role, as previously analysed, the majority of States Parties have not fully complied with the SEA-related provisions of the MLC, even after more than a decade of its implementation.

The SEAs in Vietnam's Laws in Comparison to the Seafarers Act of Korea and the MLC

The Republic of Korea is recognized as one of the most advanced and dynamic maritime nations in Asia. According to UNCTAD data from 2023, 28.28% of the world's merchant fleet was built in Korea.[37] Additionally, the fleet owned by Korean shipowners (under both national and foreign flags) totalled 97,020,891 DWT ranking Korea sixth globally.[38] Korea contributes 27,919 seafarers to the global maritime labour force, accounting for 1.26% of officers and 1.65% of ratings worldwide. Due to these notable achievements, Korea has been elected to Category A of the IMO Council, comprising states with the greatest interest in international shipping, for 12 consecutive terms.[39] Korea serves as a valuable model for other Asian countries, such as Vietnam, in the development of maritime policy and legal frameworks. Moreover, Korea operates under a civil law system similar to that of Vietnam, which makes Korean legislation particularly relevant for legal benchmarking, more so than common law systems such as those of the United Kingdom or the United States. From the perspective of seafarer supply, Vietnam and Korea share several characteristics, for instance, both maintain a seafaring labour force of approximately 30,000 individuals serving in domestic and international markets. Notably, a significant number of Vietnamese seafarers work on board Korean vessels, making them relatively familiar with Korean maritime laws and practices.

The first Seafarers Act of the Republic of Korea was enacted in 1962 and has since undergone multiple amendments, with the most recent version being Seafarers Act No. 19498, dated 21 September 2023. Article 1 of the Act states its purpose as follows: "to maintain order on a ship, guarantee and improve the basic life of seafarers, and promote the improvement of the qualification of seafarers by prescribing matters concerning duties, service, standards of labor conditions, employment security, welfare, education and training of seafarers, etc." The Act comprises 17 chapters and 180 articles, offering a comprehensive legal framework governing all aspects of seafarers' rights, obligations, and working conditions. Given its breadth and modern approach, the Korean Seafarers Act serves as a valuable reference for Vietnam in the development and enhancement of national regulations on seafarers in general and SEAs in particular.

In Vietnam's legal system, pursuant to the 2013 Constitution and the Law on International Treaties 2016, the country follows a monistic approach. To implement the MLC domestically, Vietnam issued or amended several legal instruments following ratification, including Decree No. 121/2014/ND-CP and the Vietnam Maritime Code 2015. The legal framework governing SEAs is primarily provided by the Vietnam Maritime Code 2015, Decree No. 121/2014/ND-CP, and the Labour Code 2019.

---

[37] UNCTAD (2023b).

[38] UNCTAD (2024), p. 51.

[39] IMO, Council Members n.d. https://www.imo.org/en/ourwork/ero/pages/council-members.aspx. Accessed 30 July 2025.

The development of Vietnam's maritime legislation is marked by the promulgation of the Vietnam Maritime Code in three phases: 1990, 2005, and 2015. Over this 25-year period, the legal framework concerning seafarers has gradually evolved. The 1990 Code included only four articles addressing Vietnamese seafarers, primarily outlining general principles. This reflected the nascent stage of maritime law in Vietnam during the early years of its socialist-oriented market economy.[40] In 2005, the second version of the Maritime Code was adopted to replace the 1990 Code after 15 years of implementation. However, despite expectations for advancement, the legal provisions relating to seafarers remained underdeveloped, with only five articles, including just one article specifically addressing labour contracts.[41]

Through the 1990 and 2005 Vietnam Maritime Codes, it is evident that prior to the ratification of the MLC, the legal framework governing seafarers in Vietnam was cursory, general, and vague. Vietnamese seafarers received limited attention from the government, and the maritime legislation lacked comprehensive regulation of the various aspects of seafarers' rights, duties, and employment contracts.

In 2015, the Vietnam Maritime Code was enacted for the third time, following 2 years after Vietnam ratified the MLC, and marked a fundamental reform in the legal regime concerning seafarers. The number of provisions relating to seafarers increased from 5 to 14, notably including Article 62, which governs labour contracts.

Additionally, Decree No. 121/2014/ND-CP, which elaborates on the MLC provisions related to the working conditions of seafarers on board ships, serves as a key legal instrument detailing several aspects of the Convention. These include the rights, obligations, and responsibilities of both seafarers and shipowners. Issued in 2014, 1 year after Vietnam ratified the MLC, the Decree represents the first domestic legal document to incorporate the Convention's requirements into national legislation. Regulations on SEAs are specifically addressed in Article 4 of the Decree.

SEAs between seafarers and shipowners are also governed by the Labour Code 2019. In addition to the requirements set out in Article 62 of the Vietnam Maritime Code 2015, both parties must comply with the provisions of Chapter III of the Labour Code 2019, which governs labour contracts. Furthermore, Chapter V of the Labour Code addresses collective negotiation and collective bargaining agreements, which apply to employment relationships, including those between seafarers and shipowners.

It is important to note that the Labour Code functions as a general legal framework, while the Vietnam Maritime Code serves as specialized legislation specifically regulating employment relationships in the maritime sector.

This section examines the relevant provisions of Vietnam's legal documents concerning all aspects of the SEA, in comparison with the standards set forth in the MLC.

---

40 Article 39, 40, 41, 42, Vietnam Maritime Code 1990.

41 Article 57, Vietnam Maritime Code 2005.

Seafarer

Article 59, paragraph 1, of the Vietnam Maritime Code defines a seafarer as "any person who must meet eligibility requirements and standards for holding ranks onboard a Vietnamese ship". In comparison with the definition of seafarer under the MLC, this definition is notably narrow, as it limits the scope to individuals working only on Vietnamese-flagged ships.

By contrast, Article 3, paragraph 4, of Decree 121 provides a broader and more MLC-consistent definition: a seafarer is "any person who is recruited or employed to work onboard a ship, meeting eligibility requirements and standards for holding ranks in accordance with the law". This definition is not restricted to ships flying the Vietnamese flag and, therefore, aligns more closely with the MLC, which applies to all seafarers working in any capacity on board a ship to which the Convention applies.

This discrepancy reveals a conflict between the definitions of a seafarer in the Vietnam Maritime Code and Decree 121. The definition in Decree 121 is more accurate and comprehensive, as it can encompass (i) foreign seafarers working on Vietnamese-flagged ships and (ii) both Vietnamese and foreign seafarers working on foreign-flagged ships where Vietnamese law has been contractually chosen as the applicable law.

Referring to the Seafarers Act of Korea, Article 2 paragraph 1 defines "seafarer" as a person who is employed to provide work in a ship to which this Act applies (including Korean ships, foreign ships chartered on the condition of acquiring Korean registry, and foreign ships sailing only between domestic ports).[42] This regulation demonstrates that Seafarers Act of Korea does not restrict the definition of seafarer to those working solely on Korean-flagged vessels.

Accordingly, the Vietnam Maritime Code should consider amending the definition of seafarer in Article 59, paragraph 1, by replacing the phrase "on board Vietnamese ships" with the broader phrase "onboard a ship". This revision would ensure consistency with international standards, particularly those of the MLC, and align Vietnam's legal framework more closely with comparative jurisdictions such as Korea.

Requirements of the SEAs

The MLC requires that the SEA be set out in a clear, written, and legally enforceable form, consistent with the standards stipulated in the Code.[43] Each seafarer must have a SEA signed by both the seafarer and the shipowner or the shipowner's representative, ensuring decent working and living conditions on board the ship as man-

[42] Article 3, Seafarers Act of Korea.

[43] Regulation 2.1 paragraph 1, MLC, 2006.

dated by the Convention .[44] Furthermore, both the shipowner and the seafarer must retain a signed original of the SEA.[45]

Under Vietnamese law, the Vietnam Maritime Code and Decree 121 provide that, prior to commencing work on board, a shipowner and a seafarer must enter into a SEA. In case the shipowner does not sign the SEA by himself, he shall authorize in writing his representative to sign the SEA.[46] In addition, the *Labour Code* mandates that employment contracts must be made in writing and in two copies, one for the employee and one for the employer.[47] These regulations generally satisfy the MLC's formal requirements concerning the SEA. However, the core objective of the Convention, ensuring that SEAs explicitly commit to providing seafarers with decent working and living conditions on board, is not expressly reflected in Vietnam's legal documents.

In contrast, Article 27 paragraph 1 of the Seafarers Act of Korea stipulates that, when entering into a SEA, the shipowner must clearly specify wages, working hours, and other employment conditions. If any terms fall below the minimum standards prescribed by the Seafarers Act, those provisions shall be deemed null and void (without affecting the validity of the entire SEA). In such cases, the invalid part shall be replaced by the Act's minimum standards.[48] This serves as an effective safeguard against substandard or exploitative contractual terms.

Another substantial principle under the MLC is that seafarers must be given the opportunity to review the SEA, seek advice, and freely accept the terms before signing.[49] However, this requirement is notably absent from Vietnam's current legal framework and has been highlighted by the CEACR in its review reports.[50] In contrast, the Korean Seafarers Act fully incorporates this principle, requiring shipowners to provide seafarers, upon request, an opportunity to examine the terms of the SEA and receive appropriate guidance and counsel.[51]

Moreover, Standard A2.1, paragraph 1(d), of the MLC requires that information regarding SEAs be readily available on board to seafarers (including the ship's master) and be accessible for inspection by competent authorities, including those at ports of call. This requirement is currently not addressed in either Vietnamese legislation or the Korean Seafarers Act.

---

44 Standard A2.1 paragraph 1(a), MLC, 2006.

45 Standard A2.1 paragraph 1(c), MLC, 2006.

46 Article 62 paragraph 1, Vietnam Maritime Code and Article 4, Decree 121.

47 Article 14 paragraph 1, Labour Code.

48 Article 26, Seafarers Act of Korea.

49 Regulation 2.1 paragraph 1 and Standard A2.1 paragraph 1(b), MLC, 2006.

50 CEACR (2022).

51 Article 27 paragraph 2, Seafarers Act of Korea.

Collective Bargaining Agreements (CBAs)

Regulation 2.1, paragraph 3, and Standard A2.1, paragraph 2, of the MLC stipulate that:

(i) To the extent compatible with the Member State's national laws and practices, SEAs shall be understood to incorporate any applicable CBAs.
(ii) Where a CBA constitutes all or part of a SEA, a copy of that agreement must be available on board.
(iii) If the language of the SEA or any applicable CBA is not English, a copy of the standard form of the SEA and the relevant portions of the CBA must be available in English.

In Vietnam, CBAs are regulated by the Labour Code 2019, which applies to all workers. Similarly, in Korea, CBAs are governed by the Trade Union and Labour Relations Adjustment Act 2021, providing the legal foundation for establishing CBAs across various industries, including the maritime sector. It is noteworthy that CBAs are referenced in several provisions of the Korean Seafarers Act, such as Article 33 on SEA termination, Article 39 on repatriation, Article 53 on wage payment, and Article 55 concerning the retirement allowance system.

In Vietnam, Article 63 of the Vietnam Maritime Code, which addresses working and rest hours, also refers to CBAs. These references confirm the existence and recognition of CBAs in the national legal frameworks and practices of both countries. However, neither the Korean Seafarers Act nor Vietnam's Maritime Code or Decree 121 explicitly articulates the principle governing the relationship between SEAs and CBAs, as required by the MLC.

Seafarer's Book

The MLC requires that seafarers be provided with a document containing a record of their employment on board the ship.[52] This document must not include any statement regarding the quality of the seafarers' work or details of their wages.[53]

Both Vietnam and Korea provide detailed regulations concerning the seafarer's book. The Vietnam Maritime Code stipulates that seafarers working on board Vietnamese-flagged ships must possess a seafarer's book.[54] This requirement is further elaborated in Chapter 3 of Circular No. 23/2017/TT-BGTVT, dated 28 July 2017, which regulates procedures for seafarer registration and the issuance of the seafarer's book. Similarly, the Seafarers Act of Korea dedicates five articles to the seafarer's book, addressing procedures for issuance, reissuance, invalidation, and

---

[52] Standard A2.1 paragraph 2(e), MLC, 2006.

[53] Standard A2.1 paragraph 3, MLC, 2006.

[54] Article 59 paragraph 2 (d), Vietnam Maritime Code.

the prohibition of improper use.[55] However, the crucial principle "the seafarer's book shall not contain any statement as to the quality of the seafarers' work or as to their wages" is not reflected expressly through the contents of regulations in the Korea Seafarers Act as well as in Chapter 3 of Circular 23/2017/TT-BGTVT.

Minimum Contents of the SEA

The SEA must, as a minimum, contain all the information required under Standard A2.1 paragraph 4 of the MLC, including (i) the seafarer's full name, date of birth or age, and birthplace; (ii) the shipowner's name and address; (iii) the place where and date when the SEA is entered into; (iv) the capacity in which the seafarer is to be employed; (v) the amount of the seafarer's wages or, where applicable, the formula used for calculating them; (vi) the amount of paid annual leave or, where applicable, the formula used for calculating it; (vii) the termination of the agreement and the conditions thereof; (viii) the health and social security protection benefits to be provided to the seafarer by the shipowner; (ix) the seafarer's entitlement to repatriation; (x) reference to the collective bargaining agreement, if applicable; and (xi) any other particulars which national law may require.

To meet this requirement, the Vietnam Maritime Code and Decree 121 refer to the basic contents of the employment contracts for general workers prescribed in the Labour Code[56] and add more four contents: (i) repatriation of a seafarer, (ii) accident insurance, (iii) payment for annual leave, and (iv) terms and conditions under which an employment contract is terminated.[57] However, the requirements regarding the "place and date where the SEA is entered into" and "reference to the collective bargaining agreement" are not included in these Vietnamese legal instruments. Additionally, the CEACR has urged the Vietnamese government to ensure that the SEA explicitly includes the seafarer's birthplace, as well as the place and date of signing.[58]

In contrast, the Seafarers Act of Korea and its Enforcement Rules fully satisfy all minimum requirements under the MLC.[59] Moreover, Korean law goes further by mandating the inclusion of the seafarer's nationality and specific provisions concerning working conditions. These additions represent good practice and are worthy of consideration for incorporation into Vietnam's legal framework.

[55] Articles 45, 46, 47, 49, 50, Seafarers Act of Korea.

[56] Article 21, paragraph 1, Labour Code.

[57] Article 62, paragraph 2, Vietnam Maritime Code and Article 4 paragraph 2, Decree 121.

[58] CEACR (2022), op. cit.

[59] Article 20, Enforcement Rules of the Seafarers Act.

Termination of the SEA

The MLC requires that the termination of the SEA and the conditions thereof be explicitly addressed. Specifically, it mandates the following:

- If the SEA is for an indefinite period, it must include the conditions under which either party may terminate the agreement and the required notice period, which shall not be shorter for the shipowner than for the seafarer.
- If the SEA is for a definite period, the date of expiry must be stated.
- If the SEA is for a voyage, it must indicate the port of destination and the time after arrival before the seafarer may be discharged.

In contrast, the Vietnam Maritime Code and Decree No. 121/2014/ND-CP are completely silent on the termination of SEAs. Consequently, this issue falls under the general provisions of the Labour Code, which applies broadly to all workers. Under the Labour Code, two types of employment contracts are recognized:[60]

(i) Contracts of indefinite duration
(ii) Contracts of definite duration, which may not exceed 36 months

A labour contract may be terminated in the following circumstances:[61]

- Expiry of the contract
- Completion of the tasks stated in the contract
- Mutual agreement between the parties to terminate the contract
- Unilateral termination by either the employee or the employer

However, since the Labour Code is designed for onshore and general workers, it does not address the particular nature of SEAs, such as voyage-based employment or the complex situations that may arise at sea. For example, the Labour Code does not consider scenarios in which a SEA may be terminated while a ship is in transit, sunk, or detained that are common issues in maritime employment.

In comparison, the Seafarers Act of Korea, as a sector-specific law, contains detailed and targeted provisions addressing the unique aspects of maritime employment that general labour regulations cannot adequately govern. For instance:

- Article 28(1) allows a seafarer to cancel the SEA if actual working conditions deviate from those agreed upon and to claim damages from the shipowner.
- Article 32(1) prohibits shipowners from unilaterally terminating the SEA without justifiable reasons.
- Article 35 stipulates that if a SEA is terminated while the ship is at sea, it shall remain effective until the ship enters the next port and unloads cargo or disembarks passengers. If termination occurs in a port unsuitable for embarking/dis-

[60] Article 20, Labour Contract.

[61] Article 34, Labour Contract.

embarking, the SEA continues until the ship reaches a suitable port, up to a maximum of 30 days.

- Article 33 exempts the shipowner from the obligation to pay wages during the 30-day notice period if business operations cannot continue due to natural disasters, shipwreck, or destruction.
- Article 37 entitles seafarers to unemployment compensation equivalent to 2 months' wages and a retirement allowance in the following cases:

- (i) Termination by the shipowner without the seafarer being at fault
- (ii) Termination by the seafarer due to discrepancies between promised and actual conditions
- (iii) Termination due to unavoidable causes such as shipwreck or destruction of the vessel

These provisions not only reflect the practical realities and inherent risks of seafaring but also demonstrate a humane and protective legal approach that exceeds the minimum standards of the MLC. They highlight the inadequacy of general labour laws in addressing the complexities of maritime employment and provide valuable references for enhancing Vietnam's legal framework.

Additionally, Standard A2.1(5) of the MLC mandates a minimum notice period of 7 days for early termination by either party. In contrast, Articles 33(1) and 33(2) of the Seafarers Act of Korea require a more protective 30-day minimum notice period, which could serve as a suitable model for legislative reform in Vietnam.

Termination of the SEA with Shorter Notice

Standard A2.1, paragraph 6, of the MLC provides that a seafarer shall be entitled to terminate the SEA, without penalty, either with shorter notice or without notice, where compassionate or other urgent reasons are involved. However, neither the Seafarers Act of Korea nor Vietnam's current legal framework incorporates this requirement, which allows seafarers to terminate their SEA under such exceptional circumstances.[62]

This provision is fundamentally grounded in the protection of the human rights of seafarers. From a practical perspective, seafarers may encounter personal emergencies, such as serious health issues or the death of family members, that necessitate their immediate return home. In such cases, the employer's empathy and flexibility are essential.

To ensure adequate legal protection, national legislation and collective bargaining agreements should explicitly recognize and define the scope of "compassionate or other urgent reasons" that justify early termination without penalty. Incorporating

---

[62] CEACR (2022), op. cit.

this standard would demonstrate a commitment to both international obligations under the MLC and the broader recognition of seafarers' fundamental human needs.

Validity of the SEA in Case of Piracy and Armed Robbery

Standard A2.1, paragraph 7, of the MLC stipulates that a SEA shall remain in effect while a seafarer is held captive, either on or off the ship, as a result of acts of piracy or armed robbery against ships, regardless of whether the SEA has expired or either party has given notice of its suspension or termination. This provision was introduced through the 2018 amendments to the MLC, which entered into force on 26 December 2020, as a measure to protect the human rights of seafarers. Both Korea and Vietnam are Member States to these 2018 amendments. Accordingly, after 26 December 2020, competent authorities are required to inspect ships and verify SEAs and any applicable CBAs to ensure compliance with these new requirements. However, Vietnamese legislation has yet to incorporate specific provisions stating that a SEA shall remain effective while seafarers are held captive due to acts of piracy or armed robbery against ships. Additionally, the terms piracy and armed robbery against ships are not defined under Vietnam's national legal framework.

Implications

From the above analysis, it is evident that Vietnam currently regulates seafarer employment agreements (SEAs) through three main legal documents, but many fundamental principles and detailed requirements of the MLC have not been fully incorporated. A key limitation of Vietnam's legislation is that SEAs are treated as general employment contracts under the Labour Code, which governs the process of concluding, implementing, and terminating SEAs. This framework cannot adequately address specific issues arising from the relationship between seafarers and shipowners or the unique nature of work at sea. Meanwhile, the Maritime Code and Decree 121 only briefly reference SEAs without providing comprehensive regulation.

It is therefore proposed that Vietnam establish a single, independent legal instrument specifically regulating matters related to seafarers and SEAs. This document should be based on three key foundations: comprehensive incorporation of MLC regulations, standards, and guidelines; alignment with the principles of the Vietnam Maritime Code and Labour Code; and adoption of progressive and human-centred provisions from other countries, particularly the Seafarers Act of Korea. Specific implications for legislative reform include revising the definition of "seafarer" in Article 59 of the Maritime Code for consistency, consolidating all SEA requirements from Regulation 2.1 and Standard A2.1 of the MLC into a single dedicated legal document, and ensuring SEAs provide decent working and living conditions, allow seafarers to review agreements before signing, and ensure accessibility of SEA information onboard.

Moreover, the relationship between SEAs and collective bargaining agreements (CBAs) should be clearly defined, and legislation should explicitly prohibit entries in the seafarer's book regarding work quality or wages. SEAs should include the seafarer's birthplace, the date and place of agreement, and references to applicable CBAs. Legal documents must also guarantee that seafarers can terminate SEAs under compassionate or urgent circumstances and that agreements remain in force if seafarers are held captive due to piracy or armed robbery, with the terms "piracy" and "armed robbery" clearly defined. Vietnamese lawmakers are encouraged to consult ILO guidance materials, such as the *Handbook for Implementing the MLC* and Model National Provisions, to ensure alignment with the spirit and legal intent of the Convention. While this study focuses primarily on Korea for comparison, it provides a foundational step for further research and legislative development.

Conclusion

This study examined the regulation of SEAs within Vietnam's legal system in comparison with MLC standards and the Seafarers Act of Korea. The analysis identifies significant gaps in Vietnam's legislation regarding SEAs, particularly in terms of compliance with MLC requirements. It is recommended that Vietnam enact a dedicated legal instrument to regulate SEAs and related seafarer matters. The new legal framework should fully incorporate MLC standards, align with the guiding principles of the Vietnam Maritime Code and Labour Code, and integrate comparative insights from other countries, with the Seafarers Act of Korea serving as a practical reference.

More than a decade after ratifying the MLC, Vietnam must conduct a comprehensive review of its national legal system to ensure robust protection of seafarers' rights and welfare. This is particularly important in light of the declining attractiveness of the seafaring profession and the growing international emphasis on human rights at sea. Enacting a dedicated, well-structured legal framework will provide a solid foundation for sustainable seafarer protection and compliance with international maritime labour standards.

References

CEACR (2022) Direct Request - Vietnam. https://normlex.ilo.org/dyn/nrmlx_en/f?p=1000:80031::::80031:P80031_COMMENT_ID:4125948. Accessed 30 July 2025

Chynoweth P (2008) Chapter three - legal research. In: Andrew K, Ruddock L (eds) Advanced research methods in the built environment, 1st edn. Wiley-Black Well, West Sussex, pp 28–37

Freedland M (2016) Chapter 2 - the legal structure of the contract of employment. In: Freedland M (ed) The contract of employment. Oxford University Press, Oxford, pp 28–49

ICS (2023) Shaping the Future of Shipping – Seafarer 2050: A Milestone Summit in Manila. https://www.ics-shipping.org/news-item/shaping-the-future-of-shipping-seafarer-2050-a-milestone-summit-in-manila/. Accessed 30 July 2025

ILO (2014a) Maritime Labour Convention, 2006 Ratification Progress. https://www.ilo.org/international-labour-standards/maritime-labour-convention-2006#text. Accessed 30 July 2025

ILO (2014b) Handbook Guidance on Implementing the Maritime Labour Convention, 2006 Modal National Provisions (2nd impression with modifications, 2014). https://www.ilo.org/publications/handbook-guidance-implementing-maritime-labour-convention-2006-model. Accessed 30 July 2025

IMO, Council Members n.d.. https://www.imo.org/en/ourwork/ero/pages/council-members.aspx. Accessed 30 July 2025

ITF. Before You Board. n.d. ITF Seafarers. https://www.itfseafarers.org/en/resources/you-board. Accessed 30 July 2025

Lavelle J (2014) Chapter 9 - how to determine jurisdiction and governing law in disputes arising out of a seafarer's employment agreement. In: Lavelle J (ed) The Maritime Labour Convention 2006: International Labour Law Redefined. Informa Law from Routledge, New York, pp 181–212

Moira M (2017) A delicate balance: the seafarers' employment agreement, the system of the Maritime Labour Convention, 2006 and the role of flag States. https://hal.science/hal-01470314/document. Accessed 30 July 2025

Moira M, Dominick D, Cleopatra D-H (2011) The Maritime Labour Convention, 2006: a legal primer to an emerging international regime. Martinus Nijhoff Publishers, Leiden, p vii. Preface and Acknowledgements

Tokyo MoU (2024) Annual Report on Port State Control in the Asia-Pacific Region 2024, https://www.tokyo-mou.org/wp/wp-content/uploads/ANN24.pdf. Accessed 30 July 2025

UNCTAD (2022) Review of Maritime Transport 2022. United Nations Publications, New York, pp xv (Foreword)

UNCTAD (2023a) Maritime Profile: Vietnam, UNCTADSTAT. https://unctadstat.unctad.org/CountryProfile/MaritimeProfile/en-GB/704/index.html. Accessed 30 July 2025

UNCTAD (2023b) Maritime profile: Republic of Korea, UNCTADSTAT. https://unctadstat.unctad.org/CountryProfile/MaritimeProfile/en-GB/410/index.html. Accessed 30 July 2025

UNCTAD (2024) Review of Maritime Transport 2024. https://unctad.org/publication/review-maritime-transport-2024. Accessed 30 July 2025

Chapter 14
A Comprehensive Review of the STCW Convention and Code at the 10th IMO HTW Session

Songyi Yi and Sangil Lee

This is an updated and revised version of the author's article "Adapting to Change: International maritime education and training for future seafarers – focusing on the comprehensive review of the STCW convention and code of the 10th session of the IMO HTW" published at *Journal of International Maritime Safety, Environmental Affairs, and Shipping* (Vol. 9 No. 2, 2024) under the official permission of *Journal of International Maritime Safety, Environmental Affairs, and Shipping* and the coauthor.
Songyi Yi: Instructor at International Cooperation Team, Korea Institute of Maritime and Fisheries Technology. MSc in Maritime Affairs (World Maritime Uni., Sweden), Ph.D. Candidate in Maritime Law (Korea Maritime & Ocean Uni).
Sangil Lee: Professor of Division of Division of Marine System Engineering and Director of the Seafarer Research Center, Korea Maritime & Ocean University (KMOU). B.Eng. and M.Eng. in Marine Engineering, LL.M. and Ph.D. in Maritime Law (Korea Maritime and Ocean Uni.). Former Marine Engineer (1990–2003, Chief Engineer at HMM) and Instructor at HMM (2003–2005). Professor at KMOU since 2006; served as Chief Engineer of KMOU Training Ship. Currently Vice President of the Korean Institute of Maritime Law, Public Legal Advisor, Head of Legislative Affairs at Maritime Cluster Networking in Korea.

S. Yi
Division of Marine System Engineering, Korea Maritime & Ocean University, Busan, Republic of Korea

International Cooperation Team, Korea Institute of Maritime and Fisheries Technology, Busan, Republic of Korea
e-mail: silee@kmou.ac.kr

S. Lee (✉)
Division of Marine System Engineering, Korea Maritime & Ocean University, Busan, Republic of Korea
e-mail: silee@kmou.ac.kr

J. Choi (ed.), *Public Maritime Law in Asia*, International Law in Asia,
https://doi.org/10.1007/978-981-95-7037-9_14

Background

The International Convention on Standards of Training, Certification, and Watchkeeping (hereinafter STCW) is considered one of the four major conventions of the International Maritime Organization (hereinafter IMO), focusing on international agreements related to the training, certification, and watchkeeping of seafarers. The Convention consists of a preamble, 17 articles, annexes, Code A (Mandatory Rules), and Code B (Guidance Rules). Since its adoption in 1978 and its entry into force in 1984, the STCW Convention has undergone several partial amendments, culminating in major revisions in 1995 and 2010. Although the fragmentary modifications made in the Manila Amendments of 2010 were significant, they were not an exhaustive revision but rather a broad effort to improve and reorganize.

Following the Manila Amendments, in response to the evolving policy environment in international shipping emphasizing environmental sustainability and the integration of digital technologies, the IMO Maritime Safety Committee (hereinafter MSC) adopted the "Comprehensive Review of the STCW Convention and Code" as a formal agenda item and included a completion target by 2026 in its work schedule.

Comprehensive Review of the STCW Convention and Code

During the 9th session of the IMO Sub-Committee on Human Element, Training, and Watchkeeping (herein after HTW) in 2023, the objectives and fundamental principles for the comprehensive review and revision of the STCW Convention and Code were established. Working groups gathered during the session to further discuss these tasks until the recent 10th session of the HTW, where the major scope (22 areas) and roadmap (revision schedule) for the revision of the STCW Convention were finalized.[1] From February 5 to 9, 2024, the 10th session of the HTW was held at the IMO Headquarters in London, UK. During this session, a comprehensive review and revision of the STCW Convention and Code were actively undertaken.[2] Also, the first meeting of the Inter-Sessional Working Group (ISWG)-STCW, the working group to review the STCW Convention and Code, was held from October 7 to 11, 2024.[3] The main outcomes and discussions from these meetings are summarized below.

[1] International Maritime Organization (2023b).

[2] International Maritime Organization (2024a).

[3] Ibid.

Revision Scope and Key Focus Areas

The purpose of this revision exercise being a comprehensive review of the Convention, it was decided to include the revision of the Convention's articles in its scope. However, the committee chair clarified that, based on member states' opinions, the review and revision would be clearly distinguished procedurally and the review of the articles would not presuppose revision. This decision was made due to concerns about differing requirements for entry into force between the Convention's articles and annexes. STCW Convention's Article 12 (amended) states that the "explicit acceptance" of over 2/3 of the Parties is required for the main text (Article), while the "implicit acceptance" condition for the annex is applied unless over 1/3 of the Parties object within a certain deadline.[4]

Therefore, focusing on the review of the main text during this amendment process was decided due to the potential complexities in achieving simultaneous acceptance of both the main text and the annex. In the working group sessions (June–October, 2023), 22 key review items for STCW were identified, and detailed discussions were held on each item's background and future review direction during the HTW meeting.[5] These items are shown in Table 14.1. These 22 key items will be the focus of future review and amendment efforts as decided during the meeting.

Methodology for the Amendment Process

Aiming to avoid the confusion and inefficiencies experienced during the Manila Amendment in 2010, the review categories were classified into two main groups: Category 1 for regulations requiring review due to technological advancements and

---

[4] STCW Convention's Article 12 (amended).

(v) amendments so adopted shall be communicated by the Secretary General to all Parties for acceptance; (vi) an amendment to an Article shall be deemed to have been accepted on the date on which it is accepted by two thirds of the Parties;

(vii) an amendment to the Annex shall be deemed to have been accepted:

1. at the end of two years from the date on which it is communicated to Parties for acceptance; or
2. at the end of a different period, which shall be not less than one year, if so determined at the time of its adoption by a two-thirds majority of the Parties present and voting in the expanded Maritime Safety Committee; however, the amendments shall be deemed not to have been accepted if within the specified period either more than one third of Parties, or Parties the combined merchant fleets of which constitute not less than 50% of the gross tonnage of the world's merchant shipping of ships of 100 gross register tons or more, notify the Secretary-General that they object to the amendment;

(viii) an amendment to an Article shall enter into force with respect to those Parties which have accepted it, six months after the date on which it is deemed to have been accepted, and with respect to each Party which accepts it after that date, six months after the date of that Party's acceptance.

[5] International Maritime Organization, op. cit. 3.

Table 14.1 22 key review items for STCW

1. Emerging technologies on ships and ship operations
2. Digitalization in seafarers' certification, including E-certification
3. Emerging technologies in education and training
4. Facilitation, flexibility, and quality of onboard, shore-based, and workshop skills training, including use of simulators
5. Flexibility and efficiency in implementation of new training requirements and reduction of administrative burdens
6. Requirements for sea time or practical experience in relation to new and emerging technologies including the use of simulation
7. Bullying and harassment, including sexual assault and sexual harassment (hereinafter SASH), gender diversity, and gender sensitization
8. Mental health
9. Twenty-first-century and interpersonal skills
10. Addressing inconsistencies
11. Addressing different interpretations
12. Addressing taxonomy and terminologies
13. Flexibility in revalidation and renewal of certificates and endorsements
14. Overview of the implementation of the Convention, in particular, the need to update the STCW "White List"
15. Lessons learned
16. Flexibility
17. Alternative certification under chapter VII
18. Watchkeeping arrangements and principles to be observed
19. Alignment of STCW with requirements placed on ships, seafarers, and shipowners by other IMO and relevant international instruments
20. Cybersecurity awareness
21. Implementation and transitional provisions
22. Addressing outdated training requirements

era changes and Category 2 for regulations requiring review identified during the current convention and code implementation.

On top of that, there was consensus on two-phase methodology, and MSC 108 later approved it: (1) in the first phase, there will be a review of the Convention, which will include a thorough analysis of its Articles and Code.[6] This is related to external influences such as emerging technology and the knowledge acquired from the implementation of the existing Convention and Code; and (2) in the second phase, the specific revisions to the Convention and the Code will be under consideration.[7]

[6] The first phase must be structured using provision with an identified gap, the principles associated with the proposal, explanation under the applicable criteria, and the areas associated with the gap and criterion.

[7] The second phase must be structured using provision and gaps identified, proposed amendment, and explanation.

Finalized Roadmap

To expedite the comprehensive review and revision of the STCW Convention and Code, Member States agreed to establish a biennial working group.[8] And with the approval at the 108th session of IMO Maritime Safety Committee (hereinafter MSC) (24 May 2024), a precise timetable for the biennial working group will be determined. The review is expected to be completed by 2025, and the revision and adoption are planned to be finalized by 2027.

Development of Interim Guidelines for Seafarers Training on Alternative Fuel-Powered Ships

As MSC 107 (May 23, 2023) approved the "Development of a safety regulatory framework to support the reduction of GHG (greenhouse gas) emissions from ships using new technologies and alternative fuels" as a new output, the review of guidelines and regulations required for the introduction of alternative fuel technologies is already underway.[9] At HTW, most of the Member States agreed on the need and urgency to develop training guidelines for seafarers on ships powered by alternative fuels such as methanol, hydrogen, and ammonia.[10] It was therefore decided to establish a separate working group to discuss this issue later, separate from the revision of the STCW Convention.

Thus, it is expected that HTW will consider (1) the establishment of interim guidance for training seafarers on vessels that utilize alternative fuels and (2) the draft amendments to Part B of the STCW Code related to the guidelines for training and certification of seafarers operating battery-powered vessels.

Strengthening Efforts to Prevent and Address Harassment on Board

An amendment to the STCW Code "Model Course 1.21 Personal Safety and Social Responsibility" to prevent and address SASH on board has been fully considered. Following the adoption of the amendment to STCW Code A, Table A-VI/1–4 (Specification of minimum standards of competence in personal safety and social responsibility) at MSC 108 (May 24, 2024), draft terms of reference for the revision of the Model Course 1.21 will be finalized and submitted to HTW 12 (2026) for

---

[8] It was agreed to initiate the review with individual and group submissions by Member States and interested organizations who have conducted a comprehensive review.

[9] International Maritime Organization (2023c).

[10] International Maritime Organization (2023a).

consideration and validation.[11] In the end, the basic safety training (mandatory training for embarkation) will include seafarers' human rights training and competence training on SASH and will be applied to all seafarers from 2026. Furthermore, there has been favorable discussion regarding the inclusion of curriculum on SASH in the initial training for certificates of competency (hereinafter COC) as well as in the renewal training for revalidation.

Polar Code Training Enhancement

To improve the training of polar vessel operators, Member States decided to propose the inclusion of the Polar Code requirements for seafarers working in low temperatures, minimum standards for polar vessel crews to be considered seaworthy, and capabilities of simulators as part of the review of the STCW Convention. Also, the current training requirements are limited to masters and navigating officers of polar vessels; future discussions will focus on expanding these requirements to encompass all seafarers.

Simulation and Seagoing Service

It has been agreed that the use of simulators to meet the requirements for seagoing service is appropriate only for the initial issuance of the COC at the operational level. And future discussions will address the potential inclusion of certain simulator training hours in seagoing service requirements for revalidation.

Formation of the STCW GISIS Module

The IMO has created a new Global Integrated Shipping Information System (hereinafter GISIS) module in response to a request from HTW. The module will be launched for a trial term of 2 years. The IMO secretariat has encouraged responses from Member States and international organizations to assist in the continuous enhancement of the modules. The anticipated features of the module comprise (1) STCW focal points, (2) initial communication of information (Articles IV(1) and VIII(3) and Section A-I/7, paragraph 2), (3) subsequent reports (Article IX(2) and Section A-I/7, paragraphs 3–6), (4) list of competent persons (Section A-I/7,

---

[11] International Maritime Organization, op. cit. 2.

paragraph 7, MSC.1/Circ.797 series and Circular Letter No.1882), (5) dispensations (Article VIII(3)), (6) fraudulent certificates, and (7) simulators (regulation I/12).[12]

Outlook and Implications

Emerging Technologies on Ships and Ship Operations

Existing technology enables the use of autonomous merchant ships as an appropriate replacement for traditional and crewed vessels with seafarers. The forthcoming change demands the development of education and training for professional seafarers. In this regard, a crucial component of the amendment may be the matter of educating the maritime labor force for the approaching transformation. Hence, it is recommended that Member States recognize the distinction between today's seafarers and the crew aboard the maritime autonomous surface ships (MASS) and establish new requirements to ensure exceptional performance. Technical skills required are not going to be driving a ship but controlling the systems that drive the ship, whether that is on board or remotely and whether it is navigation, engineering, or electrotechnical systems.[13] A set of those skills may include remote situation awareness, information technology proficiency, and the ability to share ship operator's attention among different assets located around the world.[14]

Bullying and Harassment, Including SASH, Gender Diversity, and Gender Sensitization

As previously indicated, a discussion at the IMO is being set up about integrating new competencies, such as SASH, about bullying and harassment on board ships into the basic safety training and social responsibility framework. Given that the basic safety training targets all crew members, it is possible to argue that the existing amendment hinders the technical approach to supervising onboard seafarers and developing managerial abilities. Therefore, there is an essential need for constant and advanced operational management training. The amended scope of education should therefore encompass fundamental understanding of gender concerns, human rights, bystander intervention training, investigation and handling protocols, victim support, onboard approaches to counseling, and methods for enhancing cultural

[12] International Maritime Organization (2024b).

[13] Nguyen (2018).

[14] Bogusławski et al. (2022), pp. 327–343.

awareness. Through such education and training, it is also expected to enhance the visibility and impact of women in the maritime industry.[15]

Considering the increasing significance of seafarers' psychological wellness, training requirements for the management level would encompass mental health awareness skills. Obviously, the improvement of seafarers' psychological safety, mental health, and physical well-being will consequently improve onboard operational maritime safety and security while supporting diversity, equality, equity, and inclusiveness.[16]

Cybersecurity Awareness

Cybersecurity threat awareness and secure working conditions are vital for the maritime industry. The lack of sufficient cybersecurity awareness and training among seafarers leads to a rise in incidents such as phishing and social engineering attacks.[17] Thus, seafarers should undergo in-depth training on the latest cybersecurity threats and response methods to enhance their ability to respond effectively in real situations. This will enable seafarers to play a crucial role in maintaining maritime safety and protecting the ship and crew from cyberattacks.

Although the IMO adopted some legal and policy instruments for maritime cybersecurity, the current international legal framework is inadequate for effectively dealing with maritime cybersecurity threats.[18] Therefore, the amendment needs to incorporate practical exercises and simulations for seafarers to offer hands-on experience.

Addressing Outdated Training Requirements

The quick progress in technology has resulted in the creation of intelligent and eco-friendly vessels. Nevertheless, the training provided to seafarers for operating these ships is unable to match the pace of these swift improvements. To cultivate a highly qualified workforce as employment patterns in the shipping industry shift with technological development, it would be necessary to change maritime education and training activities.[19]

Previous amendments to the Convention have consistently put forward additional training requirements. This makes adding extra training objectives difficult. To

[15] Österman and Boström (2022), p. 6.

[16] Veldkamp et al. (2022), p. 25.

[17] Golgota and Çerma (2024), p. 1.

[18] Karim (2022), p. 1.

[19] Kim et al. (2023), p. 3.

implement new technology-driven training requirements, outdated ones must be identified, assessed, and minimized; the outdated ones include celestial navigation, visual signaling, marine steam turbine, marine diesel engine, marine boiler, and so on.

On top of that, the historical philosophy of marine engineering education, with its emphasis on separate theoretical and practical training, has led to a disconnect between theory and practice, hindering the development of critical thinking and problem-solving skills that are crucial for future marine engineers.[20] Therefore, it seems to be essential to incorporate theoretical and practical elements in training requirements.

Review of Alternative Requirements for Onboard Training

The primary challenge of onboard training is identifying appropriate training and merchant vessels for trainees to gain practical experience in the profession and the discipline of seamanship under authentic conditions. There are only very few large shipowners having a coherent onboard training program with a serious involvement of the cadets in training activities.[21]

Moreover, regulations for the implementation of onboard training differ across IMO Member States. Some States replace a portion of the onboard training with simulator training, while others prioritize the onboard training itself. It is therefore necessary to review the extent to which simulator training can be substituted for approved seagoing service and to consider the requirements for training ships, the significance of the onboard training, the number of training hours, and other relevant factors.

Conclusion

The emphasis on safety and competence remains paramount, with the ongoing review suggesting that seafarer training must evolve to address both current and future risks, enhancing global maritime safety. Also, to keep pace with technological progress, decarbonization efforts, and digitalization, the education and qualification criteria for seafarers will be revised and reinforced. This is to ensure that they are equipped to respond to emerging technologies. Upon adoption of the Convention, there would be an immediate influence on seafarer education in the maritime industry. Therefore, it is crucial to ascertain its contents beforehand. To be specific, it is imperative to conduct or organize informative meetings to update educational institutions, labor groups, shipping companies, and other relevant industries about the

[20] Lokuketagoda et al. (2018), pp. 17–19.

[21] Albayrak and Ziarati (2010).

key matters regarding the amendments of the Convention, ensuring that they are informed of the current trends. Each government and the industry of the IMO Member States must collaborate to develop frameworks for continuous professional development that enable seafarers to stay current with technological and regulatory changes. Given the fact that the amendments are scheduled to be adopted in 2027 as per the outlined timeline, it would be necessary to take into consideration the preparatory work required for individual domestic adoption. It is anticipated that this article will aid in the understanding of the to-be-amended STCW Convention and Code by the IMO Member States.

References

Albayrak T, Ziarati R (2010) Training: onboard and simulation-based familiarisation and skill enhancement to improve the performance of seagoing crew. In: International Conference on Human Performance at Sea [conference proceeding]

Bogusławski K, Gil M, Nasur J, Wróbel K (2022) Implications of autonomous shipping for maritime education and training: the cadet's perspective. Marit Econ Logist 24(2):327–343. https://doi.org/10.1057/s41278-022-00217-x

Golgota A, Çerma U (2024) Securing Durres port's digital transformation: cybersecurity strategy for maritime industry. In: 13th Mediterranean Conference on Embedded Computing (MECO), Budva, Montenegro, p 1

International Maritime Organization (2023a) Development of interim guidance on training for seafarers on ships using alternative fuels: HTW 10/6/4. IMO, London

International Maritime Organization (2023b) Report of the Correspondence Group: HTW 10/6. IMO, London

International Maritime Organization (2023c) Report of the Maritime Safety Committee on its 107th Session: MSC 107/20. IMO, London

International Maritime Organization (2024a) Report of the Working Group: ISWG-STCW 1/WP.1. IMO, London

International Maritime Organization (2024b) Report to the Maritime Safety Committee: HTW 10/10. IMO, London

Karim MS (2022) Maritime cybersecurity and the IMO legal instruments: sluggish response to an escalating threat? Mar Policy 143:105138

Kim J, Lee C, Jeong M, Cho E, Lee Y (2023) Identifying optimal approaches for sustainable maritime education and training: addressing technological, environmental, and epidemiological challenges. Sustainability 15(10):8092

Lokuketagoda MG, Miwa T, Jayasinghe S, Dev Ranmuthugala P (2018) Training engineers for remotely operated ships of the future. In: Proceedings of the 19th Annual General Assembly (AGA), International Association of Maritime Universities (IAMU), Barcelona, Spain, pp 17–19

Nguyen L (2018) 9 experts discuss the skills seafarers need in the future. KNect365 Maritime. Available at: https://knect365.com/shipping/article/c17e1ac8-6e3a-4e33-855c-5adbb3bad9aa. Accessed 21 Sep 2024

Österman C, Boström M (2022) Workplace bullying and harassment at sea: a structured literature review. Mar Policy 136:104910

Veldkamp EL, Bygvraa DA, Dawicki HE, Dawicki MG (2022) Psychological safety, bullying, sexual assault, and harassment in the maritime sector. Med Sci Forum 13(1):25. https://doi.org/10.3390/msf2022013025

The manufacturer's authorised representative in the EU is Springer
Nature Customer Service Centre GmbH, Europaplatz 3, 69115 Heidelberg,
Germany. If you have any concerns regarding our products, please
contact ProductSafety@springernature.com

Printed and bound by CPI Group (UK) Ltd, Croydon, CR0 4YY
01/10/2026
02226264-0005